AMERICAN BATTLEFIELDS

American Battlefields

A COMPLETE GUIDE TO THE HISTORIC CONFLICTS
IN WORDS, MAPS, AND PHOTOS

Hubbard Cobb

Maps by Donald Brunelle

MACMILLAN • USA

MACMILLAN
A Simon & Schuster Macmillan Company
1633 Broadway
New York, NY 10019

Library of Congress Cataloging-in-Publication Data
Cobb, Hubbard H.
    American battlefields : a complete guide to the historic conflicts in words, maps, and photos / Hubbard Cobb.
        p.   cm.
    ISBN 0-02-860428-8 (cloth).—ISBN 0-02-860436-9 (paper)
    1. Battlefields—United States—Guidebooks.   2. United States—History, Military.   3. United States—Guidebooks.   I. Title.
E159.C65   1995   95-19504
917.304'929—dc20   CIP

Design by Nick Anderson

10 9 8 7 6 5 4 3 2 1

Printed in the United States of America

For
Elizabeth Youngblood Cobb

ACKNOWLEDGMENTS

This book would probably never have gotten very far off the ground without all the assistance provided by the scores of authorities in various fields who willingly devoted their time and expertise to the project.

Our sincere thanks to:

• Edwin Bearss, former chief historian of the National Park Service, for directing us to reliable sources for data; Odor Lantz and George Mendez, of the Park Service's Historical Division, who provided vast amounts of material covering battlefields outside as well as inside the park system; Rosa Wilson, of the still photography department, for some great shots of battlefields; the staff of the National Park Service in Washington, D.C., for all the excellent materials; and, finally, the superintendents and staff members of the numerous battlefields administered by the National Park Service who so cheerfully answered many questions and provided useful information;

• Mary Anthorp of the Tippecanoe County Historic Association, Gregory Furness of the Crown Point State Historic Site, and the personnel of other battlefields outside the National Park Service for providing data that otherwise was difficult to locate;

• James Martin of the National Archive Cartography Department in Arlington, Virginia, for many copies of old battle maps, which served as sources for our maps;

• the staff of the still photography department of the National Archives and the Library of Congress for all the time they devoted to locating so many of the book's illustrations;

• Robert W. Fisch, Curator of Arms at the West Point Museum, for all the many illustrations of arms and answering numerous questions;

• Joseph Barth and Alan Aimone, the Library of the United States Military Academy at West Point, for their suggestions on references and introducing us to the excellent "West Point Military Series";

• Elizabeth Frost Knappman, New England Publishing Associates, for helping to develop the book's concept and then going on to find it a publisher;

• the book's editors, Deirdre Mullane, who established the approach and form; and John Michel for bringing the book to completion;

• and finally, an old friend, Stanley Schuler, for providing a large quantity of Civil War material.

CONTENTS

LIST OF MAPS

Special Features

INTRODUCTION

Less than 300 years ago, the American landscape was nearly all wilderness. Unlike far older nations, we have no medieval cathedrals, ruined castles, or crumbling palaces to haunt us. But we do have a host of old battlefields, which serve as tangible reminders of our past.

There are well over 100 existing battlefields and skirmish sites scattered around the country, from Vermont to Texas, New York to Oklahoma. There are so many battlefields in Virginia alone that it would take a long summer vacation to visit them all. A few battlefields survive from wars fought on American soil a full generation before the American Revolution, while there are still a few hardy old souls who remember the massacre at Wounded Knee, South Dakota, or, more recently, the morning of December 7, 1941, when Japanese planes attacked Pearl Harbor. Some of us as youngsters encountered Civil War veterans who recalled the great battles at Shiloh, Gettysburg, Pea Ridge, and other sites as if they happened only yesterday. It seemed to take an inordinate amount of fighting to forge this nation—the battles of six wars were fought on our soil, not to mention the conflicts with Native Americans that went on for hundreds of years.

The largest and most popular of these battlefields, such as those at Gettysburg, Antietam, Cowpens, Shiloh, and Little Bighorn, are run by the National Park Service. But many other sites, maintained by individual states, historical organizations, foundations, or private owners, are also open to the public. The Civil War battlefield at New Market, Virginia, for example, is owned and operated by the Virginia Military Institute.

It seemed to us that it was time to gather information on the existing battlefields in this country and put them into a comprehensive, illustrated volume. There are, of course, illustrated guides to some of the major Civil War battles but this book includes the history of the existing battlefields of all wars fought on American soil—the French and Indian Wars, the American Revolution, the War of 1812, the War for Texas Independence, the Mexican-American War, the Civil War, and the less defined series of wars with Native Americans.

For a supposedly "peace loving" nation, we have certainly managed to do a lot of fighting, and we tend to hold certain firm notions about these wars. Many historians have cited the American Revolution as one of the major events in modern history, and they have a point; the American victory encouraged people of other countries to rid themselves of their tyrannical governments. But many Americans, and foreign visitors, consider the Civil War as "the" war. In terms of the number of people who visit Civil War battlefields and the countless books, films, and miniseries that have considered it, it remains our most "popular" war. It certainly proved the point that if one employs yesterday's tactics against newer weapons, the result is staggering casualties—as in the more than 50,000 Union and Confederate casualties at Gettysburg.

But we should not allow the romance of the Civil War to blind us to the other important conflicts. The French and Indian Wars took place a long time ago, when America was just a cluster of English colonies, but a visit to one of these rare battlefield sites can cause one to wonder what the history of America would have been if France had been the ultimate victor in this war.

Many of us have not thought much about the War of 1812 since we left school. This is unfortunate, since it was so full of drama that it has been called the "Incredible War of 1812." By the last year of the conflict, the United States was finally coming into its own, and at the battlefield at New Orleans, we can see where General Andrew Jackson mauled the British invading army. From this point on, the British had a healthier respect for the new nation.

Except for the fight at the Alamo, the battles in the two wars with Mexico represented smashing victories for American troops. And these wars certainly paid off—the United States acquired new territory in present-day Texas, New Mexico, Arizona, Nevada, Utah, and lower California. For residents of these states, these conflicts may have been the most important of all our wars.

Skirmishes with Native Americans went on for centuries, and in all but a few, the Indians were not just defeated, but almost completely eliminated. At Little Bighorn, one of the few battles that the Indians "won," George Armstrong Custer and more than 260 of his Seventh U.S. Cavalry were killed. Little Bighorn attracts great numbers of visitors, far greater than those who visit the battle of Horseshoe Bend in Alabama, where more than 900 Creek warriors, together with their women and children, were killed by American soldiers.

Each year, millions of Americans visit our battlefields and battle sites to touch base with a common heritage, learn a bit more about the course of the battle, and see firsthand where it was fought, unfiltered through the lens of Hollywood. To those who study them with an intense fascination, a battle is the most complex and deadly of all games, a lethal game of chess, where the playing field may contain hidden hazards, where the pieces do not always move where intended. It is a game where the winner at any given point may eventually lose the match, where to lose may ultimately mean disaster. And after the game is over, there is always the nagging question "What if?," prompting much second guessing of strategy and tactics.

Visitors to the battlefields at Verdun in France, where almost one million French and German soldiers were killed in the First World War, recall it as a place where death seems omnipresent. Some of the battlefields from the Indian Wars can leave a similar impression, not merely for the numbers killed, but because they included so many women and children in what was often a massacre. Most American battlefields, however, have an almost serene quality. Some seem more like pleasant parks than a place where men fought and died. The weathered monuments and headstones are too polite to ask for our sympathy, only that we remember. The once awful cannon stand now as silent, friendly sentinels. Today, the "sound of battle" is the call of visitors and the shouts of children.

Yet a troubling undercurrent remains. Some authorities are concerned that our battlefields are becoming endangered. They cite budget cuts at the National Park Service during the 1980s that reduced staff and the level of maintenance. Others argue that politicians in Washington find more glory in the fanfare surrounding the development of new parks than in funding money to properly maintain those that already exist.

One national organization that is particularly concerned with the protection of Civil War battlefields and historic areas is The Conservation Fund. They welcome support and may be reached at 1800 North Kent Road, Arlington, Virginia 22209.

The huge numbers who visit battlefields naturally attract commercial interests, such as the privately owned observation tower built a few years ago just outside the Gettysburg battlegrounds. Development is fast encroaching upon these parks, and unless state and local officials act, we may find the approach to great battlefields crowded with shopping malls.

But for the present, these sites remain places of awe and wonder, where the imagination is quickly engaged. Visit Fort Necessity in Pennsylvania and walk on the same ground that 22-year-old Colonel George Washington paced as he tasted the bitterness of his first defeat in 1754. Stand at the Union position at Gettysburg and picture nearly 15,000 Confederate soldiers, led by Pickett, Pettigrew, and Trimble, advancing, as if on parade, across the wide open field where Union artillery and riflemen stood on that July day in 1863. From a ridge overlooking the Little Bighorn Valley, one can almost smell the smoke from the Indian campfires, see distant clouds of dust raised by war ponies, hear the faint sound of an army bugle and the crack of carbines and muskets.

Each American battlefield is steeped in such a history, a site that witnessed the finest expressions of human nature, as well as the worst. We hope that this book will serve as a useful guide to the major battle sites for those who are already familiar with their history, and will encourage others to visit both familiar and unknown sites. Each battlefield has its own story to tell.

Re-creating these battlesites for the modern reader has proven a formidable challenge. Many original maps are housed in the National Archives and Library of Congress, but they are often so detailed that it would take a military genius to decipher them. Maps obtained from the West Point Military Series and the National Park Service, on the other hand, are clearer, but these collections did not include all of the significant battles we wanted to cover in this volume. Research into at least half a dozen battles involved locating someone who knew someone who knew someone who had the battle map we wanted. This method proved invaluable, with one exception: we were never able to locate a workable map of the Battle of Fallen Timbers, hence its absence here.

In some cases, the information provided by several maps of the same event proved ambiguous. For Wounded Knee, for example, our contact came through with six maps, all of them different. We assumed that each rough map had been drawn by an observer to the massacre who recorded the action as he remembered it, and from a particular vantage point. The map chosen as the most reliable source was the one that best coincided with written descriptions of the battle.

Compared to obtaining battle maps, finding information on troop strength and battle casualties was simpler. Even here, however, different sources cite different figures for the same battle. Variations are most apparent in the Civil War engagements where tens of thousands of men were involved and casualties often ran into the hundreds of thousands. Figures are most approximate for Confederate forces, who needed all their soldiers for fighting and couldn't spare troops for military bookkeeping.

At Antietam, for example, one source gives Lee's troop strength as 55,000 men while another claims he had only 38,000; depending on the source, McClellan's force ranged from 75,000 to 80,000 troops, while Lee suffered from 12,000 to 13,700 casualties. In the heat of battle one obviously has neither the time nor facilities to keep accurate figures on troop strength, casualties, and number missing in action. In this volume, figures for troop strength and casualties are approximate and represent the best estimate available. Some scholars may disagree with some of them; others will feel we're right on the money.

French and Indian Wars

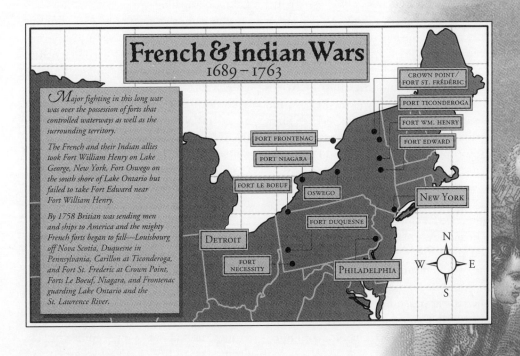

French & Indian Wars
1689 – 1763

Major fighting in this long war was over the possession of forts that controlled waterways as well as the surrounding territory.

The French and their Indian allies took Fort William Henry on Lake George, New York, Fort Oswego on the south shore of Lake Ontario but failed to take Fort Edward near Fort William Henry.

By 1758 Britian was sending men and ships to America and the mighty French forts began to fall—Louisbourg off Nova Scotia, Duquesne in Pennsylvania, Carillon at Ticonderoga, and Fort St. Frederic at Crown Point, Forts Le Boeuf, Niagara, and Frontenac guarding Lake Ontario and the St. Lawrence River.

CROWN POINT / FORT ST. FRÉDÉRIC

FORT TICONDEROGA

FORT WM. HENRY

FORT EDWARD

FORT FRONTENAC

FORT NIAGARA

FORT LE BOEUF

OSWEGO

NEW YORK

FORT DUQUESNE

DETROIT

FORT NECESSITY

PHILADELPHIA

N
W E
S

From 1689 to 1763, England and France, both colonial powers, fought a series of wars that would eventually determine which country would control North America.

These wars were primarily of European origin and were known by the English settlers as King William's War (1689–1697), Queen Anne's War (1702–1713), King George's War (1743–1748), and The French and Indian War (1755–1763). Because Native Americans played an important role in the hostilities, especially as French allies, the conflicts are collectively known as the French and Indian Wars.

In the early wars, fighting in North America was left largely to the English and French colonists, as their respective ruling countries were occupied fighting each other in Europe. When England and France became too exhausted or too impoverished to continue fighting, they would agree to a peace treaty, specifying which conquests would be retained and which were to be returned. As soon as one or both countries had recovered from fighting the last war, they would begin a new one.

But while England and France might be officially at peace for a few years between wars, fighting in North America between the English and French colonists continued without interruption.

FORTS

Forts were the "battlefields" in the French and Indian Wars. In the heavily forested and roadless wilderness of northeastern North America, the fastest and most efficient way to move trade goods and military supplies was by water. Forts, strategically sited on navigable rivers and lakes, controlled water traffic and the surrounding area.

Canada—New France—was entirely dependent on its "water highways." The St. Lawrence River was its supply line to the Atlantic and to France. The river also connected inner Canada to the west via Lakes Ontario and Erie and to the south by way of the Richelieu River and Lake Champlain. By 1755, France had established a system of forts to protect her water supply line and to assert claim to the Ohio River Valley and Lake Champlain.

The English war aim was to conquer Canada by capturing Quebec and Montreal. But the British military believed that before they marched on inner Canada, the key French forts must be taken or neutralized. These included Louisbourg on Cape Breton Island, off Nova Scotia, Fort Beausejour on the isthmus between Nova Scotia and the mainland, Fort Frontenac where Lake Ontario flows into the St. Lawrence, Fort Niagara between Lakes Ontario and Erie, Fort Duquesne on the Ohio River, and Forts St. Frédéric and Ticonderoga on Lake Champlain.

Taking some of these forts would not be easy or even necessary. In 1755, Major General Edward Braddock lost over 900 British regulars and his own life before he had even reached Fort Duquesne. But when the fort's supply line was cut by the capture of Fort Frontenac in 1758, it was abandoned and destroyed. General James Abercromby suffered 1,600 casualties in his assault on Fort Carillon at Ticonderoga in 1758. But a year later, the French abandoned and destroyed both Ticonderoga and St. Frederic as they began to concentrate their forces to defend inner Canada.

The English constructed only two forts—Oswego and William Henry. Fort Oswego was built in the early 1740s on the southeastern shore of Lake Ontario to protect the Mohawk River and the Iroquois from the French. The English thought so little

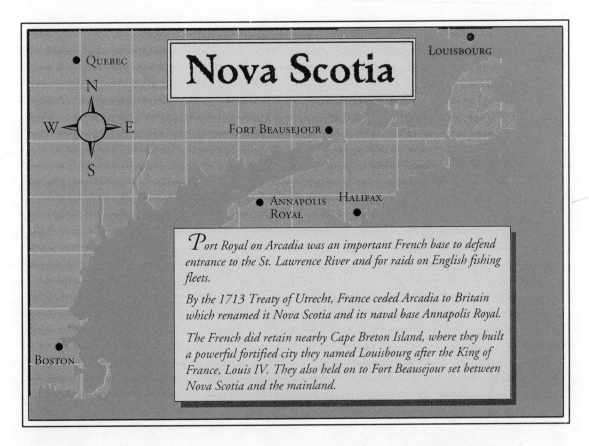

Nova Scotia

LOUISBOURG

QUEBEC

N
W E
S

FORT BEAUSEJOUR

ANNAPOLIS ROYAL HALIFAX

BOSTON

Port Royal on Arcadia was an important French base to defend entrance to the St. Lawrence River and for raids on English fishing fleets.

By the 1713 Treaty of Utrecht, France ceded Arcadia to Britain which renamed it Nova Scotia and its naval base Annapolis Royal.

The French did retain nearby Cape Breton Island, where they built a powerful fortified city they named Louisbourg after the King of France, Louis IV. They also held on to Fort Beausejour set between Nova Scotia and the mainland.

of the fort that it was not well maintained and was easily taken and destroyed by Louis Joseph, Marquis de Montcalm, in 1756. It was reoccupied and rebuilt by the British in 1759 and served as a base for the attacks on Forts Frontenac and Niagara. Fort William Henry, near Lake George, was built in 1755 by General William Johnson. It had no great military importance, and after it was captured and destroyed by Montcalm in 1757, it was not rebuilt.

COLONIAL ARMED FORCES

Until 1754, when England and France began sending large forces to fight in America, the English and French colonies fought with each other with whatever forces were available. When warfare began in 1689, the population of the English colonies was around 205,000 and that of New France was about 13,000. By 1750, it had increased to 1,250,000 and 70,000 respectively.

In spite of the almost microscopic population of this vast country, New France had certain military advantages over the English colonies. First, it had a highly centralized and autocratic government. The governor general, a man with military experience, was in complete control and answered only to the King of France. The population concentrated mainly around the citadels of Montreal and Quebec.

New France had a regiment of regulars —*la Marine Regiment.* While not a crack

*F*ORTS: TYPES, CONSTRUCTION, AND SIEGE

The earliest forts built in North America were simple affairs designed to protect settlers during an attack by Indians.

In some settlements, the inhabitants would take shelter in a fortified or "garrison" house. Larger and generally more solidly built than the surrounding houses, they provided reasonably good protection.

The simplest, most conventional fort was an enclosure surrounded by a stockade or palisade of logs. Ends of the logs were set several feet in the soil and the edges of the logs were sometimes made smooth to eliminate cracks between them, with loopholes made so defenders could fire on the attackers. The stockade could be a place where the settlers gathered when attacked or it might enclose the entire settlement, as at Schenectady, New York.

A stockade, if properly sited, defended, and supplied, provided good protection against Indian attacks. But as George Washington learned with the stockade Fort Necessity, they could not hold off an attack by experienced soldiers. No stockade or palisade fort made solely of logs could withstand cannon fire.

It was impractical, as well as all but impossible, to move a heavy cannon through a heavily forested wilderness, simply to smash a crude stockade fortification. It could be overcome in time by small arm fire or starved into submission.

Aerial view of ruins of Fort St. Frédéric, Crown Point, New York. The French destroyed this fort rather than allow it to fall into the hands of the advancing British army. (Crown Point Historic Site)

It was, however, a different story when it came to major enemy fortifications accessible by water—and all of them were. Here, it was possible to bring heavy siege guns by water to the site and manhandled into firing position.

When a fort was located where it might be attacked with cannon, it was built of logs and earth. The walls consisted of an open wood frame— cribbing—filled with packed earth and with both sides faced with logs. A wall, sometimes eight feet or more thick, could withstand cannon fire for some time—as long as the cannon were not allowed to come too close to the fort. The outside surface of the wall was sometimes faced with stone, which did not rot like logs and was sometimes effective in deflecting shot. The forts built of solid stone or masonry were very resistant to cannon shot but naturally took more skill and time to build than those made with log and earthen walls. And they were only practical where stone was readily available. Forts St. Frédéric, Crown Point, Oswego, and Niagara had solid masonry walls.

Forts came in a variety of shapes. Many were square, while others, such as Ticonderoga, were star-shaped, allowing the defenders to fire on both flanks of the attacking force. Because the French did not wish to alarm the Indians, who might consider a conventional fort as a threat to them as well as to the enemies of France, Fort Niagara was designed to resemble a large house. Forts often included outer defenses such as moats, trenches, and redoubts. Cannons were positioned to have a clear field of fire in all directions. When loaded with grape shot, the cannons could tear attacking infantry to shreds.

There were several ways to go about capturing a fort. The simplest methods were to isolate it so that it was of no further use to the enemy or to cut its supply line to starve the defenders into surrender. Artillery could sometimes be placed on nearby high ground where it would fire over the walls into the buildings behind. Another approach was to move the cannon close enough to make a breach in the fort's walls for an infantry attack. Getting cannons close enough to breach the walls was often quite a project, requiring the digging of a series of trenches, called parallels, so the cannon could be safely moved ever nearer to the wall.

Larger forts would include barracks for officers and soldiers, an infirmary, powder magazine, ovens for heating cannon shot, kitchen, storage, and sometimes a parade ground.

outfit, it did provide training for young officers and garrisoning for forts and outposts. There was also a militia made up of farmers and tradesmen that could be called out by the governor general.

Another fighting force was the *Coureurs de Bois*—"Runners of the Woods." These were men of all classes who found life in feudal New France too restrictive and had gone into the wilderness to become hunters, trappers, guides, and explorers. Many lived among the Indians, learning the language and customs and adapting Indian dress and style of warfare. They became the inspiration for the English force of scouts, "Rogers' Rangers." The French also received considerable military aid from their Indian allies, the Algonquian-speaking tribes of Canada and the Abenaki of northern Maine.

The English colonies, unlike New France, had no centralized government. Each of the colonies was almost a small independent nation, concerned with its own affairs. If the French and their Indian allies began raiding settlements in New England, it was of no concern to the mid-Atlantic and southern colonies. Each colony had a militia consisting of all able-bodied men between the ages of 16 and 60, with commanders that had little or no formal military training. This force of amateur soldiers could only be called out by the governor of the colony and for a very limited

THE INDIAN WARRIOR

During the colonial wars, both the English and French depended on their Indian allies in battles; the French more than the English because of Canada's comparatively small population and their better relationship with the Indians.

The Indian warrior was fiercely independent and was not inclined to obey all orders from a white officer, or even from his chiefs. He preferred fighting in the manner he was accustomed to, stealthily moving through the forest to surprise the enemy. He was such a superb wilderness fighter that Rogers' Rangers and the French "Coureurs de Bois" learned and employed these tactics.

Indians were excellent scouts and were often used to discover enemy plans and logistics. It is said that if Braddock had insisted on having some Indian scouts, he would not have been ambushed on the march to Fort Duquesne.

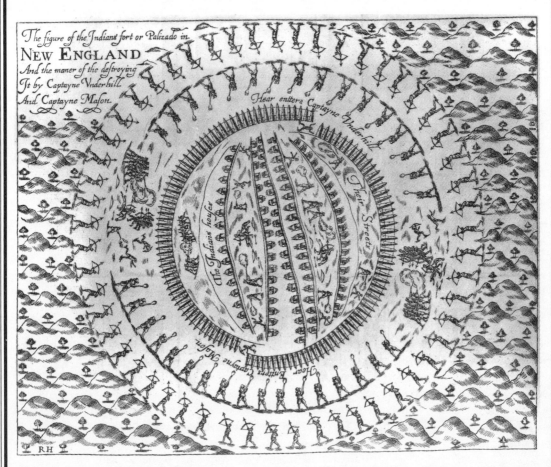

Highly imaginative woodcut illustrating attack on a Pequot fort at Mystic, Connecticut, on May 26, 1637, by troops led by Captain John Mason and John Underhill. The so-called fort was actually a Pequot Indian village and the action consisted of the massacre of women, children, and old men. (Library of Congress)

During the course of a battle, an Indian would often stop fighting to take scalps. And if he felt he had enough scalps, he might leave and go home. He would also be inclined to leave if the enemy was winning, or if he was about to fight a superior force. It was, after all, not his war.

During a prolonged siege, Indians would drift away because of boredom. Sitting around while trenches were dug and artillery was moved into place was not the Indian's way of making war.

Indians could be very cruel and would often torture their captives and sometimes roast and eat the heart and other parts of their victim. Drinking the blood and eating the flesh of killed enemy often had religious application. It was a way of absorbing the good qualities of an enemy into oneself. Sometimes the torture they inflicted was just for pleasure, but it was also done to give the warrior a chance to display his courage. On occasion, if the captive showed great courage, the torture would end, the captive was adopted into the tribe.

The French and Indian Wars were hard on the Indians of the Northeast. Many of the warriors were killed, and their villages and crops were destroyed. The tribes never recovered from these losses. The tribes of the Northeast were gradually consigned to small reservations by the new government of the independent colonies.

amount of time, and generally it would fight only within that particular colony.

During the course of wars, commanders would circumvent the many drawbacks of the militia by recruiting volunteers for a particular military campaign outside the colony. Volunteers were usually better fighters than the militia and were more inclined to remain until the job was finished and not return home because they had served their allotted time. The English also received some military support from the Iroquois confederation, which consisted of five tribes: Seneca, Cayuga, Onondaga, Oneida, and Mohawk. The French attempted to recruit the Iroquois for their own forces or at the least attempted to ensure that they remained neutral. In this effort they were fairly successful, and by around 1750, only the Mohawks actively supported the English.

War Begins in North America

In 1689, a war party of Iroquois raided the French settlement of Lachine, near Montreal, killing 200 of the inhabitants and taking 150 captive. Count Louis de Frontenac, then governor general of New France, decided to pacify the Iroquois by attacking their villages in the Finger Lake district of New York and then raiding the settlements of their English patrons. After the conflict developed into what became King William's War, raids continued as part of the French strategy to prevent the English colonists from expanding north or west by raiding settlements encroaching on these lands.

French raiding parties, often commanded by a French officer, might consist of members of the Canadian militia, the "Coureurs de Bois," and Indians. Many whites, including the officers, were often dressed as Indians. The raids would come as a surprise and were often savage and cruel. Women and children along with men were killed and scalped. Captives were often turned over to the Indians and later tortured.

In February 1690, a large French force headed down from Canada via Lake Champlain to raid Albany. Finding the town too well defended, they decided instead to take Schnectady. This former Dutch settlement was surrounded by a stockade, but on this bitter cold winter's night, no attack was expected, so the stockade gates were left open, guarded by two snowmen "sentries." When the raid was over some 60 men, women, and children had been killed, and Schnectady was reduced to a pile of smoldering ashes.

In the same year, attacks were made on Georgetown, Casco Falls, and Falmouth in Maine; Salmon Falls in New Hampshire; and Deerfield, Massachusetts. The local militia was of little help; by the time it arrived at the scene the conflict was generally over.

As these raids on outlying settlements continued, Massachusetts built four forts to protect remote settlements and supplied "Fort Number Four" at present-day Charleston, New Hampshire.

These ongoing raids soon convinced the English colonies, especially Massachusetts, who suffered the brunt of the attacks, that the only way to end them and have peace was to drive the French out of Canada. They planned to do this by taking Arcadia (Nova Scotia), which guarded the entrance to the St. Lawrence River, and then sailing up and capturing Quebec and Montreal.

This was a rather ambitious project for a force made up of the militia and volunteers and led by men with no previous military experience, but it was all that could be mustered. England was too preoccupied fighting France in Europe to do much more than send over some transport ships and a few marines. Surprisingly, the amateur English colonial force did rather well.

In May 1690, Sir William Phips, with 500 New England men, captured Port Royal in Arcadia, but it was returned to France under the treaty ending King William's War in 1697. In 1710, Port Royal was again captured by a colonial force led by Francis Nicholson. This time, England was allowed to keep the territory, along with all Arcadia, which was renamed "Nova Scotia."

France, however, retained nearby Cape Breton Island. This site was well suited to control entrance to the St. Lawrence, so the French immediately built a powerful fortress, named "Louisbourg" after the King. In June 1745, William Pepperrell, with about 3,000 volunteers from Connecticut, Massachusetts, and New Hampshire, managed to take Louisbourg, only to learn it too was to be returned to France. Thus, the projected attacks on Quebec and Montreal ended in failure.

Besides raiding English settlements and defending Arcadia, the French had been busy building forts. Fort St. Frédéric was built on the west shore of Lake Champlain to control this important waterway and serve as base for raids on New England and New York. The French also built forts to assert their claim to the Great Lakes and Ohio River Valley regions.

BATTLE AT FORT NECESSITY— JULY 3, 1754

During the period of "peace" between King George's War and The French and Indian War, Virginia and France each claimed the Ohio River Valley, a vast territory that included present-day western Pennsylvania, Ohio, Indiana, and Illinois. In 1753, Marquis Duquesne, now military commander of New France, sent 1,500 men into the area to build roads and erect Fort Le Boeuf on French Creek, just south of Lake Erie. English traders and hunters active in the valley soon informed Virginia's governor, Robert Dinwiddie, of the French activities.

Dinwiddie had a special interest in the

Ohio River Valley. He was a stockholder in the Ohio Company, which had obtained a grant from King George for over 2,000,000 acres of Ohio River Valley land, and planned to make money in its development. He ordered George Washington, then a 21-year-old major of the Virginia militia, to deliver a letter to the commander at Fort Le Boeuf, demanding that the French leave the Ohio River Valley. With a small militia force, Washington made the journey to Le Boeuf during the winter of 1753–1754. The letter was delivered, and the French commander agreed to pass it on to higher authorities.

When Washington returned, he told Dinwiddie that the point where the Allegheny and Monongahela Rivers joined to form the Ohio River would make an excellent site for a fort. Dinwiddie secured permission from England to build a fort on this site and sent out a work crew. Washington, now a lieutenant colonel, was ordered to head a small advance force to protect the crew.

By May 1754, Washington was camped just beyond Wills Creek (Cumberland, Maryland) where he was joined by Colonel Joshua Fry, the expedition's commander. Fry died shortly after arriving, and Washington, now a full colonel, was given total command. Washington and his force were about 100 miles from the construction site when members of the work crew arrived with the news that 1,000 French soldiers had reached the site, sent the work crew packing, destroyed the work, and were about to build a fort of their own—Fort Duquesne.

Washington pressed on. On May 24, he made camp at Great Meadow, near present-day Farmington, Pennsylvania. The swampy meadow was the only large open space in the area. Soon after establishing camp, Washington was told by Indian scouts, from Half King, a chief of the Senecas, that there were French soldiers hiding nearby in a glen. England and France were officially at peace, but Washington believed the French planned to attack him.

On the night of May 27, Washington and 40 of his men marched six miles to Half King's camp. Here, some Indians joined his force, and early in the morning, they marched two miles or so and surprised the French in the glen. In the brief battle, 10 French soldiers were killed and 21 taken prisoner. Among the French killed was the leader of the force, Joseph Coulon de Villiers, Sieur de Jumonville. Washington lost one and had two wounded. A French soldier who escaped carried news of the battle to Fort Duquesne.

Washington returned to Great Meadow and began to fortify his position. By June 3, his men had completed a somewhat crude stockade fort, which Washington would later refer to as "Fort Necessity."

On June 9, Washington received reinforcements, bringing his force to 293. Shortly afterwards, he was further strengthened by the arrival of nine swivel guns and 100 South Carolina volunteers under Captain James Mackay. On July 3, a force of 600 French soldiers and 100 Indians arrived around noon and attacked the fort.

The defenders first began firing outside the fort, but Washington soon ordered them into the trenches that surrounded the stockade. When it began to rain, the trenches, dug in the swampy ground, quickly filled with water. The area around the fort had not been completely cleared of trees, and the attackers climbed them and fired over the stockade. Soon all the horses and cattle, and even the dog inside the stockade, were killed.

By nightfall, Washington asked for terms of surrender. The French commander,

Louis Sieur Coulon de Villiers, whose brother was killed in the earlier battle, offered Washington very generous terms. His men could withdraw with full honors of war, retaining their arms except the nine swivel guns. On the morning of July 4, Washington and his men began their march back to Wills Creek, and the French returned to Fort Duquesne, after destroying Fort Necessity.

The surrender terms agreed to by Washington had been written in French. One of Washington's officers, who understood French, translated it for the colonel before he signed the document. The terms referred to the death of young de Jumonville as "assassination." Washington's officer thought this word simply meant "death." But in French it was the word for "murder." Having signed a document stating that he had ordered a French officer murdered eventually caused Washington great embarrassment, and the French later used it for propaganda purposes.

While it took place many months before the official declaration of war, the battle at Fort Necessity was the precursor to the coming French and Indian War.

Fort Necessity has been reconstructed and is part of the National Park System. Officially called "Fort Necessity National Battlefield," the fort area also contains Jumonville's Glen and General Edward Braddock's grave and monument.

GENERAL BRADDOCK'S CAMPAIGN

While Washington's skirmishes with the French in the Ohio River Valley in 1754 did not lead England and France to officially declare war, it hastened the day that they would. Later that year, France sent 3,000 regulars to America under the command of Baron Ludwig Dieskau, an experienced officer who had served in European wars.

William Pitt, the British prime minister, had determined that the best way to destroy France was not on European battlefields, but to strip away its colonies in North America and India. Pitt named Major General Edward Braddock to command the king's forces in America that would conquer Canada.

Braddock brought two regiments of regulars and shortly after his arrival met with the governors of several colonies to formulate an overall plan. It was finally decided to first take the four most strategically important French forts. Braddock would personally lead his regulars and take Fort Duquesne, thereby ending French control of the Ohio River Valley. William Shirley, governor of Massachusetts, would take his militiamen up the Mohawk River and capture Fort Niagara. Capture of this fort would cut off Lake Erie and surrounding territory from inner Canada. General William Johnson was to strike at Fort St. Frédéric at Crown Point on Lake Champlain, to give the British control of the lake and a clear inland route to inner Canada. The fourth force was to go by ship and take Fort Beausejour on the isthmus between Nova Scotia and the mainland.

BRADDOCK'S MARCH TO FORT DUQUESNE

In May 1755, Braddock left Wills Creek on the Potomac and headed for Fort Duquesne, some 110 miles away. His force consisted of 1,400 British regulars and 450 Virginia militia, along with artillery and supply wagons. Supplies included feed for the many horses, since there was no grazing in the forested wilderness. Washington joined

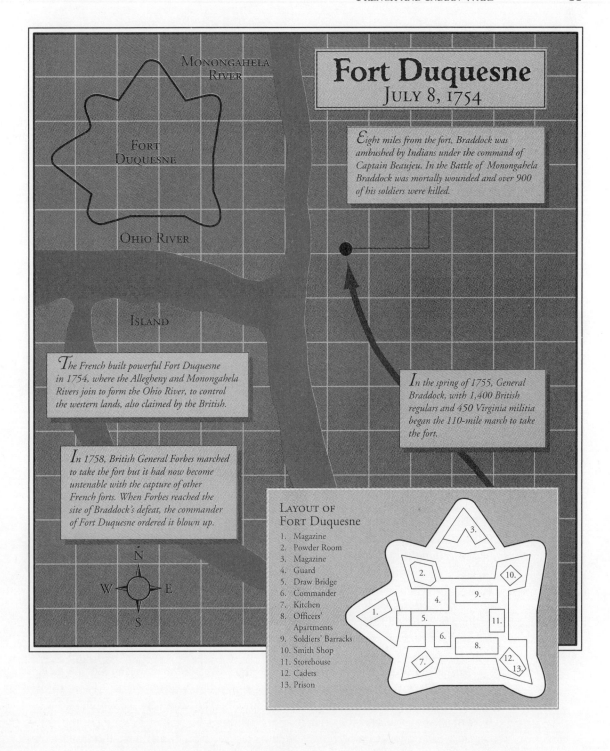

MONONGAHELA RIVER

FORT DUQUESNE

OHIO RIVER

ISLAND

Fort Duquesne
JULY 8, 1754

Eight miles from the fort, Braddock was ambushed by Indians under the command of Captain Beaujeu. In the Battle of Monongahela Braddock was mortally wounded and over 900 of his soldiers were killed.

The French built powerful Fort Duquesne in 1754, where the Allegheny and Monongahela Rivers join to form the Ohio River, to control the western lands, also claimed by the British.

In the spring of 1755, General Braddock, with 1,400 British regulars and 450 Virginia militia began the 110-mile march to take the fort.

In 1758, British General Forbes marched to take the fort but it had now become untenable with the capture of other French forts. When Forbes reached the site of Braddock's defeat, the commander of Fort Duquesne ordered it blown up.

N
W E
S

LAYOUT OF
FORT DUQUESNE

1. Magazine
2. Powder Room
3. Magazine
4. Guard
5. Draw Bridge
6. Commander
7. Kitchen
8. Officers' Apartments
9. Soldiers' Barracks
10. Smith Shop
11. Storehouse
12. Cadets
13. Prison

Burial of Major General Edward Braddock as depicted in an 1808 engraving. Completely ignorant of wilderness fighting and too arrogant to take advice, Braddock lost most of his 1,500-man army to a relatively small force of French and Indians outside Fort Duquesne in Pennsylvania. (Library of Congress)

the expedition as a civilian aide-de-camp to Braddock. He had recently resigned his commission as colonel of the Virginia militia rather than accept reduction in rank required by the reorganization of the militia.

The one element Braddock's army lacked was Indian scouts, which Braddock had not thought necessary. As was typical of many of the British officers who came to fight in America, he believed that fighting an enemy in the colonies was the same as fighting one on a tidy European battlefield. He was soon to learn how different it was to fight an unseen enemy in a wilderness.

Moving Braddock's army through the roadless wilderness was a huge undertaking. Three hundred axmen cleared away trees to make a road, which then had to be corduroyed with logs to carry the weight of the supply wagons and artillery. Often the

army only traveled twelve miles in a day. By July 9, the force was within twelve miles of the fort.

Indian scouts had kept the commander of Fort Duquesne, Captain Pierre de Contrecoeur, posted on Braddock's progress. De Contrecoeur had only 800 men and an equal number of Indians to defend his fort. He decided his best hope was to lay an ambush and defeat Braddock before he could reach the fort. He assigned this task to Captain Daniel Beaujeu, who left the fort with 100 regulars, 150 Canadian militia, and 600 Indians to take on an army of about 1,500. As they approached the fort, Braddock's army was spread out along almost 2,000 yards—close to two miles. The advance guard under Colonel Thomas Gage had 1,400 men and some pieces of light artillery. Braddock commanded the main force, with the artillery and supply wagons in the rear under Colonel Thomas Dunbar. The first enemy the advance guard saw was Beaujeu, dressed as an Indian but wearing a silver gorget and a French officer's hat. When Beaujeu waved his hat, the Indians gave their spine-chilling war cry and began firing on the red-coated British troops.

Gage was able to maneuver his light artillery pieces into action, putting the Canadian militia to flight. Beaujeu was killed early in the fighting, but Captain Daniel de Dumas took command and rallied the Indians. British troops fought as best they could, but as the Indians hid behind trees, there was nothing to aim at. Some of the Virginia militia managed to get behind fallen trees and picked off exposed Indians. Mistaking the Virginians for Indians, some British troops began shooting at them. Other British troops got behind trees to meet the Indians on even terms, but their officers used their swords to drive the men back in the open where they would be easy targets.

Gage's advance guard began an orderly retreat, but as the Indians continued to fire, the retreat soon turned into a panic. The advance guard tangled with the main army and the tightly packed troops became ideal targets. Washington and some of his officers tried to restore order, but it was an impossible task. The British troops were too terrified to follow their command. At the rear, Dunbar had heard the firing and fled, leaving behind all the artillery and baggage, including Braddock's papers, which would give the French the details of attack plans on other French forts.

In this battle near Fort Duquesne, the British lost over 900 men; the French lost only a handful. The French had apparently advised their Indians to concentrate their fire on British officers, for out of 86

Brigadier General John Forbes succeeded where Braddock had failed, occupying the French-held Fort Duquesne at present-day Pittsburgh on November 25, 1758. Forbes's success was due in great part to the fact that, by then, Britain had gained control of Lake Ontario, and Fort Duquesne was isolated from the rest of French Canada. When Forbes's army arrived on the morning of the 25th, the French garrison had blown up the fort's magazine and had all departed, heading for eastern Canada. (Library of Congress)

officers, 63 were killed. Washington had two horses shot from under him and four bullet holes through his clothing. Braddock lost four horses and was mortally wounded. What little spirit was left in the army vanished when Braddock was hit. There was a mad dash back to Wills Creek, some 100 miles away.

Braddock died soon after the battle. His last words were "We shall better know how to deal with them another time." Washington arranged to have Braddock buried near the remains of Fort Necessity.

In the early fall of 1758, General John Forbes, accompanied by George Washington, marched on Fort Duquesne with a

William Johnson, an influential landowner and merchant of the Mohawk Valley, forged an alliance between the Mohawk Indians and English during the French and Indian War. Given the rank of general during the war, he named numerous forts and lakes after members of the royal family and so was knighted by King George and returned to America as Sir William Johnson. (Library of Congress)

On the evening of November 24, Forbes and his army were camped near the site of Braddock's defeat. During the night, there was a loud explosion as the French blew up the fort. By this time, most of the French and Indians had already left and returned to Canada. In the morning, Forbes's troops arrived to find the fort in ruins. Outside the fort, stakes had been driven into the ground, each topped by a human head with a Highland kilt tied around the base.

Nonetheless, Washington had the satisfaction of raising the British flag over the ruins of Fort Duquesne. What he and Forbes did not know was that some months earlier, Lieutenant Colonel John Bradstreet had easily captured Fort Frontenac at the head of Lake Ontario, thereby cutting off Fort Duquesne's supply line. The French would have had to abandon the fort in any event.

The British built a new fort on the site, naming it Fort Pitt in honor of the prime minister. This fort would later be demolished to make space for the city of Pittsburgh.

BATTLE AT LAKE GEORGE— AUGUST 9, 1757

As Braddock was marching to disaster and his death outside Fort Duquesne, Major General William Johnson was moving north to capture Fort St. Frederic at Crown Point on Lake Champlain.

As a young man, Johnson had come from England to manage his uncle's large tract of land in the Mohawk River area of New York. He had built trading posts and eventually established close relations with the neighboring Iroquois. His influence with them became so great that the governor of New York appointed him military commander of the Iroquois Nation.

well-trained army of British regulars. As Forbes neared the fort, he ordered Major James Grant to take a detachment that included men from the 77th Regiment, which included many Scottish Highlanders, and reconnoiter the area. Grant's troops were attacked and mauled by a party of French soldiers and Indians, and Grant was forced to surrender.

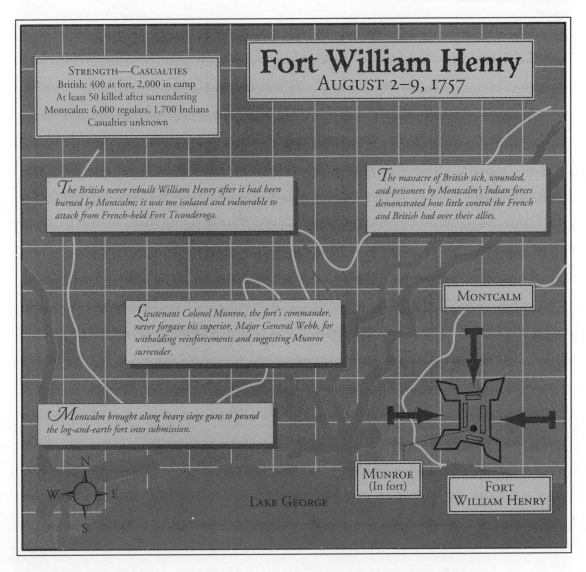

Fort William Henry
AUGUST 2–9, 1757

STRENGTH—CASUALTIES
British: 400 at fort, 2,000 in camp
At least 50 killed after surrendering
Montcalm: 6,000 regulars, 1,700 Indians
Casualties unknown

The British never rebuilt William Henry after it had been burned by Montcalm; it was too isolated and vulnerable to attack from French-held Fort Ticonderoga.

The massacre of British sick, wounded, and prisoners by Montcalm's Indian forces demonstrated how little control the French and British had over their allies.

Lieutenant Colonel Munroe, the fort's commander, never forgave his superior, Major General Webb, for witholding reinforcements and suggesting Munroe surrender.

Montcalm brought along heavy siege guns to pound the log-and-earth fort into submission.

MONTCALM

MUNROE
(In fort)

FORT
WILLIAM HENRY

LAKE GEORGE

N W E S

In July 1755, he moved up the Hudson River with a force of some 3,500 militia and artillery to Lake St. Sacrerment, which he renamed "Lake George" in honor of his king. Major General Phineas Lyman, second in command, had already created an advance base at the portage between Lake George called by the Indians "Great Carrying Place." On arrival, Johnson began to fortify this base, naming it Fort Edwards.

Baron Ludwig Dieskau, commander of the French regulars, knew of Johnson's plans from Braddock's captured papers. He had also learned that Fort Edwards was unfinished and had a garrison of only 400. He decided to attack the fort before it was completed and its garrison reinforced.

In early September, Dieskau left Fort St. Frédéric and moved south with 1,500 men. Only 200 of them were French regulars, the remainder were militia and Indians. On

September 8, Indian scouts advised Johnson that Dieskau had reached the Fort Edwards area. Johnson ordered Colonel Ephraim Williams to take 1,500 men and drive the French away. Old Hendricks, a Mohawk chief and close friend of Johnson, had seen the size of this force, and had told his friend, "If to be killed, too many. If to fight, too few." But, in spite of his misgivings, Old Hendricks joined Williams. Williams's force was ambushed by the enemy, and in the brief fighting, Williams and Old Hendricks were killed. This took the spirit out of the militia and the men rushed back to Fort Edwards. As an interesting side note, Williams's will provided funds to establish a college, which was eventually built—in Williamstown, Maine—and named Williams College.

After the easy success over Williams's force, Dieskau decided to push his luck and attack Johnson's main force. But by now, Johnson had brought up his artillery and fortified a new position closer to Lake George than Fort Edwards. Among his officers were Seth Pomeroy and Israel Putnam, who would later serve as generals in the Revolutionary War.

Dieskau's men had no chance against the grape shots that poured out of Johnson's cannon. Dieskau was wounded and then taken prisoner. The attack soon ended, and the French returned to St. Frédéric. Johnson was also wounded and decided not to press on and try to take St. Frédéric. Instead, he completed the fort he had started at the foot of Lake George, which he named Fort William Henry for King George's grandsons.

The French were also building a fort not far from Fort William Henry and a dozen or so miles south of St. Frederic. The new fort was sited on a narrow point on the west shore of Lake Champlain, adjacent to the short river connecting the lake to Lake George. The area was called Ticonderoga by the Indians, but since the river flowing over a stretch of rapids made a musical sound, the French named their fort Carillon.

Johnson's decision not to proceed to Fort St. Frederic was the third loss in Braddock's projected four-prong attack on French forts. Braddock had failed to take Duquesne, and Shirley had not even managed to get close to Fort Niagara. The only prong that was successful was the capture of Fort Beausejour by Colonel Robert Mockton and his New Englanders.

BATTLE AT FORT WILLIAM HENRY—AUGUST 2–9, 1757

In June 1756, England and France declared war over a boundary dispute and the French and Indian War officially began. In that year, the Earl of Loudoun arrived in America to take command of the British troops. The following year, he made an unsuccessful attack on Louisbourg on Cape Breton Island. But the absence of British forces—who had gone to fight in Nova Scotia—left Fort William Henry exposed to attack by the French at Ticonderoga. On August 1, the Marquis de Montcalm, military commander of the French forces, left Fort Carillon at Ticonderoga with siege cannon, 6,000 French regulars and militia, and 1,700 Indians and headed for Fort William Henry.

Constructed of logs and earth, William Henry could withstand cannon fire, provided the fort's own cannon could keep the enemy's guns from getting too close. But the fort was poorly garrisoned. Its commander, Lieutenant Colonel George Munroe, had only 50 regulars and 350

French six-pounder (circa 1761). The first time field artillery had been employed on battlefields of the northeast was in 1745 during the siege of Louisbourg where the Ancient and Honorable Artillery Company of Boston served with the British Royal Artillery. Before then, artillery had to be waterborne so its use was limited to the defense and siege of forts. (West Point Museum)

militia inside the fort and 2,000 in a nearby camp that lacked artillery.

Montcalm moved his siege cannon into position and began firing at the fort. At night, parallels (surrounding trenches) and approach trenches were dug, and the cannons were brought closer to its walls. The fort's cannon returned fire, but one by one, they were knocked out of action, and soon there were just two left to answer the enemy fire. Munroe managed to dispatch a message to his superior, Major General Daniel Webb, at Fort Edwards, asking for a 3,400 relief force.

On the seventh day of the attack, Montcalm sent in an officer under a flag of truce with a letter addressed to Munroe from Webb. Webb wrote that he could not provide assistance and instructed Monroe to ask Montcalm for the best possible terms of surrender.

Running out of provisions and ammunition, Montcalm offered Munroe generous terms. Because he did not want to feed a lot of prisoners, he indicated that he would allow the militiamen to go back to their homes and the British regulars to return to Fort Edwards after they were disarmed. Montcalm instructed his Indian allies not to harm the prisoners and ordered the French regulars to see his orders were carried out.

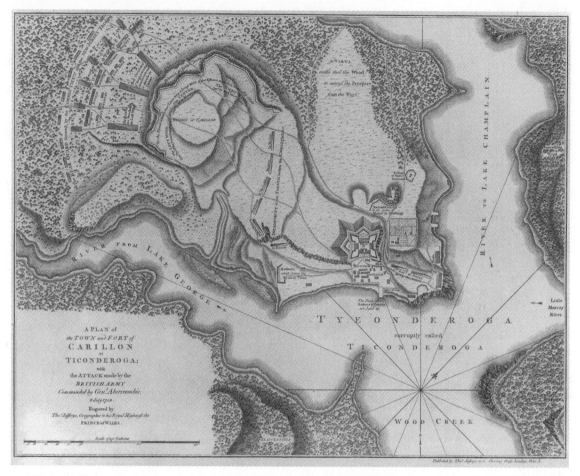

Jeffrey's map illustrates the defenses at Fort Ticonderoga—"Carillon"—that Montcalm had his French troops build. It included a high log wall with a firing platform behind, and at its front, an abatis of felled trees with sharpened ends facing the enemy.

British General Abercromby ordered seven attacks on the wall and all he had to show for it was some 2,000 casualties. (William L. Clements Library/University of Michigan at Ann Arbor)

His instructions went unheeded. As soon as the fort surrendered, the Indians dashed inside and began killing and scalping the sick and wounded. After they had finished their work in the fort, they began attacking the prisoners who were lined up outside preparing to march to Fort Edwards, tearing away at their uniforms and taking their personal possessions. Among these was rum, and after drinking it, many Indians became even more unrestrained, killing and scalping the English, including some women and children who had been at the fort. The French regulars stood by and watched, doing nothing to prevent the slaughter. Appalled at the carnage, Montcalm offered himself to the Indians if they would cease killing the English prisoners.

The Indians ignored him and continued with their bloody work. When they had finished, at least 50 of the prisoners had been killed, and as many as 200 had been taken away as captives. Many of these,

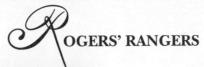OGERS' RANGERS

MAJOR ROBERT ROGERS,
Commander in Chief of the INDIANS *in the Back Settlements of* AMERICA.
Published as the Act directs Oct'r 1, 1776, by Thos Hart London.

Robert Rogers, depicted in a 1776 British engraving, was made the captain, in March 1756, of an independent ranger company fighting against the French and their Indian allies. He quickly proved his talent for recruiting and leading guerrilla raids. In 1758, British General Abercromby promoted Rogers to major, in command of nine ranger companies used for reconnaissance. During the Revolution Rogers was considered a Tory by many and sometimes accused of being a British spy. (Library of Congress)

Braddock's disastrous attempt to take Fort Duquesne emphasized the need for advance scouts to report on the enemy's activities and also showed that the British could not get reliable Indians to do this work. The idea of forming a group of "rangers" to serve as scouts had been discussed among senior officers, so when a frontiersman named Richard Rogers approached General William Shirley, the governor of Massachusetts, with a plan to recruit a force of rangers, Shirley approved it. Rogers was commissioned captain in March 1756 and recruited 60 other tough frontiersmen who knew the wilderness and were familiar with Indian war tactics. They specialized in scouting and launching guerrilla raids on small forces of the French and their Indian allies.

The rangers were a rough and undisciplined lot and were not popular with the ordinary colonial soldier. In addition to more pay, the rangers did not have to take part in routine camp duties, such as sentry duty and guarding supplies.

The rangers soon proved their value, however, and their numbers increased. General Lord August Howe thought so highly of Rogers' Rangers, as they were called, that he had them join the expedition to Fort Ticonderoga and instruct some of his British regulars in wilderness warfare.

The rangers went into Maine to raid Abenaki settlements and later used Fort Ticonderoga as a base to raid Canada. In the Revolutionary War, Rogers sided with the British and fought against Washington's army at the battle of White Plains.

however, were ransomed by the French and returned. Montcalm ordered Fort William Henry burned and then returned to Ticonderoga.

Fort William Henry was the site of much action in the novel *The Last of the Mohicans* by James Fenimore Cooper. Several motion pictures have been based on this novel.

The fort has recently been restored by a private enterprise. The fort includes a museum and a theater, and there are demonstrations of cannon and musket firing and other activities.

BATTLE AT FORT CARILLON AT TICONDEROGA—JULY 8, 1758

By 1758, the British had come up with another plan to conquer Canada. An amphibious force would go up the St. Lawrence and meet with a land army coming north by way of Lake Champlain. Before this plan could be executed, however, it was necessary to take the French bastion of Louisbourg, which guarded the entrance to the St. Lawrence, and Fort Carillon at Ticonderoga, which controlled Lake Champlain and the inland route. Major General Jeffrey Amherst was assigned the task of taking Louisbourg, and Major General James Abercromby, commander of British forces in America, was to capture Fort Carillon at Ticonderoga.

On May 5, 1758, Abercromby left his base by the ruins of Fort William Henry and moved up Lake George to Ticonderoga. It took 900 bateaus (small flat-bottom boats with raked bows and sterns), 135 of the larger whaleboats, and numerous rafts to carry 6,350 regulars, 9,000 militia, a detachment of Rogers' Rangers, and artillery and supplies. The expedition disembarked at the north end of Lake George and marched on Fort Carillon.

The fort, located on a spit of land jutting into the lake, was built in the shape of a six-pointed star after a plan originated by Sébastien Vauban, the famous French military engineer. It was said of his work that the only person who could take fortifications designed by Vauban was Vauban himself. The fort was constructed of wood cribbing filled with packed soil and faced with stone. With its many cannons, it was a formidable fortress. As Abercromby approached, the fort was garrisoned by only 4,000 troops, consisting of four regiments of French regulars and some Canadian militia. But it was commanded by Montcalm, which would help make up for the shortage of men.

Montcalm correctly guessed that Abercromby would attack the rear of the fort, the side that faced inland. He put all his men, including officers, to work felling trees to build a massive zigzag-shaped wall, anchored at each end by water and set about a mile from the rear of the fort. In front of the log wall, the men built an almost impenetrable abatis of trees laid horizontally with the sharpened ends of their branches facing out.

As the British force approached the fort, Lord Augustus Howe, second in command to Abercromby, took an advance party that included Israel Putnam, to scout the area. The force tangled with some French soldiers, and Howe was killed.

Howe's death was a serious blow to the British army. He was one of the few British officers who appreciated the fighting abilities of the colonials and had an understanding of wilderness fighting. He had arranged for some of Rogers' Rangers to join the expedition and had some of his own regulars trained in backwoods fighting. More important, Howe might have prevented Abercromby from giving the incredible order for his infantry to make a frontal attack on the log wall.

Just why Abercromby ordered the frontal attack is not known, as there were other ways to take the fort. The easiest would have been to occupy the road to Montcalm's supply base at Fort St. Frederic and starve the garrison into surrendering. He could have also hauled his artillery to the top of nearby Mount Defiance and blasted the fort to pieces. Or, he could have used the artillery to turn the abatis and log wall into kindling wood. For some reason, he took none of these options.

Some authorities believe he ordered the frontal attack because he thought that reinforcements were on the way to Montcalm. Another explanation is that he was ill. In any event, Abercromby had never personally inspected the fort's defenses but relied on the opinion of an inexperienced engineer that they were not formidable.

Seven times on July 8, the British infantry crossed the wide expanse that the French had cleared of trees and undergrowth and hurled themselves against the abatis and log wall. The French defenders, firing from platforms, were so well protected by the log wall that only the tops of their caps were visible. From these platforms, they butchered the British troops as they came within range. On the seventh, and final, attack on the wall, men of the 42nd Highlanders—the famous Black Watch—hacked at the abatis with their broadswords. It was a brave but futile attack that cost the regiment 499 men—about half its strength.

During the attack, Abercromby remained at a sawmill on the river some distance from the fort. On that one day he had lost over 1,610 men, either killed, wounded, or missing. Montcalm lost 112 killed and 275 wounded. After this disaster, Abercromby called off the attack. Though he still had more than enough men, and unused artillery to take the fort, he no longer had the will to fight. He led his army back to its base, leaving most of his supplies and all the artillery on the shore of Lake George. Montcalm's brilliant repulse of Abercromby's army, however, would be France's last major victory of the war.

On July 26, Major General James Wolfe and Brigadier General Jeffrey Amherst captured Louisbourg, clearing the way for an attack on Quebec and Montreal by way of the St. Lawrence River. Lieutenant Colonel John Bradstreet had led his force of 3,000 up the Mohawk River and across Lake Ontario to take and destroy Fort Frontenac, severing the French supply line to the west, and Fort Duquesne.

In June 1759, Amherst, who had replaced Abercromby as commander of British forces, marched with an army of 11,000 on Carillon. The fort's commander, Brigadier François Bourlemaque, had only 4,000 men and had been ordered to take them north and not waste them trying to defend the fort. After receiving word of Amherst's intentions, he withdrew his force and blew up the fort.

Amherst continued north to St. Frederic but it, too, was destroyed before he reached it. He then supervised the rebuilding of the fort at Ticonderoga, which he officially named Fort Ticonderoga, and a new fort on the site of St. Frédéric. This fort would be names "His Majesty's Fort at Crown Point" and when completed would be the largest military installation built by the British in North America.

In April 1773, a fire originating in a chimney destroyed the fort at Crown Point. But the massive gray limestone walls of some of the barracks still stand along with some of the fort's outer defenses.

The Marquis de Montcalm arrived in Canada on May 11, 1756, to take command of French forces. He was a brilliant commander who easily took Fort William Henry, smashed Abercromby's attack on Fort Carillon (Fort Ticonderoga), and gained other victories. But as the British poured more men and materials into America, Montcalm's fortune turned and he was defeated at Quebec in a battle in which both he and British General Wolfe were mortally wounded. (Library of Congress)

Crown Point is a New York State Historic Site. Forts Ticonderoga and Crown Point would play a role in the American Revolutionary War.

After the Revolutionary War, Fort Ticonderoga was allowed to disintegrate. It has now been completely restored by the Pell family.

BATTLE OF FORT NIAGARA, NEW YORK—JULY 4–15, 1759

By 1759, France's hold on Canada was slipping. Louisbourg had fallen on July 26, 1758, to Brigadier General James Wolfe, who, now a major general, was preparing a

force to sail up the St. Lawrence River and attack Quebec.

On August 26 of that same year Lieutenant Colonel James Bradstreet had captured Fort Frontenac. Fort Duquesne was now isolated, and on November 24, 1758, the French destroyed it rather than allowing it to be taken by the advancing British force under Brigadier General John Forbes.

On that same day, France blew up Fort Carillon at Ticonderoga as Major General Jeffrey Amherst approached with his army of 11,000 on its way to Canada. The fort's garrison moved north to Fort St. Frederic at Crown Point, which they destroyed on August 31 before it could be taken by Amherst's advancing army. Only Fort Niagara remained in French hands.

Amherst determined that Fort Niagara must be taken, and he assigned this task to Brigadier General John Prideaux.

Prideaux established a base at the ruins of Fort Oswego which he had rebuilt. In May he moved west over Lake Ontario to Fort Niagara with 2,000 men, accompanied by William Johnson with 900 Indians. After building Fort William Henry, Major General Johnson returned to England where he was knighted. It was said that he assured himself of this honor by naming Lake George after the king and Fort William Henry after the king's grandsons.

The invasion force landed about two miles from Fort Niagara and began the siege. The fort's commander, Captain François Pouchot, had only 486 men of whom 149 were regulars. But he had done his best to strengthen the defenses, and he had obviously succeeded because the siege lasted about two weeks. Shortly after it began, Prideaux was accidentally killed by one of his own cannon, so Johnson took over. In spite of his lack of formal military training, he conducted the siege in an excellent fash-

ion. Finally, Pouchot asked for terms, which he then accepted. Johnson was determined that the surrender of the French force would not be a repeat of the massacre at Fort William Henry. He insisted that the Indians not harm the prisoners but allowed them to raid the fort and take whatever they pleased. The strategy worked and no prisoner was hurt.

In northern New York state, Fort Niagara, now called "Old Fort Niagara," is maintained by the nonprofit Old Niagara Association, Inc.

THE CONQUEST OF CANADA

With the loss of Forts Niagara and Louisbourg, inner Canada was completely isolated, allowing Wolfe to sail up the St. Lawrence and lay siege to Quebec. It was there on the Plains of Abraham, outside the city, that the last major battle of the French and Indian Wars was fought on September 13, 1759.

It was the only formal European-style battle of the long conflict. Wolfe's 4,800 troops turned out in elaborate uniforms, faced Montcalm's equally well-attired 4,000 French regulars, and went after each other with musket, bayonet, and artillery. It was a fierce and extremely bloody affair, leaving both Wolfe and Montcalm mortally wounded. British losses were 58 killed, 577 wounded. French losses are not known exactly but may have been as high as 1,000 killed, wounded, and missing.

The French finally withdrew to their citadel of Quebec, leaving the field to the British. The siege of Quebec continued until its surrender on September 18.

Major General James Wolfe was mortally wounded during the battle on the Plains of Abraham outside the French stronghold of Quebec. Wolfe lived just long enough to learn that he had defeated the defending French army, commanded by Montcalm. (Library of Congress)

Amherst completed the conquest of the remainder of Canada. On September 8, 1760, Montral surrendered, and Canada became a British colony. By the terms of the Treaty of Paris, signed on February 10, 1763, France ceded to Britain all claims to Nova Scotia, Canada, and territory east of the Mississippi except New Orleans.

THE WAR'S LEGACY

The French and Indian Wars helped lay the foundation for the American Revolutionary War. For 65 years, the English colonies had fought against the French with little help from England until the final year of the wars, which inspired some feelings of independence. Fighting the French alone, and later alongside British regulars, gave the Americans a degree of confidence in their fighting abilities. Many Americans lost whatever esteem they had for the British military. They had seen British "redcoats" flee in panic and surrender to the enemy. Some had developed a strong dislike for the haughty British officers who spoke with contempt of the "cowardly colonials." And the wars had given valuable military experience to men who would become leaders in the Revolution: George Washington, Israel Putnam, John Stark, Seth Pomeroy, and Horatio Gates.

Most important, the wars forced the several colonies into closer communication with each other. On June 19, 1754, representatives from New York, Pennsylvania, Maryland, and New England attended the Albany Convention to improve relations with the Iroquois and discuss other matters of general concern. At this meeting, Benjamin Franklin suggested a union of the colonies to better pursue the war. His suggestion was never officially acted on at that time, but it would be considered later when the colonies became increasingly dissatisfied with British rule.

American Revolutionary War

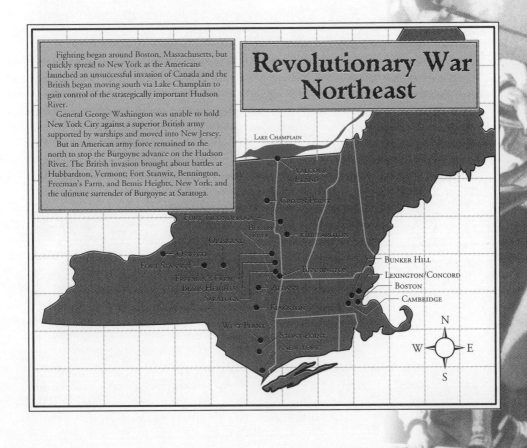

Revolutionary War Northeast

Fighting began around Boston, Massachusetts, but quickly spread to New York as the Americans launched an unsuccessful invasion of Canada and the British began moving south via Lake Champlain to gain control of the strategically important Hudson River.

General George Washington was unable to hold New York City against a superior British army supported by warships and moved into New Jersey.

But an American army force remained to the north to stop the Burgoyne advance on the Hudson River. The British invasion brought about battles at Hubbardton, Vermont; Fort Stanwix, Bennington, Freeman's Farm, and Bemis Heights, New York; and the ultimate surrender of Burgoyne at Saratoga.

LAKE CHAMPLAIN

VALCOUR ISLAND

CROWN POINT

FORT TICONDEROGA

HUDSON RIVER

HUBBARDTON

ORISKANY

OSWEGO

FORT STANWIX

BUNKER HILL

BENNINGTON

LEXINGTON/CONCORD

FREEMAN'S FARM

BOSTON

BEMIS HEIGHTS

SARATOGA

CAMBRIDGE

ALBANY

KINGSTON

WEST POINT

STONY POINT
NEW YORK

N
W   E
S

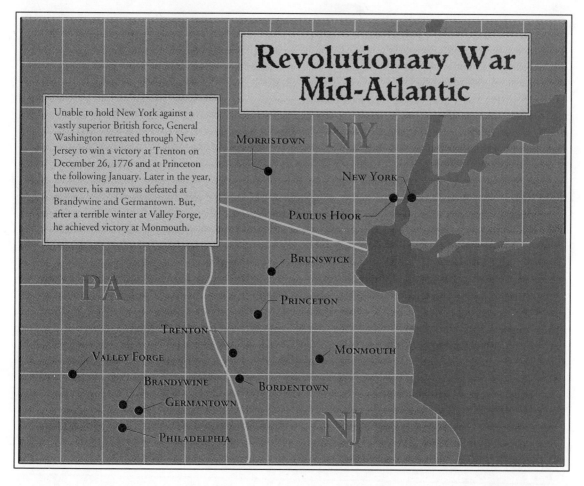

Revolutionary War Mid-Atlantic

Unable to hold New York against a vastly superior British force, General Washington retreated through New Jersey to win a victory at Trenton on December 26, 1776 and at Princeton the following January. Later in the year, however, his army was defeated at Brandywine and Germantown. But, after a terrible winter at Valley Forge, he achieved victory at Monmouth.

MORRISTOWN

NY

NEW YORK

PAULUS HOOK

BRUNSWICK

PA

PRINCETON

TRENTON

VALLEY FORGE

MONMOUTH

BRANDYWINE

BORDENTOWN

GERMANTOWN

NJ

PHILADELPHIA

CAUSES OF THE WAR

The American Revolutionary War began early on the morning of April 19, 1775, on a country road outside Boston, but its causes lay further in the past. Relations between England and the colonies in America had been strained for many years.

The basic source of the conflict was the role of the colonies. The British government believed their function was to benefit England by sending raw materials and buying manufactured goods made in England; buying sugar and tea only from English sources; providing revenue to support British regulars stationed in America,

and helping to repay the debt incurred during the French and Indian Wars.

For their part, the American colonies considered themselves on equal footing with England and particularly resented the taxes levied to provide revenue.

During the 1760s, England seemed to go out of its way to annoy and frustrate the colonies, passing a series of revenue-producing laws that included the Sugar Act and the infamous Stamp Act. Smuggling goods into America became common, and Parliament soon issued writs of assistance, allowing officials to enter and search any buildings they believed contained smuggled goods.

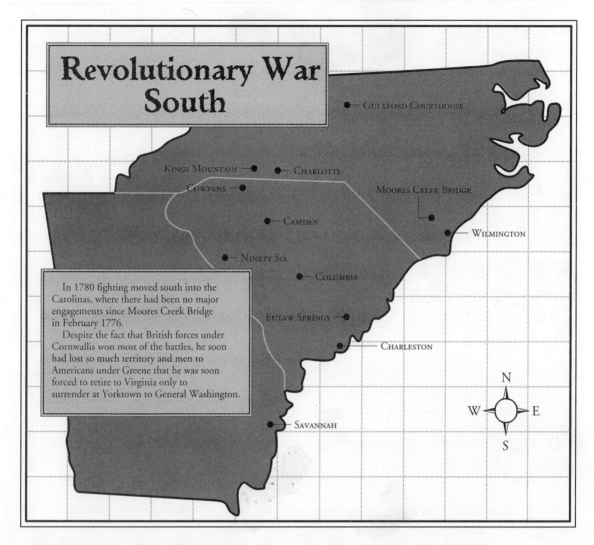

Revolutionary War South

GUILFORD COURTHOUSE

KINGS MOUNTAIN   CHARLOTTE

COWPENS

MOORES CREEK BRIDGE

CAMDEN

WILMINGTON

NINETY SIX

COLUMBIA

EUTAW SPRINGS

CHARLESTON

SAVANNAH

In 1780 fighting moved south into the Carolinas, where there had been no major engagements since Moores Creek Bridge in February 1776.

Despite the fact that British forces under Cornwallis won most of the battles, he soon had lost so much territory and men to Americans under Greene that he was soon forced to retire to Virginia only to surrender at Yorktown to General Washington.

N W E S

Tensions between the colonies and the Crown exploded into violence on March 5, 1770, when a Boston crowd pelted British soldiers with snowballs and rocks. The soldiers fired into the crowd, leaving three wounded and three dead, including Crispus Attucks, an escaped slave and seaman. The Boston silversmith and craftsman Paul Revere made an engraving of the "Boston Massacre," which helped fan the flames of rebellion.

Encouraged by radicals such as Samuel Adams and Patrick Henry, citizens in and around Boston began to attack agents of the Crown. Often supported by members of secret societies, such as the Sons of Liberty, mobs physically attacked officials and sometimes sacked or burned their houses. Ships sent from England to prevent entry of smuggled goods were also attacked. As a protest over the tea tax, an organized mob, dressed as Indians, boarded an East India Company ship at a Boston wharf on December 16, 1773, and tossed overboard $90,000 worth of tea. This "Boston Tea Party" convinced King George III that

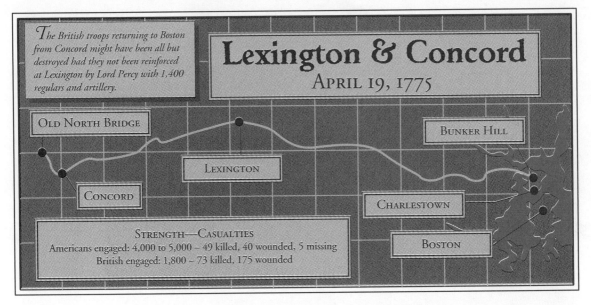

The British troops returning to Boston from Concord might have been all but destroyed had they not been reinforced at Lexington by Lord Percy with 1,400 regulars and artillery.

Lexington & Concord
APRIL 19, 1775

OLD NORTH BRIDGE

BUNKER HILL

LEXINGTON

CONCORD

CHARLESTOWN

BOSTON

STRENGTH—CASUALTIES
Americans engaged: 4,000 to 5,000 – 49 killed, 40 wounded, 5 missing
British engaged: 1,800 – 73 killed, 175 wounded

it was high time to punish Boston. On May 17, Lieutenant General Thomas Gage arrived in Boston as commander of His Majesty's Forces in America and governor of Massachusetts. His orders were to close the Port of Boston, bring the colonial government under the control of the Crown, and legalize quartering of troops in public buildings.

The other American colonies were much concerned when they learned of Gage's restrictive measures. On September 5, 1774, representatives of all the colonies, except Georgia, met in Philadelphia as the First Continental Congress. During the session, Paul Revere arrived with a copy of the Suffolk Resolve, drawn up by representatives of Massachusetts, recommending that the colony form its own government to collect taxes and withhold them from the Crown until certain restrictive acts were repealed. The Congress adopted this resolve and called for a boycott of English goods.

Massachusetts was now preparing to defend its position with force, if needed, and all military affairs were put into the hands of a Committee for Safety. Arms, ammunition, and cannon were collected and stored in relatively safe places. Militiamen, living on farms and in villages around Boston, were alerted and told to be ready in a minute (they became known as "minutemen") to assemble with their muskets and powder horns when the church bell sounded the alarm. By April 1775, the countryside around Boston had a sizable number of men ready to fight as soon as they received the word.

BATTLE AT LEXINGTON GREEN —APRIL 19, 1775

On the night of April 18, between 600 to 800 British regulars, under Lieutenant Colonel Francis Smith, left Boston by barge and crossed the bay to the mainland. Gage had ordered Smith to Lexington where Samuel Adams and John Hancock, both members of the Provincial Congress, were reported to be. After taking them prisoner, Smith was then to go on to Concord and

destroy the arms reported to be stored there.

Gage had intended to keep this mission secret, but there were no secrets in Boston in those times. Dr. Joseph Warren, a member of the Committee of Safety, quickly learned of the plan. On the morning of April 16 he sent Revere to warn Adams and Hancock, and on the night of the eighteenth, when he was certain the British force was preparing to move out, he sent Revere and William Dawes to alert the countryside.

Around 4:30 on the morning of April 19, the British advance guard, commanded by Major John Pitcairn, arrived at Lexington to find Captain John Parker with 77 rebel militia drawn up on the green about 100 yards from the road the British needed to take to reach Concord. The orders allegedly given that morning by Parker and Pitcairn to their men have become part of American folklore.

When Parker's 77 men faced the British with their shining bayonets, he is supposed to have told them "Stand your ground! Don't fire unless fired upon! But if they want war, let it begin here!" It seems doubtful however, that Parker intended to take on Smith's hundreds of regulars with 77 militiamen; when Pitcairn shouted, "Lay down your arms, you damn rebels and disperse!" Parker ordered his men not to fire and to withdraw.

As Parker's men were moving away, a British soldier fired at them; soon other troops began firing. When the fusillade stopped, eight Americans lay dead on the green. Parker moved the rest of his men out of range and at 5:30, Smith resumed his march to Concord.

The American Revolutionary War began around sunrise on April 19. At Lexington Green British troops fired on a small body of American minutemen blocking the road to Concord. In a matter of minutes the British had killed eight of them and wounded ten others. The Americans disbanded but the fighting would soon continue at Concord. (National Archives)

By this time, Revere and Dawes were spreading the word that "The Regulars are out!" and "The British are coming!" and the minutemen began to assemble. When Revere was captured by British officers, he and Dawes had been joined by young Dr. Samuel Prescott, who rode to warn Concord, spreading the news along the way.

THE RETREAT FROM CONCORD —APRIL 19, 1775

Smith's force arrived at Concord about seven in the morning and immediately began searching houses for arms. The chief depository was the home of Colonel James Barrett, but he had been given ample warning. Much of the supplies had been removed the day before and what remained were put in barrels in the attic and covered with feathers or hidden in the woods. A nearby field was plowed, and other supplies, including a cannon, were put in the furrows and then covered with earth. The British troops found precious few arms to destroy.

During the night, minutemen had been assembling at Concord. When the British arrived, they withdrew across North Bridge to the far side of the village, taking a position on high ground above the bridge. Soon this force had grown to 400 or so men. When they saw smoke coming from the village, they assumed, incorrectly, that the British intended to burn the village. Colonel Barrett ordered them to march to the village but not fire unless fired on. So off they marched, with the fifers of the Acton Company playing "The White Cockade."

British Captain Walter Laurie with about 35 men waited at the bridge and watched the Americans advance. He called for reinforcements and had his men remove some of the bridge's planks. His reinforcements arrived just as the Americans, under Major John Buttrick, came forward, and the British opened fire. The return fire from the minutemen killed three British soldiers— the first regulars killed by the minutemen. Though they lost two of their own, the Americans held the bridge.

Smith regrouped his troops and began to march back to Boston. For the first half hour, his troops marched unmolested. But when they reached Meriam's Corner, they fell under fire of minutemen concealed behind stone walls on each side of the road. The British were exhausted; had been on the march since the night before and now they found themselves attacked by an unseen foe.

Smith sent out flanking parties and some managed to get behind the Americans along the wall, killing a few of them. But for every minuteman killed, there was another to take his place. It is estimated that by the end of the day, there were about 4,000 minutemen shooting away at the British troops.

Around 2:30 P.M. British Brigadier Hugh Percy (Lord Percy) arrived at Lexington with 1,400 troops and artillery to reinforce Smith. A half hour later, Smith and his weary and discouraged force staggered in. Percy's artillery kept the Americans at bay so that Smith's men could rest and then resume the retreat to Boston.

The heaviest fighting of the march took place at present-day Arlington, where some 5,000 men from both sides were engaged. During this phase of the retreat, Percy's artillery broke up concentrations of Americans attacking the rear of the column. But as soon as the artillery fire stopped, the Americans quickly regrouped.

By nightfall, the British finally crossed Charlestown Neck and reached the safety of Bunker Hill, where they were protected by the guns of HMS *Somerset* in Boston Harbor. It had been a bad day for the British. They had lost 73 killed and 175 wounded out of a force of 1,800. American losses were far less—49 killed, 40 wounded, and 5 missing.

The day after the retreat, Percy wrote, "For my part, I never believed, I confess, that they would have attacked the King's troops, or the perseverance I found in them yesterday."

The Lexington-Concord battle road is the major element in the Minute Man National Historic Park, just outside Boston. This park system includes visitor centers in Lexington, Battle Road, and North Bridge at Concord.

BATTLE AT BUNKER HILL

After the retreat from Concord to Boston, the British found themselves cut off from the mainland by thousands of American militia. Some weeks later, Gage received reinforcements, and by June, he had about 6,500 men. At about the same time, three British major generals arrived: William Howe, Henry Clinton, and John Burgoyne. The Americans had reason to believe that Gage was planning to occupy the Charleston Peninsula, a half mile across the bay from Boston, and decided to fortify it in spite of the objections of some that the British might cut off a peninsula force and destroy it.

On the night of June 10, Colonel William Prescott and Major Israel Putnam, with some 1,000 men armed with picks, shovels, and muskets, arrived on the peninsula to build fortifications. They decided to put the major fortifications on Breed's Hill as it was closer to Boston than Bunker Hill. By morning the men had built a large redoubt with six-foot walls and dug trenches and erected

breastworks. Breastworks were also installed on Bunker Hill to cover a retreat to the mainland. Around 1 P.M., Howe landed near Moulton's Hill with about 2,000 British regulars.

Prescott correctly guessed that Howe intended to march along the edge of the Mystic River and attack the defenders from their rear and flanks. To prevent this maneuver, Prescott had his men reinforce the 100-yard rail and stone fence that ran from the Breed's Hill breastworks to the river's edge with bales of hay from the surrounding fields and sent a detachment of Connecticut troops to defend the fence.

While Howe was still assembling his men for the attack, the Americans were reinforced by the arrival of John Stark and 1,200 New Hampshiremen, who were told to join the Connecticut troops defending the wall. Stark noted that there was a smooth beach, wide enough for a column of four men marching abreast, between the end of the fence and the river. He had his men build a stone wall across the beach. Howe, seeing the arrival of Stark's men, requested reinforcements from Boston, so it was not until 3 P.M. that he ordered the attack to begin.

Howe's plan was that the light infantry would go around the end of the stone and rail fence and attack the defenders from the rear. In the meantime, his second in command, Brigadier General Robert Pigot, would take half the troops and attack the redoubt and breastworks.

American snipers began firing on Pigot's men from houses in the deserted village of Charlestown. Pigot asked the Royal Navy to take care of this nuisance, and several ships in the vicinity opened fire with incendiary shot, and soon the village was in flames.

General Howe was not aware of the stone wall that Stark had built across the beach when he ordered the Welsh Fusiliers to

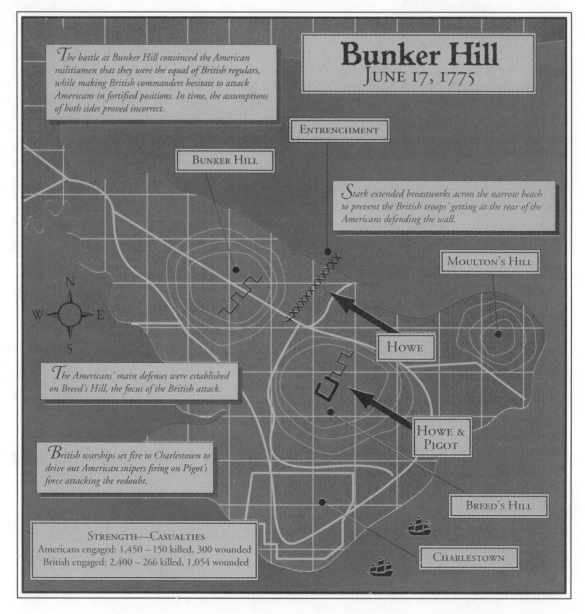

Bunker Hill
JUNE 17, 1775

The battle at Bunker Hill convinced the American militiamen that they were the equal of British regulars, while making British commanders hesitate to attack Americans in fortified positions. In time, the assumptions of both sides proved incorrect.

ENTRENCHMENT

BUNKER HILL

Stark extended breastworks across the narrow beach to prevent the British troops' getting at the rear of the Americans defending the wall.

MOULTON'S HILL

HOWE

The Americans' main defenses were established on Breed's Hill, the focus of the British attack.

HOWE & PIGOT

British warships set fire to Charlestown to drive out American snipers firing on Pigot's force attacking the redoubt.

BREED'S HILL

CHARLESTOWN

STRENGTH—CASUALTIES
Americans engaged: 1,450 – 150 killed, 300 wounded
British engaged: 2,400 – 266 killed, 1,054 wounded

attack. Stark had driven a stake into the ground 40 yards from the wall and ordered his men not to fire until the enemy reached this point. When the Fusiliers came to this point, they were cut to ribbons by the accurate fire from the wall. They managed to re-form and, with reinforcements, made another attack on the wall. Once again, the heavy and accurate fire from behind the wall broke up the attack. Howe attacked the wall a third time with his Grenadiers but this, too, ended in failure. With all of his personal staff either killed or wounded, Howe finally gave up on the wall.

Having failed to outflank the American forces, Howe decided on a frontal attack

CHARLES TOWN

BOSTON

View of The ATTACK on BUNKER'S HILL, with the
Burning of CHARLES TOWN, June 17. 1775.

Drawn by M? Millar   *Engraved by Lodge*

on the redoubt and breastworks. Guns from British warships and the battery on Coop's Hill in Boston were pounding the Americans' defenses as the British troops began the attack. The heat and the high grass in the fields leading to Breed's Hill made for tough going, and the British were ordered to shed their heavy packs and other unnecessary equipment before they began the march up the hill. They were met by withering fire and soon retreated down the hill in confusion.

Major General Henry Clinton, who had been watching the action from Coop's Hill, came over with as many reinforcements he could muster. He joined with Pigot, and the British re-formed and attacked again. Soon the ground around the breastworks and redoubt was littered with British dead.

Major John Pitcairn, who had faced the Americans at Lexington Green, was killed leading an attack on the redoubt.

But in spite of the heavy fire, some British troops managed to reach the trenches in back of the breastworks. As they did, American fire came to a stop—there was no more gunpowder. The British poured into the trenches and redoubts and attacked with bayonets. The Americans, lacking bayonets, fought back with the stocks of their muskets.

Prescott and Putnam directed a running fight, going from one position to another until their men had crossed the neck of the peninsula and reached the safety of the mainland. The majority of American casualties occurred during this retreat.

British casualties that day were stagger-

The British attack was directed at the American fortified position on Breed's Hill in front of Bunker Hill. British warships set fire to the village of Charlestown in an effort to drive off American snipers who were firing on the British left. (National Archives)

ing: out of 2,400 engaged, 1,054 had been wounded and 266 killed. American losses were 150 killed and 300 wounded out of the 1,450 or so who actually took part in the fighting. The Americans first considered the battle a defeat but would soon claim Bunker Hill as a victory, for after all, an army of untrained farmers and tradesmen had stood up to an army of British regulars and made them pay dearly.

But not all the Americans on the peninsula that day had the stomach to fight. Prescott observed that for every one man he received as reinforcements, he lost three who returned to the mainland once they viewed the fighting. Other American officers reported 20 men escorting a solitary wounded comrade from the battlefield.

After the battle of Bunker Hill, the status quo at Boston remained unchanged. The Americans continued to lay siege to the city but had no way to take it, and Gage had no way to break the siege. This stalemate continued until General George Washington arrived to break it.

The Bunker Hill Monument is now on Breed's Hill, since Bunker Hill was leveled some years ago. There is an observation platform at the top of the monument that provides an excellent view of the area, including Copps Hill in Boston.

GEORGE WASHINGTON TAKES COMMAND

The Second Continental Congress, meeting in Philadelphia on March 10, 1775, was faced with these two developments: the stalemate siege in Boston and the capture of the British fort at Ticonderoga by Benedict Arnold and Ethan Allen. Congress had little choice other than to declare the troops around Boston as the basis of a Continental Army and to assume responsi-

bility for the conduct of the war. On June 15, Congress appointed George Washington as commander of the Continental Army. At the same time, it appointed Artemas Ward, Charles Lee, Philip Schuyler, and Israel Putnam major generals and named eight brigadier generals including John Sullivan, Nathanael Greene, and Horatio Gates.

When Washington arrived at Cambridge, outside Boston, in July, he found a disorganized army of some 17,000 that lacked food, clothing, equipment, training, and discipline. He set to work to restore some form of order. As the siege of Boston continued, Washington reached the conclusion that if American forces were to win the war, they must take the initiative, which would require bold measures and certain risks. He decided that the best way to harm the British would be to invade Canada, and the Continental Congress gave its approval.

INVASION OF CANADA— AUGUST 1775–OCTOBER 1776

In July 1775, an American invasion force under General Philip Schuyler headed toward Montreal via Lake Champlain. But General Richard Montgomery, second in command, became so exasperated at the time Schuyler was wasting building ships and a base, that he marched ahead to Montreal with 1,200 men, including Ethan Allen, but without his Green Mountain Boys. Montgomery was held up at St. Johns, outside Montreal, by a small but well-deployed force led by General Guy Carleton, commander of British forces in Canada. Ethan Allen became impatient waiting outside St. Johns and with a few men dashed on to capture Montreal. But it was

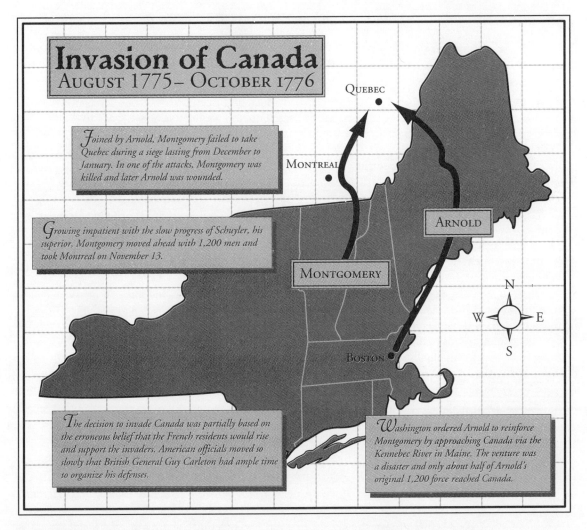

Invasion of Canada
AUGUST 1775– OCTOBER 1776

Joined by Arnold, Montgomery failed to take Quebec during a siege lasting from December to January. In one of the attacks, Montgomery was killed and later Arnold was wounded.

Growing impatient with the slow progress of Schuyler, his superior, Montgomery moved ahead with 1,200 men and took Montreal on November 13.

QUEBEC

MONTREAL

ARNOLD

MONTGOMERY

BOSTON

N W E S

The decision to invade Canada was partially based on the erroneous belief that the French residents would rise and support the invaders. American officials moved so slowly that British General Guy Carleton had ample time to organize his defenses.

Washington ordered Arnold to reinforce Montgomery by approaching Canada via the Kennebec River in Maine. The venture was a disaster and only about half of Arnold's original 1,200 force reached Canada.

Allen who was captured and eventually sent in chains to England.

Washington decided to speed up the invasion and sent a second force to Canada by way of the Kennebec River. In mid-September, Benedict Arnold and 1,200 soldiers started up the river on an incredible journey that would test the endurance of his men.

The boats, made out of green wood, leaked so the food and ammunition were ruined. Eventually, food became so scarce that, after eating a pet dog, the men boiled and ate their leather equipment— moccasins, powder pouches, and leggings. One commander and his 300 men deserted.

It rained much of the time, and by fall, there was snow and sleet. The men had to drag the heavy boats through swamps and around rapids, while being chilled to the bone by the icy cold water. On November 2, the survivors, about half the original number, reached Canada and civilization.

When Arnold heard that Montgomery had taken Montreal, he then marched on to Quebec. Montgomery joined him

ARNOLD AND ALLEN CAPTURE FORT TICONDEROGA

Benedict Arnold was living in New Haven, Connecticut, where he was a merchant and horse trader as well as a captain in the militia, when he heard the news of Lexington and Concord.

A man of great energy, Arnold immediately assembled his militia company and marched to Cambridge.

He was familiar with the Lake Champlain region and on learning that the Patriots needed cannons, he knew they could be found at Fort Ticonderoga, which he also knew was poorly defended.

The Committee of Safety approved the plan to take the fort and commissioned Arnold a colonel to lead an attack alone. He would, however, share command with Colonel Ethan Allen, who would bring his "Green Mountain Boys." These volunteers had been recruited to defend New Hampshire's claim to Vermont against New York.

Allen and Arnold arrived with 83 men by boat near the fort on the morning of May 10. The fort was taken without a shot fired by either side. One American officer was slightly wounded by the bayonet of a sentry, whom Allen then hit on the head with the back of his sword and ordered to show him the way to the fort's commander. When Allen demanded the fort's surrender, the commander asked on what authority, Allen reportedly replied, "In the name of the Great Jehovah and the Continental Congress!" (Whether Allen actually said this is questionable.)

Fort Ticonderoga would later supply Washington with the cannon he needed to drive the British out of Boston. Equally important, in October 1776, it would prevent the invasion force led by General Guy Carleton, commander of British troops in Canada, from reaching the Hudson River to join with British forces coming from New York.

outside the city, and on December 31, they struck. Montgomery, leading one column, was killed. When Arnold was also injured, the attack deteriorated. Though American forces under Brigadier John Sullivan continued trying to take the city, by this time Carleton had received reinforcements, while Sullivan's force was being reduced by smallpox and expiration of short enlistments. In June, Sullivan, joined by Arnold, moved his force out of Canada to Crown Point, a few miles above Fort Ticonderoga.

THE BATTLE AT VALCOUR ISLAND—OCTOBER 11–13, 1776

After the Americans abandoned their invasion of Canada, the British began a counterattack. Carleton was to move south by way of Lake Champlain and join at Albany with Howe coming up the Hudson from New York, thus cutting New England and New York off from the other colonies. Carleton began gathering small warships to ensure his control of Lake Champlain.

Americans learned of the British plan and Benedict Arnold, who had experience with ships from when Arnold was a merchant and sailed his own ship to the West Indies, was put in command of the small American lake fleet. Both sides began building more ships. By early September, the two fleets were ready for battle.

On September 23, Arnold's fleet of 15 ships anchored in a narrow channel between Valcour Island and the west shore of Lake Champlain. Carleton, with his

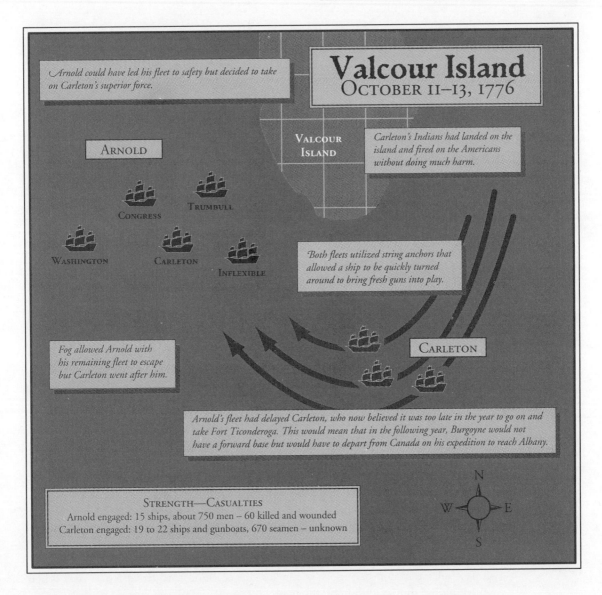

Valcour Island
OCTOBER 11–13, 1776

Arnold could have led his fleet to safety but decided to take on Carleton's superior force.

VALCOUR ISLAND

Carleton's Indians had landed on the island and fired on the Americans without doing much harm.

ARNOLD

CONGRESS

TRUMBULL

WASHINGTON

CARLETON

INFLEXIBLE

Both fleets utilized string anchors that allowed a ship to be quickly turned around to bring fresh guns into play.

CARLETON

Fog allowed Arnold with his remaining fleet to escape but Carleton went after him.

Arnold's fleet had delayed Carleton, who now believed it was too late in the year to go on and take Fort Ticonderoga. This would mean that in the following year, Burgoyne would not have a forward base but would have to depart from Canada on his expedition to reach Albany.

STRENGTH—CASUALTIES
Arnold engaged: 15 ships, about 750 men – 60 killed and wounded
Carleton engaged: 19 to 22 ships and gunboats, 670 seamen – unknown

N
W E
S

superior fleet, discovered Arnold on October 11, and the two fleets engaged in a fierce close-quarter battle. Cannonballs tore into ships while muskets fired off the men manning the cannons.

Arnold's ships fought bravely but took a terrible beating. As darkness fell, he moved his surviving ships out of enemy range. Carleton decided to wait until morning to

finish off Arnold, but during the dark and foggy night, Arnold's fleet quietly sailed away. In the morning, Carleton set out after him, and an amazing race between the two fleets began. When the wind failed, all the ships had to be propelled with oars.

Arnold finally saw no hope for retaining his few remaining ships. When he reached Buttonmould Bay, he beached and

Officers' and soldiers' barracks and parade ground, once "His Majesty's Fort of Crown Point." The fortification complex covered over three and a half square miles, making it the largest British military installation built in America. (Crown Point Historic Site)

burned them, and he and his men marched the ten miles to Crown Point. The fort's garrison, even with Arnold's men, were too few to defend the base, so they set it on fire and marched to Fort Ticonderoga. Arnold had lost 60 men and 11 of his 16 ships.

Many historians and military authorities consider Valcour Island to be one of the most important battles of the war because of its results. Carleton had spent so much time building ships and fighting the battle at Valcour that it was now too late in the year to take Ticonderoga. Instead, after Valcour, he withdrew to Canada. But if he had taken Fort Ticonderoga, Major General Burgoyne would have started out from this base the following year and very probably would have joined with Howe in Albany instead of surrendering his entire army at Saratoga.

THE BRITISH EVACUATE BOSTON—MARCH 17, 1776

In early 1776, the siege of Boston still continued. British warships in the waters prevented Washington from attacking the city, while his army was too great for Howe to break the siege.

Washington realized that he needed a lot of cannon to drive Howe out. When Arnold and Allen reported the large quantity of cannon, shot, and powder at Fort Ticonderoga, Washington decided to use them and planned to send 25-year-old Colonel Henry Knox for them. Knox, a self-taught artillery expert, waited until winter, when the ground, lakes, and rivers were frozen. Then, with 43 sleds pulled by 82 yoke of oxen along with some horses, he managed to move over 100 tons of cannon

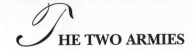HE TWO ARMIES

When the Revolutionary war started in April 1775, America's only fighting force was the militia drawn from nearby colonies. In June, Congress created the Continental Army and "adopted" into it the militiamen, then laying siege to Boston.

Congress encouraged men to join the Continental Army to serve for a longer enlistment period than the militiamen. It then became the "regular" army.

The militia were state organizations under control of state governors who also appointed commanding officers.

When Congress created the Continental Army, under its and not state control, Congress "adopted" the militia at Boston. This allowed Congress to appoint its own generals to command this force. George Washington of Virginia was one.

But all other militia units remained under state control. The Continental Army was often so short of men that it had to plead with state governors to send them some militia.

The Continental Army became an army of "regulars" who enlisted for a definite period and, unlike some militia, did not run home when the shooting began.

The Continental Army never had enough men, so commanders would often have to draw on the militia to provide additional manpower. In battle, the militia was not always dependable and would often break and run when under attack. But sometimes it stood fast, prompting one historian to state that the militia could never be counted on by a friend or ignored by the enemy,

The British troops sent from England to fight in America were the "regulars," supported on occasion by companies of Canadian militia, Loyalists or Tories, and frequently by Indians. In 1776, Parliament voted to raise an army of 55,000 to crush the American rebellion, but because the war was unpopular in England, King George III was forced to hire mercenaries from German principalities.

Since the largest number of the 33,000 German mercenaries came from Hesse-Cassel, the Americans referred to all German troops as "Hessians" (including those from the Duchy of Brunswick who fought with Borgoyne at Saratoga).

The American and British forces were organized along the same lines. The basic element was the company of about 90 men, commanded by a captain or lieutenant. A regiment, or battalion, consisted of ten companies, giving it a strength of between 450 to 800 men under a colonel or lieutenant colonel. Two or more regiments made up a brigade under a brigadier general, and two or more brigades formed a division commanded by a major general.

Regiments of both armies usually included a light infantry "flank company." These were elite troops, employed for reconnaissance, skirmishing, and protecting the regiment's flanks in battle and on the march. In German regiments, such men were called Jägers ("Huntsmen").

British regiments also included a second flank company of grenadiers. Grenadier companies were first formed during the Thirty Years War (1618–1648) to throw the "hand bomb"—an early type of hand grenade. The strongest and tallest men were selected for this task. The grenadiers wore brimless hats so they could easily swing their musket to either shoulder to free their throwing arm. In time, this hat developed into the tall miter-shaped headpiece worm by British grenadiers in the Revolutionary War.

The Americans and British did not use cavalry during the fighting in the Northeast. But when warfare moved into the more open lands of the South—Virginia and the Carolinas—the horse began to play a role. Each army used dragoons—men who rode on horses and fought on foot. But they could also fight mounted and so were, in effect, also cavalry. There were also non-dragoon cavalry units active in the southern campaigns.

hundreds of miles through forest, over mountains, and across lakes and rivers.

At the end of January, Knox arrived at Cambridge with 59 cannon and presented his commander in chief with "a noble train of artillery." Knox's artillery was placed on Dorchester Heights, and from there the cannon could sweep the harbor where the British fleet lay. As the ground was frozen solid, the breastworks for the artillery had to be prefabricated with barrels filled with earth and wooden frames filled with hay. On the night of March 3, the artillery was moved into position on the heights. In the morning, the British awoke to find more than 50 big American guns pointing at them.

The British ship's cannon could not be sufficiently elevated to fire on the American position. Rather than try to storm the heights, General Howe, who had replaced Gage, decided to evacuate Boston. By March 17, the last British troops and a number of Loyalists retreated from Boston to Nova Scotia.

THE NEW YORK CAMPAIGN— AUGUST 27–NOVEMBER 20, 1776

Washington guessed that Howe would next move on New York, since occupation of this one-square-mile town at the tip of Manhattan Island would give him control of the Hudson River, cutting off New England and New York from the colonies to the south. He believed that New York was so important that in February 1776 he sent General Charles Lee there to plan and build defenses.

On July 2—two days before Congress adopted the Declaration of Independence—which formally severed ties between England and the colonies, General Howe's army of well-trained British and Hessian troops began landing on Staten Island in New York Bay. Howe was supported by warships under the command of his brother, Admiral Earl Howe.

Washington arrived in New York with about 17,000 troops. Because of Washington's inferior, considerably smaller, and untrained army, along with unfamiliar terrain and no naval support, New York turned out to be a disaster for the American troops.

On August 27, Howe's British regulars had no difficulty driving the American force commanded by Putnam, from Flatbush, Long Island, to a defensive position on Brooklyn Heights near the East River.

When the British took the Heights, Washington had the troops ferried across the river, landing at Kip's Bay on Manhattan.

Howe crossed over and, on September 15, drove Washington's troops from the Kip's Bay area and pushed them north toward the tip of Manhattan.

Washington decided to defend a position between Harlem Heights and Kingsbridge that connected Manhattan Island to the mainland to the north.

On September 16, there was a brisk fight at Harlem Heights, and while the British got the upper hand, Howe made no effort to prevent Washington from going to Kingsbridge and continuing to the north.

On October 28, Howe caught up with Washington at White Plains, New York, but in the ensuing battle failed to destroy the American force. Rain delayed Howe's making a second attack and by the time the sky was clear, Washington had moved north to a strong defense position at North Castle, beyond the Croton River.

Instead of following Washington, Howe struck at Fort Washington on the northern end of Manhattan Island and Fort Lee

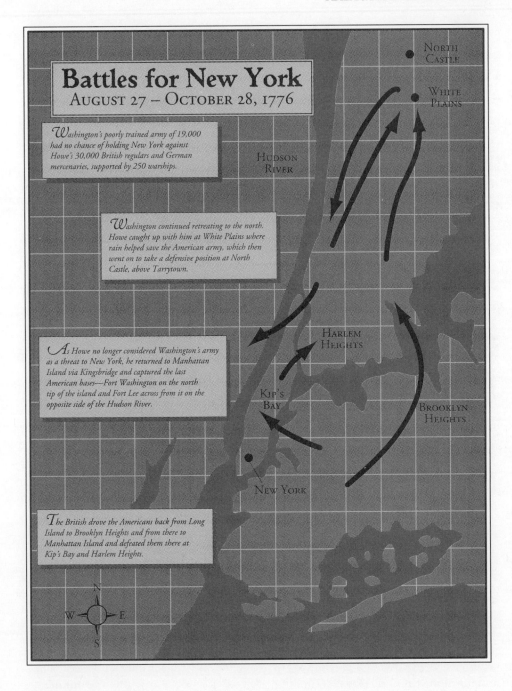

Battles for New York
AUGUST 27 – OCTOBER 28, 1776

Washington's poorly trained army of 19,000 had no chance of holding New York against Howe's 30,000 British regulars and German mercenaries, supported by 250 warships.

Washington continued retreating to the north. Howe caught up with him at White Plains where rain helped save the American army, which then went on to take a defensive position at North Castle, above Tarrytown.

As Howe no longer considered Washington's army as a threat to New York, he returned to Manhattan Island via Kingsbridge and captured the last American bases—Fort Washington on the north tip of the island and Fort Lee across from it on the opposite side of the Hudson River.

The British drove the Americans back from Long Island to Brooklyn Heights and from there to Manhattan Island and defeated them there at Kip's Bay and Harlem Heights.

NORTH CASTLE

WHITE PLAINS

HUDSON RIVER

HARLEM HEIGHTS

KIP'S BAY

BROOKLYN HEIGHTS

NEW YORK

on the opposite shore of the Hudson River. Generals Greene and Putnam had insisted to Washington that Fort Washington could be defended and therefore reinforced. They were wrong. After a brief siege, on November 16, Fort Washington surren-

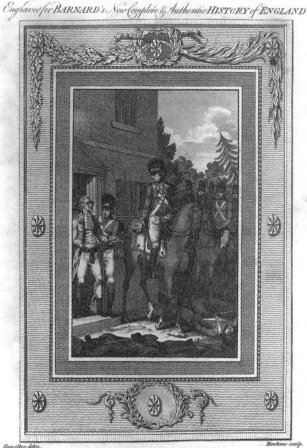

Engraved for BARNARD's *New Complete & Authentic* HISTORY *of* ENGLAND

Hamilton delin.   *Hawkins sculp.*

The American General Lee *taken* Prisoner *by* Lieutenant Colonel Harcourt *of the* ENGLISH ARMY, *in* Morris Country. New-Jersey. 1776.

Capture of General Charles Lee by the British at Widow White's tavern, near Basking Ridge, New Jersey, on December 13, 1776.

Lee, a former soldier of fortune, believed he was the best qualified to command the American army, and intrigued against Washington, but he later performed so badly at Monmouth that Congress dismissed him. (National Archives)

of the Hudson River. He and Greene retreated into New Jersey. He had lost New York and been defeated in every battle. But as would often be the case, his army remained intact. Though he would suffer other defeats in the ensuing war, Washington was always able to save his army and would continue to strike at the enemy when he believed there was a chance for success.

RETREAT THROUGH NEW JERSEY—NOVEMBER– DECEMBER 1776

Pursued by General Cornwallis, leading a superb army of 10,000 British and Hessians, Washington's army of 5,000 seemed to be about finished. When the pitiful remnant crossed the Delaware River into Pennsylvania, Cornwallis was only a few hours behind. Washington destroyed all the boats on the New Jersey side of the river that he did not need, so for a time, his army was safe from Cornwallis.

The American army was in terrible condition—exhausted and discouraged. The enlistment period for the majority of the men would end on December 30, which would leave Washington with just 1,500 men. The Continental Congress fled Philadelphia for the safety of Baltimore and left Washington in control of all military affairs.

During the retreat through New Jersey, Thomas Paine, now an aide-de-camp to General Greene, wrote a pamphlet entitled "The Crisis." His previous pamphlet, "Common Sense," had been a potent force in creating the will for independence. "The Crisis" would help gain that independence. Published around the middle of December, it had a profound effect on both civilians and soldiers. Washington ordered it read to the troops. It is not dif-

dered and over 2,600 soldiers became British prisoners. In addition, the enemy captured a huge amount of precious arms, ammunition, cannon, tents, trenching tools, and other material. Fort Lee was easily taken on November 20.

Washington left General Lee at North Castle with 4,000 men to guard that region

ficult to imagine how Paine's opening lines made these men feel:

> *These are the times that try men's souls: The summer soldier and the sunshine patriot will, in this crisis, shrink from the service of his country; but he that stands it now, deserves the love and thanks of man and woman. Tyranny, like hell, is not easily defeated; yet we have this consolation with us, that the harder the conflict, the more glorious the triumph.*

Washington had been writing General Lee at North Castle to come with reinforcements. Lee set out for New Jersey, intending to maintain separate command. Lee was captured by the British, so his second in command, General John Sullivan, reinforced Washington with Lee's 2,000 troops. Colonel John Cadwalader arrived with 2,000 Pennsylvania men. Washington now had about 6,000 men—at least until enlistments ended on December 30.

On December 14, General Howe decided it had become too cold to fight and sent the British army into winter quarters, thus ending his campaign in New Jersey. But the campaign was not over for Washington, who planned to go on the offensive. His objectives were three British military bases: Trenton, Princeton, and New Brunswick.

BATTLE OF TRENTON— DECEMBER 26, 1776

On Christmas night, Washington's army crossed the Delaware River from Pennsylvania, and on the morning of December 26, attacked the three Hessian regiments quartered in Trenton. The Germans were completely unprepared for the attack and when the battle was over they had lost 22

men, with 92 wounded and 948 taken prisoner. No Americans had been killed, and only four were wounded. Believing that his troops were too exhausted to go on to Princeton, and with almost 1,000 prisoners to deal with, Washington recrossed the Delaware.

But Washington still wanted Princeton and especially New Brunswick, where there were considerable British military supplies. On December 29, he crossed the Delaware again. At Trenton, he learned that Cornwallis was established at Princeton, some 12 miles away.

Washington's army was down to 1,600 men. But General Thomas Mifflin and Colonel Cadwalader arrived with a total of 3,600 troops, and Henry Knox and Mifflin persuaded the men whose enlistment period was up to serve for another six weeks for ten dollars. Washington now had a force of about 5,600, but only 1,600 were regulars; the others were untrained militia.

On January 2, 1777, Cornwallis reached Trenton and found Washington's army along a ridge on the south side of the Assunpink River with its back to the Delaware. He decided it was too late in the afternoon to attack but planned to strike in the morning.

Washington saw that his army was no match for Cornwallis. Rather than remain on the defensive, he would go on the offensive. Four hundred men were left on the ridge to keep the campfires burning, and by 3 A.M., the rest of the army was on its way to Princeton.

BATTLE OF PRINCETON— JANUARY 3, 1777

On the morning of January 3, the Americans attacked the forces that

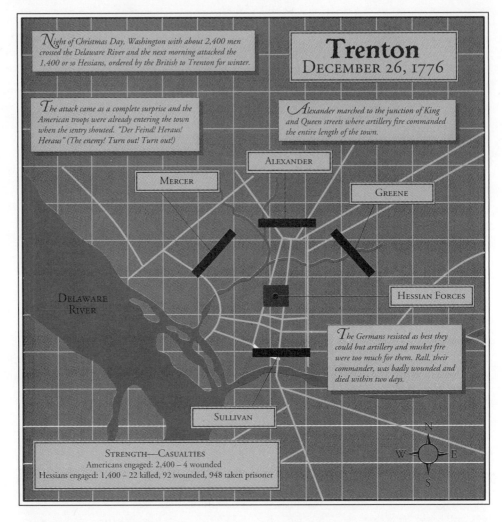

Night of Christmas Day, Washington with about 2,400 men crossed the Delaware River and the next morning attacked the 1,400 or so Hessians, ordered by the British to Trenton for winter.

Trenton
DECEMBER 26, 1776

The attack came as a complete surprise and the American troops were already entering the town when the sentry shouted, "Der Feind! Heraus! Heraus" (The enemy! Turn out! Turn out!)

Alexander marched to the junction of King and Queen streets where artillery fire commanded the entire length of the town.

ALEXANDER

MERCER

GREENE

DELAWARE RIVER

HESSIAN FORCES

The Germans resisted as best they could but artillery and musket fire were too much for them. Rall, their commander, was badly wounded and died within two days.

SULLIVAN

STRENGTH—CASUALTIES
Americans engaged: 2,400 – 4 wounded
Hessians engaged: 1,400 – 22 killed, 92 wounded, 948 taken prisoner

N W E S

Cornwallis had left at Princeton. For a time the battle did not go well for Washington. General Hugh Mercer was mortally wounded as the British came at the Americans with bayonets, and the ranks fell apart. Washington rode to within 30 yards of the enemy trying to rally his men, entreating the troops to continue fighting. Finally, Sullivan arrived and his men stormed Princeton. Alexander Hamilton's artillery put a cannonball into Nassau Hall and bagged 200 British soldiers. With the arrival of Sullivan, other troops rallied, and the British retreated.

The battle lasted only about 15 minutes, but it had been a hot fight with bayonets, muskets, and artillery. Forty Americans had been killed or wounded. Washington reported 100 British killed and 300 taken prisoner. Morale of the troops was now very good. In ten days, they had twice defeated Hessian and British troops.

Washington gave up the plan to attack New Brunswick, since his army was exhausted, and Cornwallis might appear at any time. He decided to march north to the

American base at Morristown, where the army would spend the winter.

When Congress had debated the appointment of Washington as commanding general, one member pointed out that Washington had never won a battle, which was true. But after Trenton and Princeton, he was considered by many to be a military genius equal to Frederick the Great.

While some of the original battlefield has been privately developed, there is still much to see at Princeton Battle Field State Park, including a portion of the battlefield, battle monument, the burial place of American and British soldiers, and a large oak tree, which reportedly marks the site where General Mercer fell.

BURGOYNE'S SARATOGA CAMPAIGN—JULY 5– OCTOBER 17, 1777

While Washington, in New Jersey, was trying to guess what Howe, in New York, was up to, British General John Burgoyne was on his way from Canada, heading for Albany. The plan was that he would be joined there by General Howe, coming up the Hudson River, and by General Barry St. Ledger, moving east by way of the Mohawk River Valley. Once these forces joined, New York and New England would be isolated, which, the authorities in London believed, would end the rebellion.

The surrender of Hessian troops to General George Washington following the battle at Trenton, New Jersey, December 26, 1776. This victory, after so many defeats, encouraged Washington to go on the offensive and on January 3, 1777, he moved on Princeton, New Jersey, and defeated a portion of Cornwallis's British force. (National Archives)

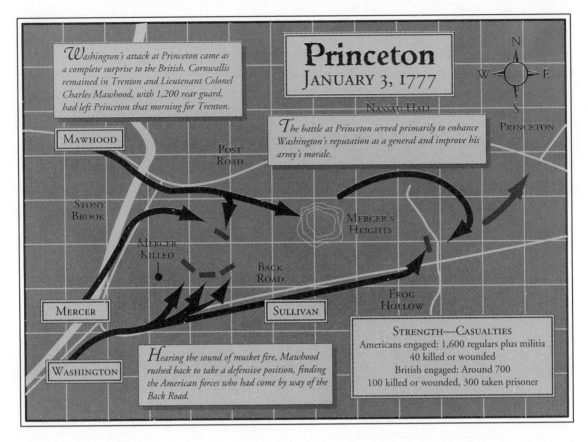

Princeton
JANUARY 3, 1777

Washington's attack at Princeton came as a complete surprise to the British. Cornwallis remained in Trenton and Lieutenant Colonel Charles Mawhood, with 1,200 rear guard, had left Princeton that morning for Trenton.

NASSAU HALL

PRINCETON

The battle at Princeton served primarily to enhance Washington's reputation as a general and improve his army's morale.

MAWHOOD

POST ROAD

STONY BROOK

MERCER'S HEIGHTS

MERCER KILLED

BACK ROAD

FROG HOLLOW

MERCER

SULLIVAN

WASHINGTON

Hearing the sound of musket fire, Mawhood rushed back to take a defensive position, finding the American forces who had come by way of the Back Road.

STRENGTH—CASUALTIES
Americans engaged: 1,600 regulars plus militia
40 killed or wounded
British engaged: Around 700
100 killed or wounded, 300 taken prisoner

There were several flaws in this plan. For example, no one was charged with overall command of troops in America, and instructions from Lord Germain, secretary of state for the American colonies, were vague and confusing. Germain, in fact, approved orders that Howe march on Philadelphia; by the time he remembered that Howe was originally supposed to go to Albany, Howe was already at sea heading south. It would also be difficult for the three forces to keep in contact in the forested wilderness of upstate New York, where it was said that a squirrel could travel the length of New York without ever touching ground.

In June, Burgoyne came down from Lake Champlain to take his first objective, Fort Ticonderoga. He commanded an impressive force: 3,000 British regulars; 3,000 German mercenaries from the Duchy of Brunswick, commanded by General Baron Friedrich von Riedesel; 250 Canadian and Loyalist militia; and about 400 Indians. There were also about 400 men to handle the 138 pieces of artillery and siege cannon.

On July 2, the invasion force reached Fort Ticonderoga. Its commander, Major General Arthur St. Clair, had about 2,500 men, and the fort's defenses had been improved. The tops of some of the surrounding hills also had been fortified. There were no fortifications on top of Mt. Defiance, however, because it was believed to be impossible to move artillery there. But Burgoyne's men managed to scale the summit, and when St. Clair saw the cannon pointing down on the fort, he realized his position was untenable. On the night of

July 4, he ordered all the fort's cannon to blast away to cover his withdrawal.

St. Clair planned to take his 2,500 men to join General Philip Schuyler at Fort Edwards, between Lake George and the Hudson River. Because there were enemy forces on the northern end of Lake George, he had to move east into Vermont and then swing south to Fort Edwards.

BATTLE OF HUBBARDTON— JULY 7, 1777

On the afternoon of July 6, St. Clair reached the tiny Vermont settlement of Hubbardton, about six miles from Castleton, where he planned to camp for the night. He ordered Colonel Seth Warner and his 150 Vermont men to wait at Hubbardton until the army's rear guard arrived and then join him that night in Castleton. The rear guard consisted of Colonel Turbott Francis's Massachusetts regiment and Colonel Nathan Hale's New Hampshire regiment—about 1,000 men in all. After their arrival, Warner ignored St. Clair's order and spent the night in Hubbardton. Worse, he did not post sentries around the camp.

Burgoyne had sent one of his best corps commanders, Brigadier General Simon Fraser, with 850 regulars to catch St. Clair's army. A but later, he ordered Baron von Riedesel to go with 200 of his Brunswickers to reinforce Fraser. On the night of July 6, Fraser camped about three miles from the American position and attacked around dawn near Sucker Creek. With no sentries posted, the attack came as a complete surprise to Warner and his men, who became badly disorganized. But they soon reformed and their first volley killed 21 of Fraser's men.

Major General Arthur St. Clair's military career as governor of the Northwest Territory ended on November 4, 1791, when his army of 2,300 was routed by Shawnee and Miami warriors, led by Little Turtle and Blue Jacket. St. Clair's army sustained a loss of close to 1,000 soldiers killed or wounded. St. Clair's previous experience in field command ended in 1777 when, for sound military reasons, he abandoned Fort Ticonderoga rather than allow his outnumbered troops to be taken by Burgoyne. (Library of Congress)

The ground was covered with standing trees: ideal for the Americans because they could have cover to shoot from; bad for the enemy because there could be no orderly fighting.

The Earl of Balcarres, who commanded the flank companies of the British advance corps, was slightly wounded.

Warner was able to establish a line extending some one thousand yards,

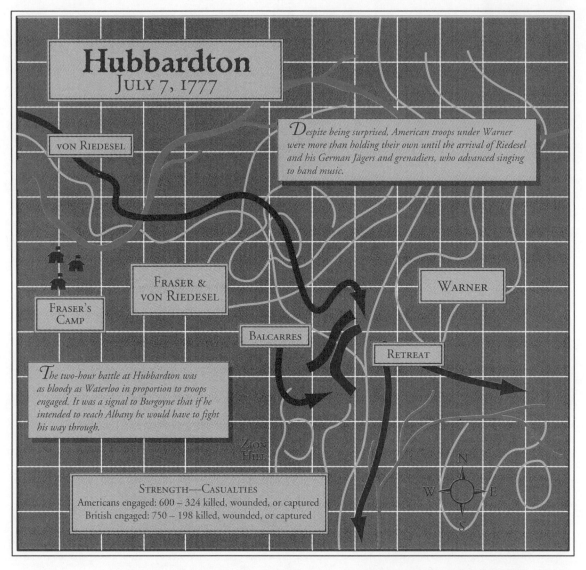

Hubbardton
July 7, 1777

Despite being surprised, American troops under Warner were more than holding their own until the arrival of Riedesel and his German Jägers and grenadiers, who advanced singing to band music.

VON RIEDESEL

FRASER & VON RIEDESEL

FRASER'S CAMP

BALCARRES

WARNER

RETREAT

The two-hour battle at Hubbardton was as bloody as Waterloo in proportion to troops engaged. It was a signal to Burgoyne that if he intended to reach Albany he would have to fight his way through.

ZION HILL

STRENGTH—CASUALTIES
Americans engaged: 600 – 324 killed, wounded, or captured
British engaged: 750 – 198 killed, wounded, or captured

N W E S

anchored on the left on the side of a hill, now called "Zion Hill."

Fraser, supported by Balcarres, attempted to turn Warner's left and occupy the Castleton road to cut off Warner's retreat. Warner pulled back his left in a maneuver called "refusing the flank" and his men continued firing.

To strengthen his attack force, Fraser had drawn men from his left. When Francis realized the weak British left, he attacked, soon reinforced by Hale's troops.

The British were faltering when they heard the sound of a German band announcing the timely arrival of von Riedesel and his force of Brunswickers. Von Riedesel immediately ordered an attack on the American flanks. For ten minutes, Francis's troops held their position and poured fire on the advancing enemy. But when Francis was mortally wounded, the Massachusetts troops fled rather than face a bayonet charge.

Warner and his Vermont men were doing more than holding their own, but when he saw much of the army leaving the field, he decided it was time for them to quit. He called out to his men, "Meet me at Manchester," and the Americans left the field.

Hubbardton, the only battle of the war fought in Vermont, was a very bloody 45-minute affair. The British lost 198 killed and wounded, and/or captured. American casualties were 312 men and 12 officers out of the 600 that actually took part in the battle. Casualties amounted to about 27 percent of all participating troops—about the same percentage as at Waterloo. The battle at Hubbardton was a clear signal to Burgoyne that if he intended to reach Albany he would have to fight his way toward it.

Hubbardton Battlefield is a State Owned Historic Site. There is a visitor center with lounge and museum along with a diorama showing the battle in its furious early stages.

BATTLE AT BENNINGTON—AUGUST 16, 1777

By the time Burgoyne reached Fort Edwards on July 29, his army was running out of basic supplies—beef and ammunition. He also needed horses for von Riedesel's dragoons and the artillery. He ordered Lieutenant Colonel Friedrich Baum, who did not speak English, to lead a foraging and raiding party into the Connecticut River region to capture cattle and horses.

On August 11, Baum marched into Vermont with a force of about 800, made up of some 375 Brunswick unmounted dragoons and infantry; 50 British sharpshooters; 30 German artillerymen; and 300 Tories, Canadians, and Indians. The advance Indian scouts turned out to be a great liability, looting houses and barns, killing cattle just for the cowbells, and so alarming the inhabitants that they took their livestock out of danger.

Local Tories had told Burgoyne that the rebels had an important military supply base at Bennington, guarded by only 300 to 400 militia. Baum was ordered to capture these supplies and started toward the town. At the same time, Brigadier General John Stark, who had been keeping tabs on Burgoyne and Baum, was also marching to Bennington, requesting that Seth Warner and his Vermonters meet him there.

On August 14, Baum encountered a small rebel scouting party at Sancoick's Mill. The Americans destroyed the bridge and withdrew. Baum sent a request to Burgoyne for reinforcements after learning that the force guarding the supplies at Bennington was far greater than a few hundred militia.

Stark arrived near Bennington about the same time as Baum, and the two forces were then only separated by the Walloomsac River. Stark withdrew to about two miles from Bennington, and the two armies camped for the night of August 14.

It rained on August 15, and Baum began to fortify his position. Trees were felled to create the "Dragoon Redoubt" manned by Germans and equipped with artillery. The "Tory Redoubt" was built beyond the bridge and on the other side of the river. Canadians and Indians occupied log cabins on each side of the river.

Around noon on August 16, the rain stopped and the battle began. Baum's army of 800 faced Stark's, which had now grown to about 2,000. Stark planned for a double envelopment of Baum's army. Colonel Moses Nichols took his 200 New Hampshire men on a long circuit to hit the Dragoon Redoubt on Baum's right. Colonel Samuel Herrick led his 300 Vermont Rangers and

THE JANE MCCREA ATROCITY—JULY 27, 1777

After the battle at Hubbardton, Burgoyne continued to pursue St. Clair, but on arrival at Skenesboro, he learned that his prey had moved south to join Schuyler at Fort Edwards. Borgoyne did not have enough boats to carry his entire force to Fort Edwards, so he decided to move the army overland and use the boats for his artillery and supplies.

Schuyler knew that crumbling Fort Edwards could not be defended but decided to delay Burgoyne as long as possible. He had 1,000 axmen fell trees, destroy bridges, divert streams to create swamps, and in general, do everything to make the 23-mile trail from Skenesboro to Fort Edwards impassable. His men did their job well, for it took Burgoyne's army about three weeks to cover the 23 miles.

On July 27, Burgoyne had reached Fort Ann, not far from Fort Edwards. While they were there, an Indian scout arrived with the scalp of Jane McCrea.

Twenty-three-year-old Jane McCrea had come to Fort Edwards from Albany in the hope of seeing her fiancé, David Jones, a Loyalist officer in Burgoyne's army. While waiting for the arrival of the army, McCrea was a guest of Mrs. McNeil, a cousin of British General Fraser.

On July 27, the two women were taken captive by a band of Burgoyne's Indians, who said they would take them to Burgoyne at Fort Ann. Mrs. McNeil arrived safely at the fort. Shortly after, an Indian arrived with the scalp that David Jones identified as belonging to Jane McCrea. Apparently, her Indian escorts had gotten drunk and argued over who would guard their captive. The result was that they killed and scalped her and then tore off her clothes.

Burgoyne was appalled at the incident and wanted to punish the Indian who killed her. But some of his officers warned him that if he did, all other Indians would desert. Finally, Burgoyne allowed the Indian to go free.

News of the murder of Jane McCrea and the fall of Fort Ticonderoga alarmed the people of Vermont and New Hampshire. New Hampshire commissioned John Stark, a brigadier general, to raise and command a force to protect the two states from Burgoyne and his Indians.

Stark had fought at Bunker Hill but had resigned from the Continental Army because he had been passed over for promotion. He agreed to help provided that his army would be completely independent and not under the control of General Philip Schuyler. Stark soon raised a force of about 1,500.

militia to turn the enemy's left. Colonels David Herrick and Thomas Stickney, with 200 men, went after the Tory Redoubt south of the bridge. Because Stark's men were not in uniform, Baum and his troops at first thought they were Tories coming for protection or to join them in the fight. By the time they realized that these men in farmers' dress were the enemy, it was too late and their flanks had been turned.

Around three o'clock, Stark mounted his horse and, calling to his men "There they are! We'll beat them, or Molly Stark is a widow tonight," led the major attack on Baum's center. The Tories in their redoubt fought hard for a few minutes, but the Americans rushed them as they were reloading their muskets, and they retreated from the field. At the first sound of musket fire, the Canadians and Indians in the log cabins fled. But Baum's dragoons and the British regulars stood fast to stand off Stark's attack, and for several hours, there was heavy fighting.

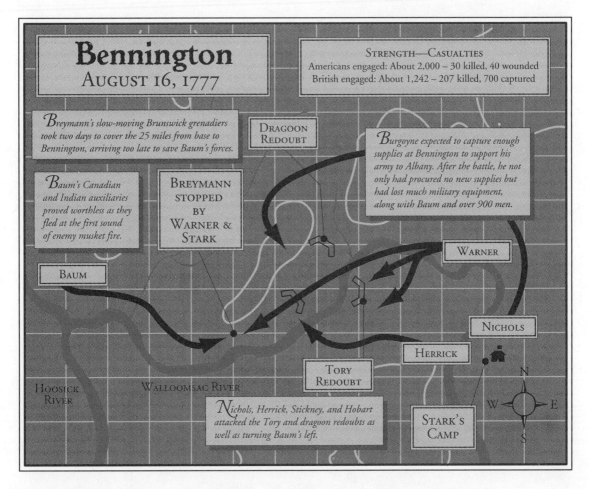

Bennington
AUGUST 16, 1777

STRENGTH—CASUALTIES
Americans engaged: About 2,000 – 30 killed, 40 wounded
British engaged: About 1,242 – 207 killed, 700 captured

Breymann's slow-moving Brunswick grenadiers took two days to cover the 25 miles from base to Bennington, arriving too late to save Baum's forces.

DRAGOON REDOUBT

Burgoyne expected to capture enough supplies at Bennington to support his army to Albany. After the battle, he not only had procured no new supplies but had lost much military equipment, along with Baum and over 900 men.

Baum's Canadian and Indian auxiliaries proved worthless as they fled at the first sound of enemy musket fire.

BREYMANN
STOPPED
BY
WARNER &
STARK

WARNER

BAUM

NICHOLS

HERRICK

TORY REDOUBT

HOOSICK RIVER   WALLOOMSAC RIVER

STARK'S CAMP

Nichols, Herrick, Stickney, and Hobart attacked the Tory and dragoon redoubts as well as turning Baum's left.

The New Hampshire men crept forward and shot down the soldiers manning the artillery. By then, Baum's men were running out of ammunition, but even after their ammunition wagon blew up, the fight was not yet over. The dragoons, with their broadswords, rushed at the Americans, who had no bayonets. The Brunswickers almost succeeded in hacking their way out, when Baum was mortally wounded. This took the heart out of the attack, and his men surrendered. The victorious Americans now went off in every direction, picking up articles left by their defeated enemy.

Around four thirty, Stark received word that Lieutenant Colonel Heinrich Breymann was approaching with 642 men intending to reinforce Baum. Stark was in trouble. His men were dispersed, still collecting the enemy's supplies. He did not have enough troops to face Breymann and was at the point of leaving the field to the enemy when Seth Warner urged him to hold out for a little longer, as he expected the rest of his command to arrive at any moment. And indeed they did; 130 men of Warner's regiment plus 200 rangers. By this time, Stark had gathered up some of his men and had found a suitable defensive position on wooded high ground.

Breymann attacked Stark's force with artillery and musket fire. There was heavy fighting until, once again, the enemy's ammunition ran out. By this time, all of Baum's artillery horses had been killed by musket fire, and he ordered a retreat. Americans continued to fire on the flanks of the retreating enemy, and Baum ordered his drums to beat for a parley to discuss surrender. Stark's men did not understand the meaning of the drums and continued firing. Breymann was wounded in the leg.

It was now getting dark, so Stark called off action. Breymann, with less than two thirds of his original force, was able to escape and return to his base. Burgoyne lost 207 of his men and 700 were captured. In addition, the Americans gained a lot of booty, including 250 broadswords, four ammunition wagons, several hundred muskets and rifles, along with four cannon. Stark had lost 30 men and 40 men were wounded. Congress had previously censured Stark for his refusal to serve under Schuyler, but Bennington stood him in good stead, and soon he was commissioned a brigadier general of the Continental Army.

Bennington came as a shock to Burgoyne. He had lost both men and arms that he could ill afford, and there was more bad news to come. St. Ledger's approach down the Mohawk River to join with him in Albany had been stopped at Fort Stanwix.

Bennington Battlefield is a New York State Historic Site and includes a relief map of the battle on the top of Hessian Hill.

BATTLES AT FORT STANWIX AND ORISKANEY—AUGUST 2–22, 1777.

In addition to Burgoyne, Colonel St. Ledger was also plagued with troubles in August 1777. His army of about 1,700—half Tory; half Indian—planned to march from Fort Oswego on Lake Ontario and join with Burgoyne and Howe at Albany. But Fort Stanwix stood between him and the Mohawk River, which provided the best passage to the Hudson River.

Fort Stanwix, at the present site of Rome, New York, was built during the French and Indian Wars and was rebuilt by the Americans in 1776. Now commanded by Colonel Peter Gansevoort, the fort had a garrison of about 700. Gansevoort had been expecting St. Ledger and had prepared the fort to withstand the attack. When St. Ledger arrived on August 2, he demanded the surrender of the fort and was refused. He laid siege to force surrender. Brigadier General Nicholas Herkimer knew of St. Ledger's advance and went about raising a force, primarily of Dutch and German farmers of Tryon County, to resist the British invasion.

On August 4, Herkimer led his army of about 800 to rescue the besieged fort. St. Ledger sent a force of British regulars, Loyalists, and Indians to meet them. Their plan was to ambush the inexperienced Americans in a swampy ravine two miles from the Oriskaney Creek and about eight miles from Stanwix.

Herkimer and his troops marched right into the ambush and suddenly found themselves subject to murderous fire coming in every direction from foes concealed by trees and undergrowth. Herkimer's horse was shot from under him and his own leg shattered. His men moved him out of range and propped his saddle against the base of a beech tree. Here, while smoking his pipe, he continued to direct his troops. The battle soon turned to hand-to-hand fighting, but the Indians, seeing no chance of a quick victory, began to leave. This action eventually forced all the others to withdraw.

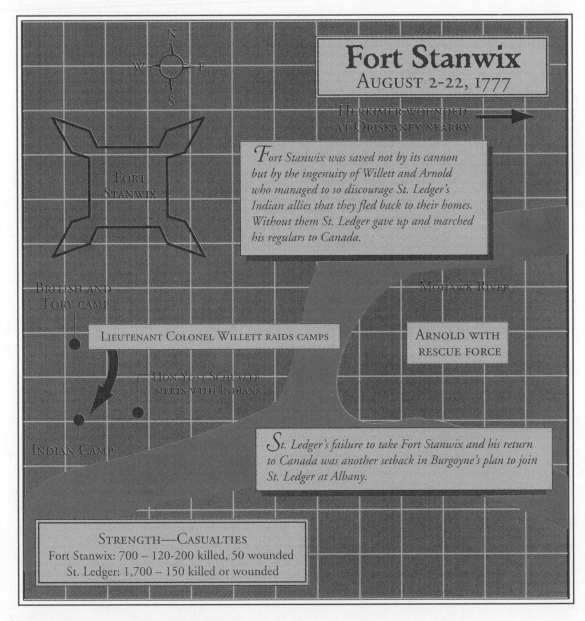

Fort Stanwix
AUGUST 2-22, 1777

HERKIMER WOUNDED
AT ORISKANEY NEARBY →

Fort Stanwix was saved not by its cannon but by the ingenuity of Willett and Arnold who managed to so discourage St. Ledger's Indian allies that they fled back to their homes. Without them St. Ledger gave up and marched his regulars to Canada.

FORT
STANWIX

N
W E
S

BRITISH AND
TORY CAMP

MOHAWK RIVER

LIEUTENANT COLONEL WILLETT RAIDS CAMPS

ARNOLD WITH
RESCUE FORCE

HON YOST SCHUYLER
MEETS WITH INDIANS

INDIAN CAMP

St. Ledger's failure to take Fort Stanwix and his return to Canada was another setback in Burgoyne's plan to join St. Ledger at Albany.

STRENGTH—CASUALTIES
Fort Stanwix: 700 – 120-200 killed, 50 wounded
St. Ledger: 1,700 – 150 killed or wounded

Gansevoort heard the sounds of the battle and sent his second in command, Lieutenant Colonel Marinus Willett, out of the fort to create a diversion. Willett and his men found the now unoccupied British and Indian camp and carried away everything they could—muskets, spears, tomahawks, kettles, blankets—and then returned to the fort. On hearing that the enemy was attacking their rear, British forces still around Oriskaney returned to their base outside the fort.

Willett left the fort again and reached Schuyler at Stillwater, New York, requesting that reinforcements be sent to the fort. Schuyler asked for volunteers to lead a

Reconstructed Fort Stanwix in Rome, New York. After failing to capture Fort Stanwix in the summer of 1777, British Colonel Barry St. Ledger gave up his attempt to join up with Burgoyne, causing Burgoyne's surrender at Saratoga. (National Park Service)

relief force but only received one response, Benedict Arnold, who headed for Stanwix with about 800 men. But they would not have to fight.

Arnold had acquired a half-wit prisoner named Hon Yost Schuyler who had been condemned to death for his Tory activities. Arnold promised him a reprieve if he would go among St. Ledger's Indians with an exaggerated report of the size of Arnold's force and encourage them to desert. Hon Yost accepted Arnold's offer with considerable enthusiasm, even putting some tiny bullet holes in his coat as an added touch.

The Indians, who looked on those who were mentally defective with a certain degree of reverence, believed Yost when he told them that Arnold was close at hand with a huge army. Yost had also brought Indians who backed his story.

This was enough for St. Ledger's Indians. They had already had chiefs killed at Oriskaney and many of their possessions taken by Willett. They had no intention of remaining to battle a large force led by such a fierce fighter as Arnold. They left for their homes, soon followed by the Tories. On August 22, St. Ledger gave up the siege and returned to Oswego. Arnold arrived at Fort Stanwix the next day.

American losses at Oriskaney were 120 to 200 killed and 50 wounded. Herkimer died of his wound shortly after he was brought to his home. The British casualties, including Indians, were around 150 killed and wounded. Of greater consequence was St. Ledger's failure to take Stanwix and reach Albany. This was another setback in the British plan for the three forces to join at Albany and end the war.

Oriskaney Battlefield is a National Historic Landmark.

Fort Stanwix, in downtown Rome, New York, has been completely reconstructed to its 1777 appearance. It is managed by the National Park Service, which also provides tours of the fort and many other related activities of interest.

BATTLE OF SARATOGA, NEW YORK: FREEMAN'S FARM, SEPTEMBER 19, 1777

Burgoyne's position in 1777 was grim. His army was down to about 6,000, his supplies were low, and he had just received word that General Howe had taken his army to Philadelphia, leaving only a rear guard in New York under General Henry Clinton. Burgoyne determined to risk everything and try to reach Albany. He wrote Clinton and asked him to join him there with reinforcements.

In August, the competent General Schuyler, who was not popular with Congress, was replaced as commander of the northern forces by the popular, yet incompetent General Horatio Gates. Gates assumed command of an army of about 9,000, along with two excellent leaders and fighters—Benedict Arnold and Daniel Morgan, who had brought along his Virginia riflemen.

On September 13, Burgoyne crossed over to the west bank of the Hudson River at Saratoga (now Schuylerville) and marched south toward Albany. Four miles north of the village of Stillwater, his army encountered Gates's force at Bemis Heights, near where the Albany road passes through a narrow defile between the surrounding hills and the river. Under the direction of the Polish military engineer Colonel Thaddeus Kosciuszko, the Americans had fortified their position on the heights, with artillery trained on the road.

Burgoyne saw that the only way to save his army was to drive the enemy from the heights and planned a three-prong attack on the American forces. General Simon Fraser with 2,200 men would march through the heavy forest, make a wide sweep, and strike the American left. Burgoyne with General Henry Hamilton would split off from Fraser and attack the enemy's center with 1,100 men. Von Riedesel with an equal-size force would march down the river road and hit the American right.

On the morning of September 19, some of Morgan's men who had climbed trees caught sight of the advancing British troops. Arnold, in command of the American left, wanted to attack at once while the British were still in the forest, where the Americans would have the advantage; Gates wanted to wait so he could fight from the recently built fortifications on Bemis Heights. Finally, Arnold held sway and launched an attack with Morgan and Benedict Dearborn's New Hampshire regiment. Fighting from the trees, Morgan's riflemen severely punished Fraser's advance guard. But when the Virginians went on to finish the job, they ran into the main force. Morgan sounded his "turkey call," and his troop returned and re-formed.

Arnold then found a weak spot in the British line at Freeman Farm between Fraser and Burgoyne. He attacked this point, and there was a vicious seesaw battle with mixed results. But Morgan's riflemen, shooting from treetops, had killed or wounded many of the officers and men serving the artillery. Arnold now saw that Burgoyne's center was beginning to falter from the insistent American fire. He asked Gates for reinforcements to finish it off. Gates took some time to consider this request so that when he finally did send reinforcements, they came too late. Von Riedesel, coming up the river road, made a sharp right turn and hit Arnold, forcing him to retreat. Gates then withdrew to the camp at Bemis Heights.

Burgoyne held the field at Freeman

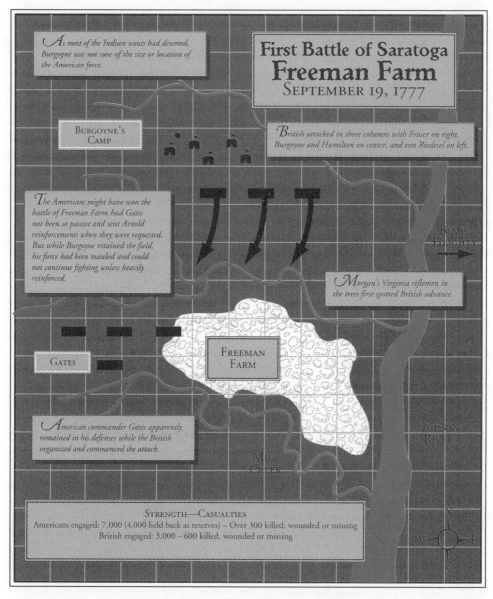

First Battle of Saratoga
Freeman Farm
SEPTEMBER 19, 1777

As most of the Indian scouts had deserted, Burgoyne was not sure of the size or location of the American force.

BURGOYNE'S CAMP

British attacked in three columns with Fraser on right, Burgoyne and Hamilton on center, and von Riedesel on left.

The Americans might have won the battle of Freeman Farm had Gates not been so passive and sent Arnold reinforcements when they were requested. But while Burgoyne retained the field, his force had been mauled and could not continue fighting unless heavily reinforced.

Morgan's Virginia riflemen in the trees first spotted British advance.

BEMIS HEIGHTS

FREEMAN FARM

GATES

American commander Gates apparently remained in his defenses while the British organized and commenced the attack.

HUDSON RIVER

MILL CREEK

STRENGTH—CASUALTIES
Americans engaged: 7,000 (4,000 held back as reserves) – Over 300 killed, wounded or missing
British engaged: 3,000 – 600 killed, wounded or missing

Farm but had paid a terrible price for it—600 killed or wounded out of a 3,000-man British force. Gates lost 300 out of the 3,000 engaged, of his 7,000-man force. Burgoyne decided to fortify his position and wait for Clinton to arrive with reinforcements. He would shortly get a letter from Clinton wishing him luck but little else. He was also not aware that an American force had taken Fort Ticonderoga, cutting his supply line and retreat route back to Canada. British troops built three powerful redoubts: "Balacarres" at Freeman Farm, "Breymann" to the northwest, and the "Great Redoubt" near the river road.

When he learned that Gates had made no mention of him in his official report of the battle, Arnold became furious with the general. The two men had a heated argument, and Gates relieved Arnold of his command. He did, however, grant Arnold's request for a pass to see Washington. But Arnold's officers persuaded him to remain.

BATTLE AT SARATOGA, NEW YORK: BEMIS HEIGHTS, OCTOBER 7, 1777

After the battle at Freeman Farm, Burgoyne decided to make a second attack and on October 7, he ordered 1,500 men with artillery to make a reconnaissance in force on the American left. At his headquarters two miles away, Gates ordered Colonel Morgan to open fire on the advancing enemy. He would soon be supported by General Ebenezer Learned and General Enoch Poor.

Brooding in his tent, Arnold heard the battle in progress. He jumped on his mare and dashed toward the site of the action. When the troops saw him galloping forward, waving his sword, they let out a cheer. With no authority, Arnold took command of Learned's brigade and smashed into the British center, which began to collapse. When he saw that General Fraser was skillfully rallying his troops, Arnold ordered Morgan to have his men concentrate their fire on Fraser, who was soon mortally wounded. The British and German troops retreated to their prepared defenses. Arnold also led an unsuccessful attack on the Balcarres Redoubt. Then he dashed off between crossfire and took the Breymann Redoubt. On entering the redoubt, he was wounded in the leg.

Nightfall saved the remains of Burgoyne's army. Leaving their campfires burning, the British force withdrew behind the Great Redoubt. The next night, after burying Fraser in the redoubt, the army marched through rain and mud to make a fortified camp on the heights of Saratoga. In three weeks, Burgoyne had suffered 1,000 casualties, as opposed to 500 Americans. He now found his force of only 6,000 surrounded by Gates with an army of 20,000.

On October 17, Borgoyne surrendered to Gates at Saratoga. This surrender was a turning point in the war, since it convinced France to now actively support the Americans with men, arms, and ships.

Some historians hold that the explanation of Arnold's incredible behavior during the battle at Bemis Heights was that he had either gone mad or was drunk. (Others feel he may have had a premonition that this would be his last battle wearing the uniform of an American officer.) But almost all agree that if the bullet had struck his heart instead of his leg, Benedict Arnold would be remembered as a great American hero and not its most infamous traitor.

The Saratoga Battlefield includes action at Freemans Farm and Bemis Heights and is a National Historic Park administered by the National Park Service. The park contains many points of interest such as Balcarres Redoubt, the Great Redoubt, and Fraser's Burial Site.

BATTLE AT BRANDYWINE— SEPTEMBER 11, 1777

In the early spring of 1777, Washington's army was down to 3,000 underfed men, many of them with smallpox. But recruits were joining his ranks, and soon his army numbered about 9,000. France, not yet officially in the war, was supplying badly needed arms, and had furnished two most useful volunteer officers: Baron de Kalb, veteran of European wars, and the young Marquis de Lafayette.

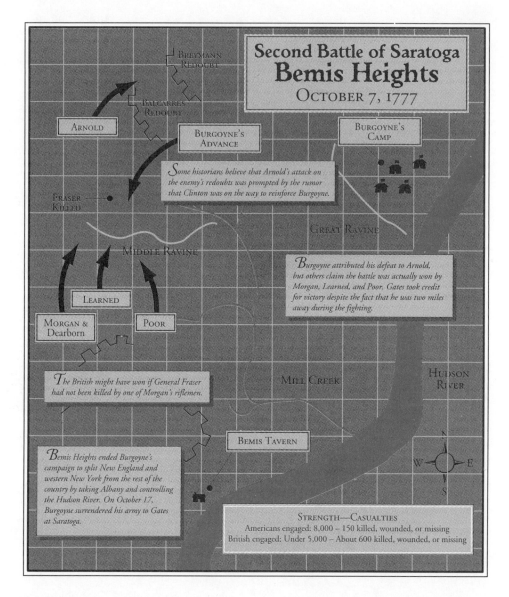

Second Battle of Saratoga
Bemis Heights
OCTOBER 7, 1777

BREYMANN REDOUBT

BALCARRES REDOUBT

ARNOLD

BURGOYNE'S ADVANCE

BURGOYNE'S CAMP

Some historians believe that Arnold's attack on the enemy's redoubts was prompted by the rumor that Clinton was on the way to reinforce Burgoyne.

FRASER KILLED

GREAT RAVINE

MIDDLE RAVINE

Burgoyne attributed his defeat to Arnold, but others claim the battle was actually won by Morgan, Learned, and Poor. Gates took credit for victory despite the fact that he was two miles away during the fighting.

LEARNED

MORGAN & Dearborn

POOR

The British might have won if General Fraser had not been killed by one of Morgan's riflemen.

MILL CREEK

HUDSON RIVER

BEMIS TAVERN

Bemis Heights ended Burgoyne's campaign to split New England and western New York from the rest of the country by taking Albany and controlling the Hudson River. On October 17, Burgoyne surrendered his army to Gates at Saratoga.

N
W · E
S

STRENGTH—CASUALTIES
Americans engaged: 8,000 – 150 killed, wounded, or missing
British engaged: Under 5,000 – About 600 killed, wounded, or missing

During that summer of 1777, General Howe intended to trap Washington in New Jersey, go on to take Philadelphia, and still have time to go up the Hudson River to support Burgoyne's campaign.

Howe failed to catch Washington in New Jersey and so returned to New York and then, on July 23, sailed away with his 15,000-man army.

Washington had reason to think that Howe was headed for Philadelphia, but when his ships failed to appear, Washington decided that he must be heading to support Burgoyne. Washington began moving north to reinforce Gates's men, but remained unsure of Howe's whereabouts until he learned British ships were seen coming up the Chesapeake.

Howe had planned to reach Philadelphia via the Delaware River, but the Americans had built forts at the river's mouth, so he continued up the Chesapeake, and on August 25, his troops began disembarking at Head of Elk, Maryland—50 miles south of Philadelphia. Howe began his march inland, attempting to flank Washington's forces and push them back against the Delaware where they would be hemmed in by Howe on one side and the fleet's cannon on the other.

Washington moved back to establish a strong defensive position on the east side of the Brandywine. He positioned his forces to protect the numerous fords—Painter's, Jones', Brinton's, Chadds, and Pyle's. But for some reason, he left Trimble's about seven miles north of Chadds, unprotected.

Finding Washington well established across the Brandywine, General Howe divided his force. He sent General Wilhelm Knyphausen and his Hessians to stage a mock attack on the American front so they would expect an attack across Chadds Ford. Howe and Cornwallis would swing north to outflank the American left and attack the rear of the main American force.

When Washington learned that Howe had divided his force, he considered it a serious blunder, and Sullivan on the right reported no sign of the enemy. When a local farmer came to Washington and told him the British were across the Brandywine, he did not believe the man. Then he received word from Sullivan that the British had crossed Trimble's Ford, were in the rear of his force, and were moving south.

Burgoyne's surrender on October 17, 1777, at Saratoga, New York, has been called the turning point of the Revolution, for it not only raised American morale but led to an alliance with France, which would provide arms, men, and warships to ensure British defeat and American independence. (National Archives)

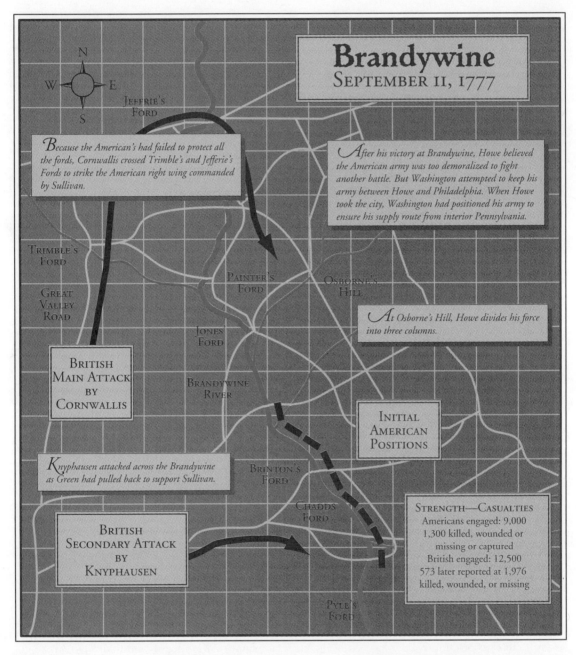

Brandywine
SEPTEMBER 11, 1777

Because the American's had failed to protect all the fords, Cornwallis crossed Trimble's and Jefferie's Fords to strike the American right wing commanded by Sullivan.

After his victory at Brandywine, Howe believed the American army was too demoralized to fight another battle. But Washington attempted to keep his army between Howe and Philadelphia. When Howe took the city, Washington had positioned his army to ensure his supply route from interior Pennsylvania.

At Osborne's Hill, Howe divides his force into three columns.

JEFFERIE'S FORD

TRIMBLE'S FORD

GREAT VALLEY ROAD

PAINTER'S FORD

OSBORNE'S HILL

JONES FORD

BRITISH MAIN ATTACK BY CORNWALLIS

BRANDYWINE RIVER

INITIAL AMERICAN POSITIONS

Knyphausen attacked across the Brandywine as Green had pulled back to support Sullivan.

BRINTON'S FORD

CHADDS FORD

BRITISH SECONDARY ATTACK BY KNYPHAUSEN

STRENGTH—CASUALTIES
Americans engaged: 9,000
1,300 killed, wounded or missing or captured
British engaged: 12,500
573 later reported at 1,976 killed, wounded, or missing

PYLE'S FORD

Washington ordered Sullivan to Birmington Meeting House, a mile on his right, to stop the British there. Just as Sullivan got his men in position, the enemy attacked and his left flank was swept away.

Lafayette then came to Sullivan's aid. The Americans drove the enemy from the hill five times and five times they were driven back by the British muskets and artillery. Hearing the artillery, Washington ordered

THE PAOLI MASSACRE

On the night of September 16, 1777, General Anthony Wayne and his division were camped near the Paoli Tavern in position to attack British General Howe's rear guard. Knowing of Wayne's location and that there were no other American forces close by, the British decided to launch a surprise raid. A detachment under Major General Charles Grey moved quietly during the night to the American camp. Grey had his men remove the flints from their muskets so no accidental shot would warn Wayne's men. The surprise was a success, and the British moved into camp and did the killing with bayonets. Wayne attempted to rally his men who, standing before the open campfire, made ideal targets. When order was finally restored, Grey and his troops had left, satisfied with a good night's work. Three hundred of Wayne's men had been killed and 100 taken prisoner. Grey's losses were only four killed and an equal number wounded.

Greene to come at once. By the time Nathanael Greene arrived, the American army was desperate. Knyphausen had broken through, and an orderly retreat of the Americans was turning into a rout. But Greene's arrival gave the troops a chance to reform, and darkness soon ended the fighting. The exhausted American army retreated to Chester, 12 miles to the southeast. The equally exhausted British army spent the night on the field.

Washington estimated his killed, wounded, and captured at 1,300. Howe first estimated his total losses at 573 but according to his papers that were later found, he gave his losses at 1,976. Washington's army had been defeated but its spirit was surprisingly high. Many men said they would fight better another time. And they would, but not before they would suffer further defeat.

Brandywine Battlefield Park is administered by the Brandywine Park Commission.

While the actual battlefield is in private hands, tours of Washington's headquarters and Lafayette's quarters can be arranged at the visitor center, for a charge.

BATTLE OF GERMANTOWN— OCTOBER 4, 1777

In spite of Washington's efforts, Howe occupied Philadelphia on September 26. He stationed about 3,000 men to guard his supply line from Head of Elk and quartered his main force of 9,000 at Germantown, about five miles north of Philadelphia.

Washington's army had been reinforced by this time, so now there were about 11,000 American troops camped some 16 miles from Germantown. Washington decided to attack the British position with four columns, reaching the British camp by different roads. Two columns would hit the enemy's center, the other two, coming from right and left, would act like pincers. It was the double envelopment used by Hannibal and might have worked, except that Nathanael Greene's guide was not familiar with the area, so Greene was two hours late arriving with his major attack force.

There was a mist on the morning of the fourth, but soon it turned into fog, which was made even more dense by the smoke from muskets and cannon. When the

Americans launched the attack, for the first time in the war, a British bugler sounded a retreat. Hearing the sounds of battle, Howe mounted his horse in Philadelphia and arrived to rally his men.

In the retreat, about 120 British barricaded themselves in a stone house belonging to Chief Justice Benjamin Chew. American General Henry Knox thought it unwise to continue the advance until the Chew House was taken and brought up his artillery. They were unable to take the house, however, and men and much valuable time were lost with no tangible result.

Despite this setback, Washington was getting ready to advance on Philadelphia, when the plan fell apart. In the dense fog, two American divisions mistook each other for the enemy and began firing. Believing the enemy was at their rear, they began to panic and flee. Officers rode among the men, swinging their swords and pleading with them to re-form, but to no avail. By about 10 A.M. the battle was over, and once again, Washington had to order a retreat. American losses had been heavy: 152 killed, 521 wounded, and 400 captured. British losses were 70 men killed and 450 wounded. Germantown was Washington's last battle of 1777. He and his army would shortly move to their winter quarters at Valley Forge.

The stone Chew House, that resisted Knox's artillery, still stands on a parklike site on Germantown Avenue. It is open to the public daily from 10 A.M. to 4 P.M. and Sundays from 1 P.M. to 5 P.M.

VALLEY FORGE
1777–1778

The winter of 1777–1778 was a miserable one for Washington's poorly clothed and underfed army at Valley Forge, but by late winter, its fortune changed.

On February 6, the formal alliance between the United States and France was signed. While some Americans took a dim view of associating with their recent enemy, the agreement meant that France would be sending money, arms, men, and warships to America to help defeat the British. Later that month, the Prussian General Baron von Steuben would arrive to transform the ragged body of troops into a first-rate army.

Washington had persuaded Greene to be quarter master general until the beginning of the next campaign and soon supply wagons with blankets, clothing, and food began to arrive. In early spring, there was a bountiful run of shad on the nearby Schuykill River. Thousands of them ended in the nets set by the soldiers. The army feasted on the fish, and there was enough to smoke and store in barrels for future meals.

The defeated and discouraged army that arrived at Valley Forge in the late fall of 1777 had been transformed over the months into a confident and effective fighting force. It would leave Valley Forge in June to defeat the British at Monmouth.

FORTS MERCER AND MIFFLIN—
OCTOBER 22–NOVEMBER 15,
1777

After occupying Philadelphia on September 26, 1777, Howe turned his attention to clearing out America's defenses at the mouth of the Delaware River, so supplies could arrive by way of the river rather than via Head of Elk, some 50 miles away.

The American river defenses included a double line of chevaux-de-frise running from the New Jersey shore to Billingston Island. These were cratelike structures of

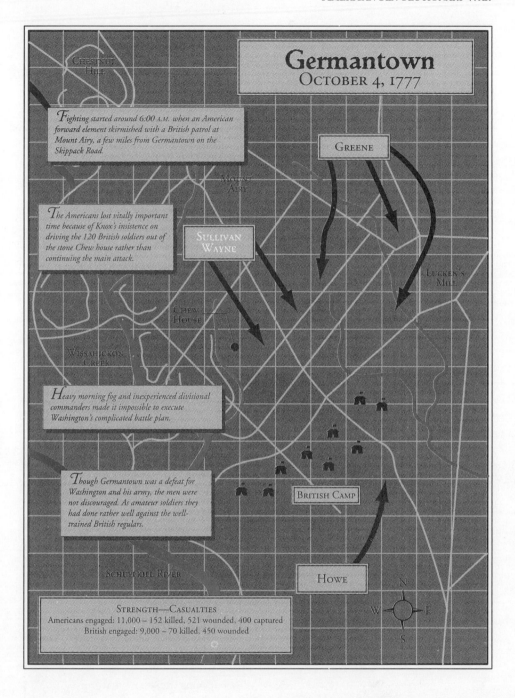

Germantown
OCTOBER 4, 1777

Fighting started around 6:00 A.M. when an American forward element skirmished with a British patrol at Mount Airy, a few miles from Germantown on the Skippack Road.

The Americans lost vitally important time because of Knox's insistence on driving the 120 British soldiers out of the stone Chew house rather than continuing the main attack.

Heavy morning fog and inexperienced divisional commanders made it impossible to execute Washington's complicated battle plan.

Though Germantown was a defeat for Washington and his army, the men were not discouraged. As amateur soldiers they had done rather well against the well-trained British regulars.

CHESTNUT HILL

MOUNT AIRY

GREENE

SULLIVAN WAYNE

LUCKEN'S MILL

CHEW HOUSE

WISSAHICKON CREEK

BRITISH CAMP

SCHUYLKILL RIVER

HOWE

N
W E
S

STRENGTH—CASUALTIES
Americans engaged: 11,000 – 152 killed, 521 wounded, 400 captured
British engaged: 9,000 – 70 killed, 450 wounded

STEUBEN CREATES AN ARMY

He claimed that he was Frederick Wilhelm August Henry Ferdinand, Baron von Steuben, former lieutenant general in the Prussian Army, inspector general of that same army and late aide-de-camp to Frederick the Great, King of Prussia. While he may have padded his resume a bit, Washington was impressed with his military knowledge when they met at Valley Forge. And unlike most of the other foreign military notables who offered help to America in its war, Steuben requested no rank and no salary, other than money to cover his expenses. Washington saw that he was appointed to the honorary rank of inspector general and assigned him to train the army at Valley Forge.

When Steuben first saw the ragged, poorly clothed, and half-starved troops shivering in the February cold, he immediately recognized the rare quality of these men. He told Washington that no European army could hold together under such conditions. And he grasped at once what was different about the American soldier. Comparing the European and American soldier in a letter to an associate in Europe he wrote, "You say to your soldiers, 'Do this,' and he doeth it, but I am obliged to say, 'This is the reason why you ought to do this,' and he does." Steuben adapted the Prussian and French military training methods to make them more suitable for Americans. Instead of leaving training to sergeants, he charged this responsibility to officers, and he chose 100 of the best men to train himself. Since he spoke only German and French, he depended on pantomime to instruct his class. Soon others gathered around to watch Steuben, wearing a magnificent uniform decorated with medals and ribbons, standing before 100 ragged American soldiers as he demonstrated the correct way to load a musket, use a bayonet, advance and retreat in formation, and all the hundreds of other important things a good soldier must know.

Steuben may not have been all he claimed to be, but his experience with the Prussian army convinced General Washington to let him train the American army at winter quarters at Valley Forge. By spring of 1778, Steuben was able to present Washington with a well-trained, disciplined force that gained its first victory at Monmouth. (National Archives)

Often, when his troops were going through some complicated maneuver, they would get tangled up with one another. He would begin to shout at them in French and German and his favorite English word, "damn." These commands usually made matters worse, and he would begin to laugh at the ill-formed troops. And they would join in the laughter. After he was satisfied that the first 100 men had learned their lessons, he sent them out to train others. By now Washington's soldiers were eager to learn and, for the first time, were taking pride in becoming real soldiers. By spring of 1778, Steuben had created a well-trained army.

In May, he had the chance to show it off at a grand review to celebrate the alliance with France. Washington watched with great satisfaction as the former rabble performed with snap and precision equal to that of a European army of regulars. The following year, Steuben drew up regulations covering order and discipline in the United States. His "Blue Book" became the foundation of the military training adapted by the United States Army.

heavy timber, filled with stones and sunk in the water. On the tops were long iron spikes, set on an angle, to rip the bottoms of passing ships. Further up the river was Fort Mercer on the east shore at Red Bank, named after General Hugh Mercer, who fell at the battle of Princeton. Fort Mifflin was set on Mud Island, almost directly across from Fort Mercer. Both were American forts.

The British began clearing the river on October 2 by taking a small redoubt and dismantling the Billingston chevaux-de-frise, and on October 22, Colonel Carl von Donop arrived with 1,200 Hessians at Fort Mercer from Haddonfield, New Jersey, to bolster the British ranks.

Mercer was defended by two Rhode Island regiments and 500 Continentals, under Colonel Christopher Greene. Since the fort had been originally designed to be defended by 1,500 men, Greene's engineer reduced its size by building a wall to cut off the northern sections. He improved the remainder by the addition of an abatis, parapetted palisade, moats, and berms. The fort's 14 cannon were placed to cover an attack from the land side.

Von Donop began his attack the afternoon of his arrival. First, his artillery opened fire, and shortly, he advanced on the fort with two columns of infantry. Greene held his fire until the Hessians had crossed the outer defenses. When they were in range, Greene gave the order, and a hail of musket shot and cannon grape poured down on von Donop's troops.

The Hessian ranks staggered. Von Donop and his officers attempted to rally the men, making themselves ideal targets. Von Donop fell, mortally wounded, but the attack continued until the Hessians retreated, after coming under additional fire from row galleys on the river. It had been a bloody battle for the Hessians—371 killed, wounded, and captured. Greene had lost 4, and 23 were wounded.

On November 10, the British were able to bring a floating battery to bombard the weak side of Fort Mifflin, and on November 15, British warships began a heavy bombardment, so that by that night, little of the fort remained and so was abandoned. Once Mifflin fell, Fort Mercer was no longer tenable, and it, too, was abandoned, giving the British control of the Delaware River to Philadelphia.

Red Bank Battlefield Park is administered by the owners, Board of Chosen Freeholders, Glouster County, New Jersey, and contains earthen remains of Fort Mercer. In a nearby display shed, adjacent to Whitehall House, are timbers from the original chevaux-de-frise.

BATTLE OF MONMOUTH COURTHOUSE—JUNE 28, 1778

In May 1777 General Howe turned over his command to General Harry Clinton, and shortly afterward sailed from Philadelphia, taking with him some 3,000 prominent Tories. Clinton, too, left Philadelphia, but because of the fear that French warships might be in the Chesapeake, he decided to march through New Jersey and reach New York via Sandy Hook or Staten Island. On June 18, he left Philadelphia with his army of 10,000 and 1,500 or so wagons loaded with equipment and supplies.

At his headquarters at Valley Forge, Washington planned to attack Clinton. Some of his senior officers were against this project, but Washington now had an army of almost 14,000 and wanted to use it. His plan was to catch Clinton before he reached Cranbury, New Jersey, where the nature of the terrain would be favorable to the Americans. He offered General Charles Lee command of the attack force, but Lee declined, and it was then offered to Lafayette. When Lee learned there would be 4,000 men in the force, he changed his mind and was given the command. Washington sent part of his force to occupy Philadelphia and sent other elements north to destroy bridges and otherwise slow Clinton's march north.

On June 27, Clinton reached Monmouth Courthouse, in Monmouth, New Jersey, and finding a site that could readily be defended, he camped there for the night. Washington, not far away, ordered Lee to attack in the morning. Clinton realized he was in danger, so about 4 A.M. on June 28, he sent General Knyphausen ahead with the wagons and followed him, leaving a rear guard of 2,000 at Monmouth.

When Lee arrived at Monmouth, he proposed to cut the rear guard off from Clinton's main army. But he had no clear idea of how this was to be done. He did not make a reconnaissance of the terrain and had no battle plan. He told his divisional commanders, Lafayette, Greene, Lord Stir-

ling (William Alexander), and Brigadier General Anthony Wayne to more or less play the battle by ear, and Lee launched the attack on the rear guard. When Clinton heard the sound of musket fire, he immediately started back to rescue his rear guard. Clinton placed his troops on the east side of the road facing the Americans on the west.

Lee ordered Lafayette to move his troops to another position and from there strike the British left. But when Lafayette achieved the new position, he found it unsuited for such an attack and moved on to a better site. This maneuver exposed other divisions, and they began to withdraw. Lee then gave orders for a general retreat. When General Henry Knox rode to tell Washington that Lee was retreating, the general exploded in rage, jumped on his white horse, and came at a gallop to confront Lee.

No one knows exactly what the furious Washington said to Lee. Lafayette, who was not there, reported that Washington called Lee "a damned poltroon." Others claimed that Washington heavily cursed Lee. In any case, he relieved Lee of command.

Washington next galloped down the road to rally his retreating men. Then he re-formed his lines to stop the British advance.

Clinton launched a major attack on Greene who was holding the American right. But heavy musket fire plus artillery repulsed the charge. Wayne, holding the center, was also hit with a major British force. He ordered his men to hold their fire until the enemy was only 40 yards away, and then, there was a crashing volley that broke the attack, killing its leader, Lieutenant Colonel Henry Monckton. Henry Knox had placed his artillery on a hill, and his guns, along with other pieces, poured fire on the enemy. The British continued

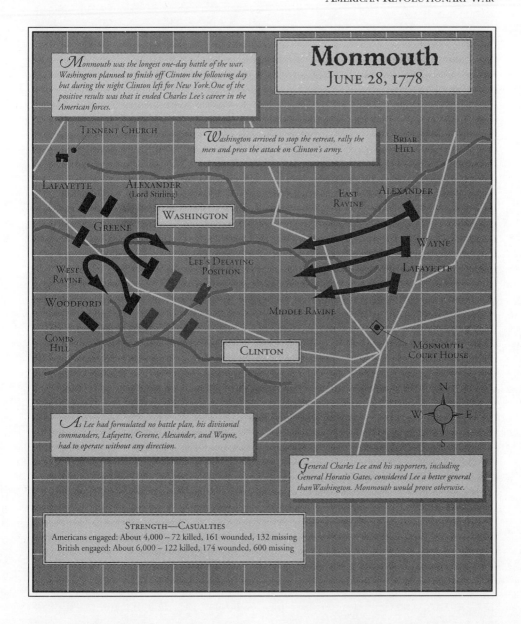

Monmouth
JUNE 28, 1778

Monmouth was the longest one-day battle of the war. Washington planned to finish off Clinton the following day but during the night Clinton left for New York. One of the positive results was that it ended Charles Lee's career in the American forces.

TENNENT CHURCH

Washington arrived to stop the retreat, rally the men and press the attack on Clinton's army.

BRIAR HILL

LAFAYETTE   ALEXANDER (Lord Stirling)

EAST RAVINE   ALEXANDER

WASHINGTON

GREENE

WAYNE

LEE'S DELAYING POSITION

LAFAYETTE

WEST RAVINE

WOODFORD

MIDDLE RAVINE

COMBS HILL

CLINTON

MONMOUTH COURT HOUSE

As Lee had formulated no battle plan, his divisional commanders, Lafayette, Greene, Alexander, and Wayne, had to operate without any direction.

General Charles Lee and his supporters, including General Horatio Gates, considered Lee a better general than Washington. Monmouth would prove otherwise.

STRENGTH—CASUALTIES
Americans engaged: About 4,000 – 72 killed, 161 wounded, 132 missing
British engaged: About 6,000 – 122 killed, 174 wounded, 600 missing

their attacks, but each time were repulsed. And, thanks to Steuben's training, the Americans made good use of their bayonets.

Eventually, the fighting ended, and both sides occupied the field that night. Washington wanted to finish Clinton the next day, but during the night the British com-mander quietly led his men away.

American losses were about 72 killed and 161 wounded, and 132 missing. The British had 122 killed, 174 wounded, and 600 missing. The day had been terribly hot—100 degrees—and many men on both sides died from the heat.

Monmouth was the last major battle

THE FORT AT WEST POINT

In 1776, the Americans built Forts Clinton and Montgomery on the west shore of the Hudson River, a few miles south of West Point to ensure control of this vital waterway. In command at New York, Henry Clinton sailed up the Hudson with 3,000 men in October 1777. His objective was to relieve pressure on Burgoyne by forcing Horatio Gates to send some of his troops to the Hudson River region.

Clinton attacked both forts simultaneously from the rear, the land side, and both fell after putting up brief resistance. George Washington was not pleased to learn that these two important forts had fallen so easily and determined to have an impregnable fort built on a high bluff overlooking the river.

This site had many advantages. It was difficult to approach from the land, high enough to be out of range of ships' cannon, and the turn in the river below caused ships to lose headway as they altered course. During the winter of 1777–1778, while Washington's army was at Valley Forge, the Polish military engineer Colonel Thaddeus Kosciuszko was busy planning and supervising the construction of the fort at West Point.

To ensure that it could not be assaulted from the rear, a system of supporting forts and redoubts were set among the surrounding hills. Cannon were positioned to have a wide sweep of the river below and, to further prevent passage of enemy ships, a 60-ton iron chain was stretched across the river between West Point and Constitution Island on the east shore.

West Point remained a fort until May of 1784 when it became the base for the United States "Corps of Artillery and Engineers." On July 4, 1802, it became the United States Military Academy.

---

of the war fought in the north, and also the last between two large armies. It also reinforced Washington's reputation as a great military leader.

As for General Charles Lee, he wrote Washington a letter listing his complaints and demanded a court martial. He got it and was found guilty of misbehavior before the enemy and ordering an unnecessary and shameful retreat. He then delivered to Congress a censorious letter; they wrote back that his services were no longer needed.

The Monmouth Battlefield is administrated by the State of New Jersey State Park Service. There is a visitor center that has a slide presentation of the battle and also a walking trail covering some of the battle site. During the summer, special events are held, including a reenactment of the battle and colonial shooting competition.

BATTLE OF STONY POINT— JULY 16, 1779

On March 28, 1779, British forces from New York easily took the American outposts of Stony Point and Verplanck's Point, about 12 miles south of West Point, thus cutting off Washington's most direct supply line. Concerned that Clinton might take the uncompleted fortifications at West Point, Washington moved his available forces to Smith's Cove, about 14 miles west of the point. When Clinton remained at Stony Point, Washington decided to take it back. "Mad Anthony" Wayne was put in the command of the attack. While he was studying the best way to take the base, which Clinton had now fortified, Steuben was drilling handpicked troops for the attack at West Point.

Wayne decided to attack Stony Point at night, and on the evening of June 15, his force of 1,200 gathered at Springsteel Farm, about a mile and a half west of the point. Wayne had issued strict security measures. Guards were posted to prevent any traitor from warning the enemy, civilians had been cleared from the line of march and ordered to remain home, and muskets of the main and secondary attack column were to stay unloaded.

The plan of attack was to hit the enemy's defenses at two points, one column coming from the north, near the ferry landing; the other to the south.

At the head was a "forlorn hope," a term used at that time to describe a group of soldiers on a difficult or suicidal mission. In this particular case, it consisted of 20 men led by a lieutenant. Their mission was to rush the barricades and force a small breach. Right behind them would be a larger force to widen the breach to allow the main column to enter and attack the garrison. Just after midnight, the two columns made contact with the enemy. In spite of enemy fire, the forlorn hope managed to chop through the wooden barricades.

Wayne had allowed one body of men, "the demonstration group," to have loaded muskets and now they charged down the center of the main road shooting and yelling. The British commander ordered a counterattack on the center and, of course, found nothing. But before they could return to the fortification, Wayne's two columns were inside the defenses, attacking the enemy with bayonets. Within 15 minutes, the British troops began to surrender. Wayne had lost 15 men, and 83 were wounded in order to take a base defended by over 600 men. British losses were 63 killed, 74 wounded, and 530 taken prisoner.

Wayne's victory was a great morale builder for the Americans and helped establish the Continental Army as a professional force to be reckoned with. But it had no strategic importance because the effort to take Verplancks Point failed. Washington would later have the fortifications at Stony Point demolished.

Stony Point Battlefield is a New York State Historic Site. There is a museum, and the walking tour includes many points of interest.

WAR IN THE SOUTH: BATTLE AT MOORES CREEK BRIDGE— FEBRUARY 27, 1776

After Monmouth, the major battles of the Revolutionary War took place in North Carolina, South Carolina, and Virginia. The South, however, had been the scene of two earlier important battles in 1776—Moores Creek, North Carolina, and Charleston's Fort Moultrie in South Carolina.

The news of hostilities at Lexington and Concord inspired the patriots in North Carolina to take action. They occupied the capital of Wilmington; forced the royal governor, Josiah Martin, to flee the colony; and formed a provincial congress. Martin convinced the British that there were many Loyalists in North Carolina who would rise up and drive the rebels out of power if they were supported by a show of force. General Henry Clinton was to provide the show of force by landing troops at New Brunswick, just below Wilmington, in late February 1776.

Martin began organizing a Loyalist uprising to occur in conjunction with Clinton's arrival. From New York, General Thomas Gage, sent Donald MacDonald and Donald McLeod to head the Loyalist force and to recruit a battalion of Scottish Highlanders who lived in the interior of

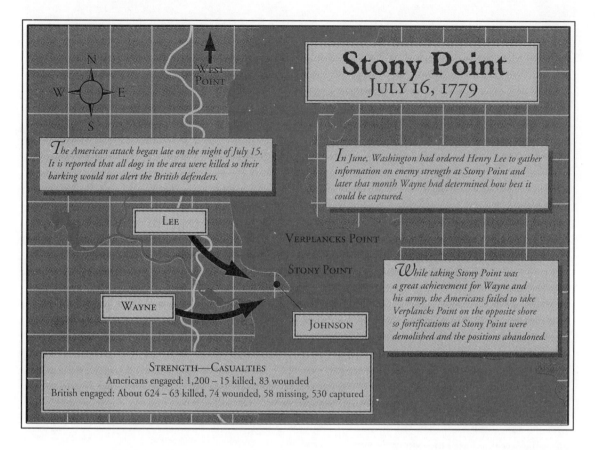

Stony Point
JULY 16, 1779

The American attack began late on the night of July 15. It is reported that all dogs in the area were killed so their barking would not alert the British defenders.

In June, Washington had ordered Henry Lee to gather information on enemy strength at Stony Point and later that month Wayne had determined how best it could be captured.

WEST POINT

LEE

VERPLANCKS POINT

STONY POINT

While taking Stony Point was a great achievement for Wayne and his army, the Americans failed to take Verplancks Point on the opposite shore so fortifications at Stony Point were demolished and the positions abandoned.

WAYNE

JOHNSON

STRENGTH—CASUALTIES
Americans engaged: 1,200 – 15 killed, 83 wounded
British engaged: About 624 – 63 killed, 74 wounded, 58 missing, 530 captured

North Carolina and were fiercely loyal to King George III. MacDonald gathered about 1,000 men from the major clans—McDowels, MacDonalds, Campbells, and Camerons.

The Patriots, aware of the preparations, built breastworks to defend Wilmington. The militia was called up under the command of Colonel Richard Caswell, and the leader of the 1st North Carolina Continentals, Colonel James Moore, was given command of all Patriot forces. With about 650 men and some artillery, Moore left Wilmington on February 15 and camped about 12 miles from MacDonald's base at Cross Creek. There, he was reinforced by 450 men under Colonel John Alexander Littington.

MacDonald saw the enemy around him growing in strength and decided to march at once to the coast. On February 20, he left Cross Creek, but since Moore blocked the main route, he headed east, to cross the Cape Fear and South Rivers and move through backcountry to the coast. MacDonald's force now numbered 1,500 including 1,000 Highlanders. Many wore kilts and were armed by huge double-edged broadswords. They marched to the beat of drums and the skirl of bagpipes.

Moore realized that MacDonald's route would force him to cross the bridge at Moores Creek, a sluggish stream about 35 feet wide. He notified Caswell of this movement and sent Colonel Alexander Lillington with reinforcements, which

ARNOLD'S TREASON

Henry Clinton appreciated the importance and strength of the fort at West Point and wanted to take it, if he could. He would almost find a way through Benedict Arnold.

Arnold was one of the most capable of the American military commanders, but he had been repeatedly passed over for promotion and harbored many other resentments. He also had financial problems and faced court martial for misuse of public funds.

In April 1779, while in command of Philadelphia, Arnold married 19-year-old Peggy Shippen, who had been a close friend of British army captain John André. Arnold and his new wife began living far beyond his means and soon he needed a lot of money. Through a Philadelphia Loyalist, Arnold began to correspond with André in New York, now with British intelligence.

Arnold managed to persuade Washington to name him commander at West Point. After much waggling, André told him that Clinton was willing to pay him 10,000 (pounds) and a general's commission in the British army if he could deliver the fort and its garrison.

On the night of September 21, André sailed up the Hudson on the sloop *Vulture* to meet with Arnold at Haverstraw and confirm the final details of the surrender of West Point. Fire from American batteries drove *Vulture* away, and André was forced to go overland back to New York. On his way, incriminating papers were found under his stocking, and he was arrested and later executed by Washington's order.

Arnold managed to escape. The British kept their end of the bargain, making Arnold a brigadier

Benedict Arnold, the nation's most famous traitor, remains an enigma. To some, he was an outstanding military leader, brought down by the jealousy of others. But there are many who don't consider him a great general and believe he caused his own downfall in his desire for glory, resentment of supposed slights, and greed for money.

general, awarding him over 6,000 pounds, plus a yearly pension for his wife.

Arnold fought against the Americans in Virginia in 1780 and, in September 1781, led the attack on Fort Griswold, near New London, Connecticut. This engagement was the last one of the war that occurred in the northeast.

General "Mad Anthony" Wayne took over command in the old northwest after St. Clair's defeat on the Wabash, November 4, 1791. Wayne formed a new force "Legion of the United States" and on August 20, 1794, routed Blue Jacket's Shawnee force at Fallen Timbers. (Library of Congress)

arrived at the bridge on February 25. Lillington built some fortifications overlooking the bridge; the next day Caswell arrived with 850 men and fortified the west end of the bridge.

The Loyalist army arrived in the vicinity of the bridge on the night of February 26. MacDonald had fallen ill, and Donald McLeod was in command. He decided to attack Caswell's position before dawn, but during the night, Caswell had crossed over to the east side of the bridge. He had some of the bridge planks removed and greased the exposed stringers. Artillery was positioned to cover the bridge.

At daybreak on the twenty-seventh, McLeod attacked. An advance party picked its way across the partially demolished bridge with bagpipes skirling and brandishing their broadswords. When they were within 30 or so paces of the Patriots' breastworks, the Highlanders were struck by a

withering fire of muskets and artillery. The advance party simply disintegrated and all of McLeod's army retreated. The battle lasted only about 15 minutes, but in that time, 30 of the Highland Loyalists had been killed and 40 were wounded. Caswell lost just one man.

Soon after the skirmish, the Patriots captured 850 Loyalist soldiers, disarmed them, and sent them home. The spoils included 1,500 muskets, 150 swords and dirks, and 15,000 pounds sterling.

Moores Creek Battlefield is administered by the National Park Service. There is a visitor center with exhibits that include a Highland broadsword and swivel gun. There are also audiovisual program and diorama.

BATTLE OF FORT MOULTRIE— JUNE 28, 1776

Clinton's seaborne force arrived in North Carolina waters in May and, since the battle at Moores Creek Bridge had squelched Loyalist activity in that area, sailed south to attack Charleston in South Carolina. When Washington learned that the British were mounting a seaborne operation, he sent General Charles Lee from Boston to help with Charleston's defenses—the largest port south of Philadelphia. But the commander of Charleston's defenses, Colonel William Moultrie, really didn't need any help.

He had constructed a fort on Sullivan Island to protect the entrance into the harbor. The fort's walls were made of two walls of palmetto logs with the sixteen feet between two wood walls filled with sand. In addition to 30 smooth-bore cannon, Moultrie had some good men—over 300 riflemen and 400 or so North and South Carolina regulars.

THE OLD FOX AND THE BOY

CONCLUSION DE LA CAMPAGNE ... DE 1781 EN VIRGINIE
To his Excellency General Washington this Likeness of his friend,
the Marquess de la Fayette is humbly dedicated

Portrait of himself that Lafayette presented to his friend, General George Washington. Washington had taken an immediate liking to the young French nobleman whom Congress made a major general in June 1777. (National Archives)

A British bugler sounded the hunting call "the fox has gone to ground" when George Washington's advanced troops withdrew at the start of the battle at Harlem Heights, New York. Washington, who had often ridden with the hounds, took this as the insult it was intended. He rallied his men and stopped the enemy before withdrawing to White Plains. British generals began to refer to Washington as "the old fox," as a pejorative, when they believed they finally had him trapped, but with a degree of admiration on finding he had escaped the snare. On the evening of January 1, 1777, Lord Charles Cornwallis was so sure he had Washington trapped along the Assumpink Creek that he decided to rest for the night and "bag the old fox in the morning." By morning, "the old fox" had left and was headed to defeat Cornwallis's force at Princeton.

At the same time, British commanders called the relatively inexperienced 20-year-old Major General Marquis de Lafayette "the boy." On May 18, 1778, Brigadier General George Howe and Clinton with 14,000 troops, were so sure they could bag "the boy" and his 2,000 men at Barren Hill, Pennsylvania, that Howe already invited friends for dinner to meet his young prisoner. One of Lafayette's officers, however, found an obscure road to safety, and by the time Howe and Clinton's forces arrived on the hill, "the boy" and his men were back at Valley Forge. In May 1781, Cornwallis tried several times to trap Lafayette in Virginia but without success. By late summer, Lafayette's force had been reinforced and Cornwallis soon found himself trapped at Yorktown by "the boy."

Clinton's attack force consisted of about 2,000 regulars, 500 or more seamen, and warships having a total of 200 cannon.

On June 16, Clinton's regulars had landed on Long Island, a deserted and swampy strip of mainland east of Sullivan Island. Long Island turned out to be so unsuited for land attack on the fort that it was agreed to take it with ship's cannon fire.

On June 28, the British warships began bombarding the fort, but the cannonballs did little or no harm. The soft palmetto logs

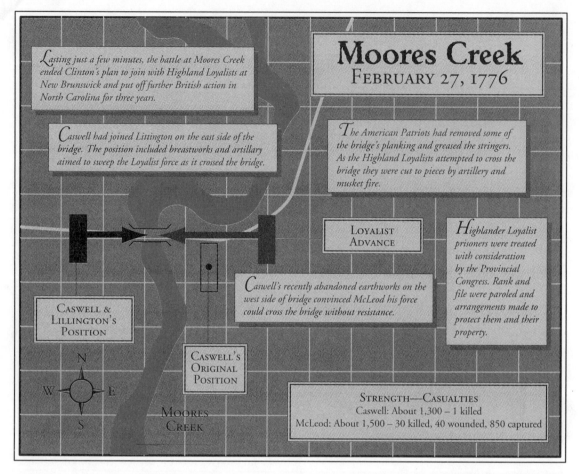

Moores Creek
FEBRUARY 27, 1776

Lasting just a few minutes, the battle at Moores Creek ended Clinton's plan to join with Highland Loyalists at New Brunswick and put off further British action in North Carolina for three years.

Caswell had joined Littington on the east side of the bridge. The position included breastworks and artillary aimed to sweep the Loyalist force as it crossed the bridge.

The American Patriots had removed some of the bridge's planking and greased the stringers. As the Highland Loyalists attempted to cross the bridge they were cut to pieces by artillery and musket fire.

LOYALIST
ADVANCE

Highlander Loyalist prisoners were treated with consideration by the Provincial Congress. Rank and file were paroled and arrangements made to protect them and their property.

Caswell's recently abandoned earthworks on the west side of bridge convinced McLeod his force could cross the bridge without resistance.

CASWELL &
LILLINGTON'S
POSITION

N
W   E
S

CASWELL'S
ORIGINAL
POSITION

MOORES
CREEK

STRENGTH—CASUALTIES
Caswell: About 1,300 – 1 killed
McLeod: About 1,500 – 30 killed, 40 wounded, 850 captured

absorbed most of the shot; the rest disappeared in the 16 feet of sand. The bombardment continued all day but by night the attack had failed. Clinton soon sailed away.

The Sullivan Island Fort, later named "Fort Moultrie," gave up over 7,000 British cannonballs buried in the logs and sand.

Fort Moultrie would go through many transformations in order to serve in the Civil War and in World Wars I and II.

Fort Moultrie is part of Fort Sumter National Monument, administered by the National Park Service. The fort, now fully restored, contains visuals showing its appearance over the years and a reconstructed section of the original palmetto log construction.

There was no major fighting in the South after Clinton's repulse at Fort Moultrie until 1778, when Savannah was captured by the British. In 1779, a joint force consisting of American troops and the French fleet, commanded by Admiral Charles D'Estain, failed to recapture it and the fleet sailed off.

With the French fleet out of American waters, Clinton decided to leave his base in New York and move south. Leaving General Knyphausen in New York, Clinton and his second in command, Cornwallis, sailed from New York on December 26, 1779. He had about 8,500 men, and his transports were escorted by five warships with 600 cannon and 5,000 seamen and

Fort Moultrie, named after its first commander Major General William Moultrie, was built on Sullivan Island in 1776 to protect Charlestown from British attack and constructed of two palmetto log walls set 16 feet apart with the space between filled with sand. On June 28, 1776, the fort's cannon drove off a fleet of British warships. Over the years the logs were replaced by masonry walls with sand filling. The fort played an active role in the Civil War. With constant improvements, it remained a part of the country's harbor defenses until 1947. In 1960, it was taken over by the National Park Service. (National Park Service)

marines. The first objective was a return trip to Charleston.

Clinton laid siege to Charleston on April 1, 1780. He had better luck than on his earlier attack. The port's defenses were commanded by General Benjamin Lincoln, who had a force of about 5,000—Continentals, militia, and armed townspeople. Clinton's siege was well organized, and on May 12, Lincoln surrendered the city and over 5,000 men were taken prisoner. This was the largest number of American prisoners taken at one time during the war. After taking Charleston, Clinton put

Cornwallis in command of further operations in the south and returned to New York to keep an eye on Washington.

British occupation of Charleston encouraged the southern Loyalists, who soon unleashed what amounted to a civil war in the South with colonials fighting colonials, neighbor fighting neighbor, even fighting between relatives. One major Loyalist force was led by Lieutenant Colonel Banastre Tarleton, a 26-year-old British cavalryman. His force, "The American Legion," included a troop of dragoons. Soon after the arrival of Clinton, Tarleton and his force

Eight-inch bronze howitzer, Revolutionary War period. The howitzer, with a shorter barrel than standard cannon and more mobile than a mortar, was designed to deliver shot at a high trajectory against targets behind earthworks, hills, and ridges that could otherwise not be hit with an ordinary fieldpiece with its relatively flat trajectory. (West Point Museum)

attacked about 400 rebels under Colonel Abraham Buford. After a short but brisk fight, Buford surrendered and ordered his men to lay down their arms. When they obeyed, Tarleton's men went after them with bayonets and swords, killing 131 and wounding over 200. This incident gave the rebels two battlecries to be heard in future battles—"Buford! Buford!" and "Tarleton's Quarters!"

Another British officer who commanded a force of Loyalists whose group became known as the "American Volunteers" was Major Patrick Ferguson. Ferguson was a rather remarkable young man who had invented a breachloading rifle that could be fired five or six times before having to be reloaded. Like Tarleton, he hated rebels, and he and his men roamed the countryside hunting them down and burning and looting their houses and barns.

The Patriots had their own guerrilla leaders who operated independently and with the American army. The most famous of these was Francis "Swamp Fox" Marion. Among the others were Thomas "Carolina Gamecock" Sumter and Andrew "Wizard Owl" Pickens. Unlike the heavily wooded north, large areas of the South were open and suitable for cavalry and mounted troops, allowing the guerrillas on both sides to move quickly over considerable distances.

When Clinton attacked Charleston, Washington had sent some troops under Major General Johann de Kalb to reinforce Lincoln. After the surrender of the city, de Kalb remained as commander of the southern forces. Upon learning of the surrender, Washington wanted Nathanael Greene to take over command in the south. But Congress selected their favorite, Horatio Gates, for the job.

BATTLE OF CAMDEN— AUGUST 16, 1780

Gates arrived in North Carolina on July 25 and took control of the southern force from de Kalb, whom he appointed a divisional commander. The army consisted of the small force of Continentals under de Kalb who had moved into North Carolina to await further orders. A few days after Gates took over, 3,000 southern militia arrived, giving him a force of about 5,000.

On hearing that Cornwallis was in Charleston and had left Lieutenant Colonel Francis Rawdon (Lord Rawdon) in Camden, Gates decided to strike at Camden immediately. Some of his officers suggested that he wait until supplies arrived, since the countryside they would be marching through had been picked clean. But Gates insisted on going forward with the plan. On July 27, the army was on the march south. The countryside was desolated and the men had to subsist on green corn and peaches. Many began to suffer from diarrhea.

On August 15, the army encamped near Camden. Of about 4,100 men, only 3,000 or so were fit for duty. Gates, however, believed he had 7,000 troops, and over the objections of his officers, decided on a night attack on Rawdon at Camden. By now, Cornwallis had returned to Camden, sending Rawdon on to the British base at Ninety Six. Cornwallis also decided on a night attack on Gates and the armies collided around 2:00 A.M. on August 16. After a short flight, both armies fell back, waiting for dawn in order to continue.

Gates deployed his troops in a line of battle with the Continentals on the right and militia on the left. Cornwallis began the battle with an assault on the American left. The British hit the militia with a bayonet charge and the raw troops broke and fled.

Gates, some 60 yards in the rear, was swept away by the tide of fleeing men, and by the time he had regained control of his horse, he was in Charlotte, North Carolina, some 60 miles from Camden. De Kalb and his Continentals continued fighting.

Cornwallis threw 2,000 men against de Kalb's 600, but the Americans almost broke through with a bayonet charge. Then de Kalb was killed after receiving many wounds, and the surviving Continentals surrendered.

The British lost 68, and 238 were wounded. Gates's defeat was so complete that there are no accurate casualties, but some sources claim that 900 were killed and 1,000 captured, in one of America's most crushing defeats of the war. The battle ended all hope for a quick victory in the South. It also ended Gates's military career. He was removed from command, and Congress decided it was wise to let Washington select his replacement. Washington, of course, chose the best man—Nathanael Greene.

BATTLE AT KINGS MOUNTAIN —OCTOBER 7, 1780

After his victory at Camden on August 16, Cornwallis began his move into North Carolina, ordering Major Patrick Ferguson into northwestern South Carolina to secure his left inland flank. Ferguson succeeded in recruiting several thousand "up country" Loyalists to "punish" rebel settlements.

Beyond the mountains in the west, in what today is southern Tennessee, were the Wautauga Settlements, peopled by hardy frontier folk of Scots-Irish descent, often referred to as "over the mountain" men. Some of them had joined in partisan raids on the Loyalists, and Ferguson had responded by

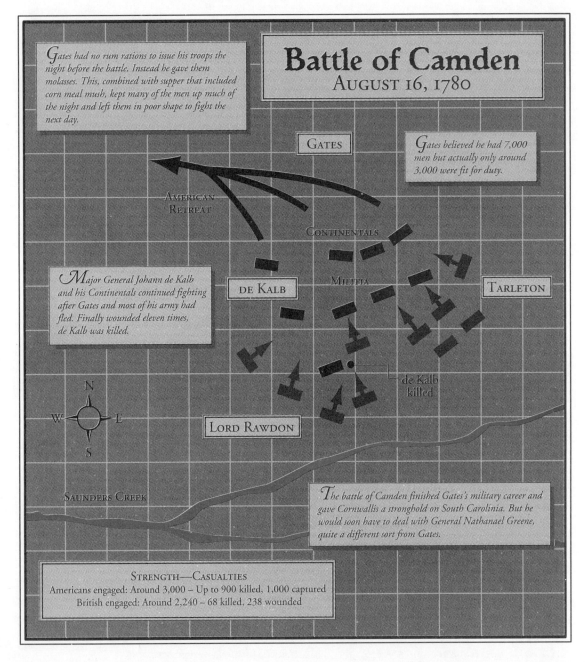

Battle of Camden
AUGUST 16, 1780

Gates had no rum rations to issue his troops the night before the battle. Instead he gave them molasses. This, combined with supper that included corn meal mush, kept many of the men up much of the night and left them in poor shape to fight the next day.

GATES

Gates believed he had 7,000 men but actually only around 3,000 were fit for duty.

AMERICAN RETREAT

CONTINENTALS

Major General Johann de Kalb and his Continentals continued fighting after Gates and most of his army had fled. Finally wounded eleven times, de Kalb was killed.

DE KALB

MILITIA

TARLETON

de Kalb killed

N
W — E
S

LORD RAWDON

SAUNDERS CREEK

The battle of Camden finished Gates's military career and gave Cornwallis a stronghold on South Carolinia. But he would soon have to deal with General Nathanael Greene, quite a different sort from Gates.

STRENGTH—CASUALTIES
Americans engaged: Around 3,000 – Up to 900 killed, 1,000 captured
British engaged: Around 2,240 – 68 killed, 238 wounded

raiding some of the Wautauga Settlements, winning the intense hatred of those mountain people. When they received word from Ferguson that unless they ceased their op- position to royal authority, he would cross the mountains and destroy their settle- ments, they assembled a force to fight him before he crossed the mountains.

Soon the Patriots had a force of about 1,000. Colonel William Campbell arrived with 400 Virginians, Charles McDowell came with 160 men from North Carolina, and there were 240 over the mountain men accompanied by Shelby and Sevier. The entire force consisted of tough frontiersmen—men who could ride a horse through the woods, were crack shots with rifles, and were accustomed to hardships.

Ferguson was now being pressured by Patriot forces moving up from the south. He wrote Cornwallis at Charlotte for reinforcements and then began moving westward to be closer to Cornwallis's troops. On the march, Ferguson took up a position on Kings Mountain, a wooded and rocky spur of the Blue Ridge mountains that rises about 60 feet above the plains, just south of the North Carolina border. Ferguson selected the site because the plateau on the top made an excellent defensive position. The plateau was 600 yards long, 70 yards long on one end, and 120 yards on the opposite end, and so could easily accommodate his force of about 900.

After marching through a rainy night and morning, the rebels arrived near Kings Mountain in the early afternoon of October 7. When they were about a mile away, they hitched their horses and moved into attack position. The plan was to encircle the base of the mountain and then move up in four columns. Their approach was so quiet and Ferguson's security so poor that Shelby's force was within a quarter of a mile from the plateau before the first shot was fired. Moving in from the opposite side, Campbell had also come near the top before the surprised Ferguson became fully aware of the attack.

A major flaw in Ferguson's position was that the trees and rocks covering the slopes were a tremendous advantage to the attackers but a decided disadvantage to the defenders. When Shelby's force was nearing the top, Ferguson ordered an attack with bayonets. Shelby's men had to give ground but his riflemen killed so many of the Loyalists in the charge that they, too, had to fall back. Coming up the other side, Campbell shouted to his troops, "Here are the boys! Shout like hell and fight like devils." The Loyalists' charge on Campbell's Virginians was repulsed, and soon Sevier's men were also on the crest. The air on the crest was continually shattered by rifle fire and yells.

Ferguson dashed about on his horse, blowing the silver whistle he used to maneuver his men and giving them encouragement. Wearing his checkered hunting shirt, he made a perfect target and he fell from his horse, one foot caught in the stirrup and several bullet holes in his body. He had been the only British officer at the battle. All the rest, on both sides, were "Americans." His second in command, Captain Abraham De Pyster, took over and seeing a hopeless situation, raised a white flag of surrender.

It took Shelby and Campbell some time, however, to get their men to stop firing, and there were reports that a number of Loyalists were killed after they had surrendered and been taken captive.

It had been a bad day for the Loyalists—157 killed, 164 wounded, and 698 prisoners. Patriots lost 28, and 64 were wounded out of the 900 or so engaged. The prisoners were marched to Gilbert Town where 30 or 40 were tried for helping the British loot and raid. Twelve were convicted, and ten were executed.

The battle at Kings Mountain, which had

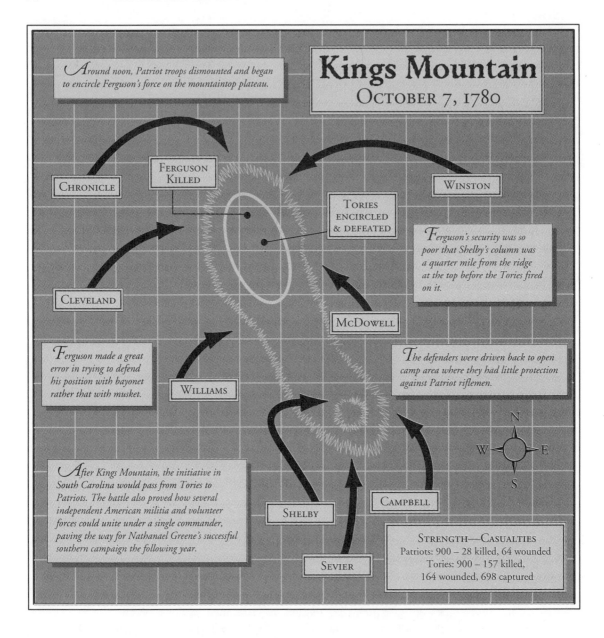

Kings Mountain
OCTOBER 7, 1780

Around noon, Patriot troops dismounted and began to encircle Ferguson's force on the mountaintop plateau.

CHRONICLE

FERGUSON KILLED

WINSTON

TORIES ENCIRCLED & DEFEATED

Ferguson's security was so poor that Shelby's column was a quarter mile from the ridge at the top before the Tories fired on it.

CLEVELAND

Ferguson made a great error in trying to defend his position with bayonet rather that with musket.

WILLIAMS

McDOWELL

The defenders were driven back to open camp area where they had little protection against Patriot riflemen.

After Kings Mountain, the initiative in South Carolina would pass from Tories to Patriots. The battle also proved how several independent American militia and volunteer forces could unite under a single commander, paving the way for Nathanael Greene's successful southern campaign the following year.

CAMPBELL

SHELBY

N
W   E
S

SEVIER

STRENGTH—CASUALTIES
Patriots: 900 – 28 killed, 64 wounded
Tories: 900 – 157 killed,
164 wounded, 698 captured

lasted only about an hour, gave a great boost to the southern rebels and grief to the Loyalists. It also delayed Cornwallis's plan by three months. Within that time, General Nathanael Greene would take command of the Continental Army in the south. The tide of the war there would soon turn in favor of the Americans.

Kings Mountain Military Park is administered by the National Park Service. It includes a center where exhibits help the visitor interpret the battle.

BATTLE AT COWPENS— JANUARY 17, 1781

The army that Gates turned over to Nathanael Greene on December 2, 1780, at Charlotte, North Carolina, was a ragged and discouraged force of about 3,000 men, of which 1,000 were Continentals, the remainder semitrained militia. But while Greene realized his army was no match for Cornwallis's well-trained force of 4,000, he could not risk a retreat, as it would further demoralize his army as well as the civilians. He decided the best strategy was to divide his force. By doing this, each force could live off the country and be sufficiently mobile to keep clear of the heavily equipped British forces.

One flank of the army, which Greene would accompany, was commanded by Isaac Huger. The other flank was under Daniel Morgan, a splendid tactician who had shown his worth at Freeman Farms and Bemis Heights. He understood his men well and always told them exactly what he expected in battle. As he had once been a teamster, his men called him the "Old Wagoner."

Morgan was instructed to move west from Charlotte, while Huger would move east with Greene, creating a problem for Cornwallis: If he moved against one of Greene's forces, his bases would be open to attack by the other wing. His solution was the same as Greene's—to divide his army. He sent Banastre Tarleton to take care of Morgan, while he would take care of Greene. Tarleton went after Morgan with about 1,100 men—cavalry and infantry, mostly veterans. He pressed hard and on the morning of January 16 his troops enjoyed the breakfast rations left by the hurriedly departing Patriots.

When Morgan saw he could not get away from Tarleton, he decided to fight him. The place he chose was an open wood known as "Hannah's Cowpen." The ground sloped gently toward the south—Tarleton's approach. At the far end were two low crests, separated by a wide swale. This was not an ideal site for the Patriots, and while Morgan had 900 men, many were untrained and would break if hit by cavalry or the bayonet. Morgan devised a plan to suit his men and the terrain.

In the morning, Morgan positioned his troops in three lines, straddling the dirt road that curved through the field. In the front line were 120 sharpshooters, told to fire two well-aimed volleys and then fall back. Behind them were the Carolina and Georgia militia, under Andrew Pickens. Their orders were to fire two rounds and then leave (if they so wished). One hundred fifty yards in back of the militia were 500 Continentals under John Eager Howard. Morgan told these men to fire slowly and deliberately and not to break. If forced to retreat, they were to rally on the main crest. Behind the crest, Morgan placed his 120-man cavalry under William Washington.

Before dawn, the British stumbled on the American position. Wanting a better look at the American line, Tarleton sent a detachment of cavalry forward. The American sharpshooters emptied 15 saddles in a matter of minutes. Tarleton then formed his troops into line and advanced on the American position, some 400 yards away— infantry straddling the road with 50 dragoons, 200 cavalry, and a brigade of cavalry as reserves.

As soon as the British were in range, the militia delivered a murderous fire and then broke for the flanks. Dragoons on the right went after them but were soon driven off by a fierce charge of Washington's cavalry. Pickens was now able to re-form his broken ranks.

The British now attacked Morgan's third line. When the advance faltered because of the heavy American fire, Tarleton ordered up the Highlanders. The fighting now was both violent and confusing. Howard ordered his right to fall back and present a new front. When asked by Morgan the reason for a retreat, Howard answered him with another question, "Do men who march like that look as though they were beaten?" Morgan saw the point and found a new position for Howard's troops. Tarleton also believed that Howard was retreating and that victory was almost certain. He ordered all his troops into a final attack.

Howard's command reached its new position and began a deadly fire into the massed British ranks. When the line staggered, the Continentals moved in with bayonets. When the British began to surrender, there were calls from the Americans, "Tarleton's Quarters, Tarleton's Quarters," recalling the earlier massacre of American troops. American officers had to hold back some of their men and even use bayonets to protect surrendered wounded enemy from harm by Americans seeking revenge.

The Highlanders held out to the end but finally surrendered. Tarleton tried to organize one last charge with his dragoons but the men refused. He then withdrew from the field, taking his horsemen with him.

It had been a stunning victory for Morgan and his men. The British had lost 100 men, with 229 wounded and 600 captured. Morgan had lost only 12 men, with 60 wounded. Cowpens provided a tremendous boost for the morale of the Americans, especially the southern Patriots. The battle would also make it easier for Greene to wage his war of attrition against the limited British forces in the south.

Cowpens National Battlefield is administered by the National Park Service. There is a visitor center with exhibits and also exhibits along the tour road and walking rails.

BATTLE AT GUILFORD COURTHOUSE—MARCH 15, 1781

After whipping Tarleton at Cowpens, Morgan learned that Cornwallis and his army were nearby and, having no intention of tangling with such a superior force, marched northeast to join Greene. For his part, Cornwallis was concerned that, in just a few months, British forces had suffered two serious blows: Kings Mountain and Cowpens. He believed a British victory in South Carolina was essential; defeating Greene offered that opportunity.

After joining with Greene, Morgan advised him to retreat to the western mountains, where his army would be safe from Cornwallis. But Greene was determined to go north into Virginia, where he expected reinforcements recruited by Steuben.

As Greene moved north, Cornwallis was hard on his trail. To increase his mobility, he destroyed all but the most essential supplies and equipment. The race between Greene and Cornwallis continued through rain and snow for almost 100 miles. Sometimes the two armies were only a dozen or so miles apart. Greene was finally able to cross the Dan River into Virginia, and since he had taken all the boats, Cornwallis could not follow.

A few days after he had arrived in Virginia, Greene recrossed the Dan into North Carolina. Though he had lost Morgan, who had resigned because of poor health,

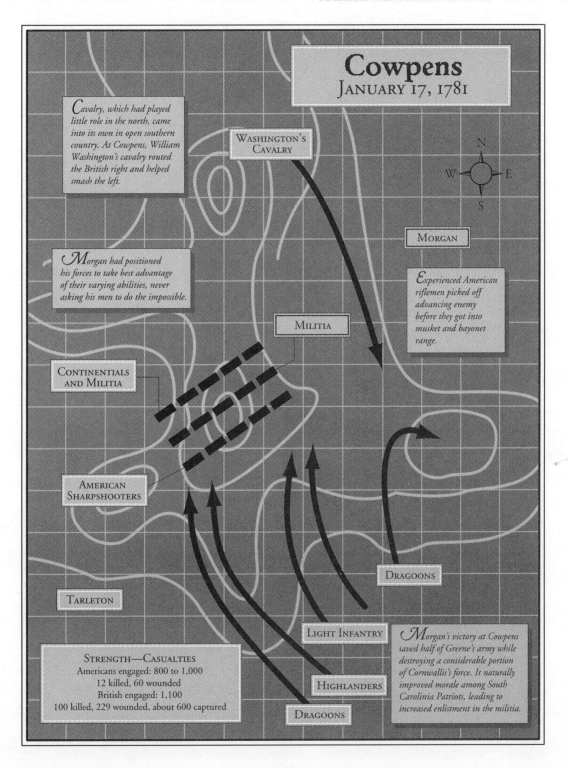

Cowpens
JANUARY 17, 1781

*C*avalry, which had played little role in the north, came into its own in open southern country. At Cowpens, William Washington's cavalry routed the British right and helped smash the left.

WASHINGTON'S CAVALRY

N
W · E
S

MORGAN

*M*organ had positioned his forces to take best advantage of their varying abilities, never asking his men to do the impossible.

*E*xperienced American riflemen picked off advancing enemy before they got into musket and bayonet range.

MILITIA

CONTINENTIALS AND MILITIA

AMERICAN SHARPSHOOTERS

TARLETON

DRAGOONS

LIGHT INFANTRY

*M*organ's victory at Cowpens saved half of Greene's army while destroying a considerable portion of Cornwallis's force. It naturally improved morale among South Carolinia Patriots, leading to increased enlistment in the militia.

STRENGTH—CASUALTIES
Americans engaged: 800 to 1,000
12 killed, 60 wounded
British engaged: 1,100
100 killed, 229 wounded, about 600 captured

HIGHLANDERS

DRAGOONS

Colonel William Washington and his cavalry smashed the British right at Cowpens then hit the left and finally chased Banastre Tarleton and his dragoons off the field. (National Archives)

he had received reinforcements of Virginia militiamen. While he sparred with Cornwallis, more reinforcements arrived, and by March 11, he had 4,300 men. The majority of them, however, were inexperienced soldiers. Cornwallis had only 1,900 troops, but these were battle-hardened veterans. When Cornwallis found Greene at Guilford Courthouse, he attacked.

Greene had decided to make a stand here because he had studied the area on his way to Virginia. The courthouse stood alone on a clearing by the Salisbury Road. From it the road sloped westward through woods to a creek about a mile away, before disappearing into woodlands. Near the creek on both sides of the road were cornfields, with zigzag fences along their upper boundaries.

Greene saw that Cornwallis would have to come east on the road to the creek and up through the cornfields. So behind the fences, backed against the woods, Greene placed his first line—North Carolina militia. On the wings, he put riflemen, Delaware regulars, and cavalry. To the rear of the front line was the second line of Virginia militia and in back of this his best troops—Virginia and Maryland Continentals. He placed his artillery in the road and at the center of his third line.

On the clear and chilly morning of March 15, Tarleton's advanced guard clashed with some of Lee's cavalry. But it was not until early in the afternoon that the main British force advanced through the woods and approached the creek. Greene's artillery opened fire, and British cannon replied.

After about 30 minutes, Greene ordered his guns to the rear. By then, the British ranks were moving forward to the sound of their drums and bagpipes. They came across the cornfield toward the rail fence. When they were about 150 yards away, the North Carolina militia fired their first volley, tearing great holes in the British ranks. But these regulars quickly re-formed and continued uphill. After firing their muskets, they went after the militia with bayonets. Some of the militia fired another round, but shortly, all fled to the rear. The wings on the line held until Cornwallis sent his reserves against them. With the American flanks driven aside, the re-formed British troops moved into the woods to attack Greene's second line.

In dense underbrush, there was heavy, savage fighting, but finally, the British turned the Virginian's right flank and drove through the third line. In the cleared field, the action swayed back and forth. Then, for the first time in the battle, the American cavalry came smashing into the fight, and Cornwallis saw that what had appeared to be a victory could now turn into a defeat. He ordered his artillery to fire grapeshot into the struggling mass of men. Firing on his own men was a harsh measure but one he felt was required to save his army. His plan worked; the cavalry charge was checked, and the American infantry was driven back.

Greene learned that the British were moving around to his rear. He had lost his artillery, and the tide was turning against him. He ordered his army to disengage and later withdrew "leisurely" from the field to camp about 15 miles away. American casualties were about 78 killed and 183 wounded. Out of his 1,900 or so men engaged, Cornwallis lost 532 out of which 93 were killed and 50 shortly died of wounds.

After Guilford Courthouse, Cornwallis moved into Virginia, leaving Rawdon to deal with Greene.

Guilford Courthouse Battlefield is administered by the National Park Service. There is a visitor center with exhibits, films, and related activities. Along the driving and walking trail are reproductions of cannon, numerous monuments and a large equestrian statue of Nathanael Greene.

BATTLE OF HOBKIRK'S HILL— APRIL 25, 1781

Cornwallis's victory at Guildford Courthouse cost him 30 percent of his force. He felt he could not fight Greene again, so he marched to the coast to gather reinforcements.

The ever-resilient Greene turned his attention on South Carolina and Georgia, now defended by Loyalist Lieutenant Colonel Francis Rawdon. Rawdon had about 8,000 men—2,000 at Camden and the remainder scattered among small outposts. Greene's army was down to 1,500 Continentals because the six-week militia enlistment period had expired. Nevertheless, Greene marched his small force to fight Rawdon at Camden. In the meantime, he sent Lee, Marion, Pickens, and Thomas Sumter to take the numerous small British outposts.

Greene planned to surprise Rawdon at Camden, but when he reached Hobkirk's Hill, he learned Rawdon was too strong, so he waited for reinforcements. While he and some of his officers were sitting down for breakfast, the British attacked.

The 26-year-old Rawdon gave Greene quite a beating but did his army no serious harm. However, Marion had cut his supply lines, so Rawdon was forced to retreat toward Charleston. Greene suffered about 266 casualties with 18 killed. Rawdon had 38 killed out of a total of 258.

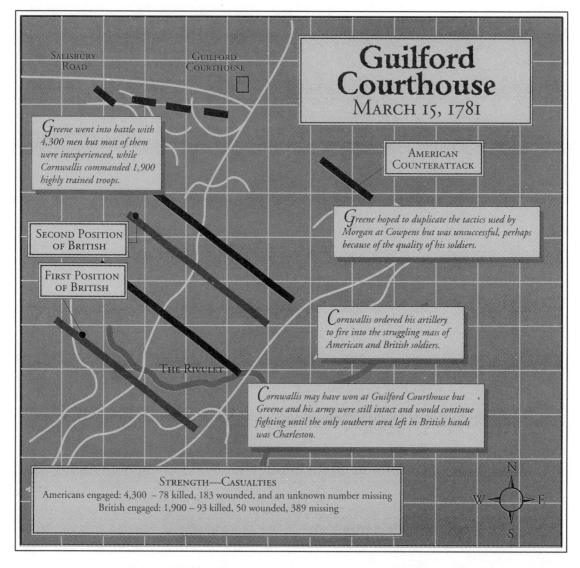

Guilford Courthouse
MARCH 15, 1781

SALISBURY ROAD

GUILFORD COURTHOUSE

Greene went into battle with 4,300 men but most of them were inexperienced, while Cornwallis commanded 1,900 highly trained troops.

AMERICAN COUNTERATTACK

Greene hoped to duplicate the tactics used by Morgan at Cowpens but was unsuccessful, perhaps because of the quality of his soldiers.

SECOND POSITION OF BRITISH

FIRST POSITION OF BRITISH

Cornwallis ordered his artillery to fire into the struggling mass of American and British soldiers.

THE RIVULET

Cornwallis may have won at Guilford Courthouse but Greene and his army were still intact and would continue fighting until the only southern area left in British hands was Charleston.

STRENGTH—CASUALTIES
Americans engaged: 4,300 – 78 killed, 183 wounded, and an unknown number missing
British engaged: 1,900 – 93 killed, 50 wounded, 389 missing

N
W   E
S

SIEGE OF NINETY SIX— MAY 22–JUNE 20, 1781

As Rawdon marched toward Charleston, Greene, with 1,000 men, headed west to take Ninety Six, a major British base in South Carolina. It had been so named because the early settlement was thought to be 96 miles from the Cherokee village of Keowee on the "Charleston Path," a crude trail road. The first fort was built on the site to protect the settlers from Indian attacks. Later, a more substantial fort was constructed, and, in the early years of the war, was defended by rebels against an attack by Loyalists. Eventually, the fort was captured by British forces and turned into an important military base.

Ninety Six now consisted of three major elements. First, there was the small village surrounded by a log stockade. To the north-east was the main defense, a formidable star-shaped redoubt (Star Redoubt) circled by trenches and an abatis of logs with pointed tops. A covered walkway connected the redoubt to the village. To the west, also connected by a covered walkway, was another stronghold, Fort Holmes (The Stockade Fort), which guarded the village's water supply. The base was garrisoned by 550 Loyalists under the command of Colonel John Cruger.

When Greene arrived on May 22, he had not brought along heavy enough cannon to reduce Star Redoubt, so his engineer, Colonel Thaddeus Kosciuszko, laid out plans for a formal siege, consisting of parallels and approach trenches. The first parallels were set too close to the redoubt so the night after they were dug, forces from the redoubt drove the work crews away and filled in the trenches. New parallels had to be dug further away from the redoubt.

Cruger had a gun platform built on the redoubt, so the crews working on parallels were under artillery as well as musket fire. Greene, in turn, built a 40-foot tower so his men could fire on the redoubt, as well as into the village. Cruger used sandbags to increase the height of the stockade.

The village continued to be under fire and the women and children had to take shelter in hastily dug trenches. To add to the general discomfort, the weather turned very hot and the village was low on water. There was almost continuous firing by both sides but with little result.

Lee arrived with his legion on June 10, and the next day, Greene received word that Rawdon was on his way with 2,200 troops to rescue the base. He decided he must take the base before Rawdon arrived, and on June 16, he launched a coordinated two-prong attack. Lee and his force attacked

Fort Holmes and succeeded in taking it, thus cutting off the village's water supply. Colonel Richard Campbell, with Maryland and Virginia Continentals, attacked Star Redoubt and prepared to plant a mine to blow a breech in the structure. The redoubt's defenders launched a counter-attack, however, and, after some very hard fighting, drove Campbell's men away.

Greene realized he did not have time to launch another attack, so on the nineteenth, he marched off in the direction of Charlotte. The siege lasted 28 days, and Greene lost about 57 men, with 70 wounded. Cruger's losses were 27 killed and 58 wounded.

When Rawdon arrived at Ninety Six on June 21, he started off after Greene but, after seeing that his quarry was too far away, returned to the base and shortly thereafter ordered the Ninety Six abandoned and destroyed.

Greene had lost another battle but, once again, he was the strategic winner. The British forces in South Carolina no longer held this former important stronghold.

Ninety Six Historical Site is administered by the National Park Service. There is a visitor center, and the site includes the ruins of fortifications and siege trenches. The stockade fort has been rebuilt.

BATTLE AT EUTAW SPRINGS— SEPTEMBER 8, 1781

Greene was resting his army after their efforts to take Ninety Six when Lee brought word that Lieutenant Colonel Alexander Stewart had replaced Rawdon and was now camped at Eutaw Springs, about midway between Charleston and Camden, with a force of about 2,000.

Greene had been reinforced and now had a slightly larger force. Besides Lee's

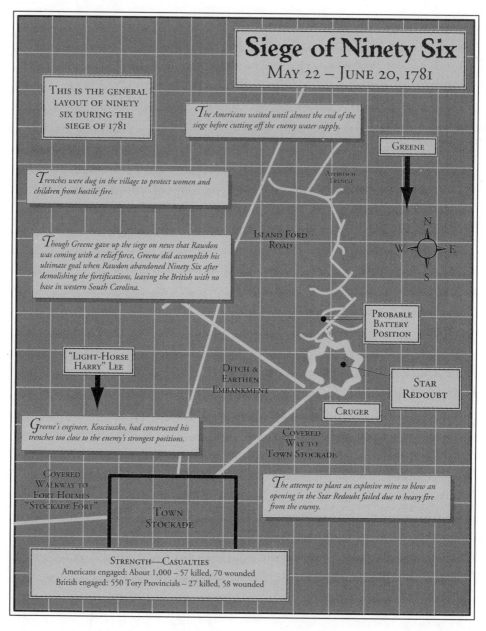

Siege of Ninety Six
MAY 22 – JUNE 20, 1781

THIS IS THE GENERAL LAYOUT OF NINETY SIX DURING THE SIEGE OF 1781

The Americans waited until almost the end of the siege before cutting off the enemy water supply.

GREENE

APPROACH TRENCH

Trenches were dug in the village to protect women and children from hostile fire.

ISLAND FORD ROAD

N
W   E
S

Though Greene gave up the siege on news that Rawdon was coming with a relief force, Greene did accomplish his ultimate goal when Rawdon abandoned Ninety Six after demolishing the fortifications, leaving the British with no base in western South Carolina.

PROBABLE BATTERY POSITION

"LIGHT-HORSE HARRY" LEE

DITCH & EARTHEN EMBANKMENT

STAR REDOUBT

CRUGER

Greene's engineer, Kosciuszko, had constructed his trenches too close to the enemy's strongest positions.

COVERED WAY TO TOWN STOCKADE

COVERED WALKWAY TO FORT HOLMES "STOCKADE FORT"

The attempt to plant an explosive mine to blow an opening in the Star Redoubt failed due to heavy fire from the enemy.

TOWN STOCKADE

STRENGTH—CASUALTIES
Americans engaged: About 1,000 – 57 killed, 70 wounded
British engaged: 550 Tory Provincials – 27 killed, 58 wounded

legion, he had Pickens and Marion's North and South Carolina militias; Maryland, Virginia, and North Carolina Continentals under Williams, Campbell, and Sumner, and Washington and Hamton's cavalry. On the morning of September 8, Greene broke camp and began the seven-mile march to Stewart's camp at Eutaw Springs. He laid out his forces in the Cowpens manner, with a front line of militia, the Continentals behind them, and cavalry at the rear and on the left.

The battle began around 9 A.M., and for a time, it seemed that Greene was certain of a victory. The militia fired 17 rounds without retreating, and when one unit did falter, Sumner's Continentals moved forward to fill the gap.

Stewart launched a major counterattack, but it was broken by the Continentals who held their fire until the enemy was within 40 yards and then followed up with a bayonet charge, causing them to retreat.

But now things began to fall apart for Greene. When he sent Washington with his cavalry to strike at Stewart's right flank, half the command was wiped out, and Washington was wounded and captured. As the remaining troops advanced into the British camp, they found food along with rum and brandy in the tents. The food and liquor soon took control of much of the infantry. When the British shortly drove them out of the camp, they were an undisciplined rabble. Both sides struggled to hold the Brick House, a strong point in the British camp, and the British won. When they counterattacked, Greene finally had to retreat. He had lost 139 men, with 375 wounded and 8 missing. The British losses were 85 killed, 351 wounded, and 257 missing.

For the fourth time, Greene had failed to win a battle. But in some sense he had won the campaign. He had forced Cornwallis into Virginia and so wore down British forces in South Carolina that after Eutaw Springs, they were relegated to the vicinity of Charleston.

THE WAR IN VIRGINIA

On December 9, 1775, Colonel William Woodford, with a regiment of Continentals and militia, marched on Norfolk, Virginia. At the battle of Great Bridge, he defeated a force of Loyalists assembled by the royal governor, Lord Dunmore, and soon occupied the city. Dunmore and many of the Loyalists took refuge on a British warship. Finding little food and water on board, Dunmore ordered the ship to open fire on Norfolk and drive the rebels away. Shortly, the largest town in Virginia was on fire. Dunmore returned to try and set up a base among the ashes but rebels cut off his supplies and forced him to leave—never to return to Norfolk.

After the battle at Great Bridge, there was no fighting in Virginia until 1779. In that year, the British began raiding the countryside for supplies and tobacco to use in securing loans from foreign banks and governments. In December 1780, Benedict Arnold landed at Hampton Roads with 1,600 men to begin his first assignment as a British brigadier general. He occupied Richmond on January 7 and then ordered his men to burn buildings and tobacco.

George Washington, then headquartered on the Hudson River highlands, sent Lafayette to Virginia with 1,200 men to take advantage of Arnold's isolated position. Lafayette reached Virginia in March, and about that same time, Brigadier General William Phillips arrived to assume overall command, bringing with him 2,000 more troops.

On May 20, Cornwallis arrived at Petersburg after marching from Wilmington, North Carolina. His original force of 1,500 was soon increased to 7,200 with the arrival of reinforcements sent by Clinton. As commander of the British forces in America, Clinton took a rather dim view of Cornwallis leaving South Carolina for Virginia. But after his victory in Camden, Cornwallis was now held in such high regard by Lord Germain, who was overseeing the war from his London office, that he felt confident in taking the initiative, no matter what Clinton

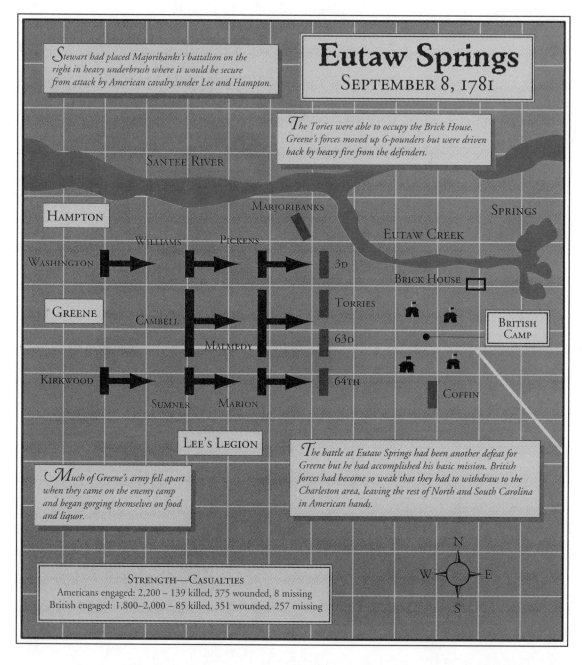

Stewart had placed Majoribanks's battalion on the right in heavy underbrush where it would be secure from attack by American cavalry under Lee and Hampton.

Eutaw Springs
SEPTEMBER 8, 1781

The Tories were able to occupy the Brick House. Greene's forces moved up 6-pounders but were driven back by heavy fire from the defenders.

SANTEE RIVER

HAMPTON

MARJORIBANKS

SPRINGS

WILLIAMS   PICKENS

EUTAW CREEK

WASHINGTON   3D

BRICK HOUSE

GREENE

TORRIES

CAMBELL.

BRITISH CAMP

MALMEDY   63D

KIRKWOOD   64TH

SUMNER   MARION   COFFIN

LEE'S LEGION

The battle at Eutaw Springs had been another defeat for Greene but he had accomplished his basic mission. British forces had become so weak that they had to withdraw to the Charleston area, leaving the rest of North and South Carolina in American hands.

Much of Greene's army fell apart when they came on the enemy camp and began gorging themselves on food and liquor.

N
W   E
S

STRENGTH—CASUALTIES
Americans engaged: 2,200 – 139 killed, 375 wounded, 8 missing
British engaged: 1,800–2,000 – 85 killed, 351 wounded, 257 missing

thought. Cornwallis was convinced that if Virginia were occupied, the colonies would be split in half and thus the war would end.

Lafayette's small force now faced a powerful enemy; he wrote to Washington, "I am not strong enough even to get beaten." General Anthony Wayne soon arrived with 1,000 well-trained troops. Although Lafayette could still not afford to fight a battle with Cornwallis, he could prevent some British raids on supplies and settlements.

On May 21, 1781, Washington met with Comte Rochambeau, commander of French forces in America, to plan the next major campaign. In July 1778, a joint American and French force had attacked Newport, Rhode Island. Their effort failed, partially because of poor communications between the Americans on land and the supporting French warships, but Washington and Rochambeau liked and respected each other. Though Washington wanted to concentrate on capturing New York, the scene of his early defeats, when he and Rochambeau studied its defenses, they realized that even with the support of the French fleet it would be impossible to dislodge Clinton with his force of 15,000. Rochambeau favored moving into the Chesapeake Bay area at once, rather than wasting time with New York. His plan received added emphasis when they received word from Admiral François de Grasse that he would sail from the West Indies on August 13 with 3,000 men directly to the Chesapeake and would return to his base on October 31. On August 21, Washington left the New York area and headed south, shortly followed by Rochambeau.

When Clinton finally realized that an American-French force was on its way to Virginia, he instructed Cornwallis to find a defensive position where he could be evacuated by ship. On June 15, Cornwallis left his base at Elk Hill, northwest of Richmond, and marched toward Williamsburg.

Washington ordered Lafayette to follow. Lafayette's force had now grown to about 5,200 with the recent arrival of Campbell's 600 riflemen and Steuben's 450 Virginians. Clinton now wrote Cornwallis to take a defensive position at Old Point Comfort or Yorktown and that he was sending him

reinforcements. Cornwallis selected Yorktown as the better site.

SIEGE OF YORKTOWN— OCTOBER 6–20, 1781

On his way south from Philadelphia in early September, Washington was delighted to learn that De Grasse's fleet had arrived at the Chesapeake, bringing 3,000 French troops for Lafayette. Washington asked Lafayette to contain Cornwallis so that he could not escape by moving up the peninsula and into the Carolinas.

On September 5, De Grasse sailed out of the bay to fight the British fleet commanded by Admiral Thomas Graves. There was no clear winner in the ensuing battle, but the British ships were so badly damaged that Graves sailed back to New York for repairs. While the battle was in progress, Admiral Comte de Barras slipped in and delivered Rochambeau's siege guns brought from Newport, Rhode Island.

Washington, now commander in chief of the allied forces, arrived at Williamsburg on September 14 with Rochambeau. By the twenty-sixth, the armies were concentrated in the area ready to attack Yorktown.

A village of several hundred houses, Yorktown faced the York River, which separated it from Glouscester Point, a half mile away. While the land at the rear of the village was relatively flat sandy soil, a swampy area formed to the west where Yorktown Creek flowed into the river. Cornwallis's defenses were built about 300 yards to the rear of the village and extended in a 1,000-yard curve with the east end anchored by the York River and the other by the swamp.

Of the trenches and ten redoubts that Cornwallis constructed, the most formidable was positioned at the west near

Yorktown Creek. Because it was garrisoned by a detachment of Welsh Fusiliers, it was called the "Fusilier's Redoubt." The remaining redoubts were identified by numbers. Cornwallis had about 65 cannon and 9,000 troops to defend his position. He had also fortified Gloucester Point with trenches, redoubts, and artillery and sent Lieutenant Colonel Thomas Dundas and Tarleton with a detachment to garrison this position.

When Washington arrived, he saw that Cornwallis could escape by way of Gloucester Point and sent General George Weedon with 1,500 men to take and hold a position behind Dundas. Weedon would be reinforced later by Lauzen, and finally General de Choisy would arrive to take command of the 3,000 allied troops on the point. Cornwallis countered the allied move by sending over Tarleton with 1,000 men.

On September 28, the allied army of 29,000 moved from Williamsburg to within a mile or so of Yorktown's defenses. Washington's army of 20,000 was divided into three divisions under Lafayette, Steuben, and Lincoln, with Henry Knox commanding artillery.

Rochambeau's force of 9,000 was divided into two wings, commanded by generals Marquis de Saint-Simon and Baron Charles de Viomenil.

The day after the allied forces reached Yorktown, they saw that Cornwallis had abandoned three of his redoubts covering the approaches to the inner defenses. He had received word from Clinton that a relief fleet bringing 5,000 men would leave New York on October 5 and decided to concentrate his limited force on holding some of the outer works. The allied force was now positioned to encircle Cornwallis's defenses—the French on the left and the Americans on the right.

The siege began on October 6. That night 1,500 men set to work digging a 2,000-yard trench parallel to the defenses. Because of the sandy soil, by morning they had completed the trench and added some redoubts. Artillery was brought up, and soon, almost 50 cannon were pounding the British positions, but redoubts 9 and 10 had to be taken before the American end of the parallel trench could be completed. Alexander Hamilton of Lafayette's division led the attack on redoubt 10, which he was able to take with the loss of only 9 men and 25 wounded.

The French attack on redoubt 9 did not go nearly as well. When it was eventually taken, 15 had been killed and 77 wounded. In the two redoubts, Cornwallis lost about 20 men and 50 or so were captured. A second parallel, closer to the defense, was completed, and now the artillery was able to bombard the defenses and town from several angles and at close range. By this time, most of Cornwallis's guns had been put out of action.

Cornwallis now sent a force of 350 to silence some of the batteries, and he managed to disable a few guns, but they were shortly back in use. He decided his only chance to avoid defeat was to take his army to Gloucester Point and retreat overland to the Delaware River, where British ships could take him back to New York. On the night of October 16, he tried to ferry his men across the river, but there were not enough boats, and there was a severe storm.

The allied cannon continued pounding the defenses and the village of Yorktown. But on the morning of the seventeenth, they gradually became silent as a British officer with a white handkerchief came out in front of the defenses. After corresponding several times with Washington over terms, Cornwallis surrendered his army.

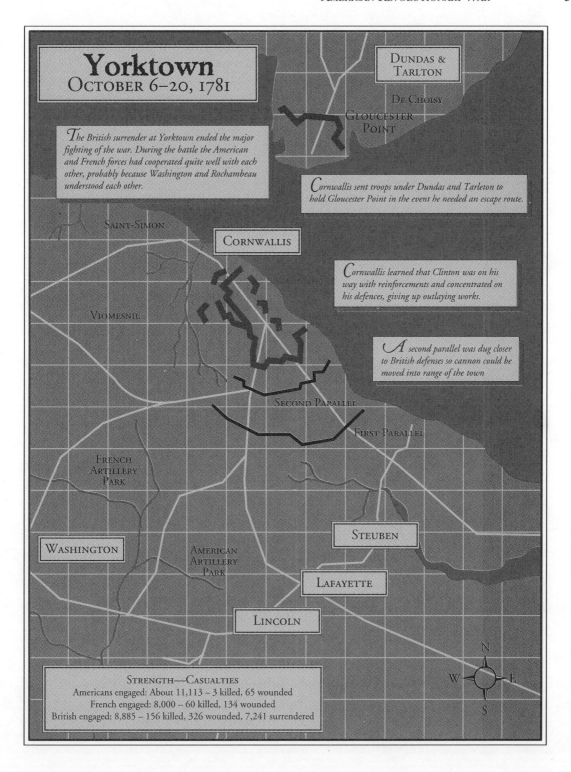

Yorktown
OCTOBER 6–20, 1781

The British surrender at Yorktown ended the major fighting of the war. During the battle the American and French forces had cooperated quite well with each other, probably because Washington and Rochambeau understood each other.

DUNDAS & TARLTON

DE CHOISY

GLOUCESTER POINT

Cornwallis sent troops under Dundas and Tarleton to hold Gloucester Point in the event he needed an escape route.

SAINT-SIMON

CORNWALLIS

Cornwallis learned that Clinton was on his way with reinforcements and concentrated on his defences, giving up outlaying works.

VIOMESNIL

A second parallel was dug closer to British defenses so cannon could be moved into range of the town

SECOND PARALLEL

FIRST PARALLEL

FRENCH ARTILLERY PARK

STEUBEN

WASHINGTON

AMERICAN ARTILLERY PARK

LAFAYETTE

LINCOLN

N
W E
S

STRENGTH—CASUALTIES
Americans engaged: About 11,113 – 3 killed, 65 wounded
French engaged: 8,000 – 60 killed, 134 wounded
British engaged: 8,885 – 156 killed, 326 wounded, 7,241 surrendered

The siege produced relatively light casualties on both sides. Americans lost 3 men, with 65 wounded. The French lost 60 men, with 134 wounded, while the British losses were 156 killed and 326 wounded.

The reinforcements that Clinton had promised Cornwallis arrived from New York at the Chesapeake on October 24, 1781. It is interesting to speculate on what might have happened if those 7,000 troops and 25 ships-of-the-line arrived a few weeks before.

The formal surrender on October 20 was impressive, to say the least. American and French troops were drawn up in two lines, dressed in their best uniforms; those of the French, of course, much more colorful than the Americans'. When Lord Percy had marched from Boston on April 19, 1775, to rescue the column returning from Concord, his band played "Yankee Doodle" to mock the rebels. As the British troops now came to lay down their arms at Yorktown, their band played a different tune—"The World Turned Upside Down." Cornwallis was not on hand for the formal surrender, claiming he was ill, and he sent General O'Hara with his sword to represent him.

The generally accepted version of the actual surrender is that O'Hara first offered the sword to Rochambeau who graciously pointed to Washington. O'Hara then offered the sword to Washington. But Washington had no intention of accepting Cornwallis's sword from one of his officers and directed O'Hara to General Lincoln. Lincoln accepted the sword and immediately returned it to O'Hara. After that exercise, some 8,000 British and Hessian troops marched past the line of American and French troops and laid down their arms and cased flags.

When the British prime minister, Lord North, heard of Cornwallis's surrender, he cried out, "Oh God! It is all over." And so it was, but it would not be until September 3, 1783, that the peace treaty between Britain and the United States was signed.

Battlegrounds at Yorktown are a portion of the Virginia National Historical Park that also includes Jamestown. There is a visitor center at Yorktown with a diorama and reconstructed section of a British warship with objects recovered from the York River along with cannon. There is also a museum with a film describing the battle, for a charge. On the grounds are remains of American lines and British fortifications.

War of 1812

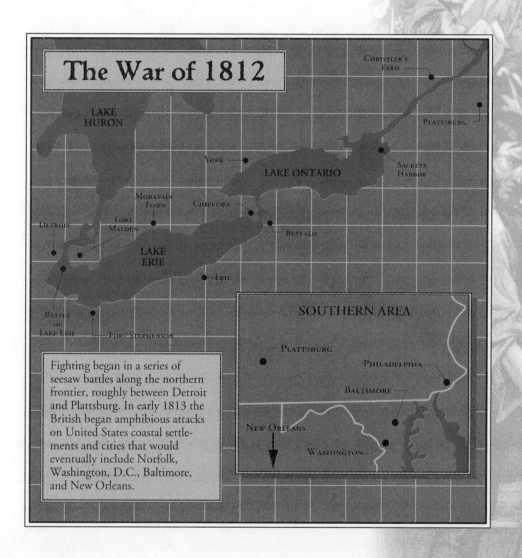

The War of 1812

LAKE HURON

CHRISTLER'S FARM

PLATTSBURG

YORK

LAKE ONTARIO

SACKETS HARBOR

MORAVAIN TOWN

CHIPPEWA

DETROIT

FORT MALDEN

BUFFALO

LAKE ERIE

ERIE

BATTLE OF LAKE ERIE

FORT STEPHENSON

SOUTHERN AREA

PLATTSBURG

PHILADELPHIA

BALTIMORE

NEW ORLEANS

WASHINGTON

Fighting began in a series of seesaw battles along the northern frontier, roughly between Detroit and Plattsburg. In early 1813 the British began amphibious attacks on United States coastal settlements and cities that would eventually include Norfolk, Washington, D.C., Baltimore, and New Orleans.

America's second war with Great Britain is sometimes called "The Incredible War of 1812," which is not a bad description, considering how it started and was fought. But this small and unpopular war left its stamp on our American heritage.

The British bombardment of Fort McHenry on the night of September 13–14, 1814, inspired Francis Scott Key to write verses that he entitled "The Star Spangled Banner." "Don't give up the ship," the last command of mortally wounded Captain James Lawrence of the frigate USS *Chesapeake*, became the motto of the United States Navy. John Randolph of Virginia coined the term "war hawks" to describe the young members of Congress who were pushing for war with Great Britain. These days, "hawk" applies to anyone who favors the more aggressive solution to a problem. The frigate USS *Constitution*—"Old Ironsides"—that lifted the spirits of America with her victory over the British frigate HMS *Guerriere* on August 9, 1812, still floats at Boston, the oldest commissioned warship in the world.

The dress uniform of West Point cadets is a reminder of those worn by Brigadier General Winfield Scott's brigade of regulars when they defeated the British forces at Chippawa, Canada, on July 5, 1814.

After defeating the British fleet on Lake Erie, Commodore Oliver Perry sent a brief message to his superior, General William Harrison, that began, "We have met the enemy and they are ours." And finally, the campaign of 1812 was the only U.S. war from which two generals—William Henry Harrison and Andrew Jackson—went on to be elected President.

There was no single crisis that drove the United States to declare war on Great Britain on June 18, 1812, but rather, it was years of frustration over unsuccessful efforts to maintain its honor and national economic interests. These imperatives became tangled up in the war between Great Britain and Napoleon's France. In 1792, these two countries began a war that lasted with a few brief interruptions, until Napoleon's final defeat at Waterloo in 1815.

In 1805, British naval commander Horatio Nelson defeated the combined French and Spanish fleets at Trafalgar, giving Britain control of the world's seas. Napoleon Bonaparte, however, was making himself master of western Europe. The war developed into a life-and-death struggle between these two colonial powers and as neither one could physically attack the other, both attempted to harm the enemy economically by restrictions on trade.

Napoleon closed off continental ports to neutral ships that traded with Britain. Britain issued orders that forbade neutral ships from entering French ports unless they first visited British ports and had cargo inspected. Napoleon countered this by issuing a decree to the effect that any neutral ship that allowed the British to inspect its cargo would be seized on entering a French port.

Since the United States had the largest neutral merchant fleet in the world, this put American shippers in something of a bind. Americans were also becoming angry that British warships cruised off its ports to stop and inspect departing vessels for contraband goods that night be intended for French ports.

Of far greater concern to American honor was the arrogant action of British warships, which stopped merchant ships flying the American flag to inspect the crew and remove those whom the British officer believed to be deserters or British citizens.

Over the years, many thousands of men were removed from American ships and "impressed" into service in the Royal Navy.

This affront to American national honor reached crisis proportions over the "Chesapeake-Leopard Affair," an altercation between a British and an American ship near Norfolk, on June 21, 1807. Most Americans were so enraged over this incident that almost the entire country was ready to declare war. But President Thomas Jefferson, aware of the unprepared state of the country's military, preferred to settle matters through negotiations.

Great Britain, however, was not sympathetic to American complaints as Britain was convinced that it was helping all free nations with her war against Napoleon and any means needed to win the war would eventually benefit all such nations.

In 1807, Jefferson sought to punish both Great Britain and France through an embargo act that prevented the departure of American ships bound for foreign ports. All this act accomplished, however, was to harm American shippers, and it was repealed in 1808 shortly after James Monroe became president.

The election of 1810 brought to Congress a number of younger men who were impatient with the national government's efforts to maintain peace. Representatives from western and southern states, such as Henry Clay of Kentucky and John Calhoun of South Carolina, were particularly aggressive, and they and their followers were soon known as "war hawks."

The war hawks took up the popular cry "Free Trade and Sailor's Rights!" and "Free Ships Make Free Trade," but they had other reasons for wanting war. Many were convinced, and with good reason, that the British in Canada were supporting and encouraging Indians to raid western American settlements. War could also lead to the annexation of portions of Canada as well as Spanish Florida.

Portions of the country, especially New England, were not in favor of war. Many believed the nation was unprepared for such a conflict in spite of Clay's claim that the Kentucky militia alone could conquer Canada. There were also those who felt that the real enemy was not Britain but France. But the war hawks prevailed, and war against Britain was declared on June 18, 1812.

In the first two or so years of the war, most of the battles took place along the northern frontier, which adjoined British territory in North America, including the sparsely settled areas on and around Lakes Erie and Ontario, the Niagara River, and western parts of the St. Lawrence River. By the summer of 1813, Great Britain was receiving help in its war with Napoleon from Russia, Prussia, and Austria, allowing it to send more troops and warships to fight in America.

In 1814, Britain launched a major counteroffensive, which resulted in the significant battles of the war fought at Plattsburg, New York; Washington, D.C.; Baltimore; and New Orleans.

THE UNITED STATES AND CANADA BEFORE 1812

In 1812, with a population of about 7,500,000, the United States was made up of the original 13 colonies, plus the additional states of Louisiana, Ohio, Tennessee, and Kentucky. The regular army consisted of about 7,500 men, although its authorized strength was 35,000. With the approach of

THE CHESAPEAKE-LEOPARD AFFAIR

On June 21, 1807, the U.S. 38-gun frigate *Chesapeake*, fresh from the Washington navy yard, sailed from Norfolk, Virginia, flying the flag of Commodore James Barron. *Chesapeake*'s guns were still unmounted and the crew not yet organized, but there was ample time to take care of these matters during the long voyage to the Mediterranean, where the ship was headed.

Just after passing the three-mile limit, *Chesapeake* was hailed by the British 32-gun frigate HMS *Leopard*. Believing the *Leopard* had a message she wanted brought to Europe, *Chesapeake* hoved to. A British officer boarded and said there were four British deserters on board, and his captain demanded the crew be mustered and inspected by an officer. Barron, of course, refused, saying there were no deserters among his crew and that it was against U.S. Navy regulations to allow any foreign officer to muster the crew.

The British officer returned to his ship, and shortly afterward, and a call through a trumpet demanded that Barron comply. Barron refused even to reply and *Leopold* fired a shot across his bow, followed by a broadside. For about 15 minutes firing continued on helpless *Chesapeake*. Barron managed to get off one shot to preserve his ship's honor and then lowered his flag in surrender. Three of his men had been killed and 18 or more wounded, including Barron.

A few minutes after the surrender, Captain Humphries of the *Leopard* came aboard, declined Barron's offered sword, and apologized for the damage his ship had done but, nevertheless, insisted on inspecting the crew and removing four men he claimed were deserters. There was general uproar throughout the nation when *Chesapeake* limped back to Norfolk to tell her story.

The Federalists and Jefferson's Republicans were united in the cry for revenge, even if it meant war with Great Britain. But Jefferson, aware of the poor state of America's fighting force, let the moment slip away, and by the time war was declared in 1812, President Madison had to fight it with a divided nation.

war, Congress voted to increase the army to 50,000, but there were few enlistments. The states were also ordered to raise a force of 80,000 militia. Massachusetts, Connecticut, and Rhode Island refused to do so, and it later turned out that the militia from other states would refuse to cross into Canada.

Competent military leadership was almost nonexistent. There was no general staff and no well-planned strategy for the proposed invasion of Canada. President James Madison knew little of warfare, and the only military experience of Dr. William Eustis, the secretary of war, had been that of an army surgeon in the Revolutionary War. The senior major general, Henry "Granny" Dearborn who would plan the Canada invasion, was a 61-year-old veteran of the revolution. James Wilkerson, the senior regular army brigadier, was better at winning court martials than battles. At the start of the war, he was in command along the Florida border. (Later papers belonging to Spanish authorities listed him as "Spy No. 13.") By 1814, capable men such as Jacob Brown, Winfield Scott, and Andrew Jackson were in command, but two years and many men had been wasted because of poor leadership.

Canada's population at the time was only around 400,000 non-Indians. The huge area was divided into two provinces: Upper Canada with its capital at York (present-day Toronto) and Lower Canada with Montreal as its capital. The designation "upper" and "lower" referred to the location on the St. Lawrence River. Canada was governed by men with military experience: Lieutenant General George Prevost was governor general of Lower Canada and governor in chief of all provinces; Major General Isaac Brock was governor of Upper Canada.

In 1812, Great Britain was too involved fighting Napoleon to send much help to Canada, so Prevost and Brock had to defend Canada with what they had at hand: an army of about 7,000 British and Canadian regulars, plus about 10,000 Canadian militia. Many of these men, of course, were French, and there was some doubt as to how well they would fight against the enemy of their British conquerors, but most of them proved loyal.

Canada also had a force of some 3,500 Indian warriors, and many of them accepted Shawnee chief Tecumseh as their leader. Tecumseh's village at Tippecanoe had been destroyed by General William Henry Harrison's army on November 7, 1811, but Tecumseh was away at the time. After the battle, he left for Canada to join with the British in fighting the Americans. Brock established good relations with Tecumseh, and together, they gained a number of victories over the invaders.

BATTLES ALONG THE NORTHERN FRONTIER

The U.S. military objective was to invade Canada and force Great Britain to respect its interests, as well as to provide a valuable chip for future peace negotiations.

Even before war was declared, General Dearborn had President Madison's approval of an invasion plan that called for Dearborn to take a major force down Lake Champlain and capture Montreal and be supported by attacks on Upper Canada from Sackets Harbor, New York, Niagara, and Detroit. This projected invasion, however, turned into a series of disasters and lost opportunities filled with incompetency and stupidity.

On July 5, the elderly and somewhat infirm Brigadier General William Hull, governor of Michigan territory, with 2,000 militia arrived at Detroit, a settlement of some 800 people. Hull had lost the chance to take the poorly defended important British base of Fort Malden on the opposite side of the Detroit River, which was soon reinforced by the arrival of General Brock with some soldiers and a large band of Indian warriors.

Brock warned Hull of what his Indians would do if Detroit was stormed and paraded the Indians in war paint in full view of the occupants of Detroit. Hull became so afraid that on August 16, he surrendered his army and Detroit.

In October, inexperienced General Stephen Van Rensselaer, with 6,000 militia, was preparing to cross the Niagara River to capture Queenstown, supported by General Alexander Smyth and his 1,650 regulars, who would attack Fort George, some ten miles from Queenstown. Smyth, however, refused to take part in the expedition because he did not approve of the embarkation site that Van Rensselaer had selected.

Van Rensselaer went ahead anyway and, on the night of October 11, crossed the river and attacked Queenstown. The attack

BATTLE AT FORT MEIGS—MAY 1–9, 1813

During the winter of 1812–1813 American General William Henry Harrison built Fort Meigs (named in honor of the governor of Ohio) near the mouth of the Maumee River as a base in striking distance of Detroit. Harrison had only about 1,000 men, and when he learned that General Henry Proctor was on his way to attack the fort, sent word to General Clay at Fort Defiance on the lower Maumee River to come with his 1,200 men.

In late April, Proctor arrived with 522 British regulars, 450 or so Canadian militia, 1,500 of Tecumseh's Indians, and artillery. Proctor placed his artillery on the north side of the river, opposite the fort, and on May 1 opened fire. Harrison received word that Clay was well on his way and instructed him to send part of his force to the north side of the river to take out Proctor's cannon.

Clay gave task to Colonel William Dudley. He and his men drove off the artillerymen and spiked the cannon, but instead of recrossing the river to the fort, Dudley went after the retreating artillerymen and was ambushed by some of Tecumseh's Indians. Dudley's 800 men put up a stiff fight, but they were completely surrounded, and only about 170 managed to reach the safety of the fort. Reinforced by Clay's 400 troops, the fort's garrison went on the offensive, capturing the remaining artillery. Under this pressure, Proctor gave up the attack and returned to his base at Malden.

On the way, some of the Indians began to kill and scalp the 20 or so captives. A British soldier tried to stop the killing but ended up being killed himself. Tecumseh asked Proctor why he did not order the killing to stop, and Proctor replied that Indians could not be controlled. Tecumseh gave Proctor a contemptuous look and said, "You are unfit to command. Go put on petticoats!"

Fort Meigs has been reconstructed by the Ohio Historical Society to look as it did in 1813. There is a visitor center, and several of the fort's blockhouses contain exhibits and a diorama of the War of 1812.

might have succeeded with support but none was forthcoming. Brock, at nearby Fort George, arrived with some British troops and eventually the Americans surrendered, including young Lieutenant Colonel Winfield Scott. Scott was soon exchanged and would fight again in this war and the war with Mexico and head the U.S. Army at the start of the Civil War. For their part, the British paid a high price for their victory at Queenstown since the brilliant Brock was killed leading a charge.

The projected invasion from Sackets Harbor never materialized, and the attack on Montreal ended in failure. With 6,000 militia, Dearborn had moved north from Plattsburg and, on the night of November 19 tangled with 1,900 Canadian militia. After a brief skirmish, the Canadians retreated into Canada, but Dearborn's militia refused to pursue them, since it would mean crossing the border. Dearborn returned to Plattsburg to establish winter quarters.

Eigthteen thirteen was a better year for American forces along the frontier. William Henry Harrison, the 39-year-old hero of the 1811 battle of Tippecanoe, was made commander of the northern armies and moved north to attempt to retake Detroit. During the winter of 1812–1813, he built Fort Meigs on the Maumee River to serve as his base for the attack. He soon realized, however, that Detroit could never be taken and held

as long as the British fleet controlled Lake Erie. On September 10, American Commodore Oliver Hazard Perry defeated the British lake fleet, and Harrison was able to recapture Detroit from General Henry Proctor, who had taken over command of British forces after Brock's death.

Proctor moved his small force of regulars and some 1,000 Indians under Tecumseh out of the Detroit area and up the Thames River on the north shore of Lake Erie. Perry's fleet carried Harrison's force across the lake, and on October 5, it defeated Proctor's army near Moravain Town. Tecumseh was killed in the battle, robbing the British of a valuable ally. Proctor escaped capture but played no further part in the war. The United States now, however, controlled Lake Erie and the territory to the west. The war was not

proceeding nearly as well on Lake Ontario. John Armstrong, now the secretary of war, developed a campaign plan that called for Dearborn to capture Kingston on the eastern end of the lake, then go on to take York, and finally to cooperate with a force from Buffalo to secure the Niagara River. Dearborn and Commodore Isaac Chauncey, commander of naval forces on Lake Ontario, determined that Kingston was too well defended and received Armstrong's approval to pass it over and go on to York. The failure to attempt to take Kingston was one of the great lost opportunities of the war, for if it were held by the United States, it would have cut off the supplies to all British bases and forts to the west.

On April 27, Dearborn and Chauncey attacked York, which was easily taken, since the defenders had retreated before the

Perry's Victory and International Peace Memorial was completed in 1915 and designated a national monument in 1936. From an observation platform 317 feet above the lake the battle site of Lake Erie, some ten miles away, can easily be seen on a clear day. (National Park Service)

DON'T JUDGE A SOLDIER BY THE COLOR OF HIS UNIFORM

In early July 1813, Major General Jacob Brown's well-trained and highly disciplined force of about 3,500 regulars, including Brigadier General Winfield Scott's brigade, were on their way to Fort Erie. The rather inefficient War Department had run out of the blue cloth needed for the uniforms of the regular army. So Scott's brigade, along with the West Point cadets, had to make do for uniforms with what cloth was available—militia gray. A few miles outside Fort Erie, near Chippewa, Scott halted his brigade, while Brown and the remainder of the army encamped at another site.

On the following morning, July 5, Brigadier General Phineas Riall with 1,500 regulars and about 600 militia and Indians attacked Brown's position. The British attack forced one of Brown's brigades to retreat, and he ordered Scott to come forward with his troops. Scott had drawn up his men for parade and immediately moved forward. One of Riall's officers observed, through a spyglass, the color of the uniforms of Scott's troops and reported to Riall that they were nothing more than militia. This assured Riall who had been considering retreating when he first noted Scott's advance.

Scott's brigade marched in perfect formation, as if they were still on parade, and as men began to fall under the British artillery, the ranks closed up and the advance continued at an even pace. Riall took notice of the superb action of Scott's men and exclaimed in surprise, "Those are Regulars, by God!"

The British regulars advanced on Scott's regulars until the two forces were only about 70 yards apart. Then, Scott ordered a bayonet charge. The British forces collapsed under the force of the charge, and Riall retreated.

American troops entered the town. The British, however, had planted explosives in some buildings, and these killed 52 Americans (including General Zebulon Pike, explorer and the first non-Indian to view "Pike's Peak," in Colorado. Dearborn's troops set fire to some public buildings and committed various other acts of vandalism, which the British would remember when they entered Washington, D.C., on September 13, 1814. Dearborn did manage to mount an attack across the Niagara River but failed to follow through; he was then relieved of his command.

On May 27, Perry's fleet bombarded Fort George on the Niagara River, and Winfield Scott, now a full colonel after his exchange, forced British General James Vincent to abandon it. Two days later, Prevost launched an attack on the important American naval base at Sackets Harbor, but it was repulsed by the defenders under General Jacob Brown.

In the fall of 1813, Secretary of War Armstrong decided to make one last attempt to capture Montreal with a two-prong attack. Major James Wilkerson, who had replaced Dearborn, moved eastward with 5,000 troops, until he suffered a humiliating defeat by a far smaller British force at Christler's Farm, about halfway between Sackets Harbor and Montreal. Wade Hampton, who did not trust either Armstrong or Wilkerson, moved north from Burlington, Vermont, and gave up after running into resistance. With this, the Montreal campaign ended.

American forces along the Niagara

River, however, were commanded by two young, competent officer, Major General Jacob Brown and Brigadier General Winfield Scott, who would fight two fierce battles with British regulars, commanded by Lieutenant General Gordon Drummonds and Brigadier General Phineas Riall.

The first encounter was on July 5, 1813, at Chippewa on the Niagara River. In the first battle of the war fought between regulars of both armies, Brown and Scott forced Riall to retreat, leaving 500 killed or wounded compared to Brown's loss of 300 killed or wounded.

On July 25, the two forces met again at Lundy's Lane north of Chippewa. By this time, Brown was down to 2,600 men, and Drummond had about 3,000. The battle began in late afternoon and continued during the night and into early morning, since neither side wanted to stop short of victory. It finally ended with inclusive results. It had been a bloody affair with 171 Americans killed, 572 wounded, and 110 missing. Drummond lost 84 men, 559 were wounded, and 193 were missing. This was the last battle fought along the Canadian border. The British would now bring the war into America, extending the battle zone all the way from Plattsburg, New York, to New Orleans, Louisiana.

British Raids on Chesapeake Bay and the Battle of Norfolk.

In early 1813, the British began bringing the war far inland and in February, a large

"Those are Regulars, by God!" British General Riall exclaimed at the battle at Chippewa when he realized that the advancing American troops were not militiamen, as an aide had reported, but Winfield Scott's magnificently trained brigade of United States Army regulars. (West Point Museum)

BATTLE AT FORT STEPHENSON—JULY 31, 1813

Only July 20, British General Henry Proctor and Tecumseh paid Fort Meigs a return visit, but finding it still too well defended, moved on to Fort Stephenson, near the mouth of the Sandusky River. The fort's defenses consisted of 160 men and one six pounder cannon, under the command of 22-year-old Major George Croghan.

When General William Henry Harrison learned that Proctor was on his way with artillery, he ordered Croghan to abandon the fort rather than put up a pointless defense. Croghan, however, wanted to defend his fort and sent Harrison a message, "We have determined to maintain this place, and, by Heaven's we can."

Harrison did not like his orders disobeyed, especially by a boy major, and relieved Croghan of command and ordered him to report to him immediately. But when he heard from Croghan how he planned to defend the fort, he changed his mind and let Croghan return to his post.

Proctor reached Fort Stephenson on July 31 with 400 regulars, artillery, and 2,000 of Tecumseh's Indians. He sent word to Croghan to surrender or else expose his men to the Indians. The offer was declined.

Procter then launched an attack on the weakest point, just as Croghan had expected him to do. For it was here that he had set his single cannon, masked, so it would not be visible to the attackers.

As Proctor's troops came in range, the mask was ripped off the cannon, and it poured out a hail of grapeshot that tore great holes in their ranks. The British soldiers fell back, reformed, and made a second charge with the same disastrous results. The ground in the cannon's range was now covered with the 100 bodies of killed or wounded.

Proctor had too few regulars to make a third charge and ordered his Indians to attack, but they had too much respect for the fort's cannon and refused to join in the fight. Proctor gave up and that night returned by barge to Malden.

Proctor lost over 100 killed or wounded, while Croghan had only one killed and 7 wounded.

British amphibious force sailed up Chesapeake Bay intending to burn Norfolk, Virginia, the frigate USS *Constellation*, anchored in the Elizabeth River there, and the navy base at nearby Portsmouth.

Finding Norfolk too well defended, Vice Admiral George Cockburn had to be satisfied with raiding and plundering the countryside in and around Lynnhaven Bay, Frenchtown, Havre de Grace, and Georgetown.

On June 22, the British took another crack at Norfolk by sending Admiral John Warren with the largest invasion fleet ever sent into American waters—8 ships of the line, 12 frigates, and transports with 5,000 regulars.

Norfolk had been expecting another attack, and Brigadier General Robert Taylor made sure it was well defended. Besides securing the two stone forts of Nelson and Norfolk, he had anchored a line of gunboats across the Elizabeth River from Craney Island on the west to just above Norfolk on the east. He also had the guns of the *Constellation*. For their part, the British planned to first take Craney Island and then neutralize the gunboats so their warships could come in close to bombard the forts and the *Constellation*.

At daybreak on June 22, British General Sidney Beckworth took 2,500 men by barge to the mainland east of Craney, intending to reach it by marching across the shallow waters. But he never got across because of the heavy artillery fire from Craney Island. Unaware that Beckworth's attack had failed, Warren, with 50 barges and 1,500 men, left the ships and headed for the north shore of Craney. Members of his expedition were so confident they could easily take the American gunboats, and their warships could get in range to bombard the forts and destroy the *Constellation*, that some officers brought along their pet dogs.

The American artillery on the island held fire until the barges were in close range, at which time Captain Arthur Emerson called out, "Now my brave boys, are you ready to open fire?" His men replied that they were more than ready, so he gave the order "Fire!" The island's artillery roared in unison. Warren's barge—50 feet long with a brass cannon at the bow—was the first one sunk by the heavy fire. Other barges were soon shattered, and many of the soldiers drowned, pulled down by their heavy uniforms and equipment.

After Warren's barge had gone down, the remaining barges began returning to the fleet, and the attack on Norfolk was over. The British lost over 200 men—killed, wounded, or taken prisoner. There were no American losses.

A monument to the battle stands on Fleet Street, in Norfolk, near the Corps of Engineers' Headquarters. The Headquarters can also furnish visitors with more information on the battle and arrange a visit to Fort Norfolk.

At this writing, Craney Island is being developed into a park.

BATTLE OF LAKE ERIE— SEPTEMBER 10, 1813

On the morning of September 10, 1813, a few minutes before the first shots were exchanged, in the next major confrontation between the Americans and the British, Commodore Oliver Hazard Perry ran up his battle flag. It was a large blue banner with the crudely inscribed words "Don't give up the ship." This was the last command of the mortally wounded American Captain James Lawrence, a friend of Perry, who had given his life in the June 1, 1813, battle between his ship frigate USS *Chesapeake* and frigate HMS *Sharron*. In honor of his friend, Perry had named his flagship *Lawrence*.

In early 1813, it had been obvious to General Harrison and others that Detroit could not be retaken and held, until the British fleet was driven off Lake Erie. The U.S. Navy Department assigned this task to the 28-year-old Perry.

Perry arrived at the naval base at Erie in March to supervise the completion of the four recently built ships. He felt the four vessels were insufficient and managed to get another five from Black Rock on the Niagara River. On August 5, he moved his nine ships across the sandbar outside Erie and into open water. The crews consisted of a few experienced sailors; the majority were untrained militia and blacks. Shortly, however, Lieutenant Jesse Elliott arrived with 90 trained sailors, and afterward, General Harrison sent 100 Kentucky riflemen to serve as "marines."

On August 25, Perry located the British fleet at its Malden base on the Detroit River, and he sailed to Put-in-Bay where he could keep an eye on it. On September 9, he learned that the British fleet, under

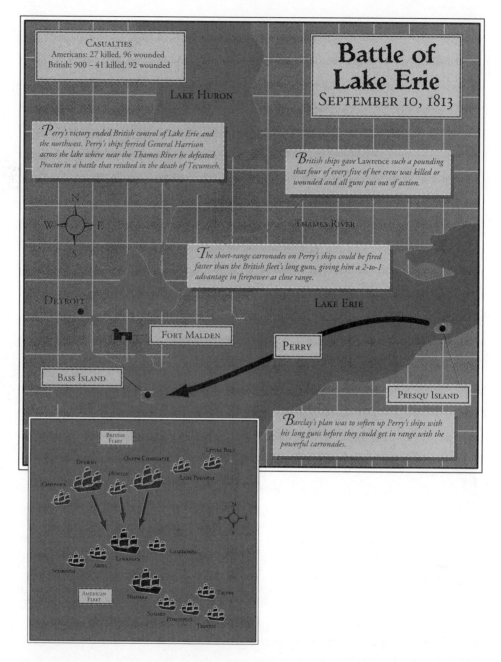

CASUALTIES
Americans: 27 killed, 96 wounded
British: 900 – 41 killed, 92 wounded

LAKE HURON

Battle of Lake Erie
SEPTEMBER 10, 1813

Perry's victory ended British control of Lake Erie and the northwest. Perry's ships ferried General Harrison across the lake where near the Thames River he defeated Proctor in a battle that resulted in the death of Tecumseh.

British ships gave Lawrence such a pounding that four of every five of her crew was killed or wounded and all guns put out of action.

N
W   E
S

THAMES RIVER

The short-range carronades on Perry's ships could be fired faster than the British fleet's long guns, giving him a 2-to-1 advantage in firepower at close range.

DETROIT

LAKE ERIE

FORT MALDEN

PERRY

BASS ISLAND

PRESQU ISLAND

Barclay's plan was to soften up Perry's ships with his long guns before they could get in range with the powerful carronades.

BRITISH FLEET

LITTLE BELT

DETROIT   QUEEN CHARLOTTE

HUNTER   LADY PREVOST

CHIPPAWA

N
W   E
S

CALEDONIA

LAWRENCE

SCORPION   ARIEL

AMERICAN FLEET

NIAGARA

TRIPPE

SOMERS   PORCUPINE

TIGRESS

Captain Robert Barclay, had sailed up the Detroit River into Lake Erie, preparing for battle.

Barclay, who had lost an arm at the battle of Trafalgar, had six ships: his flagship, the

19-gun *Detroit*; 10-gun *Hunter*; 17-gun *Queen Charlotte*; 13-gun *Lady Prevost*; 3-gun *Little Belt*, and 1-gun, plus a swivel gun, *Chippawa*. Perry's principal ships were his flagship *Lawrence* and her sister ship *Niagara*, each

with 20 guns. In support was the 3-gun *Caladonia*, one long 24-pounder *Scorpion*, four long 12-pounder *Ariel*, and schooners *Somers*, *Trippe*, *Porcupine*, and *Tigress*, each with 3 guns.

The two fleets were just about equal, with Perry having a slight advantage; Barclay had more guns, 63 compared to Perry's 54, but he had three less ships. Most of Perry's guns were the powerful short-range carronades, while Barclay's were the lighter long guns but with twice the range of carronades. The type of cannon determined Perry's and Barclay's battle tactics. Perry would move close to the enemy so his short-range guns would be most effective, while Barclay would keep out of their range and pound away with his long guns.

On the night of September 9, Perry had learned how Barclay planned to position his ships and met with his ships' commanders to give assignments for the coming battle. He reserved for his own *Lawrence* the honor of engaging Barclay's flagship *Detroit*. *Caladonia* was to take on *Hunter*; *Niagara*, under *Elliott*, would engage *Queen Charlotte*; and the four schooners were assigned to *Lady Prevost*, *Chappawa*, and *Little Belt*.

Late on the morning of September 10, Perry's fleet cleared Put-in-Bay and made

"Don't give up the ship. Fight her until she sinks," the last command of mortally wounded Captain James Lawrence as he was carried below on his ship, USS frigate Chesapeake during the June 1, 1813, battle with HMS frigate Shannon.

contact with Barclay's fleet. As the two were coming in range, there was a change in wind direction that favored Perry, and Barclay turned his ships westward, furled his sails, and prepared to fight in a line of battle.

The ship's cannon opened fire around midday, and *Detroit* drew first blood when her second broadside crashed into *Lawrence,* killing and wounding many of the crew. *Ariel* and *Scorpion* opened fire on *Detroit* with their long guns, but by the time *Lawrence* was able to get within range, it had already suffered from the fire of almost all British ships. But even so, once in range, its guns crashed into *Detroit* and its supporting ships. During this intense action, Perry saw, to his disappointment, that *Niagara* was holding back, leaving *Queen Charlotte* free to assist *Detroit.* He also noted that the four schooners had not arrived.

With *Niagara* out of range, *Lawrence* faced the broadsides of three British ships that pounded her for two hours. She fought back, but by 2:30 P.M., she was a floating wreck, with all her guns out of action and 83 of her 103 crew killed or wounded.

Perry, however, was not about to give up the fight. He saw the *Niagara,* still out of range and hardly hurt, and decided to board it and continue the battle. Taking down his battle flag, he had four sailors row him in an open boat to the *Niagara.* He sent Elliott to take the boat and round up the four schooners, and then, with the guns double shotted (loaded with two balls to increase total firepower), sailed *Niagara* into the line of British ships.

As the *Niagara* approached, the British attempted to turn some of their ships around to bring the starboard guns to bare, but because many of their experienced officers were killed or wounded, this maneuver became a disaster when the *Detroit* and the *Queen Charlotte* rammed each other and ended up locked together. The *Niagara* sailed between the British line, pouring broadside after broadside on the now almost helpless British ships. Perry then set *Niagara's* sails to hold it almost motionless as its cannon pounded the enemy. The wind increased, and Elliott arrived with the four tardy schooners, but now the battle was almost over, and a little after three o'clock, the British ships lowered their colors in surrender.

Perry accepted the surrender on the torn and bloody decks of the *Lawrence.* He graciously declined to accept the tendered swords and asked about Barclay, whom he learned had been wounded. Perry and Barclay would continue their relations but as friends and not as enemies.

After the surrender, Perry wrote his famous report to General Harrison: "Dear General, We have met the enemy and they are ours. Two ships, two brigs, one schooner and one sloop. Yours with great respect and esteem, O. H. Perry."

Perry's victory was one of the most decisive of the war, for it forced the British to abandon Lake Erie and the northwest.

Perry's Victory and International Peace Memorial is administered by the National Park Service. An observation platform 317 feet above the lake is reached by elevator for a small fee. The battle site ten miles northwest can easily be seen on a clear day.

BATTLE AT SACKETS HARBOR— MAY 29, 1813

Sackets Harbor, a port on eastern Lake Ontario, was an important base for American naval and military operations for the upper St. Lawrence Valley and Lake

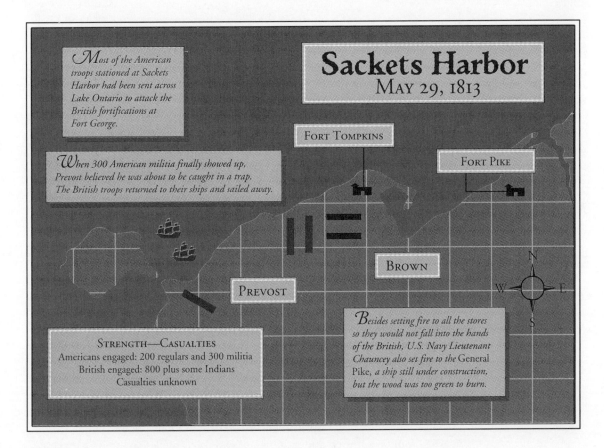

Sackets Harbor
MAY 29, 1813

*M*ost of the American troops stationed at Sackets Harbor had been sent across Lake Ontario to attack the British fortifications at Fort George.

*W*hen 300 American militia finally showed up, Prevost believed he was about to be caught in a trap. The British troops returned to their ships and sailed away.

FORT TOMPKINS

FORT PIKE

BROWN

PREVOST

N
W   E
S

STRENGTH—CASUALTIES
Americans engaged: 200 regulars and 300 militia
British engaged: 800 plus some Indians
Casualties unknown

*B*esides setting fire to all the stores so they would not fall into the hands of the British, U.S. Navy Lieutenant Chauncey also set fire to the General Pike, *a ship still under construction, but the wood was too green to burn.*

Ontario. General Jacob Brown, commander at Sackets Harbor, had only 200 regulars to defend the large base, so when he learned that George Prevost was on his way, he called on the militia for support.

On May 29, the base was attacked by Prevost with a force of about 1,200 soldiers and Indians, but Brown's regulars put up such resistance that Prevost made little progress. The militia, however, kept its distance and did not take any part in the fight.

Brown believed he could drive Prevost and his troops back to their ships if he could get some of the militia to fight, so he told them that the Americans had won the battle. This news persuaded 300 of them to join in the fight in order to be part of the great victory. The arrival of these men convinced Prevost that Brown was being heavily reinforced. He broke off action, returned to his ships, and sailed away.

But the conflict was not a complete waste of Prevost's time and effort. During the battle, U.S. Navy Lieutenant Woolcott Chauncey saw some of Brown's men retiring and decided that the British had won. To prevent them from capturing the considerable quantity of naval stores, he set them on fire, and $500,000 worth of supplies—an enormous sum at that time—went up in smoke.

Sackets Harbor Battlefield is administered by New York State Office of Parks, Recreation and Historic Preservation.

There are 1812 military exhibits and many other points of interest. Brigadier General Zebulon

Pike's body was returned to Sackets Harbor and lies in the military cemetery.

BATTLE FOR WASHINGTON— AUGUST 24, 1814

The war with the British was being waged vigorously to the South as well.

After routing the Americans early in the day on August 24, at Bladensburg, Maryland, the British force continued the march and by evening entered the almost deserted U.S. capital of Washington. The British immediately went about setting fire to the White House, the Capitol, other public buildings, and the Navy Yard. Heavy rain put out the fires, but the British soldiers relit them in the morning before they marched back to their transport ships.

The attack on Washington was the first in a series of attacks on important American coastal cities, which was intended to relieve pressure on the British troops in Canada, repay the Americans for burning the Canadian capital of York and other Canadian towns and villages, and weaken the United States' position in peace negotiations.

On August 14, a British fleet anchored at the mouth of the Patuxent River. Under the joint command of Vice Admiral Alexander Cochrane, Major General Robert Ross, and Rear Admiral George Cockburn, the impressive force consisted of 4 ship of the line (similar to modern-day battleships); 20 frigates, sloops, and transports; and 4,000 regulars.

The original invasion plan was to strike first at Baltimore and then Washington, but Cockburn convinced Ross and Cockrane to hit Washington first, primarily because he hated the Washington newspaper *National Intelligence* for its harsh criticism of him

when he raided the Chesapeake Bay area the year before.

Washington's major defenses consisted of gunboats commanded by Commodore Joshua Barney. When the British fleet arrived in the area, he moved the gunboats up the Patuxent River where the water was too shallow for British warships to follow. A detachment of British troops landed, at Benedict and marched up the river to capture the boats, but before they arrived, Barney blew up his ships saving the cannon.

With the gunboats gone, Washington had no defenses, not even an army. Secretary of War John Armstrong and his military leaders had been too involved dreaming up impractical plans to invade Canada to pay attention to the defense of the capital or other major coastal cities.

As Ross's army of 4,000 advanced from Benedict toward Washington, U.S. officials there went into what can only be described as a "flap." Everybody, including President Madison and Secretary of State James Monroe, dashed about organizing an army to defend the capital. Eventually, a makeshift force of 4,000 was organized under Brigadier General William Winder, the overall commander of the defense of the city. He was shortly reinforced by 2,000 Maryland militia under Brigadier General Tobias Stansbury. It was by now common knowledge that Ross was heading for Washington and would come by way of Blandensberg, but no steps were taken to fortify positions on his route or even destroy bridges over the creeks his army would cross.

Stansbury remained on the Bladensberg Road, while Winder returned to Washington. But on word that Ross was near Blandensberg, he rushed back and positioned his army on a ridge on Ross's line of march. Ross's army attacked, and the

S THE FLAG STILL THERE?

On the night of September 13, Francis Scott Key stood on the deck of a small schooner and watched the nearby British fleet bombard Fort McHenry. A few days before, the young attorney had come to the British flagship on a cartel boat flying a white flag. Accompanied by Colonel John S. Skinner, U.S. commissioner general of prisoners, Key's purpose was to obtain the release of Dr. William Beanes of Maryland who was held prisoner by the British. Dr. Beanes had violated his pledge of good conduct, and some British officers thought he should be hanged.

Key apparently did an excellent job in pleading his client's case because Dr. Beanes was released. But because the British believed Key and Beanes knew of the impending bombardment of the fort, they required them to remain with the fleet for the night.

Shortly after the British began firing, the fort's cannon fell silent because they did not have sufficient range to reach the British warships. Key and Beanes stood on the deck of their little schooner watching as the bombs and rockets fell on the fort. As night fell, they saw the big flag still flying above the fort. Then the flag disappeared into the night.

All night two men stood on the deck watching the bombardment, praying the fort would hold.

At the first blush of dawn, Dr. Beanes asked Key, who had better eyesight, "Is the flag still there?" Key replied that it was.

The sight of the flag still flying after such a terrible bombardment had a profound effect on Key. Inspired by Dr. Beanes's question, he made some notes that he later worked into the words of what later became the national anthem, "The Star-Spangled Banner."

---

ensuing battle went about as one could expect considering that the American troops were poorly trained, there were no experienced commanders, and no thought was given to how the defensive forces should be employed.

At the beginning, Stansbury's artillery did damage the British advance, but when they began firing Congreve rockets on the Americans, which did little harm, their roar frightened the inexperienced militia and they ran away. Soon the rest of the Americans were on the run. This prompted the British to refer to the battle as the "Bladensberg Races."

At the battle of Bladensburg, the American casualties were very light with only 26 men killed with 51 wounded because so many men ran away when the shooting started. But those who remained to fight resulted in British casualties of 150 men killed with about 300 wounded.

One American force that did not run were the 400 sailors commanded by Commodore Barney. He had joined up with Winder, bringing along some of his gunboat cannon, and when Ross continued his advance, Barney blocked his path. Not only did Barney's men try to stop Ross, they even mounted an attack, with the sailors and marines shouting "Board 'em! Board 'em!" as they went after the British. But they received no support from the militia, and their valiant effort achieved nothing, except perhaps to preserve a bit of the Americans' honor. Barney was wounded and captured, but Ross and Cockburn knew his reputation as a gallant fighter and treated him with

kindness, making sure that his wounds received proper attention.

America's first lady, Dolley Madison, was the other hero that day. Alone, in a practically deserted Washington, she went to work loading a wagon with the White House silver and china, cabinet papers, and Gilbert Stewart's famous portrait of George Washington and then drove to join her husband in Virginia.

The day after burning Washington, British warships sailed up the Potomac River to take Fort Warburton and then continued to nearby Alexandria, Virginia. In face of certain destruction of his fort, Captain Samuel Dyson evacuated his men and blew up the fort. It was rebuilt as Fort

Washington and would be an important coastal defense in the Civil War, the Spanish-American War, and World War II.

Fort Washington and the surrounding area is now Fort Washington Park, Maryland, administered by the National Park Service. There is a visitor center and many exhibits and special events.

BATTLE OF BALTIMORE AND FORT MCHENRY, MARYLAND— SEPTEMBER 12–14, 1814

After torching Washington and attempting to take Warburton, the British invasion fleet

CONGREVE ROCKETS

The rockets that produced the now-familiar "red glare" over Fort McHenry on the night of September 13, 1814, were developed for the British forces in the late eighteenth century by William Congreve. Congreve's rockets carried an explosive or incendiary charge, had a range of about two miles, and fired from troughlike launching stands that could be set on land or mounted on warships. The British began using them around 1806 and employed them in Europe, at the battle of Waterloo, as well as against Americans in the War of 1812.

These rockets, while not very accurate, made a terrifying sound and had a demoralizing effect on unprotected troops, especially poorly trained troops such as the American militia that faced them at Bladensberg on August 24, 1814. But the rockets did no great harm to Fort McHenry.

The U.S. Army shortly developed a similar rocket and continued to use it through the 1846–48 war with Mexico. Improved artillery soon made these rockets obsolete, and it would not be until World War II that rockets would again be an important weapon.

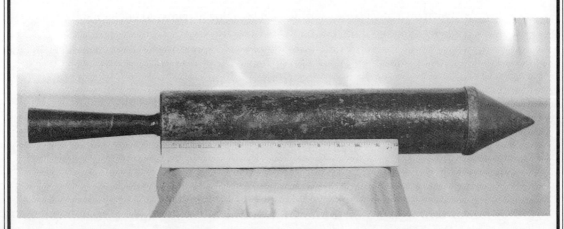

With a range of two miles this terrifying new weapon was used by the British on ships and land. It made a crazy roar and while doing little harm to entrenched troops was a serious threat to those in the open. (West Point Museum)

sailed up the Patapsco River and prepared to attack Baltimore, Maryland. Baltimore was a far greater prize than Washington because not only was it the fourth largest American city, but it was also home port for a nest of privateers who roamed the seas capturing or destroying British merchant vessels.

But British General Ross and Admiral Cochrane found Baltimore a far harder nut to crack than the capital.

The port city had been improving its defenses since 1813 when Admiral Cockburn sailed around the Chesapeake raiding the countryside. Commanded by Major George Armistead, Fort McHenry was the key to the defense system because it guarded an attack from the Patapsco. It was a well-maintained earth and masonry fort with 36-pounder cannon and a garrison of 1,000.

When Armistead learned the British fleet was on its way, he wanted a flag for his fort big enough so "that the British will have no difficulty in seeing it from a distance." Mary Pickersguill made him such a flag measuring 42 by 30 feet—the flag that Francis Scott Key saw still flying over the fort by "the dawn's early light."

Fort McHenry was supported by batteries on the east and west: Lazaretto Battery, Battery Babcock, Fort Look-Out, and Fort Covington.

Baltimore's inner harbor was guarded by a sunken cable and ships' hulls, and the city was protected from a land attack by a system of trenched and Rodgers Bastion, built with the help of Baltimore residents. These defenses were manned by some 15,000 troops, many of them volunteers from Pennsylvania, Maryland, and Virginia, under the command of Major General Samuel Smith, a U.S. Senator and a tough, active, and competent Revolutionary War veteran.

The British plan of attack on Baltimore provided for a naval force to take Fort McHenry, and then a land force would capture the city from the east. On the morning of September 12, Ross and about 4,000 troops landed at North Point and marched up the peninsula. Along the way, they encountered about 3,000 American militia under Brigadier General John Strickler. After a brief fight, Strickler retreated, but two of his sharpshooters killed Ross. Colonel Author Brooke took command and continued the march north.

Not far from the eastern defenses, Strickler's army made a very strong stand, and in the battle, the British suffered 300

casualties to 200 Americans. Brooke halted, deciding not to attack the American fortified position until he learned the results at Fort McHenry.

The bombardment of the fort began at dawn on September 13. Cockrane's fleet consisted of some 50 vessels that included ships of the line, frigates, bomb ships, and ships especially modified to fire the Congreve rocket. Fortunately for Fort McHenry, the shallow waters and line of sunken hulls prevented Cockrane's heavily armed ships from getting in range, so the bombardment was made with the shallow draft bomb and rocket ships. When the ships first opened fire, the fort's guns returned the blasts. But when Armistead saw that his guns did not have sufficient range, he ordered them to cease fire.

For the next 25 hours, Fort McHenry was pounded by bombs and rockets. Armistead estimated that the British fleet had fired 1,500 to 1,800 cannon and rocket shots at the fort, and 400 or so had found their mark. Around midnight of the thirteenth, Cochrane realized that McHenry could not be taken by bombardment. He decided to mount an attack on the rear of the fort by way of Ferry Branch, which would also distract the Americans, so Brooke could storm the land defenses.

It was dark and rainy when the British troops left by barge for Ferry Branch. On the trip, one barge lost its way and fired off a rocket, which lit up the sky and the invasion force. Immediately, every American cannon opened fire and the attack was called off. Unlike Ross, Brooke was no fighter and made no attempt to storm Rodgers Bastion and the other defenses.

The bombardment of Fort McHenry continued until 7 A.M. on the fourteenth and then the battle was over. The Americans lost about 200 men during the battle

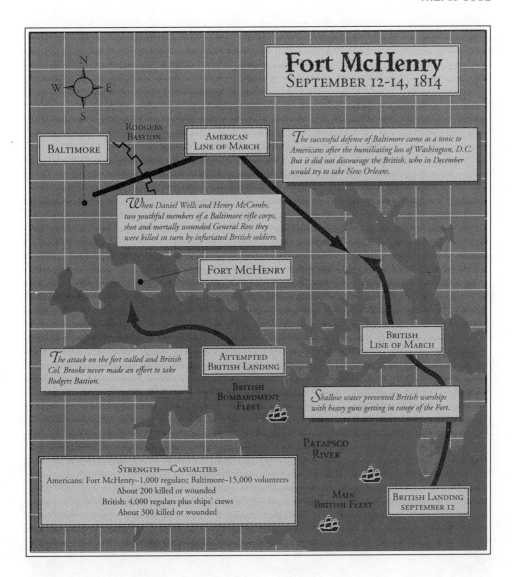

Fort McHenry
SEPTEMBER 12-14, 1814

N W E S

RODGERS BASTION

BALTIMORE

AMERICAN LINE OF MARCH

The successful defense of Baltimore came as a tonic to Americans after the humiliating loss of Washington, D.C. But it did not discourage the British, who in December would try to take New Orleans.

When Daniel Wells and Henry McCombs, two youthful members of a Baltimore rifle corps, shot and mortally wounded General Ross they were killed in turn by infuriated British soldiers.

FORT McHENRY

BRITISH LINE OF MARCH

The attack on the fort stalled and British Col. Brooke never made an effort to take Rodgers Bastion.

ATTEMPTED BRITISH LANDING

BRITISH BOMBARDMENT FLEET

Shallow water prevented British warships with heavy guns getting in range of the Fort.

PATAPSCO RIVER

STRENGTH—CASUALTIES
Americans: Fort McHenry–1,000 regulars; Baltimore–15,000 volunteers
About 200 killed or wounded
British: 4,000 regulars plus ships' crews
About 300 killed or wounded

MAIN BRITISH FLEET

BRITISH LANDING SEPTEMBER 12

around Baltimore, and British casualties were around 300. In spite of the severe bombardment, Fort McHenry suffered only two killed and several wounded.

As the British fleet sailed back to Chesapeake Bay, an American band struck up "Yankee Doodle."

Fort McHenry is administered by the National Park Service. Guided tours of the fort are available in summer months but self-guided tours can *be taken the year round. A theater at the fort runs a film on the battle every half hour.*

BATTLE OF PLATTSBURG— SEPTEMBER 11, 1814

On August 3, General George Prevost with 11,000 regulars moved from Canada, intending to capture the important American base at Plattsburg, New York, and then

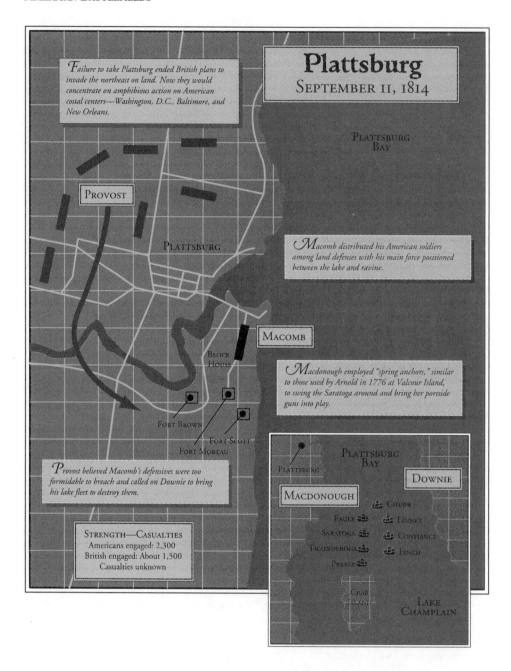

Failure to take Plattsburg ended British plans to invade the northeast on land. Now they would concentrate on amphibious action on American costal centers—Washington, D.C., Baltimore, and New Orleans.

Plattsburg
SEPTEMBER 11, 1814

PLATTSBURG BAY

PROVOST

PLATTSBURG

Macomb distributed his American soldiers among land defenses with his main force positioned between the lake and ravine.

MACOMB

BLOCK HOUSE

Macdonough employed "spring anchors," similar to those used by Arnold in 1776 at Valcour Island, to swing the Saratoga around and bring her portside guns into play.

FORT BROWN

FORT SCOTT
FORT MOREAU

Provost believed Macomb's defensives were too formidable to breach and called on Downie to bring his lake fleet to destroy them.

PLATTSBURG

PLATTSBURG BAY

DOWNIE

MACDONOUGH

CHUBB

EAGLE   LINNET

SARATOGA   CONFIANCE

TICONDEROGA   FINCH

PREBLE

CRAB ISLAND

LAKE CHAMPLAIN

STRENGTH—CASUALTIES
Americans engaged: 2,300
British engaged: About 1,500
Casualties unknown

continue south to occupy much of New England and New York.

Brigadier General Alexander Macomb, in command at Plattsburg, had a force of only 1,500 men, but when he learned of Prevost's approach, he managed to get 800 New York militia and 2,500 Vermont volunteers. His land defenses were concentrated on a spit of land bounded by the Saranac River and Plattsburg Bay and included redoubts, blockhouses, and trenches. While these provided good protection from a land attack, they would be readily demolished by ship in the bay firing artillery.

On September 6, Prevost probed the defenses of the town. He decided they were too formidable for an attack from land and asked Captain George Downie to come with his Lake Champlain fleet to destroy them. But before Downie could do this, he first had to knock out the American lake fleet that Captain Thomas Macdonough had recently built. The two fleets were about equal in number of ships, although Downie had more long guns, and Macdonough had more short-range carronades. Macdonough, therefore, decided to fight Downie in the bay where close quarters would be to the advantage of his short-range guns.

On September 11, Downie arrived to find Macdonough's ships anchored across the bay. Four gunboats beaded the line, followed by the 26-gun *Eagle*, Macdonough's flagship; the 26-gun frigate *Saratoga*; the 17-gun schooner *Ticonderoga*; and the 7-gun sloop *Preble*. Macdonough had fitted his ships with spring anchors so that if the guns on one side were put out of action, the ship could be quickly turned around to bring the guns on the other side into play.

Downie's fleet sailed into the bay in line led by the 11-gun sloop *Chubb* and followed by the 16-gun brig *Linnet*, Downie's flagship; the 38-gun frigate *Confiance*; the 11-gun sloop *Finch*; and finally a small fleet of gun-boats.

At the start of the battle, *Confiance* sailed too close to *Saratoga* and received a blistering broadside before she moved out of range, dropping anchor, and began pounding *Saratoga* with long guns, killing 40 of the crew with the first broadside. *Linnet* pounded away at *Eagle*, doing that ship so much damage that it moved to safety between *Ticonderoga* and *Saratoga*.

Downie was killed but his *Confiance* and *Linnet* soon put all of Saratoga's starboard guns out of action. But here Macdonough's anchoring system proved its worth; *Saratoga* was turned around and was soon pounding *Confiance* with its port guns. The cannon fire overwhelmed *Confiance*, and it struck colors. When the other British ships saw their flagship surrender, they, too, quit. In the battle, 52 Americans were killed and 58 wounded, and British casualties were estimated at 200.

During the battle, Prevost's men had crossed the Saranac and were preparing to attack Plattsburg's defenses when Prevost learned of Downie's death and the defeat of his fleet. Some of his officers encouraged him to go ahead with the attack, as they were confident the defenses could be taken in 20 minutes or so. But all the spirit was out of Prevost, and he led his army back to Canada, giving up the planned occupation of northeast America.

Macdonough's important victory at Plattsburg would probably be better remembered if he had Perry's gift for words. But he did not, and sent a simple message to the secretary of navy: "Sir; The Almighty has been pleased to grant us a signal victory on Lake Champlain the capture of one frigate, one brig and two sloops of war of the enemy."

There is a diorama of the Battle of Plattsburg, as well as the Revolutionary War battle of Valcour Island, at the Clinton County Historical Museum.

BATTLE OF NEW ORLEANS— DECEMBER 23, 1814– JANUARY 8, 1815

On December 1, 1814, the day General Andrew Jackson arrived to take command at New Orleans, a British invasion fleet was already on its way from Jamaica. The British considered the city a handsome prize, for not only were its warehouses full of valuable goods, but its capture would give them control of the Mississippi River and surrounding territory.

Jackson set about improving the city's defenses. Crews went to work felling trees to block passage on the numerous bayous leading to the city from Lake Borgne to the east; fortifications around New Orleans were improved, and two armed schooners, *Carolina* and *Louisiana*, moved down the Mississippi so their cannon would add to the defenses.

Jackson had sent for additional troops and by the time the battle began had a wonderful mix of fighting men. Among them were General John Coffee with his 2,300 mounted riflemen, General William Carroll with 2,000 Tennessee volunteers, two battalions of free blacks under Major Louis Daquin and Major Pierre Lacoste, Jean Laffite and his Barataria pirates, a battalion of young New Orleans aristocrats under Major Jean Plauché, Major Thomas Beale's "New Orleans Sharpshooters," and a band of Choctaw Indians under Major Pierre Jugeat. In early January, Jackson was further reinforced by 2,500 Kentuckians commanded by General John Adler, giving Jackson a force of about 5,700.

The British invasion army consisted of about 8,000 regulars. Until General Sir Edward Pakenham's arrival on Christmas Day, Major General John Keane was in command.

Action began with the British capture of the gunboats on Lake Borgne, allowing them to move to the west end of the lake. Here a pro-British Spanish resident told them that Bayou Bienview was one route from the lake to the city that, for some reason, had not been blocked. Keane's men followed this route, and on the afternoon of December 23, Jackson was unpleasantly surprised to hear that there were about 1,800 British troops camped on a wide plain near the Villere Plantation, only a dozen or so miles south of New Orleans. In spite of the late hour, Jackson told his officers, "Gentlemen, the British are below. We must fight them tonight."

The *Carolina* quietly slipped down the river with orders to begin firing at 7:30 P.M. and stop at 8, when Jackson's forces would attack. The British soldiers were gathered around their campfires recovering from the long and difficult march made even more exhausting by rain and cold. Suddenly, they found themselves under fire from the unseen *Carolina*. Some of them panicked, while others rushed to take cover on the river's levee. Campfires were put out, and the troops soon were restored to order. The *Carolina*'s gun ceased fire, and Jackson's men attacked in a typical night fight, with squad against squad, man against man. Jackson suspected that the British would soon be reinforced and broke off the attack around midnight.

The nasty fight had cost the British 46 men killed, 167 wounded, and 64 captured. Jackson lost 24 men, 115 wounded, and 74 captured. But the night battle had been a blow to the morale of the British troops. The battle of Bladensburg outside Washington had reinforced their contempt for the fighting qualities of American troops, but now they realized they were up against an army of fighters.

Jackson moved to a position on the Rodriguez Canal, some five miles south of the city. The canal was a dry ditch about 4 feet deep, 20 feet wide, and extending about three-eighths of a mile from the river to a large cypress swamp on the east.

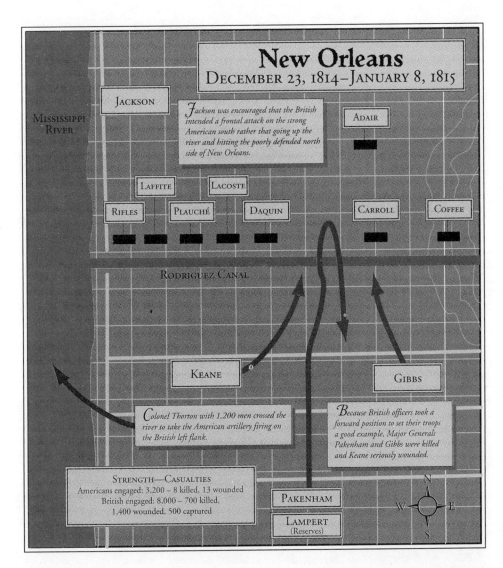

New Orleans
DECEMBER 23, 1814–JANUARY 8, 1815

MISSISSIPPI
RIVER

JACKSON

Jackson was encouraged that the British intended a frontal attack on the strong American south rather that going up the river and hitting the poorly defended north side of New Orleans.

ADAIR

LAFFITE   LACOSTE

RIFLES   PLAUCHÉ   DAQUIN   CARROLL   COFFEE

RODRIGUEZ CANAL

KEANE

GIBBS

Colonel Thorton with 1,200 men crossed the river to take the American artillery firing on the British left flank.

Because British officers took a forward position to set their troops a good example, Major Generals Pakenham and Gibbs were killed and Keane seriously wounded.

STRENGTH—CASUALTIES
Americans engaged: 3,200 – 8 killed, 13 wounded
British engaged: 8,000 – 700 killed,
1,400 wounded, 500 captured

PAKENHAM

LAMPERT
(Reserves)

N
W   E
S

General Pakenham arrived on Christmas Day, took over command from Keane, and two days later, the British artillery opened fire on the two schooners. *Louisiana* managed to escape, but *Carolina* was blown up. Jackson put his men to work digging a trench about 30 feet in back of the canal as a second line of defense.

On December 28, Pakenham began bombarding the American positions along the canal to soften them up for a frontal attack. When he assumed the shells and rockets had done their work, he sent two columns forward. One of them came close to turning the American left held by Coffee and Carroll, but the second column advancing on the American right was cut to pieces by fire from the *Louisiana* and Laffite's artillery.

Pakenham decided that he needed heavier cannon to blast the American defenses, and Cockrane's sailors managed

BIRD'S-EYE VIEW OF THE BATTLE NEAR NEW ORLEANS, JANUARY 8, 1815.—FROM A SKETCH BY LATOUR, JACKSON'S CHIEF ENGINEER.

he author of this volume is indebted to the late General Palfrey, of New Orleans, who was a participant in the | talion ; 7. Lieutenants Crawley and Ross ; 8. Colonel Perry ; 9. General Garrigue ; 10. Lieutenant Spotts ; le, for the privilege of copying Major Latour's interesting drawing, above given. The following explanations, | Divisions of Generals Carroll and Adair, and, further to the left, General Coffee's ; 13. Cavalry and dragoo means of the reference figures, were made in the drawing by Major Latour : *American Arms*—1. General Jack- | 15. Line of intrenchments ; 16. Macarte's, Jackson's headquarters ; 17. Rodriguez's house.   *British Arms*— and his staff ; 2. Major Plauche ; 3. Captain Humphrey ; 4. Beale's riflemen and a company of the Seventh | British Army in two columns ; C. The right column making the principal attack, under the command of Pak ment ; 5. Redoubt on the bank of the river ; 6. Captains Dominique You and Beluche, of Major La Coste's bat- | E, F. Left column, commanded by Colonel Rennie ; I. Battery ; M. Ruins of Chalmette's buildings.

The battle of New Orleans ended on January 8 with a major assault by British forces on Jackson's command along the Rodriguez Canal. In a short time the attack was repulsed. There were 2,000 casualties, including the deaths of two British generals. (National Archives)

to manhandle some of the fleet's heavy cannon 70 miles across water and swamps to the British base in front of the canal.

On New Year's Day, Jackson was reviewing his troops when there was a tremendous roar as heavy guns opened fire, doing so much harm to Jackson's defenses that the British troops waiting to attack began to cheer. But the cheering soon stopped when Jackson's artillery opened up with effective and continuous fire that caused the attack to be called off.

For a week, there was no serious action as each side prepared for the next battle. Jackson spent this time improving his defenses while Pakenham readied his artillery and troops for another assault on the American line. Pakenham now had about 8,000 well-trained regulars, plus some sailors and West Indian troops. Jackson had a force of about 5,700, consisting of regulars, volunteers, and militia, but his defenses had space for only 3,200 or so. He sent 500 men to join Brigadier General David Morgan's

550-man force, which was protecting Captain David Patterson's battery on the west side of the Mississippi River.

Jackson received reports that the British were busy building scaling ladders and fascines of corn stalks needed to cross the Rodriguez Canal, but they were also hauling boats overland from Lake Borgne to the Mississippi. Jackson was unsure of the intent of Pakenham's plan. In fact, Pakenham's plan was to use the boats to ferry Colonel William Thornton and 1,200 troops across the river to capture Patterson's artillery and turn the guns on the American line. This would be the signal for the frontal attack on Jackson's line. General Keane would head a 1,200-man column and strike the American right. Major General John Lampert's 1,400 force would be at center rear of the two columns to move where needed.

Pakenham had acquired a healthy respect for American marksmanship and so planned to attack before daylight on

January 8, 1815. During the night of the seventh, Thornton moved to cross the river, while Keane and Gibbs moved their troops to within a quarter of a mile from the American line to wait for the signal from Thornton.

With the approach of dawn, Pakenham's plan began to fall apart. Thornton found that there were only enough boats for half his force, and then the river's current carried the boats downstream so they landed some distance from Patterson's battery. By the time Thornton reached the battery, it was too late to help Pakenham.

As the morning sun began to dissipate the fog, American artillery started firing on the massed scarlet ranks only a quarter of a mile away. Pakenham had been waiting for a signal from Thornton that he had taken Patterson's battery, but now he felt he could wait no longer. It would be better to attack than leave the troops exposed to the artillery blast. A signal rocket was fired and answered by one set off by Keane, and the frontal attack was launched. A portion of Keane's column moved up by the levee and managed to capture a bastion in front of the American line but were then driven off by a savage counterattack.

As Gibbs's column advanced on the American line, it was discovered that the scaling ladders and fascines had been left behind, and men were sent back to fetch them. The column continued the advance to face the most deadly fire then imaginable. Carroll's Tennessee riflemen held their fire until Gibbs's troops were within range and then opened up on them with a murderous hail of lead. One British officer later stated he had never faced such rapid and deadly fire.

Jackson saw that the smoke from the artillery was spoiling the riflemen's aim and ordered the left forward batteries to cease fire. But a cannon on the right was angled to plow across the line of advancing column.

In spite of the heavy rifle and artillery fire, groups of Gibbs's men continued to try to cross the canal. The scaling ladders and fascines finally arrived, and Gibbs's officers restored order and made a final organized assault on the canal. But only a handful of men managed to cross it before being shot down. A Highland regiment of 900, sent to reinforce Gibbs, made a brave assault on the canal. Only 130 of the 900 survived the attack.

Gibbs was killed while rallying his men. Keane was seriously wounded and had to leave the field. Pakenham was mortally wounded but before dying ordered Lambert to come forward with his reserve troops. But Lambert, viewing the plain covered with dead and wounded British soldiers, disobeyed the order and withdrew the remains of the once proud British army from the field. The following morning he recalled Thornton from the west side of the river.

January 8 was a dreadful day for the British army. It suffered over 2,000 casualties— 700 killed, 1,400 wounded, and 500 taken prisoner. The Americans lost 8 men, and 13 were founded.

The battle of New Orleans was a great victory for Jackson and his army, but ironically, it took place after the War of 1812 had actually ended for on December 24, a peace treaty had been signed at Ghent.

The Battlefield at New Orleans is at the Chalmette Unit of Jean Lafitte National Historic Park and Preserve administered by the National Park Service.

Chalmette Unit preserves three battle sites that include restored earthworks and artillery positions. At the visitor center there are exhibits and an audiovisual program.

Texas War for Independence and War with Mexico

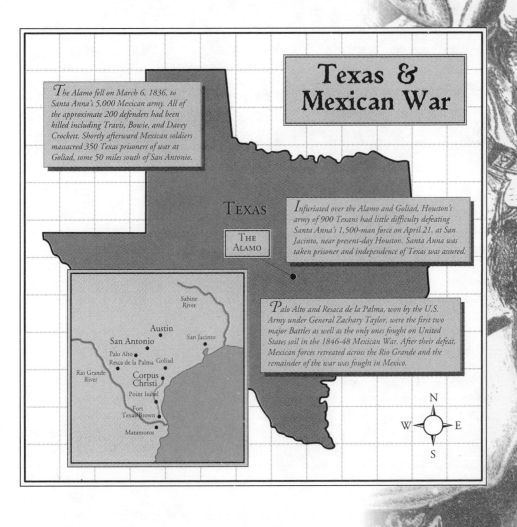

Texas & Mexican War

The Alamo fell on March 6, 1836, to Santa Anna's 5,000 Mexican army. All of the approximate 200 defenders had been killed including Travis, Bowie, and Davey Crockett. Shortly afterward Mexican soldiers massacred 350 Texas prisoners of war at Goliad, some 50 miles south of San Antonio.

TEXAS

THE ALAMO

Infuriated over the Alamo and Goliad, Houston's army of 900 Texans had little difficulty defeating Santa Anna's 1,500-man force on April 21, at San Jacinto, near present-day Houston. Santa Anna was taken prisoner and independence of Texas was assured.

Palo Alto and Resaca de la Palma, won by the U.S. Army under General Zachary Taylor, were the first two major Battles as well as the only ones fought on United States soil in the 1846-48 Mexican War. After their defeat, Mexican forces retreated across the Rio Grande and the remainder of the war was fought in Mexico.

Sabine River

Austin

San Antonio

San Jacinto

Palo Alto

Resaca de la Palma · Goliad

Rio Grande River

Corpus Christi

Point Isabel

Fort Texas/Brown

Matamoros

N
W E
S

Battlefield at Palo Alto as it appears today. (National Park Service)

No one knows exactly why in 1821 the Mexican authorities began to encourage Americans to settle in the province of Texas. It may be that they wanted more whites in this unsettled land to help contain the Indians, or thus may have wanted a buffer between Mexican land and the United States' Louisiana.

In any event, in that year Mexico granted Moses Austin a huge tract of land in east Texas on the condition that he bring in American settlers. Although Austin died before the terms of the deal were agreed upon, his son Stephen worked out another arrangement with Mexico and brought in settlers.

Soon other land speculators, called "empresarios," obtained large land grants on very favorable terms. Because the land in east Texas was fertile, good for crops and cattle, and cost almost nothing, there were soon 20,000 Yankees in Texas.

The original grant required all settlers to be Catholic or convert to the faith and many did, believing this condition acceptable to obtain cheap land. Mexican law also forbade slavery but many settlers brought and kept their slaves.

In those early years, the center of Mexican authority was far away, and the Yankee Texans could do more or less as they pleased. While there was a difference in language, customs, and culture, the Yankees and Mexicans got along without too much friction. Most of the Americans had come to farm and had no intention of wresting control of Texas away from Mexico.

By 1830, however, there were signs of trouble. Both Presidents John Adams and Andrew Jackson had made offers to buy Mexico, which had irritated and alarmed the Mexican government. As a response, Mexico passed a law in 1830 prohibiting immigration to certain areas of the territory. With the help of Austin the Texas state legislature was able to have these laws modified, but they were signs of future problems. In addition, the new immigrants were impatient with the operation of the Mexican government and believed conditions would improve if Americans took over.

The attitude of almost all American Texans was to undergo a radical change in 1835 when General Antonio López de Santa Anna became dictator of Mexico. He replaced the 1824 Constitution with one that officially prohibited future immigration to Texas and put affairs in Texas under his control.

At this time, there were about 30,000 Yankees in Texas, making up about 60 percent of the total population. Since there had been an elected state legislature, the Texans could be readily organized. When Santa Anna changed the governmental policy, the legislature met, and on March 2, 1836, declared Texas independent from Mexico.

THE ALAMO

The Alamo was part of a Franciscan missionary complex created in 1718. In the early nineteenth century, the mission compound was changed from religious to military use. In 1803 a company of Spanish soldiers from Alamo del Parras, Mexico, occupied the abandoned mission for barracks. Some historians believe that it was from this association that the old mission complex got its name. Others believe the name came from the cottonwood tree that grew nearby, which is called in Spanish *alamo.*

During a revolution in Mexico in 1812–1813, the Alamo was occupied by the Republican army. But the Royalist army recaptured it, and over 800 people in what is now San Antonio who had sided with the Republicans were executed. The Alamo building then had no official use until the beginning of the Texas war for independence.

In 1835, General Santa Anna sent his cousin, General Martin Perfecto de Cos, to San Antonio to crush the Texas rebellion. De Cos converted the mission compound into a fort in late 1835. But in the siege of Bexar in early December, Texans defeated the Mexican troops and forced de Cos to surrender. This act infuriated Santa Anna and he was soon on his way with an army of 5,000 to deal with the rebellious Texans in San Antonio.

On February 23, Santa Anna and his army of 5,000 reached San Antonio and began an attack on the fortified Alamo.

General Sam Houston had directed James Bowie—inventor of the famous knife—to destroy the old mission, but Bowie, who was a commander of volunteers, decided to defend it. The day before Santa Anna's arrival at San Antonio, Colonel William Travis, Bowie, and about 145 men, including frontiersman Davy Crockett, entered the Alamo compound. They would later be joined by 32 men from Gonzale.

Upon his arrival outside the Alamo, Santa Anna ordered a red flag indicating "No Quarter" flown from a nearby church tower. As the siege got underway, tensions developed between Bowie and Travis. This was soon eliminated when Bowie came down with fever and spent the rest of the siege in bed.

On the second day, Travis sent out his famous appeal for help that ended, "To the People of Texas and all Americans in the world, I shall never surrender—I am determined to sustain myself as long as possible and die like a soldier who never forgets what is due to his honor and that of his country—VICTORY OR DEATH."

During the siege, the Texans watched and waited but also kept busy improving

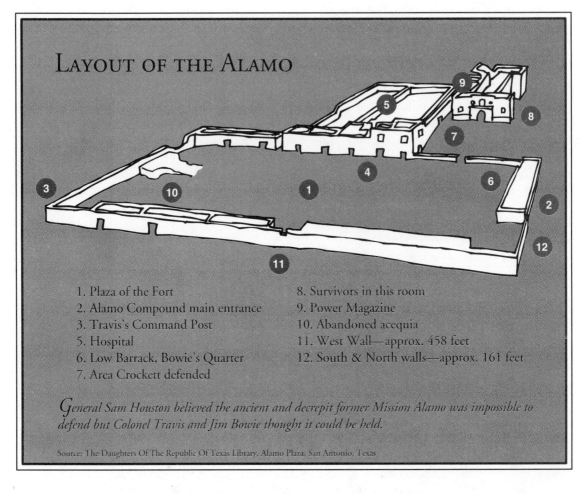

LAYOUT OF THE ALAMO

1. Plaza of the Fort
2. Alamo Compound main entrance
3. Travis's Command Post
5. Hospital
6. Low Barrack, Bowie's Quarter
7. Area Crockett defended
8. Survivors in this room
9. Power Magazine
10. Abandoned acequia
11. West Wall—approx. 458 feet
12. South & North walls—approx. 161 feet

General Sam Houston believed the ancient and decrepit former Mission Alamo was impossible to defend but Colonel Travis and Jim Bowie thought it could be held.

Source: The Daughters Of The Republic Of Texas Library, Alamo Plaza, San Antonio, Texas

defenses and employing their 18 pieces of artillery cannon to destroy houses and anything else that might shelter Mexican troops. On March 4, the Mexicans began a day-long bombardment of the fort. Then, before dawn on the sixth, the Mexicans who had crept up near the walls launched a major attack.

Three Mexican columns massed under the north wall. The Texans drove back two waves, but then the third attack began, and the Mexicans came over the parapet. But no matter how many the defenders killed, there were more men to take their place. Both sides fought fiercely for almost an hour and a half. There was no way for the Texans to retreat, and soon, the fighting was hand to hand. By 8 A.M. on the seventh, every Texan at the Alamo was dead including Travis, Bowie, and Crockett. But for the lives of 200 Texans, Santa Anna had lost 1,544 men in 13 days.

Though the Alamo was a famous and bloody battle, it decided little more than that Mexican soldiers were as brave in battle as Texans. It was also an unnecessary battle. Santa Anna could have just as easily left a force large enough to prevent supplies coming into the Alamo and forced the defenders to surrender from starvation.

Three weeks after the fall of the Alamo, Mexicans shot and killed 350 Texas prisoners at Goliad. This bloody affair only gave Texans another cause for revenge.

The Alamo is under the custody of the Daughters of the Republic of Texas. Many of the original buildings are open to visitors and there is also a museum and a film describing the battle.

BATTLE OF SAN JACINTO— APRIL 21, 1836

Four days before the fall of the Alamo, Texans declared their independence from Mexico, and appointed Sam Houston commander of the Republic of Texas's armed forces. As a young ensign, Houston had fought under Andrew Jackson against the Creek Indians at Horseshoe Bend in 1814 and had been wounded leading an attack on Creek warriors in a ravine beyond the breastworks. After the fall of the Alamo, Houston had time only to raise an army of 600 before he was pursued by Santa Anna with a far larger Mexican force. Houston retreated eastward, and after crossing the Brazos River, Santa Anna caught up with him.

By this time Houston's army had about 900 men. Santa Anna's original force was far greater but he had divided it with his cousin, General de Cos, leaving him with only 600 soldiers. The Mexicans took up a position where the San Jacinto River joins Buffalo Bayou, with an open prairie on the left, the San Jacinto on the right, and Buffalo Bayou at the front. Santa Anna believed he had trapped Houston, for the bridge on the only road across the Brazos River had been destroyed, so retreat westward was impossible.

Houston had, however, managed to intercept messages that gave him Santa Anna's plans. Nevertheless, for unknown reasons he did not attack the Mexican position until after General de Cos had arrived, bringing the Mexican force to 1,200.

On the afternoon of April 21, Houston prepared for the attack on the Mexican position. Along the 1,000-yard front, he put a line of infantry with two batteries of artillery set at intervals. The 60-man cavalry was placed on the right flank to prevent a Mexican breakthrough to the prairie.

At half past three, Houston ordered his troops to attack. A slight swell in the terrain provided cover for the attacking forces until they were within 200 yards of the enemy. But why the attack came as such a complete surprise to the Mexican forces is hard to explain. One report is that Santa Anna was occupied by an attractive young woman named Jenny and was not even aware of the immediate presence of the Texans until they attacked.

When the command to attack was given, the entire line of Texans advanced in double quick time to the Mexicans' position, raising their new war cry, "Remember the Alamo!" They waited until they were within point-blank range before pouring deadly fire on the enemy. The cavalry moved to clear the wooded area on the left. The two batteries of artillery moved to within 70 yards of the Mexican breastworks and then blasted them apart.

The battle lasted for only 18 minutes before all the surviving Mexican soldiers surrendered. Santa Anna, dressed as a private, was captured the following day. In the brief battle, 630 Mexicans were killed, 208 wounded, and 730 taken prisoner. Houston lost 9 men, and 30 were wounded. San Jacinto was the decisive event in the war for independence of the Texas Republic. Santa Anna was held captive until he signed an agreement to remove all Mexican troops

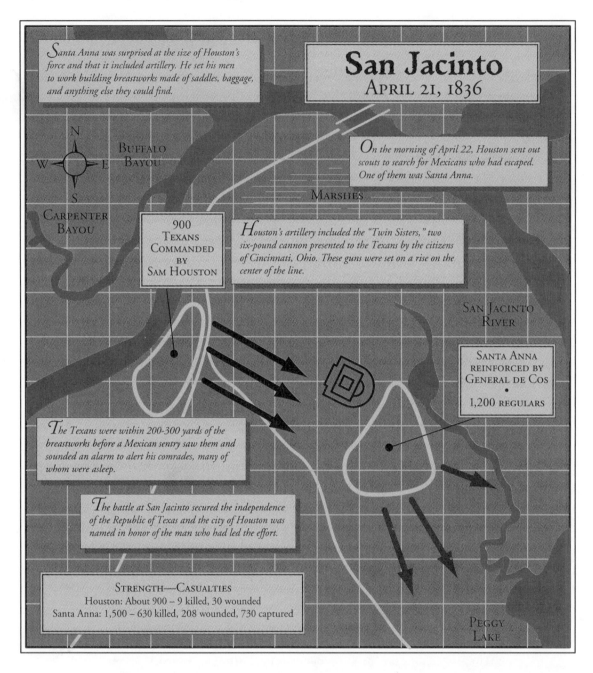

San Jacinto
APRIL 21, 1836

*S*anta Anna was surprised at the size of Houston's force and that it included artillery. He set his men to work building breastworks made of saddles, baggage, and anything else they could find.

BUFFALO BAYOU

N
W   E
S

*O*n the morning of April 22, Houston sent out scouts to search for Mexicans who had escaped. One of them was Santa Anna.

MARSHES

CARPENTER BAYOU

900
TEXANS
COMMANDED
BY
SAM HOUSTON

*H*ouston's artillery included the "Twin Sisters," two six-pound cannon presented to the Texans by the citizens of Cincinnati, Ohio. These guns were set on a rise on the center of the line.

SAN JACINTO RIVER

SANTA ANNA
REINFORCED BY
GENERAL DE COS
•
1,200 REGULARS

*T*he Texans were within 200-300 yards of the breastworks before a Mexican sentry saw them and sounded an alarm to alert his comrades, many of whom were asleep.

*T*he battle at San Jacinto secured the independence of the Republic of Texas and the city of Houston was named in honor of the man who had led the effort.

STRENGTH—CASUALTIES
Houston: About 900 – 9 killed, 30 wounded
Santa Anna: 1,500 – 630 killed, 208 wounded, 730 captured

PEGGY
LAKE

from the Republic of Texas and to use his influence to persuade Mexico to recognize Texas as an independent nation.

Santa Anna's government never recognized the Republic of Texas but the dictator did keep part of his word and withdrew his 3,000 to 4,000 troops from Texas. With no Mexican army on its soil, Texas was not concerned over the lack of formal recognition by Mexico.

As a result of independence, Texas eventually joined the Union, which triggered the U.S. war with Mexico in 1846.

San Jacinto Battlefield is administered by Texas State Park and Wildlife Department. The park includes a 570-foot high monument with an observation floor and a museum at the base. Markers at various points help explain the battle. The film Texas Forever! The Battle of San Jacinto *is shown daily every hour for a charge at the Jesse H. Jone Theatre in the monument.*

War with Mexico— 1846–1848

On February 28, 1845, the U.S. Congress passed a joint resolution providing for the annexation of Texas, which would become the twenty-eighth state. Because of this act, Mexico broke off diplomatic relations with the Unites States on March 6.

At that time, Mexico also had other grievances with her powerful land-hungry neighbor to the north. It was deeply offended over U.S. efforts to buy Texas, along with California and large areas of its southwestern lands. In addition, there was a smoldering dispute as to the location of the southern border of Texas. (The United States claimed the Rio Grande River as the border, but Mexico insisted it had always been further north at the Nueces River.)

President James Polk hoped to solve some of these differences and in the fall of 1845 sent John Slidell to Mexico City to negotiate a solution. But Polk also prepared for war. On May 29, he ordered Brigadier General Zachary Taylor to take 1,500 regulars to a position near the Rio Grande. By the end of July, Taylor was camped at Corpus Cristi, on the Gulf of Mexico, near the mouth of the Nueces.

On January 12, 1846, Polk learned that Slidell's mission had ended in failure to reach an agreement, and he ordered Taylor to advance to the Rio Grande. On March 8, Taylor and his troops left Corpus Cristi on the 150-mile march to the river. It was a hard journey over difficult terrain, made worse by heat and dust. Taylor shared the hardships with his men, who gave him a nickname that would be revived in the presidential election of 1848—"Old Rough and Ready." On the long march south, Taylor left a detachment at Point Isabel to establish a supply base called Fort Polk.

Taylor and his army arrived at the Rio Grande, opposite the Mexican town of Matamoros on March 28. The Mexican troops there made no attempt to attack Taylor, and he ordered his men to build an earthen wall fort, christened Fort Texas.

The Mexicans, however, had been building fortifications and gun emplacements at Matamoros and had begun sending in more troops. On April 28, Mexico declared a state of war against the United States, and on the following day, General Mariano Arista, commander of Mexican forces in the north, notified Taylor that hostilities between the two countries had begun. To make his point, Arista ordered General Anastasio Torrejón to cross the Rio Grande with 1,600 cavalry and cut Taylor's supply line to Point Isabel.

Taylor sent Captain Seth Thornton and a detachment of dragoons to determine Torrejón's purpose. Thornton's force tangled with some enemy cavalry and lost 11 men killed, with 6 wounded and 46 captured. Taylor notified Washington of the incident and that American blood had been spilled. On May 12, Polk declared war between the United States and Mexico.

Mexico appeared to be very confident of victory in this coming war in spite of the fact that its population was only 7 million compared to 20 million in the United

States. The Mexican generals seemed to have forgotten that only ten years earlier Sam Houston, with a small makeshift force of Texans, had beaten Santa Anna's Mexican army at San Jacinto.

Taylor learned that Arista was starting to move his army across the Rio Grande and became concerned for the safety of his supply line to Point Isabel. He put Major Jacob Brown in command of Fort Texas, providing him with 500 men and some artillery, while he took the major force of 2,300 to Point Isabel to strengthen Fort Polk and pick up supplies. Arista crossed the Rio Grande too late to stop Taylor's march north to Fort Polk and so decided to take Fort Texas.

On May 3, the guns at Matamoros began to bombard the fort and continued to do so for the next six days. But they did little damage as the earthen walls absorbed most of the impact of the cannonballs. On the morning of May 6, Brown was mortally wounded and Captain E. S. Hawkins took over. Arista demanded the fort surrender; Hawkins refused. On May 9, the attack ended with 2 Americans killed and 11 wounded.

On May 7, Taylor began the return march to Fort Texas. On the following morning, about 15 miles south of Point Isabel, he found his road blocked by Arista with a large force of Mexican soldiers.

BATTLE OF PALO ALTO— MAY 8, 1846

Taylor had a force of some 2,300 soldiers, mostly infantry, two squadrons (companies) of dragoons, a battery of 18-pounder siege guns, 200 wagons of supplies, and, most important for the coming battle, two

batteries of 6-pounder howitzers known as "flying batteries." The howitzers were a creation of Major Samuel Ringgold who recognized the need for highly mobile artillery during the Seminole Indian Wars. Mounted on large-wheeled horse-drawn carriages, the artillery was light and highly mobile. The guns could be quickly moved into position, unlimbered, fired, and move again in far less time than required by conventional artillery pieces. Ringgold would command one of these batteries in action and Captain James Duncan the other.

Arista commanded 4,000 men, artillery, and cavalry, armed with lances and carbines.

About 2 P.M., Taylor ordered his troops to advance on the Mexican line. The Americans got within 800 yards of the line before Arista ordered his cannon to open fire. Most of the Mexican shells fell short, but one hit an American artillery caisson.

Taylor halted the advance and ordered the artillery forward. With their flying batteries, Ringgold and Duncan moved into position and began rapid fire. The 18-pounders came up and concentrated on the Mexican cavalry on the left. The American artillery fire tore gaping holes in the Mexican line but while disrupting maneuvers, the soldiers stood fast and moved to fill the breach.

After some hesitation, Arista ordered General Torrejón to lead his cavalry through the chaparral, flank the Americans, and take the wagon train. When this plan became apparent to Taylor, he sent Colonel James McIntosh and his Fifth Infantry forward to the right. The Fifth formed a square before the Mexican cavalry could attack. And when it did, a single volley from the square stopped the charge. Torrejón then went after the supply train

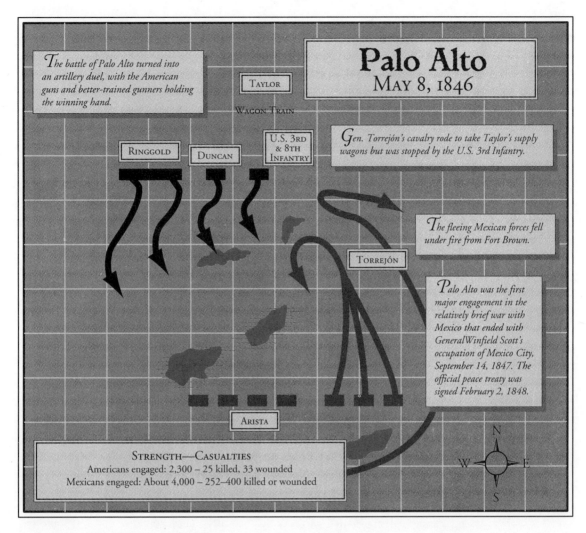

The battle of Palo Alto turned into an artillery duel, with the American guns and better-trained gunners holding the winning hand.

TAYLOR

Palo Alto
MAY 8, 1846

WAGON TRAIN

RINGGOLD   DUNCAN   U.S. 3RD & 8TH INFANTRY

Gen. Torrejón's cavalry rode to take Taylor's supply wagons but was stopped by the U.S. 3rd Infantry.

The fleeing Mexican forces fell under fire from Fort Brown.

TORREJÓN

Palo Alto was the first major engagement in the relatively brief war with Mexico that ended with GeneralWinfield Scott's occupation of Mexico City, September 14, 1847. The official peace treaty was signed February 2, 1848.

ARISTA

STRENGTH—CASUALTIES
Americans engaged: 2,300 – 25 killed, 33 wounded
Mexicans engaged: About 4,000 – 252–400 killed or wounded

N
W   E
S

but the Third Infantry had moved into a position to stop him. Torrejón retired.

Artillery came to support the Fifth Infantry and raked the Mexican cavalry with canisters, grape, and shot. The bombardment proved too much for the Mexican lancers and they retreated out of range. By four o'clock, cannons had set fire to the prairie, and there was a pause in the battle until the heavy smoke cleared.

Around five o'clock the battle resumed. Mexican cannon opened fire on the Fourth

Infantry, which suffered many casualties. Taylor ordered the dragoons under Captain Charles May to hit the Mexican left. After advancing under heavy cannon fire, they were met by Torrejón with massed cavalry and were forced to retreat. The Fourth Infantry under Major G. W. Allen was also pulled back, and Major Ringgold was seriously wounded and died two days later.

Arista sent his light cavalry, supported by infantry, to turn the American left flank. Under cover of smoke, Duncan moved his battery to the left so the Mexican troops were at point-blank range. A force of Mexican cavalry was detached to take Duncan's gun while the remaining soldiers continued with the flanking movement.

Duncan's highly mobile guns were able to withstand both of these forces, delivering round after round of solid shot, grape, and canisters. In spite of the large number of cavalry and infantry killed by these guns, the Mexicans tried to return the fire but were hampered by the blinding light of the setting sun.

The Mexican cavalry finally retired in face of the heavy artillery fire, colliding with other elements of the army, which resulted in general confusion. Arista pulled all his force back and set up a camp a few miles from the Americans.

Taylor did not follow. He knew that though he had weakened Arista's army, he had not defeated it. Arista still had more men than Taylor and was also familiar with the terrain.

At Palo Alto, it was the artillery, especially Ringgold's flying batteries, that were the "Queen of the Battle." The highly mobile American artillery smashed Mexican cavalry and infantry attacks before they reached American lines. This accounted for the low casualties suffered by Taylor's army. During the four hours of battle, American artillery fired over 3,580 rounds. The inferior Mexican guns fired only 850 rounds.

Americans lost 15 killed and 43 wounded of which 10 would later die from their wounds. Arista claimed losses at 252 killed but others gave the figure as close to 400.

In June 1992, President George Bush signed into law a bill authorizing and providing funds to establish a national park to be called Palo Alto National Battlefield.

Until this project is completed, the battle site consists of a roadside area maintained by the Palo Alto National Park Committee, an umbrella organization of the Brownsville Kiwanis. The site includes a monument, marker, cannon, and map of the battle.

BATTLE OF RESACA DE LA PALMA—MAY 9, 1846

A short distance from Palo Alto, another battle took place at Resaca de la Palma, the site from which Taylor launched another attack on Arista's Mexican forces, who had taken defensive positions at Resaca de Guerrero.

Early on the morning of May 9, General Mariano Arista withdrew from Palo Alto and headed for the Rio Grande. He took up a defensive position at Resaca de Guerrero, which extended east and west across the route to Fort Texas and about seven miles from the Rio Grande.

The resaca was an ancient channel of the river, about 200 feet wide and 3 to 4 feet deep. Unlike the open prairie at Palo Alto, the ground around the resaca was covered by thickets and chaparral.

Arista placed artillery on his right to cover the road from Palo Alto and his infantry on both sides of the road. Torrejón's cavalry massed on the road but some distance from the infantry. The heavy growth in the area would impede Taylor's cavalry, but it would also work to the disadvantage of the lance-carrying Mexican cavalry.

Taylor did not go after Arista until he had erected earthworks and gun positions to protect his 200 supply wagons. It was early afternoon before his army reached Resaca de la Palma, where he intended to determine Arista's strategy, and sent Captain George McCall forward with an advance force. Coming around a turn in the road, they faced Mexican cannon. Six of his

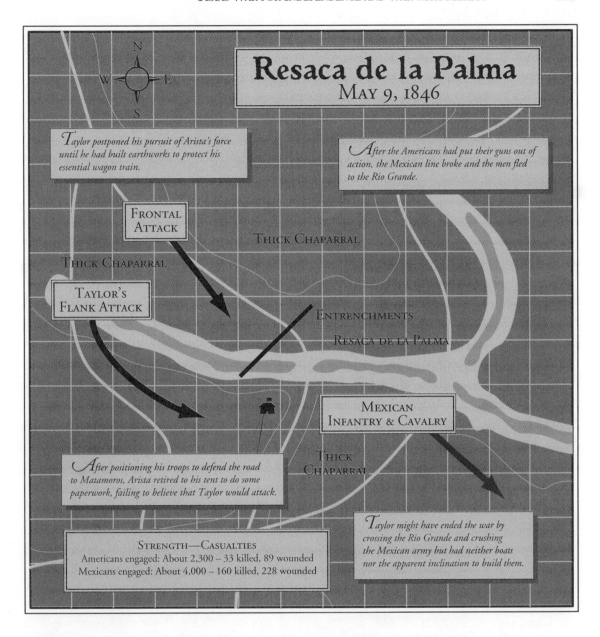

Resaca de la Palma
MAY 9, 1846

Taylor postponed his pursuit of Arista's force until he had built earthworks to protect his essential wagon train.

After the Americans had put their guns out of action, the Mexican line broke and the men fled to the Rio Grande.

FRONTAL ATTACK

THICK CHAPARRAL

THICK CHAPARRAL

TAYLOR'S FLANK ATTACK

ENTRENCHMENTS

RESACA DE LA PALMA

MEXICAN INFANTRY & CAVALRY

After positioning his troops to defend the road to Matamoros, Arista retired to his tent to do some paperwork, failing to believe that Taylor would attack.

THICK CHAPARRAL

Taylor might have ended the war by crossing the Rio Grande and crushing the Mexican army but had neither boats nor the apparent inclination to build them.

STRENGTH—CASUALTIES
Americans engaged: About 2,300 – 33 killed, 89 wounded
Mexicans engaged: About 4,000 – 160 killed, 228 wounded

soldiers were killed before McCall retreated and reported back to Taylor.

Taylor moved toward the Mexican defenses. Captain Randolph Ridgley, now in command of Ringgold's artillery, was ordered to attack. McCall's inability to provide support did not faze Ridgley. His flying battery dashed forward, firing as they galloped toward the enemy. A body of lancers charged his guns, but with courage, skill, and a bit of luck, Ridgley's force routed them.

He soon reached some Mexican artillery and drove off the men and then swept a

wooded area with canister, which frightened many of the enemy, reminding them of the deaths the same artillery had caused the day before at Palo Alto.

The American infantry now moved to attack, and soon there was fierce fighting within the dense vegetation. The struggle came down to man-to-man combat with swords and bayonets, slashing at the growth to reach the enemy. Lieutenant George Meade, who would participate in the battle at Gettysburg, was there in the chaparral fighting along with his soldiers.

On the morning of the battle, the morale of the Mexican army was reportedly very poor. Many of them had been without food for 24 hours, and all had seen their dead comrades left unburied at Palo Alto because Arista wanted to march on. But if morale was poor, the mood was not apparent by the way the Mexican soldiers fought in this battle of the underbrush. Their Twenty-first Light Infantry lost most of its field officers, and it was reported that in one company every man was either killed or wounded. Eventually the Mexican troops withdrew.

Taylor decided that to gain total victory the Mexican artillery must be taken by Charles May and his dragoons. So off they rode, slashing with their sabers as they moved in among the cannon and then beyond. But when they returned, the Mexican gunners that they drove off had resumed position and began to fire on May's troopers. In spite of May's failure, Taylor was determined to take the cannon. He turned to Lieutenant Colonel William Belknap and exclaimed. "Take those guns, and by God, keep them!"

WAR WITH MEXICO—A WAR OF MANY "FIRSTS"

The war with Mexico was a war of many "firsts." It was the first offensive war the United States had ever fought. All the other wars, including the War of 1812, were defensive operations.

The battles at Palo Alto and Resaca de la Palma were the first U.S. Army military operations to be reported by the recently developed telegraph, and during the war, the military would use the telegraph to communicate with officials in Washington. Also, railroads and steamboats were extensively employed to transport men and military supplies.

In this war, U.S. Army surgeons introduced ether as an anesthetic. Previously, seriously wounded soldiers were either held down, given opium, if available; or a bullet to bite on while the surgeon amputated their shattered limbs.

Combat photography made its first appearance in this war, and Samuel Colt's new revolver made such a big hit with officers in the field that the War Department contracted for many more of them.

Finally, it was during the Mexican campaign that West Point-trained officers came into their own. Young officers such as Captain Robert E. Lee and Lieutenants U. S. Grant, George Meade, George McClellan, and P. G. T. Beauregard would fight with distinction in the war. Later, in the Civil War they would fight against other West Pointers of their time—Thomas (Stonewall) Jackson, Joseph Hooker, and Albert Sidney Johnson, along with many others.

But it was the last war for American "dragoons," henceforth, all mounted soldiers would be known as "cavalry."

A part of the Fifth Infantry joined Belknap's Eighth, and they all rushed furiously toward the guns, yelling like fiends. The Mexican gunners put up stiff resistance, but when the supporting infantry withdrew, the Americans had the cannon. The battle was almost won for the Americans.

Arista's behavior during this battle was somewhat bizarre. For some reason, he did not believe Taylor would attack, so when the battle began, he was at the rear of his tent writing. It was not until the battle was almost over that he left his tent and rushed around, cursing his soldiers for being cowards.

After Torrejón refused to attack, Arista took command of the cavalry and dashed up the road, lancing a few American

dragoons, and then, with his army torn to pieces and the Americans holding the chaparral, rode off with his cavalry and crossed the Rio Grande.

The survivors of his army crossed the river as best they could. Panic-striken soldiers threw away their uniforms, equipment, and muskets as they fought for space in the boats that would get them away from Taylor's army. It had been a hard battle for Mexico—160 killed, 228 wounded, and 159 missing. American losses were 33 killed and 89 wounded.

Resaca de la Palma/Resaca de Guerrero was the last battle in the War with Mexico fought on American soil. In fact, it would not be until December 7, 1941, that Americans would again see a foreign force on their own land.

The battlefield today merely suggests conditions as they were at the time of the battle, since the once dense chaparral has been cleared for a citrus orchard. The site includes a monument and cannon mounted in concrete.

THE INVASION OF MEXICO AND THE SURRENDER OF MEXICO CITY—SEPTEMBER 8, 1847

After Resaca de la Palma, Taylor crossed the Rio Grande and moved north into Mexico, taking Monterrey on November 24, 1847. But to end the war, President Polk decided that it was essential to capture the capital, Mexico City. He appointed Winfield Scott commander of this operation. Taylor had to send men to Scott, so when he engaged the 15,000 troops under Santa Anna at Buena Vista on February 23, he had only 5,000 troops, but thanks to his artillery and dragoons, he eventually won the day. It was General Zachary Taylor's last battle but it would help him gain the presidency in 1848.

General Scott with his 13,000-man army landed at Vera Cruz in March and began the march to Mexico City. After several battles they took the city on September 14.

On February 2, 1848, the war was formally over with the signing of the Treaty of Guadalupe Hidalgo, whereby Mexico ceded to the United States some 1,193,061 square miles of territory that included the disputed land in Texas north of the Rio Grande, New Mexico, Arizona, California, Nevada, and Utah. In return, the United States paid Mexico $15,000,000 and assumed American citizen's claims for their property taken by the Mexican authorities during the course of the war.

The conclusion of the war was an expression of the popular national belief in "manifest destiny," a term first introduced in an 1845 editorial in the *New York Morning News*. It included the phrase, "our manifest destiny to overspread and to possess the whole continent which Providence has given us."

The Civil War

Eastern Campaigns of the Civil War

Gettysburg
Washington, D.C.
Harpers Ferry
Antietam
New Market
Chancellorsville
Fredericksburg
Gaines' Mill
Cold Harbor
The Wilderness
Seven Pines
Spotsylvania
Malvern Hill
Sayler's Creek
Richmond
Lynchburg
Appomattox Court House
Petersburg
Fort Monroe
Danville
Five Forks
Norfolk
Raleigh
New Bern
Wilmington
Columbia
Fort Fisher
Charleston
Fort Sumter

N
W   E
S

Most battles in this region took place in Northern Virginia as Federal troops attempted to take the Confederate capital of Richmond.

Southern strategy was to keep Union commanders off balance by sending forces up the Shenandoah Valley to threaten Washington and invading Maryland and Pennsylvania.

When Grant took command in 1864, he concluded that to win the war, Lee's army protecting Richmond must be destroyed and so the final battles took place in that area.

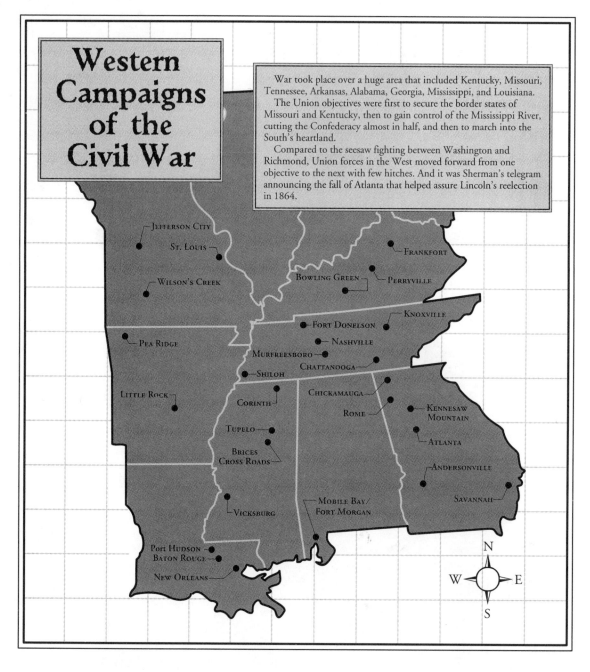

Western Campaigns of the Civil War

War took place over a huge area that included Kentucky, Missouri, Tennessee, Arkansas, Alabama, Georgia, Mississippi, and Louisiana.

The Union objectives were first to secure the border states of Missouri and Kentucky, then to gain control of the Mississippi River, cutting the Confederacy almost in half, and then to march into the South's heartland.

Compared to the seesaw fighting between Washington and Richmond, Union forces in the West moved forward from one objective to the next with few hitches. And it was Sherman's telegram announcing the fall of Atlanta that helped assure Lincoln's reelection in 1864.

The Civil War was the titanic event in America's history. By the time this four-year war had run its course, of the over two million Union and Confederate soldiers who served, about 620,000 would die, more dead than the nation had suffered in any single war, before or since including World War II. While peace in 1865 brought freedom to some 3.5 million Southern slaves, it left the South's social structure and economy in tatters. Hundreds of thousands of dollars' worth of Southern property was destroyed—crops, barns, houses, railroads—and whole cities, such as Atlanta and Columbia, were left virtually in ruins.

But the postwar peace also energized the nation. The transcontinental railroad brought thousands upon thousands of Northern and Southern settlers into western lands to farm, mine, and otherwise exploit the great natural resources of the West. The nation's industry and economy flourished, and only 33 years after General Robert E. Lee surrendered at Appomattox on April 9, 1865, the United States emerged from the Spanish-American War as a colonial and naval power.

THE CAUSES OF WAR

Many learned books have been written on the causes of the Civil War, but the inventor Eli Whitney and writer Harriet Beecher Stowe certainly played major parts in bringing it about.

In 1792, Whitney introduced his cotton gin, a mechanical device that speeded and simplified the processing of cotton just as the textile mills that increased demand were being established, especially in Britain. The Southern climate proved to be perfectly suited to growing cotton and the cotton gin allowed it to increase production from 70,000 bales in 1800 to 4,000,000 bales by 1860. The cotton crop determined the Southern agrarian economy, dependent on slave labor to plant and pick the cotton. In time the entire social system of the South depended on slavery, that "peculiar institution," and encouraged the growth of huge plantations with a feudal character. It also discouraged industry in the South because the export of cotton provided all funds needed to import manufactured goods from Europe or the North.

The North with its small farms and growing industries had no need for slave labor. In 1852, Harriet Beecher Stowe's *Uncle Tom's Cabin* was published, effectively demonstrating the evils of slavery and the complicity of all society in allowing a system that debased the "master" as well as his slaves.

Uncle Tom's Cabin was a tremendous success—in the North. It was the first serialized in a magazine to be read by thousands and in book form sold 300,000 copies in less than a year. Mrs. Stowe's book so aroused the conscience of the North against slavery that when she met President Abraham Lincoln at the White House during the war he greeted her saying, "So this is the little lady who made this big war."

The conflict over slavery was almost as old as the nation. The South had sought to ensure its survival by acquiring congressional support for the extension of slavery in western territories. The question of slavery began to become a major issue as the new nation expanded into new territory following the War of 1812.

In 1820, Congress passed the Missouri Compromise, allowing Maine to enter the Union as a free state and Missouri as a slave state. It also prohibited slavery in the remainder of the Louisiana Purchase north of the southern boundary of Missouri of 36 degrees 30'.

By 1850, slavery had become a political issue. The South insisted it was essential for its economic and social survival; the North opposed slavery on moral grounds and reminded the South that it was now outlawed in all civilized nations. In July 1854, a group of "Free Soilers," who opposed the extension of slavery, met in

Milwaukee, Wisconsin, to form the Republican Party. A few days after James Buchanan became president in 1857, the U.S. Supreme Court rendered its decision in the Dred Scott Case. A slave whose master took him from Missouri into free territory for two years, Scott sued for liberty in a Missouri court after his return, on grounds that living in a free state conferred freedom on him.

The case went to the Supreme Court, which ruled that a slave was not a citizen and, therefore, could not sue in court, and living in a free state could not confer freedom. It was also ruled that the Missouri Compromise was unconstitutional and Congress had no right to pass any law that deprived a person of his or her rightful property, including slaves.

The Dred Scott Decision was bitterly criticized in the North, for now no slave could escape to freedom in a free state without fear of being taken and returned to his or her master.

The only place a runaway slave could be safe was Canada, which could be reached by the recently organized Underground Railroad. This system consisted of safe houses or barns where the runaway could hide during the day and, if undetected, move northward to another safe house and on until reaching Canada. Owners of safe houses were in danger not only because they were breaking the law but also from men paid to capture and return runaways.

Abolitionist sentiment continued to grow in the North. John Brown's raid on the federal arsenal at Harpers Ferry on October 19, 1859, aroused passions on both sides. The armed assault by Brown also reinforced the South's major concern—an insurrection by its 3.5 million slaves. In 1860, its representatives in Washington introduced a resolution for a federal law demanding protection of slave property in all territories.

That same year, the Republican Party held its convention in Chicago and nominated Abraham Lincoln as its candidate for president. His views on slavery were well known. Two years before, Lincoln had stated, "Slavery is founded on the selfishness of man's nature—opposition to it in his love of justice."

The Democrats—the major political party of that time—met in Charleston, South Carolina, to nominate their own candidate. The convention split over the slavery issue. The Southern slave states nominated John Beckinridge, and the Northern delegates nominated Stephen A. Douglas of Illinois.

The Democrats' division ensured Lincoln's election. In protest, South Carolina adopted an Ordinance of Secession on December 20 and cut all ties with the Union. A few weeks later, it was joined by Mississippi, Alabama, Florida, Georgia, Louisiana, and Texas. On February 4, 1861, delegates from these seven states met in Montgomery, Alabama, to form the Confederate States of America and elected Jefferson Davis of Mississippi as provincial president. As they left the Union, the succeeding states took over federal property—mints, arsenals, shipyards, and military bases. One piece of federal property that remained fatefully beyond their reach was Fort Sumter in Charleston Harbor.

In spite of the South's belligerent actions, Lincoln was anxious to avoid war. His paramount objective was to preserve the Union. "In your hands, my dissatisfied fellow-countrymen, and not mine," he told the South, "is the momentous issue of civil war."

The newly formed Confederate government was also not anxious for war but eventually came to the conclusion that it would be necessary in order to bring Virginia, the South's most populous and important state, into the Confederacy. On April 12, 1861, on order by President Davis, Confederate artillery along the shore opened fire on Fort Sumter, and the Civil War began. The opening shots brought Virginia into the Confederacy along with North Carolina, Arkansas, and Tennessee.

Shortly after Virginia seceded, Richmond, a little more than 100 miles from Washington, became the capital of the Confederacy.

The western counties of Virginia, pro-Union and long unhappy over the treatment they received from the aristocratic slaveholders of the tidewater region, formed a free state, later called West Virginia. It remained in the Union thanks to General George McClellan, who in the first few months of the war defeated a Confederate force that had come to reclaim the western counties.

The so-called border states—Maryland, Delaware, Kentucky, and Missouri—created a problem for both sides. These states retained southern traditions but their population was divided on the slavery issue. Maryland and Delaware were so close to Washington, D.C., where federal troops were gathering, that a show of force was enough to keep them in the Union. But Kentucky and Missouri were too far away for this approach.

Kentucky's governor leaned toward the Confederacy and favored neutrality for his state, in spite of strong Unionist sentiment among the population. For his part, Lincoln remarked that while in war he merely hoped to have God on his side, he had to have Kentucky. In early September 1861, Kentucky's neutrality vanished when a Confederate force invaded it and occupied Columbus on the Mississippi River. Brigadier General Ulysses S. Grant promptly left his base at Cario, Illinois, to occupy Paducah, Kentucky, thus gaining control of the mouth of the Tennessee River. The Confederate army left the state, and Kentucky remained in the Union.

Missouri also remained in the Union but at the cost of much bloodshed. Two battles at *Wilson Creek*, August 10, 1861, and at *Pea Ridge*, March 7–8, 1862, were waged over control of the state, and even after the Union victory at Pea Ridge, Missouri, throughout the war was torn by savage partisan guerrilla warfare.

By now thousands of men were volunteering to serve in the Union and Confederate armed forces in what most believed would be a quick war and victory.

THE OPPOSING FORCES

The Union and Confederacy each possessed advantages as well as disadvantages as they entered the war.

The North had a far larger population—19 million compared to the South's 9 million, including 3.5 million slaves. Northern industries were capable of making all that was needed to equip and maintain armies that would eventually total over 1 million soldiers. It had a superior railroad system with some 31,000 miles of track, compared to the South's 9,000 miles. The North was also a formidable seapower with ships to blockade Confederate ports, transports to carry troops, and gunships to control rivers.

But one thing the Union lacked in the early years of the war was competent military leadership, and this was most apparent in the eastern theater of the war. President Lincoln's only previous military experience had been as captain of the militia in the Black Hawk War of 1829. Generals George McClellan, Ambrose Burnside, and Joseph Hooker took turns at leading the Union Army of the Potomac with unfortunate results. It was not until Ulysses S. Grant took over in 1864 that this army achieved lasting successes.

Major Union armies were generally named after rivers, hence Army of the Potomac, Army of the Tennessee, and Army of the Cumberland. Confederate armies were named after states—Army of Northern Virginia, Army of Tennessee, and Army of Mississippi.

The South's greatest assets included the enthusiasm, devotion, and courage of its people, who were convinced of the justice of their cause and were fighting to preserve their homes, families, and way of life. From the beginning of the war, the South was blessed with good leadership. President Davis, a graduate of West Point, served as an officer in the war with Mexico and had been Secretary of War.

Of the 900 or so trained U.S. officers in 1860, almost a third of them joined the Confederate army. Among them was Robert E. Lee.

Aside from the Tredegor Iron Works at Richmond that supplied cannon for its armies, the Confederacy had few facilities for making military equipment. The Union blockade of Southern ports prevented the export of cotton and the import of military needs. Blockade runners were able to bring in some arms from Europe, and the South was also able to build plants to make small arms and ammunition.

The Confederate lack of adequate transportation was one of its greatest handicaps. Even though there was often ample food available, soldiers and civilians went hungry because there was no way to deliver it to where it was needed.

STRATEGY

The South's war objective was to defend itself against occupation by Union forces, so its strategy was simple: repel an invasion force.

The Union, however, had a far more complex problem: to force the Southern states back into the Union.

In the early weeks of the war, General Winfield Scott, then in command of the Union army, developed a plan for winning the war that called for an effective blockade of all southern ports and the control of the Mississippi to the Gulf of Mexico, thereby cutting the Confederacy in half. Northern newspapers referred to this as the "Anaconda Plan" and often pictured it as a giant snake slowly squeezing the life out of the Confederacy.

The Northern public and press, however, were too impatient for this slow process. The popular cry was "Forward to Richmond," as many believed that the war could quickly be won by the capture of the Confederate capital of Richmond. By the same token, the South was convinced that if they captured Washington, the North would give up the fight. It also knew that the North would not stand for prolonged warfare.

In the east, the war developed into a seesaw contest of land between the two capitals. But in the west, the Union developed clear objectives: control of central and eastern Tennessee, south to Vicksburg, control of the Mississippi, east to Chattanooga and the South's heartland, and then south to Atlanta.

THE CAMPAIGNS

The four years of protracted battles in the east led to the Union attempt to smash the

Confederate army defending Richmond and taking the capital. Two famous armies were raised for this conflict—the Union's Army of the Potomac and the Confederate Army of Northern Virginia, forever associated with its great commander, General Robert E. Lee. Tens of thousands of men on each side were killed as these two mighty forces battled each other, and thousands of Union troops were tied down in Washington to repulse a Southern attack.

But victory for the Union armies in the east was a long time coming. After it suffered its first defeat in the 1861 *First Bull Run Campaign,* General McClellan turned the Union force into the well-trained Army of the Potomac and in March 1863 launched the *Peninsula Campaign,* intending to reach Richmond by moving up the interior peninsula and by ship via the Potomac River. In the course of this four-month drive, battles took place at *Fair Oaks* and *Seven Pines* on May 31, 1862, and during the *Seven Days Campaign,* June 25 to July 1, at *Mechanicsville, Gaines' Mill,* and *Malvern Hill.* But Lee outgeneraled McClellan, who never reached Richmond.

Meanwhile, Confederate General Thomas Jackson's *Shenandoah Campaign,* from January to June 1862, proved a success. Fighting battles at *McDowell,* May 8, and *Port Republic* on June 9, along with *Kernstown,* March 23, *Front Royal,* May 23, *Winchester,* May 24, and *Cross Keys,* June 8. Aside from reaching Harpers Ferry and threatening Washington with attack, the campaign tied up thousands of Federal troops that McClellan needed for the *Peninsula Campaign.*

On June 24, Jackson moved south to join with Lee, and the Union forces continued to suffer serious defeats and high casualties during the *Second Bull Run Campaign* of August 29–30, 1862; *Fredericksburg Campaign,* November 19 to December 13, 1862; and the *Wilderness* and *Chancellorsville Campaigns,* April 30 to May 6, 1863. The Army of the Potomac performed better when Lee took the risk of invading Northern territory. The *Antietam Campaign* into Maryland might have ended in a smashing Union victory instead of a draw on September 17, 1862, if McClellan had thrown in his reserves at the critical moment.

But while Antietam was not a great Union victory, it did halt Lee's invasion of the North, which gave Lincoln opportunity to finally issue the Emancipation Proclamation on September 22, 1862, stating that all slaves held in any state in rebellion were "henceforth and forever free."

The proclamation, of course, failed to free any slaves until the Union forces occupied states in rebellion, but it made a profound change in Union war objectives. Now the Northern cause was not only to reunite the nation, but also to end slavery. It dashed the Confederacy's hope of an alliance with Britain or France; no foreign power could hope for popular support against a nation armed with the abolitionist cause.

The Army of the Potomac again clashed with the Army of Northern Virginia when Lee invaded the north during the Pennsylvania *Gettysburg Campaign,* June 19 to July 3, 1863. In the final battle of the campaign, Lee suffered a serious defeat, and his retreating army might have been destroyed if General George Meade, recently appointed the Army of the Potomac's commander, had pursued it.

On March 2, 1864, Grant was put in command of the Union forces and came east to supervise the capture of Richmond and the destruction of Lee's forces. Grant was a true fighter and launched a series of offensives that included fierce battles fought in the *Wilderness Campaign,* May 5 to 6, 1864; *Spotsylvania,* May 8 to 21; *Cold Harbor,* June 3; and the *Siege of Petersburg,* June 15, 1864, to April 1, 1865.

Because Grant was determined to achieve his goals, these campaigns cost the lives of tens of thousands of Union soldiers. But while Grant could afford to lose men because he could always replace them, Lee could not. Grant simply wore down the Army of Northern Virginia. Eventually, Lee was forced to give up Richmond and start down the road west toward Appomattox Courthouse.

Union victory in the east might not have been possible had not the western armies accomplished their own goals so quickly. At the same time that Grant finally took Richmond, General William Tecumseh Sherman and his western armies had already smashed their way from Atlanta to Savannah and were pursuing Joseph E. Johnston's Confederate forces through North Carolina.

The major campaigns in the west began with Union forces under Grant capturing two important Confederate forts in February 1862, *Fort Henry* on the Tennessee River, and *Fort Donelson* on the Cumberland River. On April 6, 1862, a Confederate force of 40,000 under Johnston attacked Grant's 33,000 on the south side of the Tennessee River near Pittsburg Landing. Grant came close to losing the *Shiloh Campaign,* but he was able to rally his troops and achieved a somewhat tarnished victory.

In August, Confederate General Braxton Bragg, who had taken command after Johnston was killed at Shiloh, moved north and invaded Kentucky. On reaching Louisville, he found no support and retreated to Perryville. Here on October 8, 1862, he encountered Union forces under General Don Carlos Buell. *The Battle of Perrysville* was a bloody affair, and while neither side could claim victory, Bragg continued his retreat.

Bragg's next battle was at Murfreesboro, Tennessee, where he engaged Union forces under General William Rosecrans at *Stones River* on December 31, 1862, to January 2, 1863. The battle was a narrow victory for Rosecrans, and after it Bragg continued to move south.

By late 1862, Grant began the *Vicksburg Campaign,* intending to capture this heavily fortified city that controlled the upper Mississippi River. The siege lasted for months, and the city was finally taken on July 3, 1863. In the course of the campaign, several battles were fought in the general area including *Port Gibson,* May 1, 1862, and *Champions Hill,* May 16, 1862.

In late April 1862, Rear Admiral David Farragut's U.S. fleet captured New Orleans which was then occupied by Union troops. On July 9, 1863, Union forces under General Nathaniel Banks, after a long siege, captured the Confederate bastion of *Port Hudson* on the Louisiana side of the Mississippi River. With the fall of Vicksburg, New Orleans, and Port Hudson, the Union now controlled the Mississippi River and the Confederacy was cut in half.

Union forces in the west now concentrated on invading the Confederate heartland. This campaign resulted in two major battles: *Chickamauga,* Georgia, September 19–20, where Bragg's Confederate force triumphed, and *Chattanooga,* Tennessee, November 23–25, which was a Union victory.

After Chattanooga, Bragg continued his southward retreat, pursued by General Sherman, whom Grant had named overall commander in the west. Sherman's orders were to advance into Georgia and inflict as much damage on the state's resources as possible. As he moved south toward Atlanta with 100,000 men, he was opposed by General Joseph E. Johnston's 65,000-man army.

Johnston managed to slow Sherman's advance, but since he could not completely stop it, he was replaced by General John B. Hood from Texas, who thought he could whip Sherman's army; when he found out he could not, Johnston resumed command, but by then, it was too late. On September 3, Sherman wired Washington, "Atlanta is ours and fairly won"—the news would help President Lincoln win reelection.

From Atlanta, Sherman marched to Savannah and from there headed north through the Carolinas, opposed only by Johnston's weakened army. By now the Confederate States of America had nearly ceased to exist. Its once splendid armies were all but nonexistent and its territory so reduced to ash and rubble that when Grant and Lee faced each other at Appomattox, there were only about 300 miles separating the Confederate's eastern and western armies.

FALL OF FORT SUMTER— APRIL 12–14, 1861

In the months immediately following the secession of South Carolina and the other six states, most federal property—mints, shipyards, arsenals—was peacefully occupied. The exceptions were some coastal fortifications that could be defended by the Union Navy. Chief among these was Fort Sumter at Charleston, South Carolina—the birthplace of the Confederacy.

Built on an artificial island in Charleston Harbor, Sumter is a 300-by-350- feet or so pentagonal brick structure with walls from five to 12 feet thick and rising 40 feet above the water.

Begun in 1829, it was designed to carry three tiers of cannon. The guns in the two lower tiers were protected by casements but the heavier cannon on the upper tier—the barbette—were exposed to enemy fire.

In late December 1860, Major Robert Anderson, a Kentuckian, moved his 84 men from nearby vulnerable Fort Moultrie to the as yet unfinished Fort Sumter. Only 48 of the 140 cannon were in position, half in the two lower tiers with the heavy howitzers and Columbiads on the unprotected barbette. The fort was also low on ammunition and food.

The South, especially South Carolina, resented the northern occupation of the fort and the now despised American flag flying over it. The Union, on the other hand, considered Sumter as a symbol of national sovereignty.

On January 6, 1861, Confederate batteries drove off the *Star of the West,* a ship chartered by the federal government to bring reinforcements and supplies to Anderson.

Just one day after Lincoln took office as president, he received word from Major Anderson that the fort's garrison would run out of supplies within six weeks. Only one of Lincoln's advisers thought that he should answer this plea for help; the others felt he should give up the fort, fearing that the remaining Southern states would join those that had already seceded.

Lincoln's decision, reached after long deliberation, was to send food to the Sumter garrison but to make no effort to send men. He advised the governor of South Carolina accordingly. This was strictly a relief mission, and no military force would be used by the federal government unless the relief ship or fort were attacked, Thus, in the event of conflict, the onus for breaking the shaky peace between North and South would be borne by the South.

Jefferson Davis, the new president of the secessionist government, answered Lincoln's decision by ordering Brigadier General Pierre Gustave Toutant Beauregard, the Confederacy's commander in Charleston, to demand that Fort Sumter surrender before the relief ship arrived. Futile negotiations followed, and Anderson rejected the ultimatum.

On 4:30 A.M., April 12, Confederate batteries positioned on three sides of Fort Sumter opened fire. At 7:30 A.M., Captain Abner Doubleday, often incorrectly cited as the developer of modern baseball, fired the fort's first answering shot. The fort's cannon in casements did not have sufficient range to damage the Confederate batteries and, as Anderson did not wish to send his men to man the long-range guns in the unprotected barbette, there was nothing to do but take the punishment from the enemy guns.

Confederate bombardment was intense and quite accurate. The gunners, however, observed that the shells were doing little harm to the fort's thick walls. They trained their guns to fire shells, heated in a furnace until they were red hot, over the walls and to set fire to the interior wood structure.

The bombardment continued for 30 hours. By then much of the fort's interior was burned or on fire. Ammunition and food were running out and a storm at sea prevented a second relief expedition's coming to the rescue.

Finally, on April 14, Anderson surrendered his fort on terms previously made by Beauregard that provided, "All proper facilities will be afforded for the removal of yourself and command together with company arms and property, to any post in the United States which you may select. The flag which you have upheld so long with much fortitude, under the most trying circumstances, may be saluted by you on taking down."

During the lowering of the flag, one of the fort's guns firing the salute exploded and killed Private Daniel Hough, the first casualty of the war.

Taking along the flag, Anderson and his men boarded a ship to return to the North. The flag of the Confederate States of America now flew over Fort Sumter.

The bombardment of the fort had accomplished President Davis's goal of bringing Virginia into the Confederacy. And with Virginia came North Carolina, Arkansas, and Tennessee.

The firing on Fort Sumter was the beginning of the four-year-long Civil War that would cost the lives of over six hundred thousand Union and Confederate soldiers and sailors.

During the terrible war that followed, the federal government made several attempts to retake the fort. On April 7, 1863, a fleet of monitors under Rear Admiral Samuel F. DuPont made a carefully planned run into Charleston Harbor but was badly mauled by fire from Sumter, nearby Fort Moultrie, and other Confederate batteries. Sumter was extensively damaged but not enough to prevent retaliation. In the end, the fleet withdrew.

On August 17 of the same year, after federal army troops had gained a foothold on Morris Island at the entrance to Charleston Harbor, a combined army and navy attack was made on Fort Sumter and the Confederate battery in the middle of the island. The bombardment lasted seven days, at the end of which the fort was reduced to rubble, with only one usable gun remaining. The men manning the Morris Island battery were forced to flee. But the federal ships could not get past Fort Moultrie and its associated batteries, and General

On December 26, 1860, Major Robert Anderson abandoned vulnerable Fort Moultrie and moved his small Union force to Fort Sumter in Charleston Harbor. Confederate forces then occupied Fort Moultrie, the site of a Revolutionary War battle. On April 12, 1861, the artillery positioned at the fort joined with each other batteries in bombarding Sumter. (National Park Service)

Beauregard refused to surrender Fort Sumter. This refusal encouraged further attacks on the fort until one of the monitors ran aground and was refloated only with the aid of its companion ships.

The next day, the navy put ashore a force of sailors and marines to seize Fort Sumter. (This was supposed to have been a joint army-navy project, but the commanders of the two forces could not agree on who should direct the attack.) What the Union forces did not realize was that the Confederates knew of their plans. When the Union

soldiers landed, they were mowed down by gunfire, and most of those who were not killed or injured were taken prisoner.

Union forces continued to make occasional jabs at Fort Sumter and Charleston, but there were no more official assaults. So it was not until April 14, 1865, roughly a month after the approach of Sherman's Union army had forced the evacuation of Charleston, that the fort finally came back under Federal control. The United States flag that had once flown over it had been retained by Anderson, who was on hand to see it raised over the fort he had defended in 1861.

Fort Sumter National Monument is four miles from Charleston Harbor and can be reached by Park Service tour boats that leave from the City Marina on Parkwood Drive and from the Naval Museum at Patriots Point in Mount Pleasant.

Much of the fort has been reconstructed but the ruins of the officers' and enlisted men's barracks still remain as do some of the guns used in its defense.

FIRST BATTLE OF BULL RUN (MANASSAS)—JULY 21, 1861

The day after the fall of Fort Sumter, Lincoln called for 75,000 state militia to reinforce the 15,000-man regular army to put down the rebellion. On July 4, 1861, Congress authorized the call for an additional 500,000 three-month volunteers.

The Confederate Congress authorized President Davis to take charge of military operations and to call out the states' militia and accept 100,000 volunteers for one-year service.

The sight of large bodies of troops, even if poorly trained, gave each side a sense of pride and confidence that it would be a short and victorious war.

Union troops poured into Washington, D.C., prepared to march south and end the war by taking the Confederate capital of Richmond, Virginia. The equally confident Confederate forces moved north to defend their new capital.

Lincoln was aware that his forces were not as yet prepared for a major battle but found it hard to resist the call of the press and public, "Forward to Richmond" and "The Rebel Congress must not be allowed to meet there on July 20."

More importantly, he had learned that a large Confederate army under Beauregard was moving north from Richmond and could pose a threat to Washington. He ordered Brigadier General Irvin McDowell to use his 39,000-man army to stop the Confederate advance, resulting in the first major battle of the Civil War.

Both sides, especially the North, were badly prepared. The officers had been promoted to positions beyond their abilities, and were unaccustomed to commanding units as large as those they were given. The top commanders lacked staff assistance to train raw troops to carry out directions rapidly during battle. McDowell was also under tremendous public and political pressure to defeat the rebels, and he had to do it quickly because a high percentage of his soldiers had volunteered for only three months of service and those three months were nearing an end.

McDowell started moving his army from Washington on July 16, 1861, heading toward the important railroad junction at Manassas. To get there, he intended to strike southward—at right angles to his line of march. This would bring him up against Beauregard's force at Blackburn's Ford.

Recognizing the encounter he was facing, Beauregard asked that the 12,000 men under Brigadier General Joseph E. Johnston at Winchester beyond the Blue Ridge join him. Johnston was being watched by an 18,000-man Union force just south of Harpers Ferry, but his observers proved negligent, because Johnston gave them the slip and began arriving undetected at Manassas Junction the day before McDowell opened battle. Johnston was also reinforced by the arrival of Brigadier General T. H. Holmes's brigade and Colonel Wade Hampton's Legion to bring his total force to about 32,232.

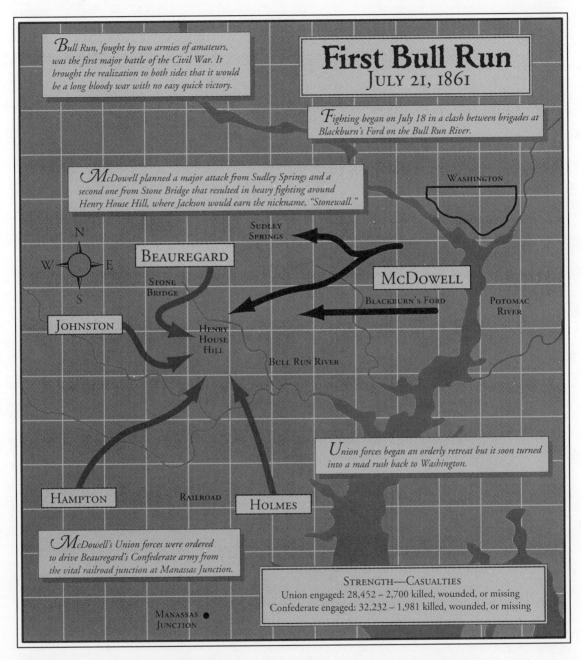

Bull Run, fought by two armies of amateurs, was the first major battle of the Civil War. It brought the realization to both sides that it would be a long bloody war with no easy quick victory.

First Bull Run
JULY 21, 1861

Fighting began on July 18 in a clash between brigades at Blackburn's Ford on the Bull Run River.

McDowell planned a major attack from Sudley Springs and a second one from Stone Bridge that resulted in heavy fighting around Henry House Hill, where Jackson would earn the nickname, "Stonewall."

WASHINGTON

N
W E
S

SUDLEY SPRINGS

BEAUREGARD

STONE BRIDGE

McDOWELL

JOHNSTON

HENRY HOUSE HILL

BLACKBURN'S FORD

POTOMAC RIVER

BULL RUN RIVER

Union forces began an orderly retreat but it soon turned into a mad rush back to Washington.

HAMPTON   RAILROAD   HOLMES

McDowell's Union forces were ordered to drive Beauregard's Confederate army from the vital railroad junction at Manassas Junction.

STRENGTH—CASUALTIES
Union engaged: 28,452 – 2,700 killed, wounded, or missing
Confederate engaged: 32,232 – 1,981 killed, wounded, or missing

MANASSAS ●
JUNCTION

In the meantime, McDowell changed his plans, and instead of marching directly toward Manassas, he sent most of his men westward. His plan now was to make his main attack at Sudley Springs, a secondary attack at Stone Bridge, and a feint at Blackburn's Ford. Nothing, however, worked out as planned. Neither Beauregard nor his subordinates were fooled by the feint at the ford nor the secondary attack

at the bridge: consequently, they shifted most of their men westward to meet the Union main force marching south on the Manassas-Sudley Road. At Henry House Hill, the fighting became violent.

The Confederate forces, under the direct command of Nathan Evans, Barnard Bee, and Francis Bartow, had a hard time holding back the Union forces until Bee rallied them around Brigadier General Jackson's newly arrived brigade. "There stands Jackson like a stone wall!" Bee shouted. "Rally behind the Virginians." At about this same time, Beauregard and Johnston arrived from their command post and helped revive the Southerners in the face of the heavy Union attack.

But while the Federals seemed on the verge of carrying the day, their attack began to unravel because it lacked organization. An hour's lull in the fighting did not improve matters. When the fighting resumed, with each force trying to drive the other from the hill, the Union troops were too tired to withstand the fresh

Confederate troops that were brought from the rear.

Shortly after 4 P.M. the Federals began to withdraw. At first they did so in an orderly fashion, but soon the retreat, led by the 90-day volunteers, turned into a rout. As they crossed Bull Run, they found the road to Washington jammed with Congressmen and others who had come out from the city to watch what almost all Northerners felt would be the first and last battle of the war. Thoroughly demoralized and exhausted, the soldiers did not stop retreating until they reached the Potomac River, 20 miles distant.

Before the battle, many soldiers on each side believed war would be an exciting lark where all would soon return home to a hero's welcome. They and their families would view war a bit differently when the casualties were added up.

Of the 28,452 Union troops engaged, 2,700 were killed, wounded, or missing. Similar casualties of the 32,232 Confederate forces amounted to 1,981.

The disaster at Bull Run was a blow to the North, shattering its hope to end the war with once decisive victory.

Now Lincoln's major concern was the defense of Washington. Large numbers of soldiers were assigned to this task and posters calling for volunteers often included in large type, "An Attack Upon Washington Anticipated."

Along with many others, Lincoln was now convinced the Union was in for a long war and would need more than short-term militiamen to win it. He ordered Major General George B. McClellan, who had made a name for himself by driving Confederate forces in what was to become West Virginia, to take command of the Union troops around Washington. This force would soon be known as "The Army of the Potomac."

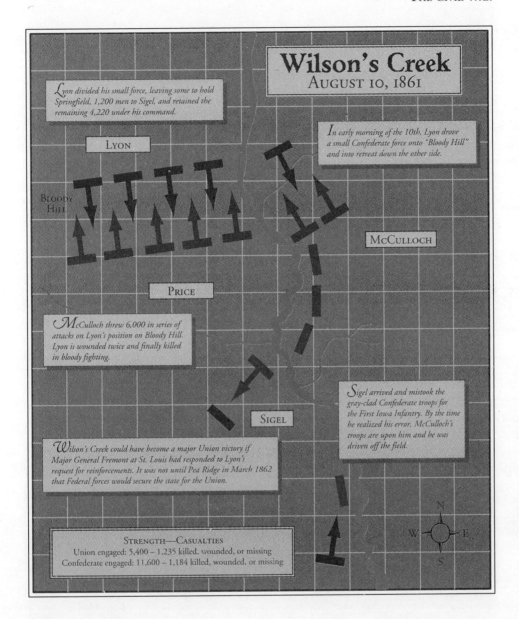

Wilson's Creek
AUGUST 10, 1861

Lyon divided his small force, leaving some to hold Springfield, 1,200 men to Sigel, and retained the remaining 4,220 under his command.

LYON

BLOODY HILL

In early morning of the 10th, Lyon drove a small Confederate force onto "Bloody Hill" and into retreat down the other side.

McCULLOCH

PRICE

McCulloch threw 6,000 in series of attacks on Lyon's position on Bloody Hill. Lyon is wounded twice and finally killed in bloody fighting.

SIGEL

Sigel arrived and mistook the gray-clad Confederate troops for the First Iowa Infantry. By the time he realized his error, McCulloch's troops are upon him and he was driven off the field.

Wilson's Creek could have become a major Union victory if Major General Fremont at St. Louis had responded to Lyon's request for reinforcements. It was not until Pea Ridge in March 1862 that Federal forces would secure the state for the Union.

STRENGTH—CASUALTIES
Union engaged: 5,400 – 1,235 killed, wounded, or missing
Confederate engaged: 11,600 – 1,184 killed, wounded, or missing

BATTLE OF WILSON'S CREEK— AUGUST 10, 1861

The battle at Wilson's Creek, the first battle of the war west of the Mississippi River, resulted from the desire of both North and South to control strategically important Missouri.

Like the people in Kentucky, most Missourians preferred neutrality but there was an active pro-Confederate group led by the state's governor, Clairborne F. Jackson, who had refused Lincoln's call for troops. Instead, Jackson ordered the state militia to Camp Jackson, outside St. Louis, intending to take the U.S. arsenal there.

RIFLES AND THE MINIÉ BALL

At the First Battle at Bull Run, both sides were armed with smooth-bore muzzle-loading muskets. Because these had an effective range of only 100 yards or so, attacking troops only had time to fire one volley before going ahead with bayonets.

The smooth-bore muskets were soon replaced with the muzzle-loading Springfield musket with a rifled barrel. Rifling caused the bullet to spin when leaving the muzzle, increasing accuracy and range.

The rifled musket was further improved by use of the famous "Minié bullet." Introduced to the French army by Captain Claude E. Minié, after whom it was named, this cylindrical bullet was made of relatively soft lead with a hollowed area at its base, and was small enough to be easily rammed down a rifled barrel. When fired, gas pressure at the base caused the bullet to expand and seal the bore. This gave the rifled weapon a deadly accurate range of over 200 yards and a killing range of up to 1,000. When the soft Minié ball struck a man it would expand, leaving a terrible wound.

Rate of fire was increased by incorporating the Minié ball into a paper cartridge. With this development, all the soldier had to do to reload was to bite

Top: The deadly .58 and .69 caliber Minié Bullet, which greatly increased the range of a muzzle-loading rifle or musket but created a dreadful wound.

Below: The .58 caliber William's "cleaner" bullet, the Confederate .57 and .69 caliber English bullet, and .58 caliber Gardner cartridge. (West Point Museum)

through the paper, pour the powder and ball down the barrel, add the wadded paper, and tamp with a ramrod.

By 1861, U.S. arsenals were producing standard muzzle-loading rifles well suited to the Minié ball. Confederate forces continued to use smooth-bore muskets until they were able to get rifled muskets from Europe or capture them from Union arsenals and Union soldiers.

The first breech-loaded rifle was developed at Harpers Ferry in 1859 and used by cavalry. Toward the end of the war, Union cavalry were often armed with the 16-shot Henry or the 7-shot Spencer carbines.

U.S. Army Special Model 1861 Colt .58 caliber rifle-musket. The Confederacy had limited means of producing such weapons and had to depend on imports from Europe and what their soldiers captured or took from the Union dead. (West Point Museum)

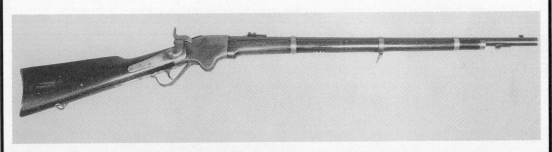

The Spencer .52 caliber breech-loading repeating rifled carbine was the first successful weapon of its type. Its magazine held seven cartridges that vastly increased Union soldiers' firepower. By 1864, it was the standard firearm of the United States Cavalry and later played an important role in the conquest of the West. (West Point Museum)

The commander of the St. Louis arsenal was aggressive, redheaded Unionist Captain Nathaniel Lyon. Captain Lyon was concerned about Jackson's intent and moved the arsenal's weapons across the river to safety in Illinois. Then he began raising an army.

On May 10, Lyon with 7,000 men marched on Camp Jackson, which promptly surrendered. From there he moved to take Jefferson City, the state capital, and by July 13, was encamped outside Springfield with 6,000 men and joined there by troops under Colonel Franz Sigel.

The pro-Confederate element had no intention of giving up Missouri and by August 10, Brigadier General Benjamin McCulloch and Major General Sterling

THE SWORD, SABER, AND CUTLASS

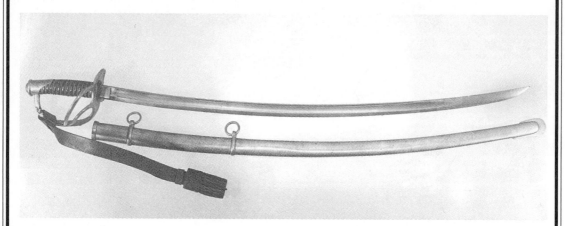

U.S. light cavalry saber, Model 1860. This slashing and piercing weapon was carried by officers and troopers and was augmented by the carbine and pistol. (West Point Museum)

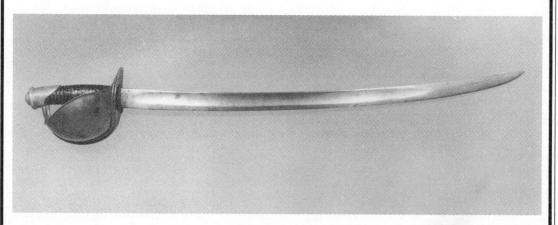

1860 model naval cutlass used by sailors in hand-to-hand fighting when boarding an enemy vessel or repulsing an enemy attack. (West Point Museum)

The sword is man's oldest manufactured metal weapon and is still carried today at formal military ceremonies. In the early years of the American Revolution, foot soldiers and officers carried swords. In the later years of the war, the ordinary soldier gave up the sword in favor of the bayonet. But officers, and many noncommissioned officers, continued to carry swords and this practice continued beyond the Civil War.

For the officer, the sword was more than a weapon; it stood for his rank and his honor. It was often a prized possession that had been in his family for years and passed down from one generation to the next. If forced to surrender, the officer in command of the defeated force would offer his sword to the victorious commander who would accept it and usually immediately return it.

This custom was breached, however, on September 6, 1781, when the American leader Colonel William Ledyard surrendered his force at Fort Griswold, Connecticut, to Lieutenant Colonel Bushkirk, commander of the Tory force. Bushkirk accepted the sword and then promptly ran the blade into Ledyard, killing him.

Swords would play a far more positive role at the surrender of Appomattox on April 9, 1865.

As General Grant was writing the terms of surrender, he was certainly aware of the magnificent dress sword General Lee was wearing for this unpleasant occasion. It had been a gift to the general from some of his many admirers.

The sight of Lee's sword may have prompted Grant to include in the surrender terms that Confederate officers would be allowed to retain their "sidearms"—or swords. This consideration on Grant's part would help heal the wounds of the war, for when the Confederate officer returned home, the sword at his side announced that while the South had lost the war, it had not lost its honor.

In all wars fought on American soil up to and including the Civil War, the sword may not have been an essential weapon but it served in other important functions. Many a battle in these wars was won by troops inspired by their commander, astride his horse, waving his sword, and calling for his men to rally and mount another attack.

At the Battle of Gettysburg, Brigadier General Lewis Armistead led the attack on the Union line, cheering his troops long with his cap on the point of his raised sword.

No two fine swords were identical, which may account for some of the sword's mystique, but a typical eighteenth- and nineteenth-century weapon had a single- or double-edge blade, pointed at the tip, around 30 to 39 inches long and $1/2$ to $1^3/4$ inch width. With its hilt, the sword weighed around a pound.

Blades of fine swords were forged in Toledo, Spain; Soligen, Germany; and other foreign centers famous for quality steel. Sword hilts and hand guards, however, were made locally and then attached to the blade. Hilts and hand guards came in many different shapes, the more common being the simple cross bar, the stirrup, and wire basket. Some of them were very elaborate and even studded with jewels. Many fine expensive swords were worn just for show but the ordinary kind were used in battles of the Revolution and Civil War where officers fought with their swords along with their men with bayonets.

While the sword was designed for piercing and cutting, the saber was meant for slashing. The single-edge saber blade was either straight or curved and generally around $1^1/2$ inches in width. The blade length was around 36 inches giving the saber an overall length of 40 inches or over and weight up to about 2 pounds. The saber was the weapon of the horse soldier, dragoon, and cavalry, for it could strike at a man on the ground as well as one on horseback. Sabers continued to be an important cavalry weapon in the Civil War although some troops turned to the revolver and carbine.

The U.S. Cavalry was equipped with sabers during the Plains Indian Wars of the post–Civil War period. The Indians had considerable respect for the "long knives" and some authorities suggest that Custer should have allowed his men to take their sabers when they rode into the Little Bighorn Valley in June of 1876.

The Cutlass was a short version of the saber. The single-edge blade was from 19 to 32 inches long and around $1^1/2$ inches in width. Its weight was from 1 to 2 pounds. This weapon was favored by sailors and was very handy for close-in fighting when boarding an enemy ship and repelling an enemy boarding party. But the cutlass belonged to the age of wood sail warships, and the introduction of the iron steam-drive warships ended its use.

Price, commander of the state guard, with a force of over 12,000 men were moving along Telegraph Road toward Springfield.

Lyon, now a brigadier general, found himself in a difficult position. His request for reinforcements had been denied by Major General John Fremont, Union Commander of the Western Department. Lyon decided to seize the initiative and attack McCulloch's superior-size force.

Lyon divided his small army into three parts, one of which he left behind in Springfield, Missouri, to guard the city. The second unit, with 4,200 men, was commanded by Lyon.

Marching down the west side of Wilson's Creek, Lyon hit a small Confederate cavalry unit at dawn and drove it onto what came to be known as Bloody Hill and down the other side. He almost immediately came under fire from Confederate artillery across the creek but managed to hold his strategic position.

When the shooting started at Bloody Hill, Sigel, who was east of Wilson's Creek and about two miles farther south, hit the Confederates' main camp. The surprised Southerners fled, and for the moment, the Federals claimed victory. But not for long.

Regrouping his forces, McCulloch first went after Sigel. The latter mistook the advancing Rebels for an Iowa infantry unit that also wore gray and allowed them to approach. The result was disaster for the Federals, who fled the field.

Then McCulloch launched a series of major attacks against Bloody Hill. The first three were turned back, but the fourth was made in mid-morning by 6,000 Southerners drawn up in a 1,000-yard line. In places, they advanced to within 20 feet of the Federals, who were fighting shoulder to shoulder; but they could go no farther and

finally withdrew down the hill. The Northerners, however, were exhausted and running out of ammunition. General Lyon had been killed, becoming the first Union general to fall in the Civil War. Their comrades, fighting under Sigel, were nowhere to be seen.

What was left of Lyon's brave force retired to Springfield, leaving the battered Confederates to claim victory, even though by a narrow margin.

It had been a small but fiercely fought battle. Union losses were 1,235 out of the 5,400 engaged. Confederate casualties were 1,184 out of 11,600 troops engaged.

Soon after the battle, the pro-Confederate members of the Missouri State Legislature passed an ordinance of secession. The pro-Union members declared the state would remain in the Union, so for a time, Missouri had two state governments with representatives in both the United States and Confederate Congresses.

The battle of Pea Ridge on March 6, 1862, would ensure that Missouri remained in the Union.

BATTLE OF FORT DONELSON— FEBRUARY 12–16, 1862

By the beginning of 1862, Lincoln had become impatient with the progress of the war and issued War Order No. 1, which directed all union military units to make a joint move against the Confederates on February 22. Major General Henry W. Halleck, who was at that time in command of the Department of Missouri; Brigadier General Ulysses S. Grant; and Flag Officer Andrew Foote of the navy were in favor of attacking the Confederate forts guarding the Tennessee and Cumberland rivers just south of the Kentucky-Tennessee line.

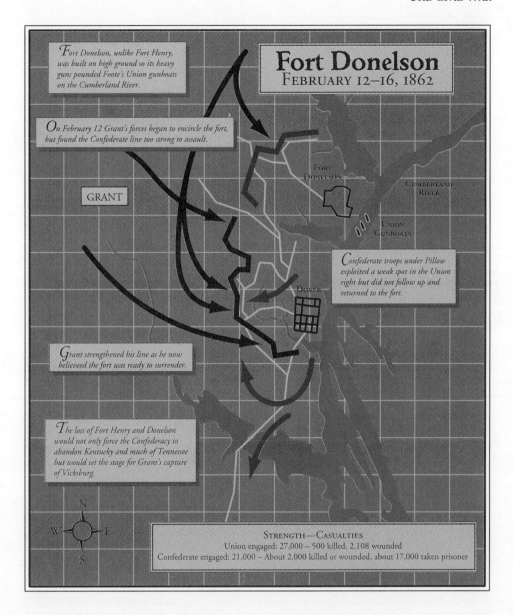

Fort Donelson, unlike Fort Henry, was built on high ground so its heavy guns pounded Foote's Union gunboats on the Cumberland River.

On February 12 Grant's forces began to encircle the fort, but found the Confederate line too strong to assault.

Fort Donelson
FEBRUARY 12–16, 1862

GRANT

FORT DONELSON

CUMBERLAND RIVER

UNION GUNBOATS

Confederate troops under Pillow exploited a weak spot in the Union right but did not follow up and returned to the fort.

DOVER

Grant strengthened his line as he now believed the fort was ready to surrender.

The loss of Fort Henry and Donelson would not only force the Confederacy to abandon Kentucky and much of Tennessee but would set the stage for Grant's capture of Vicksburg.

N
W   E
S

STRENGTH—CASUALTIES
Union engaged: 27,000 – 500 killed, 2,108 wounded
Confederate engaged: 21,000 – About 2,000 killed or wounded, about 17,000 taken prisoner

On February 5, while Grant was still bringing up his troops, Foote, with four ironclads supported by three unarmored gunboats, began shelling Fort Henry on the Tennessee River. The fort was on low ground; the river was almost at flood stage. As a result, the guns in the fort had to fire up at the boats. Even so, they scored 59 hits.

But the boats were not seriously damaged and brought the fort to its knees—but only after the 1,500 Confederate troops in it had escaped to Fort Donelson.

Donelson, about 11 miles away on the Cumberland River, was next, in the federal army's path. This time, Grant was determined that no Confederates would escape, and he set out to encircle the fort completely. General A. S. Johnston, who commanded the Confederacy's western army, was equally determined that the Union would not prevail. He reinforced the garrison so it numbered about 20,000, and placed Brigadier General John Buchanan Floyd in command, supported by troops under Brigadier Generals Johnson Pillow and Simon Bolivar Buckner. Of the three generals, only Buckner was a trained officer.

Johnston had also ordered Colonel Nathen Bedford Forrest to bring his cavalry to help defend Fort Donelson.

On February 12, the Union ironclad *Carondelet* arrived at Donelson and lobbed a few shells into it. The next day, as Grant continued his encirclement of the fort, *Carondelet* made an all-out attack.

But unlike Fort Henry, Fort Donelson was on high ground and had heavy batteries on three levels.

On February 14, at 3 P.M., Foote arrived with three more ironclads, and the four boats attacked Donelson as they had Fort Henry. But within 90 minutes, two of the boats were forced out of action with damaged steering gear. The remaining two, taking the brunt of the action, were driven off. Each of the boats had been hit at least 30 times.

The following morning, as Grant and Foote were on a gunboat discussing their next move. Pillow hit the union right and by noon had broken through the line, opening a route to Nashville.

The fort's three generals now had the choice of using all available men to exploit Pillow's victory and strike at Grant's entire line or abandon the fort and save the 20,000 men by marching to Nashville. After some heated discussion, Floyd decided to do neither and ordered Pillow to bring his men back into the fort.

But it was then decided that further defense of Donelson was hopeless. Floyd, who had been President Buchanan's secretary of war, was afraid that if captured he would be tried for treason, and escaped from the fort after turning over command to Pillow, who joined him after giving the command over to Buckner. Their behavior finished Floyd's and Pillow's military careers.

Forrest obtained permission to take his cavalry to safety, leaving Buckner to face the music alone.

On the morning of the sixteenth, he sent a message to Grant asking him to name a delegation to negotiate surrender terms. He was both surprised and shocked at his old friend and West Point schoolmate's reply, "No terms except unconditional surrender can be accepted. I propose to move immediately on your works."

Buckner had no choice but to accept these harsh terms and surrendered his fort with around 14,000 men and 40 pieces of artillery.

Casualties had been relatively light. Of Grant's 27,000, 500 were killed and 2,108 wounded. Confederate losses were 2,000 killed 17,000 taken prisoner from the 21,000 engaged.

His victory at Fort Donelson gave U.S. Grant a new nickname, "Unconditional Surrender Grant." The loss of Forts Henry and Donelson would soon force the Confederates to abandon Kentucky and much of Tennessee and set the stage for the Union gaining control of the Mississippi River.

BATTLE OF PEA RIDGE— MARCH 7–8, 1862

During the first year of the Civil War, the Union and Confederacy struggled to

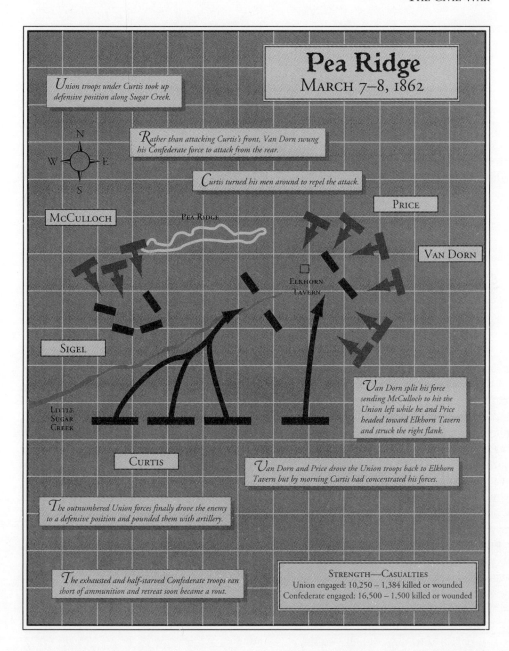

Pea Ridge
MARCH 7–8, 1862

*U*nion troops under Curtis took up defensive position along Sugar Creek.

*R*ather than attacking Curtis's front, Van Dorn swung his Confederate force to attack from the rear.

*C*urtis turned his men around to repel the attack.

PRICE

McCULLOCH

PEA RIDGE

VAN DORN

SIGEL

ELKHORN TAVERN

*V*an Dorn split his force sending McCulloch to hit the Union left while he and Price headed toward Elkhorn Tavern and struck the right flank.

LITTLE SUGAR CREEK

CURTIS

*V*an Dorn and Price drove the Union troops back to Elkhorn Tavern but by morning Curtis had concentrated his forces.

*T*he outnumbered Union forces finally drove the enemy to a defensive position and pounded them with artillery.

*T*he exhausted and half-starved Confederate troops ran short of ammunition and retreat soon became a rout.

STRENGTH—CASUALTIES
Union engaged: 10,250 – 1,384 killed or wounded
Confederate engaged: 16,500 – 1,500 killed or wounded

control Missouri, a border state that had allegiances to both sides. This struggle continued throughout the war but was waged principally by guerrillas. Only a few real battles were fought, the largest at Pea Ridge in Arkansas.

When Brigadier General Samuel R. Curtis was appointed commander of Federal forces in the Southwestern District of Missouri at the end of 1861, he immediately set out to push all Confederate forces out of the state. Within a few weeks, he

RONCLADS

At the beginning of the Civil War, conventional warships of all nations were constructed of wood, even those that were steam driven. In April 1861, when Union forces abandoned the Norfolk Navy Yard, they burned and scuttled the 40-gun frigate *Merrimac*, rather than allow it to be taken by the Confederates.

The Confederates raised the hull and transformed it into a heavily armored vessel. The hull was cut down, a barn-shaped superstructure added and the ship was equipped with six 9-inch smoothbore and four rifled cannon. The hull and superstructure were sheathed with 4-inch-thick wrought iron and a long wrought iron ram was attached to the bow.

On March 9, 1862, this formidable warship, renamed *Virginia*, but still referred to as *Merrimac*, sailed out of Norfolk to attack U.S. warships at Hampton Roads. The U.S. war ships' cannonball just bounced off *Merrimac*'s armor and in a few hours she had achieved a stunning victory. The 30-gun USS *Cumberland* had been sunk and 50-gun USS *Congress* was so heavily damaged that she surrendered. Only low tide prevented the *Merrimac* from destroying the 50-gun USS *Minnesota* so she returned to Norfolk and planned to finish off the federal ship on the following morning. When *Merrimac* arrived at Hampton Roads the next day, she was surprised to find the *Minnesota* protected by a mighty strange looking craft, USS *Monitor.*

If *Merrimac* was herself different from conventional warships, the *Monitor* was even more so. Designed by the Swedish inventor, John Ericsson, who had persuaded the Federal Navy to build her, this heavily armored vessel well suited her nickname, "Cheesebox on a raft." The hull was below waterline so that her armored deck was awash and only the 9-foot-high rotating turret and small pilot house exposed. The turret was covered with 8 inches of iron plates and housed two eleven-inch smooth-bores.

Monitor had left New York on March 6, and bad weather had slowed her progress, but she arrived on Hampton Roads in time for a historic battle with *Merrimac.* On the morning of March 9, these two ironclads poured cannon fire on each other, but neither was able to inflict much damage—cannonballs just could not penetrate the ships' heavy armor. After about two hours of fighting, *Monitor* had to withdraw to secure more ammunition, then the battle continued. *Merrimac* began concentrating her fire on *Monitor*'s pilot house and commander Lieutenant Lorimer Worden was wounded. *Monitor* withdrew and shortly afterward *Merrimac* returned to Norfolk.

The outcome of the battle between the two ironclads may have been inconclusive, though North and South claimed victory. But the Union was the actual winner as it ended the threat of *Merrimac* sailing north to destroy Union warships and attack coastal defenses and cities. The battle had also, in a matter of hours, made all warships obsolete as navies around the world rushed the construction of ironclad vessels.

This engagement would be the only time when either *Monitor* or *Merrimac* saw action. *Merrimac* was destroyed by the Confederates when they vacated Norfolk on May 9, 1862, because it was not seaworthy enough to move to another coastal port. *Monitor* was lost in a gale off Cape Hatteras on December 31, 1862, while being towed North.

A few years ago, divers located the *Monitor* in water off Cape Hatteras, North Carolina, and left it undisturbed; it is now a protected site.

Union forces in the western theater had already begun to use armor to protect river gunboats, an important tactical component where so many campaigns took place in areas served by navigable rivers, which were used to support land troops, destroy enemy fortifications, and protect river transport of men and materials.

At the attack on Fort Henry in early December 1862, Flag Officer Andrew Foote observed that the low position of the fort's cannon would force them to fire on his gunboat's armored prows. When Foote attacked the fort, his gunboats sustained almost 60 hits, which did little harm, while their fire tore into the defenders and their earthworks.

succeeded in chasing Confederate troops under Major General Price into the Boston Mountains of northern Arkansas, where he was joined by Brigadier General McCulloch and Major General Earl Van Dorn. Van Dorn took charge, and at the head of a 16,000-man army, he headed north toward Pea Ridge, where Curtis, with 10,250 men, had dug into the rough terrain along Sugar Creek.

Disliking the prospect of battling the entrenched Federals, Van Dorn decided to swing northward around them and attack the Federal rear on March 7. But his men were tired and fell behind schedule; Curtis, learning of Van Dorn's movements, turned his troops completely around to face north.

Now it was Van Dorn's turn to change plans. Instead of hitting the Federals in one great assault, he split his force. McCulloch was to swing around the west end of Pea Ridge toward Leetown and the Federal left; Price and Van Dorn were to swing around the east end of the ridge toward Elkhorn Tavern and the Federal right.

McCulloch's force, which included two regiments of Cherokee Indians, did not fare well. At first, they took a Federal battery and cavalry unit, but a little later, McCulloch was killed; then his second in command, Brigadier General James McIntosh, was mortally wounded and still later, the ranking colonel was captured. Stripped of their leaders, the Confederate foot soldiers scattered.

Price and Van Dorn were more successful. After softening up the Federals with cannon fire, the Confederate infantry moved in and slowly but steadily drove the Northerners back to Elkhorn Tavern. There, during the night, Curtis concentrated his forces. At the same time, Price and Van Dorn were being reinforced by many of the men who had been with McCulloch. In all, the Confederates outnumbered the Federals at Elkhorn Tavern by almost 3,000 men. But the Confederates were exhausted by marching and fighting without enough food, and they could not hold back the Federal attack the next day.

The Confederates had formed into a defensive "V." But as they were hammered by the Federal artillery, and as the Federal infantry wheeled in toward them, thus forming their own "V," the Confederates began to fall back. When they ran short of ammunition, the retreat became a rout, with men in gray scattering in every direction.

Out of the 10,250 Union troops engaged, 1,384 were casualties. The larger Confederate force of between 14,000 and 16,500 lost around 1,500 men.

The Union victory ended any future threat of the Confederates' retaking Missouri. The state was now solidly in Union hands and would remain so, despite some minor battles and guerrilla skirmishes.

BATTLE OF GLORIETA PASS— MARCH 26–28, 1862

In the summer of 1861, President Jefferson Davis ordered Brigadier General Henry H. Sibley to raise a brigade of Texas volunteers

*B*UTTERFIELD'S LULLABY

In the Civil War, as in other wars before the age of electronics, armies depended on the drum and especially the bugle to communicate orders from the commander to his men.

In 1860, the U.S. army had several dozen different bugle calls to direct tactics and regulate camp life. The most familiar battle call was the "Charge," the two most common in camp life were "Reveille," sounded in the morning, and the last call at night, "Lights Out."

Union Brigadier General Daniel Butterfield, who composed bugle calls, believed that the army's official "Lights Out" call was too harsh and martial sounding to put his civilians-turned-soldiers into the proper frame of mind for a good night's sleep. In 1862, he wrote another call to replace "Lights Out" and gave it to his bugler to play.

When his soldiers first heard the sad and strangely haunting notes of the new call, they seemed to be saying, "Go to sleep—all is well." It established just the mood that Butterfield wanted, and his men soon began to refer to it as "Butterfield's Lullaby." Commanders and buglers of nearby brigades heard it, liked it, and it spread through the army. It soon became the official call for "Lights Out," now called "Taps."

"Taps" today is primarily associated with loss, and is sounded at funerals and at ceremonies honoring war dead.

As of 1995, there were still a few former soldiers who remembered its original purpose. In the early months of World War II, there were still buglers who would play "Taps" at night. The sad and lovely sound brought much comfort to those new soldiers, so far away from loved ones and home, so afraid of what the future might hold. To them, the bugler was not playing of death but rather a lullaby telling all in hearing distance, "Go to sleep—all is well."

---

and march west to bring the territory of New Mexico into the Confederacy, and continue to open a route to the silver and gold mines of California and Colorado.

By January of 1862, Sibley's Army of New Mexico, consisting of 2,500 mounted infantry, had reached New Mexico and on February 21, engaged 3,800 Union troops under Colonel Edward Canby, who had marched from their base at Fort Craig, between Albuquerque and El Paso.

A brief battle took place at Valverde and the defeated Union troops returned to Fort Craig.

The Texans continued north and in early March had occupied Albuquerque and Sante Fe to discover that the supplies Sibley expected to find had been destroyed before Union troops had abandoned the area.

Sibley then went for the Federal supply depot at Fort Union, about sixty miles northeast of Sante Fe on the Santa Fe Trail.

On March 1, Colonel John Slough with 900 Colorado volunteers arrived at Fort Union and ordered the garrison to join in stopping the Confederate offensive.

On March 22, he moved out of the fort with 1,340 men and headed towards Sibley's force in the area of Santa Fe.

On March 26, a Confederate advance guard under Major Charles D. Pyron clashed with a Union advance guard under Major John M. Chivington about a mile west of Glorieta Pass on the Santa Fe Trail. When Chivington's men outflanked the Confederates by climbing the hills bordering the trail, the Confederates withdrew westward. But instead of avoiding trouble, they found

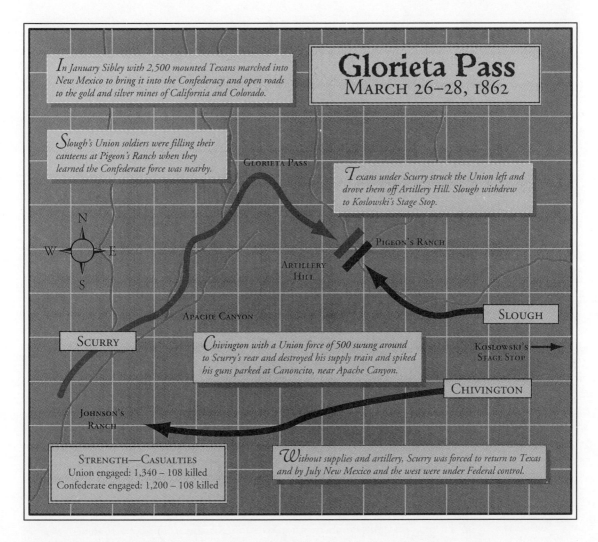

Glorieta Pass
MARCH 26–28, 1862

In January Sibley with 2,500 mounted Texans marched into New Mexico to bring it into the Confederacy and open roads to the gold and silver mines of California and Colorado.

Slough's Union soldiers were filling their canteens at Pigeon's Ranch when they learned the Confederate force was nearby.

GLORIETA PASS

Texans under Scurry struck the Union left and drove them off Artillery Hill. Slough withdrew to Koslowski's Stage Stop.

PIGEON'S RANCH

ARTILLERY HILL

SLOUGH

APACHE CANYON

SCURRY

KOSLOWSKI'S STAGE STOP

Chivington with a Union force of 500 swung around to Scurry's rear and destroyed his supply train and spiked his guns parked at Canoncito, near Apache Canyon.

CHIVINGTON

JOHNSON'S RANCH

STRENGTH—CASUALTIES
Union engaged: 1,340 – 108 killed
Confederate engaged: 1,200 – 108 killed

Without supplies and artillery, Scurry was forced to return to Texas and by July New Mexico and the west were under Federal control.

themselves almost encircled and beset from every side. At what became known as the Battle of Apache Canyon, the Confederates lost almost 100 men when day ended. Even so, they managed to retreat to safety.

The next day was quiet. But on March 28 the Confederates left their large supply train at their camp at Canoncito and marched eastward to do battle with the Federal force, which was marching westward from its camp at Koslowski's Stage Stop. Now 1,200 strong, the Confederates were commanded by Lieutenant Colonel

William R. Scurry. Colonel Slough's Federal force numbered about 850 men, plus two four-gun artillery companies.

The battle opened at 11 A.M. near Pigeon's Ranch, a mile east of Glorieta Pass. Having learned from the fight at Apache Canyon, the Confederates outflanked the Federals by climbing the hillsides above them, and after six hours, Slough broke off the action and retired once again to Koslowski's Stage Stop. The Confederates, left in possession of the battlefield, felt that they had scored a triumph. But the victory was short lived, as they received word that their supply camp had been destroyed.

While the fight was raging at the pass, Chivington, unbeknownst to the Confederates, had marched cross-country with a force of about 500 men toward Johnson's Ranch and then to the Confederate camp at Canoncito, near Apache Canyon. There, the men roped themselves down the steep slopes to the valley, where they drove off or captured the few men on guard. Unable to take the supplies with them, they destroyed the 80-wagon supply train, including all the horses and mules, reserve ammunition, and food.

With no supplies left to subsist on or fight with, the Confederates were compelled to withdraw completely from the area and escape southward.

The Confederate forces never recovered from the catastrophe. They continued to retreat, with the Federal troops close on their heels, until they eventually returned to Texas, where most of the men had come from.

For a two-day battle, casualties on each side were relatively light. Union lost 108 of the 1,340 engaged. Confederate losses were the same out of 1,200 engaged.

The Battle of Glorieta Pass has become known as the "Gettysburg of the West" for in both instances, Confederate invasion of Union-held territory ended in defeat.

Battle of Shiloh— April 6–7, 1862

Grant's capture of Fort Henry and Fort Donaldson in February 1862 broke the northwestern Confederate defense line and cut the east-west rail line between Nashville and Memphis.

Grant now intended to move south to destroy the Confederate forces around Corinth, Mississippi. But in early March he had a run-in with his superior, Major General Henry ("Old Brains") Halleck, now commander of the Department of the Mississippi, headquartered at St. Louis. Halleck more or less gave Grant's Army of the Tennessee to Major General C. T. Smith, who moved it to Pittsburg Landing on the south side of the Tennessee River.

By March 17, Halleck and Grant had pretty well patched up their differences. Grant resumed command of his army and was ordered to wait at headquarters at Savannah, across the river from Pittsburg Landing, for the arrival of Brigadier General Don Carlos Buell, who was marching very slowly from Nashville, with his 50,000-man Army of the Ohio.

Grant's army was now encamped in the vicinity of Shiloh Church, a couple of miles or so inland from Pittsburg Landing and nine miles from Savannah.

General A. S. Johnston, with General P.G.T. Beauregard as second in command, assembled an army of around 40,000, consisting of Major Generals William Hardee's and Braxton Bragg's corps and additional troops under Major General Leonidas Polk and Brigadier General John C. Breckinridge. On April 3, the force left Corinth for the 20-mile march to Shiloh.

The Union divisions at that time were loosely spread about the vicinity of Shiloh Methodist Church. Each division had made camp in any spot they found suitable, without regard for its tactical value in event of an attack. Brigadier Generals William T. Sherman's and John McClernand's divisions were on the right, near the Shiloh Church, while divisions under Brigadier Generals W.H.L. Wallace and Stephen Hurlbut were on the left, with Brigadier General Benjamin Prentiss some distance in front of them.

The clearing around Shiloh Church and

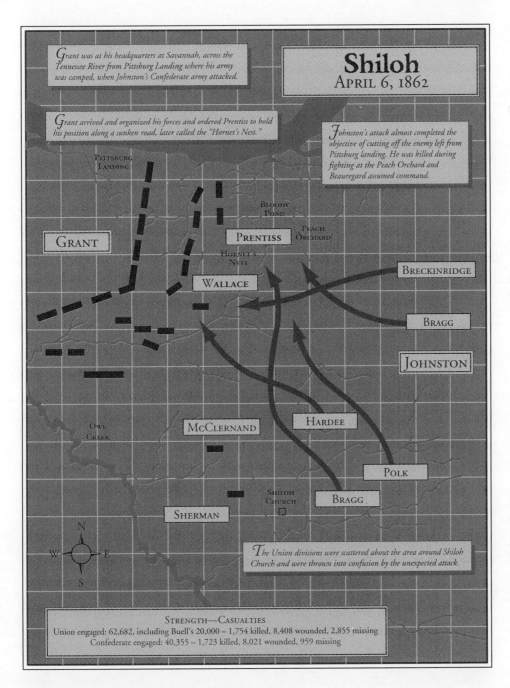

Grant was at his headquarters at Savannah, across the Tennessee River from Pittsburg Landing where his army was camped, when Johnston's Confederate army attacked.

Grant arrived and organized his forces and ordered Prentiss to hold his position along a sunken road, later called the "Hornet's Nest."

Johnston's attack almost completed the objective of cutting off the enemy left from Pittsburg landing. He was killed during fighting at the Peach Orchard and Beauregard assumed command.

Shiloh
APRIL 6, 1862

PITTSBURG LANDING

BLOODY POND

PEACH ORCHARD

GRANT

PRENTISS

HORNET'S NEST

WALLACE

BRECKINRIDGE

BRAGG

JOHNSTON

HARDEE

McCLERNAND

OWL CREEK

POLK

SHILOH CHURCH

BRAGG

SHERMAN

The Union divisions were scattered about the area around Shiloh Church and were thrown into confusion by the unexpected attack.

STRENGTH—CASUALTIES
Union engaged: 62,682, including Buell's 20,000 – 1,754 killed, 8,408 wounded, 2,855 missing
Confederate engaged: 40,355 – 1,723 killed, 8,021 wounded, 959 missing

its immediate area consisted of small farms and orchards. The surrounding terrain was covered with dense woods and underbrush, along with swamps, creeks, and ravines. There were few roads, many no more than trails.

Grant and his commanders believed they would have to go to Corinth to get at

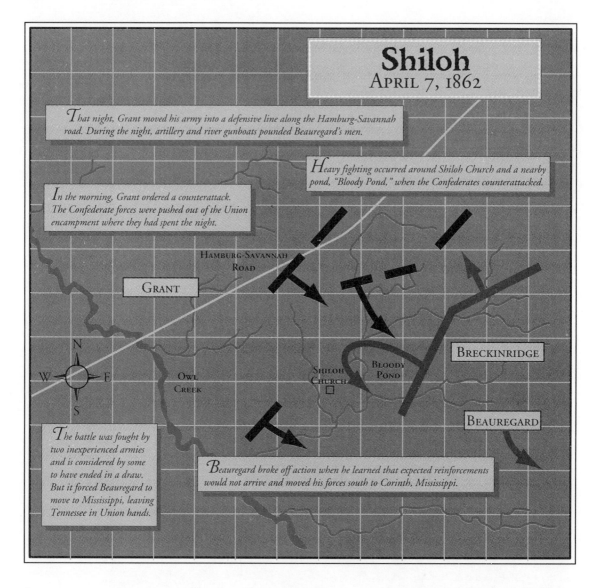

Shiloh
APRIL 7, 1862

That night, Grant moved his army into a defensive line along the Hamburg-Savannah road. During the night, artillery and river gunboats pounded Beauregard's men.

Heavy fighting occurred around Shiloh Church and a nearby pond, "Bloody Pond," when the Confederates counterattacked.

In the morning, Grant ordered a counterattack. The Confederate forces were pushed out of the Union encampment where they had spent the night.

HAMBURG-SAVANNAH ROAD

GRANT

N
W   E
S

OWL CREEK

SHILOH CHURCH

BLOODY POND

BRECKINRIDGE

BEAUREGARD

The battle was fought by two inexperienced armies and is considered by some to have ended in a draw. But it forced Beauregard to move to Mississippi, leaving Tennessee in Union hands.

Beauregard broke off action when he learned that expected reinforcements would not arrive and moved his forces south to Corinth, Mississippi.

Johnston and did not consider the possibility that he might attack them at Pittsburg Landing. Few divisions sent out scouts or posted pickets. There was not much effort made to dig entrenchments, because, in the early years of the war, most officers believed defenses were more hindrance than help.

Johnston planned to attack on the fourth, but his inexperienced troops moved so slowly that it was April 6 before the army was in position to take on the Yankees.

Despite the fact that the Confederate army had camped the night of the fifth only a mile or so from the Union position, the attack that began around 6:00 A.M. came as a surprise. Many of the men were cooking or eating breakfast and some were still asleep in their bedrolls. Grant, of course, was nine miles away at Savannah.

Johnston's original plan was to make a concentrated attack on the left to cut the Union force off from Pittsburg Landing and roll it into the swamps north and west of the landing in the areas around Owl Creek.

Beauregard, who was to direct the attack, had other ideas, so instead of following Johnston's plan, he ordered a general frontal attack along the entire Union line.

Hardee, with some of General Bragg's force, hit Sherman and McClernand, driving them to the rear and occupying Shiloh Church. Breckinridge, Polk, and the remaining troops of Bragg's command struck the Union left held by Prentiss, Hurlbut, and W.H.L. Wallace. Prentiss was driven back all the way to Hurlbut's position, adding to the general confusion.

By this time, the Union forces were becoming disorganized. At his headquarters on the steamer *Tigress*, docked near Savannah, Grant heard the sound of battle and immediately left for the battlefield, but not before sending a message to General Lewis Wallace at Crump's Landing to come with his division. Grant also ordered Major General William Nelson of Buell's army to bring his division into the battle.

By 7:30 A.M., when Grant arrived on the scene, he found a confused situation. There was no single battle, but rather a series of small ones. The troops on each side were inexperienced so command often broke down and groups of soldiers fought as they saw fit.

Grant talked with his commanders in an effort to restore some sort of order. He ordered Prentiss and Wallace to hold their positions at all cost. Prentiss's position was along a sunken road, later named the "Hornet's Nest."

Further to the left, Johnston was directing a series of attacks on Union troops, holding the areas around the Peach Orchard. Around 2:30 P.M. Johnston was killed and Beauregard took over command of the Confederate forces.

The 6,000 or so Union troops holding the Hornet's Nest were under heavy attack by Bragg. Instead of mounting a major attack in force, Bragg continued to attack piecemeal. Prentiss and Wallace were able to hold on for seven and a half hours in spite of repeated attacks and pounding by 62 Confederate cannon. At 5:30 P.M. the Union attempted to withdraw, but it was too late. Wallace was killed and Prestiss was forced to surrender with the 2,100 men that remained of his division.

Beauregard advanced almost to Pittsburg Landing, but his forces were stopped by Union artillery on the heights and from river gunboats.

Grant established a strong defense line along the Hamburg-Savannah Road and placed 53 cannon nearby on Dill's Branch.

Confederate forces made an attack on the Union line that required them to climb down a 65-foot-high bluff, cross a swamp, and climb the banks on the far side, where they faced the 53 cannon and 20,000 or so Union troops. Some of Beauregard's men did reach the top but were soon driven back.

After this final assault, Beauregard broke off further action, intending to finish off Grant the next day. Beauregard believed that Buell would not arrive in time to reinforce Grant, but he expected to be strengthened by 20,000 troops under Major General Earl Van Dorn coming north from Arkansas.

Confederate forces spent the night in the campsites previously occupied by Grant's divisions.

April 6 had been a good day for the South, all but destroying one Union division and badly mauling the other four. But there was trouble ahead for Beauregard.

The National Cemetery at Shiloh stands on a bluff overlooking Pittsburg Landing and the Tennessee River. The 10-acre cemetery contains the graves of 3,746 men, 2,370 of which are those of soldiers killed in surrounding battles. (National Park Service)

During the rainy night his men were kept awake by Union artillery pounding their position and morning found Grant's army reinforced by the arrival of Buell and Lew Wallace.

Supported by these fresh divisions, Grant ordered an attack the following morning that initially regained most of the ground lost the previous day. Beauregard launched a savage counterattack, driving Union troops back to the peach orchard.

Bitter fighting continued for hours in the dense undergrowth at the crossroads area near Shiloh Church, and little by little the superior-size Union force pushed the enemy back.

Around 2:00 P.M., Beauregard ordered one last counterattack at Water Oaks Pond, "Bloody Pond," and then, on learning that Van Dorn was not coming to his aid, broke off action and withdrew south toward Corinth, Mississippi.

Grant's impulse was to pursue and defeat Beauregard before he could reach Corinth but "had not the heart to order the men who had fought desperately for two days, lying in mud and rain whenever not fighting" to immediately go after Beauregard. Grant also did not believe he had the authority to order Buell to go after Beauregard.

The battle of Shiloh, or, as it is sometimes called, Pittsburg Landing, had been a mean and bloody fight, the largest battle so far in the war. In less than two days, the Union army of some 62,682 suffered 13,017 casualties and the smaller Confederate force of 40,355 had 10,703 casualties.

The outcome of the battle is sometimes described as a draw but actually it was a decisive Union victory. It ended Confederate hopes of gaining control of the iron-producing regions of Tennessee and opened the way for a Union attack on the important rail center of Corinth.

After the battle, Grant was criticized for allowing his army to be surprised at Shiloh. Word even went around that Grant was drunk at his headquarters in Savannah when the Confederates attacked. This rumor may have originated with Halleck, no friend of Grant's, who had recently written to McClellan that Grant was "up to his old bad habits."

But when Lincoln was urged by some to dismiss Grant after Shiloh, he replied, "I can't spare this man—he fights."

ATTACK ON FORT PULASKI— APRIL 10–11, 1862

Construction of Fort Pulaski on Cockspur Island was begun by the federal government after the War of 1812 to guard the river approaches to Savannah, Georgia. The massive brick structure, covering about five acres of the low marshy island, was named in honor of Count Casimir Pulaski, the Polish hero of the American Revolution who had been mortally wounded during the unsuccessful attack on Savannah in 1779.

Between its thick walls and the fact that the nearest solid ground suitable for heavy siege guns was Big Tybee Island, too far away to be effective, Fort Pulaski was believed by many to be unbreachable. Joseph G. Totten, U.S. Chief of Army Engineers had proclaimed that "you might as well bombard the Rocky Mountains."

When the Civil War began, the fort's armament was still not completed and the entire garrison consisted of a sergeant and a caretaker.

On January 3, 1861, two weeks after South Carolina seceded from the Union, the Georgia militia seized the fort and after Georgia seceded on January 19, transferred it to the Confederate States of America.

Late in the summer of 1861, the federal troops instituted a tight blockade of southern ports and soon it was decided to retake Fort Pulaski in order to make sure that Savannah was sealed off from the sea. The first step was to land a force on Hilton Head Island. Then, after the Confederates abandoned nearby Tybee Island, Federal troops under Engineer Captain Quincy A. Gillmore landed there and proceeded to establish 11 artillery batteries aimed at Fort Pulaski just a mile across the water.

The Southerners were not worried about the Federal cannon aiming at the fort because it was well known that mortars and smooth-bore cannon did not have the strength to do much damage beyond 700 yards. But what the Confederates did not know—or if they knew, ignored—was that Gillmore had brought with his force ten new experimental cannon with rifled (spiral) barrels. These 30-pounder Parrott guns had an effective range of 8,453 yards. The spiral grooves in the barrel gave the Parrott guns greater accuracy, range, and penetrating power than all earlier cannon.

Before he opened fire on Fort Pulaski, Gillmore urged the defenders to surrender. Not knowing what they faced, they refused. When the Federal artillerymen opened fire on April 10, as expected, the old-style cannon and mortars did little damage, but the Parrott guns were devastating. By noon the next day, they had blasted huge holes in the thick brick walls. Fearing that explosive shells would soon penetrate the main powder magazine, the commander of the fort, Colonel Charles H. Olmstead, surrendered.

NAPOLEONS, PARROTTS, AND GATLING GUNS

Confederate copy of U.S. 1857 bronze, smooth-bore, muzzle-loading 12-pounder gun howitzer, the standard fieldpiece of both armies. When bronze was no longer available to the South, the guns were made of cast iron with a reinforced breech. (West Point Museum)

NAPOLEONS

The basic artillery piece of both Union and Confederate armies was the 12-pounder Napoleon, developed for the French army during the reign of Napoleon III. This bronze smooth-bore, muzzle-loading howitzer-gun fired a 4 1/2-inch ball with maximum range of about one mile. It was best used for close-range work, 800 yards or less, and when loaded with canister, a collection of pellets as in a shotgun shell. When firing a canister against advancing troops, such as at Cemetery Ridge, the impact of the Napoleon was devastating.

The Union army had adopted the Napoleon before the Civil War. Until the Confederate States began to manufacture this kind of cannon, they depended on those captured from Union troops. When bronze was no longer available, the Confederate Napoleons were made of cast iron with a reinforcing jacket at the breech.

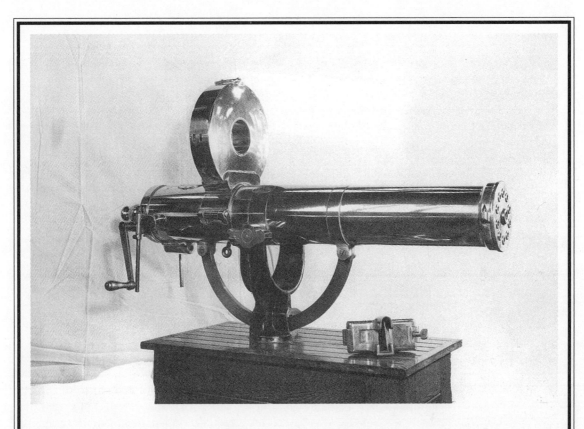

Horse-drawn 1883 model, 10 barrel, .45 caliber Gatling gun. Custer was offered use of these guns with a rate of fire of around 350 rounds a minute, but refused them because they would slow up the U.S. 7th Cavalry ride to the Little Bighorn. (West Point Museum)

PARROTT GUNS

During the course of the war, the Parrott gun replaced the Napoleon for long-range work.

Invented and manufactured by Robert Parrott, a New Hampshire West Pointer who became superintendent of the West Point foundry, the guns were different from the earlier Napoleons because the barrels were rifled. This gave them much greater range and accuracy. There were seven classes of Parrott guns, ranging from a 10-pounder with a 2.9-inch bore to a 100-pounder with a 6.9-inch bore to a 300-pounder with a 10-inch bore. The shells used in the guns were actually somewhat smaller than the stated size. A 200-pounder, for example, fired a 150-pound shell. If elevated to 35 degrees, a 100-pounder could fire an 80-pound shell almost five miles.

The 300-pounder Parrotts, used by the Union army at sieges such as Forts Pulaski and Sumter, weighed 13 tons. Getting a battery into position within 1,750- to 4,290-yard range of the target was a complicated engineering operation involving landing the guns through surf and then hauling them over difficult terrain.

GATLING GUN

The Gatling gun, patented in 1862 by its inventor, Richard Gatling, was the first effective machine gun. Operated by a hand crank, it consisted of a cluster of six barrels rotating around a common axis with ammunition fed from a hopper and had a rate of fire of around 350 rounds a minute.

Major General Benjamin Butler employed Gatling guns during the siege of Petersburg in 1864–1865 but the Gatling was not adopted by the U.S. army until 1866. It required a special .58 caliber rimfire cartridge, and during the Civil War the army had difficulty trying to supply over 100 different kinds of ammunition for the various other firearms.

Horse-drawn Gatlings were used in the 1868–1890 wars with the western Plains Indians, and there is debate about the consequences of Custer's refusal of three Gatlings offered to him by General Alfred H. Terry before Custer rode to Little Bighorn.

For about 50 years, the Gatling was an important weapon of the army and underwent many improvements; late models had ten barrels and fired 450 rounds a minute. But it was eventually made obsolete with the development of the automatic reciprocating machine gun.

Around 1990, the U.S. air force began to use a modernized version of the Gatling gun for fighters, bombers, and especially for gunships because it had a higher rate of fire—up to 6,000 rounds a minute—than the conventional machine gun, and its multiple barrels allowed it to maintain continuous rate of fire without the barrels' overheating.

The Gatling gun was the source of the term "gat"—slang for a pistol and other forms of handguns.

The "unbreachable" defense system, 50 years in the making, had been made obsolete in 30 hours, thanks to the modern rifled Parrott guns.

The Federal soldiers moved into the fort at once and did not leave it until the end of the war. For his bold use of the new Parrott guns, Gillmore was hailed as a hero and promoted at once to brevet brigadier general.

Despite the fact that during the bombardment, over 5,000 shells were fired on the fort, casualties were very light. One Union soldier was killed and one Confederate was mortally wounded.

After surrendering, Olmstead, with 384 of his officers and men, was sent north and imprisoned on Governor's Island in New York City's harbor. In the fall of 1862, Olmstead was exchanged and served with distinction for the remainder of the war.

BATTLE OF MCDOWELL— MAY 8, 1862

The battlefield near McDowell, Virginia, is one of the few that has not been changed or "improved" over the years, allowing the visitor to appreciate how difficult the battle was for the men who fought there and how the terrain influenced the outcome.

In the weeks before the battle, the 9000-man force under Stonewall Jackson had been keeping the Federal troops in the Shenandoah Valley so occupied that they could not be sent east to interfere with the Confederate army's attempt to stop the advance of McClellan's huge army toward Richmond. At McDowell, Virginia, a tiny town 23 miles west of Staunton, Jackson clashed with a 6,000-man force under Brigadier General Robert H. Milroy.

The battle was actually fought on a high ridge east of the Bull Pasture River. Called Sitlington's Hill, the ridge was topped by an open field about a mile long. The ground fell away from the ridge in a precipitous, heavily wooded, rocky slope, which was so rough that cannon could not be dragged up it and cannon firing from the base of the hill could not reach the top. So the battle that was fought was strictly an infantry engagement.

Jackson reached the hill first and established his men on top. Milroy's force

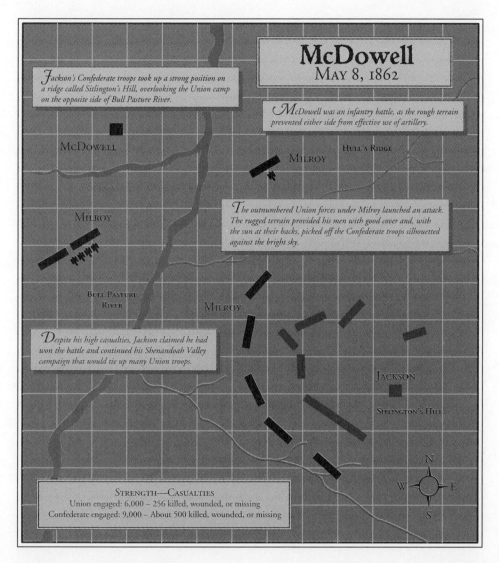

McDowell
MAY 8, 1862

Jackson's Confederate troops took up a strong position on a ridge called Sitlington's Hill, overlooking the Union camp on the opposite side of Bull Pasture River.

McDowell was an infantry battle, as the rough terrain prevented either side from effective use of artillery.

McDOWELL

MILROY

HULL'S RIDGE

MILROY

The outnumbered Union forces under Milroy launched an attack. The rugged terrain provided his men with good cover and, with the sun at their backs, picked off the Confederate troops silhouetted against the bright sky.

BULL PASTURE RIVER

MILROY

Despite his high casualties, Jackson claimed he had won the battle and continued his Shenandoah Valley campaign that would tie up many Union troops.

JACKSON

SITLINGTON'S HILL

N
W   E
S

STRENGTH—CASUALTIES
Union engaged: 6,000 – 256 killed, wounded, or missing
Confederate engaged: 9,000 – About 500 killed, wounded, or missing

attacked soon afterward. The sun behind the Federals blinded the Confederates firing down from their vantage point and made it comparatively easy for the Federals to hide behind trees and rocks as they clawed their way upward. In addition, the Confederates were silhouetted against the sky so that the Federal riflemen could pick them off easily. As a result, although the Confederates theoretically should have had an advantage over the Federals, they did

not. In fact, Jackson had to send a force down the right side of the hill to hold the attackers.

It was a vicious fight. A Georgia brigade in the center of the hill lost a third of its men; even so, the survivors flatly refused to seek protection. On the other hand, the Union soldiers made little progress in taking the hill, and as darkness fell, Milroy withdrew the entire force from the McDowell area.

Battery of 13-inch mortars of the 1st Connecticut Heavy Artillery at Yorktown, Virginia, positioned to defend Washington from attack by way of the Chesapeake Bay. (National Archives)

In a report to Richmond the next day, Jackson claimed victory, but he had lost 500 men versus the Union's 256. But there was no disputing the fact that Jackson had tied up the Federal army and made it reconsider its plan to send troops from the Shenandoah Valley to reinforce McClellan in Richmond.

McDowell Battlefield is at McDowell, Virginia. McDowell Battlefield is open to the public if prior permission for a visit is secured.

Battle of Port Republic— June 9, 1862

After the battle in McDowell, Virginia, Jackson chased some of the Union forces across the Potomac River, but learning that Union troops under Major General John C. Fremont and Brigadier General James Shields were trying to trap him, he headed south. Fremont followed Jackson directly south through the Shenandoah Valley, while Shields followed through the Luray Valley on the east side of the Massanutten mountain range.

Jackson halted his 6,000-man force at Port Republic, Virginia, where he meant to take on both pursuers. First, Major General Richard S. Ewell would hit Shields at nearby Cross Keys; then Jackson, with Ewell's support, would hit Fremont. But the plan failed when Shields was slow in arriving. Instead, Fremont attacked Ewell on June 8 at Cross Keys. The next day, when Brigadier General Erastus B. Tyler, in the vanguard of Shields's division, reached Port Republic,

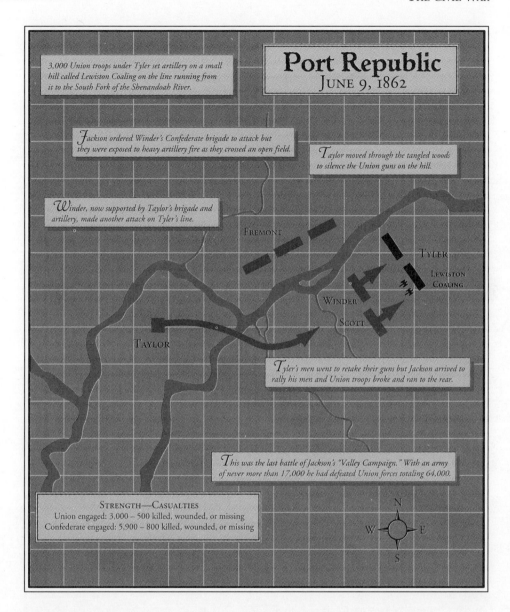

Port Republic
JUNE 9, 1862

3,000 Union troops under Tyler set artillery on a small hill called Lewiston Coaling on the line running from it to the South Fork of the Shenandoah River.

Jackson ordered Winder's Confederate brigade to attack but they were exposed to heavy artillery fire as they crossed an open field.

Taylor moved through the tangled woods to silence the Union guns on the hill.

Winder, now supported by Taylor's brigade and artillery, made another attack on Tyler's line.

FREMONT

TYLER

LEWISTON COALING

WINDER

SCOTT

TAYLOR

Tyler's men went to retake their guns but Jackson arrived to rally his men and Union troops broke and ran to the rear.

This was the last battle of Jackson's "Valley Campaign." With an army of never more than 17,000 he had defeated Union forces totaling 64,000.

STRENGTH—CASUALTIES
Union engaged: 3,000 – 500 killed, wounded, or missing
Confederate engaged: 5,900 – 800 killed, wounded, or missing

N
W E
S

Jackson ordered Brigadier General Charles Winder to confront him.

With 3,000 men, Tyler was positioned in a line from the South Fork of the Shenandoah River to a little hill called Lewiston Coaling. As Winder's Confederates crossed the open plain facing the Federal line, the Northerners opened up with rifle fire and cannonballs from seven guns positioned on the hill. The Rebel advance was stalled, unable to move until finally a brigade under Brigadier General Richard Taylor appeared. While the Confederates attacked the battery on the hill, Winder's men resumed their advance until they were stalled once again and running out of

UNION BALLOON CORPS

Entered according to Act of Congress, in the year 1862, by M. B. BRADY, in the Clerk's Office of the District Court of the District of Columbia.

Professor Lowe's balloon Intrepid *being filled with hydrogen at Fair Oaks, Virginia. (National Archives)*

President Lincoln was so impressed at a demonstration of Professor Thaddeus S. C. Lowe's hydrogen-filled balloon in June 1861 that he named Lowe chief of a balloon corps that would gather useful military information for what would soon become the Army of the Potomac.

Shortly afterward, the professor and his assistants had seven balloons in operation keeping track of enemy troop movements around Washington.

During the Peninsula Campaign, balloons were used to direct artillery fire by means of a telegraph cable running from the balloon's passenger basket to the artillery's battery commander.

Despite the fact that balloons did prove their worth, Union Army commanders did not seem ready to accept an "Air Corps" and created so many problems for Professor Lowe that by mid 1863 he resigned, and that ended the Balloon Corps.

ammunition. Now, as the Federals charged, the Confederates fled. But for a second time, they were saved by the arrival of reinforcements: two of the regiments that had fought Fremont the day before.

Shortly after that, Taylor's men, working their way through a thick stand of mountain laurel, charged the artillery unit on Lewiston Coaling and, after hand-to-hand fighting, took it. Seeing what had happened, the nearby Confederate infantrymen pulled out of their line and charged the hill.

Now Jackson rallied Tyler's stalled infantry, which resumed its charge and put the Federals to flight. In the fierce four-hour battle, the northern force lost 500 men. But they had killed or wounded 800 Confederates. The rest were so battle weary that, instead of leading them across the river and doing battle with Fremont once again, Jackson withdrew them so they could rest.

Port Republic was the last battle Jackson fought on his famous Shenandoah Valley campaign that began on March 23, with the battle of Kernstown, Virginia, and extended as far north as outskirts of Harpers Ferry. With never more than 17,000 men, he had outmaneuvered Federal forces totaling 64,000 and inflicted 7,000 casualties, at a cost of 2,500 of his own men, and established his reputation as a brilliant tactician.

In addition, Jackson had so occupied and terrorized the Union forces that Lee, on the eastern side of the Blue Ridge, was able to more than hold his own against the much larger Union army.

On June 24, 1862, Jackson moved south to join Lee, forming an effective team that won the great battles of Second Bull Run (Second Manassas), Fredericksburg, and Chancellorsville.

Only nine acres of the Port Republic Battlefield are open to the public.

THE PENINSULA AND THE SEVEN DAYS CAMPAIGNS

The day after the union disaster at Bull Run, July 21, Lincoln appointed Major General George McClellan commander of the Division of the Potomac and called for 100,000 long-term enlistments. In the early weeks of the war, McClellan had made a name for himself by driving Confederate forces out of what is today West Virginia. He now applied his recognized organization abilities in training and equipping 100,000 men for the Army of the Potomac.

By November, McClellan had replaced the infirm 76-year-old Lieutenant General Winfield Scott as general in chief of Union forces, but instead of engaging the enemy he continued to train and review his troops. In March, Lincoln fired McClellan from his post but kept him in command of the Army of the Potomac, urging him to use it for actually fighting the enemy.

McClellan developed a plan to take Richmond by marching up the Richmond Peninsula. Lincoln approved and by late March a Union force of some 100,000 troops began arriving by ship at Fort Monroe, on the tip of the peninsula, preparing to march north to the capital.

The march to Richmond only got about 15 miles, however, when it was stopped on April 5, outside Yorktown by a Confederate force of 15,000, positioned behind hastily dug earthworks. McClellan moved slowly and with great caution as his intelligence agent, Allan Pinkerton, informed him Yorktown was defended by 200,000 Confederate soldiers. In fact, Lieutenant General Joseph Johnston, who was responsible for the defense of Richmond, had altogether just 60,000 men. Throughout the conflict, Pinkerton would continue to wildly exaggerate the size of the opposing force and McClellan would continue to rely on him. It was not until May 5 that Yorktown was taken, also removing the threat of the Confederate ironclad *Virginia* (formerly the *Merimack*) interfering with Union shipping on the mouth of the James River.

At the same time that the Army of the Potomac was slowly crawling up the peninsula, Confederate Major General Thomas

"Stonewall" Jackson was raising hell during his famous "Shenandoah Valley Campaign."

Jackson had first moved into the valley with 6,000 men to protect the valley as an important source of food and as an invasion route into the heart of the North. In April, Jackson was reinforced by Major General Richard Ewell with 8,500 men, and eventually bought his total force to 16,000.

Jackson was able to get as far north as Harpers Ferry, and in the course of his campaigns fought battles at *Kernstown* (March 23), *McDowell* (May 8), *Front Royal* (May 23), *Winchester* (May 24), *Cross Keys* (June 8), and *Port Republic* (June 9).

Major General Nathaniel Banks with 38,000 was initially Jackson's major opponent in the Valley but in time Union strength had grown to 64,000.

On June 24, Jackson left the valley that had made him famous in the North and the South, and with his "foot cavalry" moved south to help General Lee defend Richmond.

Jackson's valley campaign had alarmed Washington, and Lincoln had ordered Major General Irvin McDowell to remain in the area with his 40,000-man force to confront Jackson, rather than sending a portion of it to join McClellan on the peninsula. At the end of May, McClellan was finally in striking distance of Richmond, with his army divided by the flood-swollen Chickahominy River.

Johnston decided to attack the two Union corps south of the river on May 31. The battle, known as "Seven Pines" or "Fair Oaks," was bloody—5,031 Union and 6,134 Confederate casualties—but inconclusive. It was a calamity for McClellan and his army in another respect as well, because Johnston was wounded, and on June 1, President Davis gave command of the army to his military advisor, General Robert E. Lee.

At the beginning of the war, General Scott had offered Lee command of the Union forces, having first recognized his abilities during the War with Mexico. The Virginia-born Lee refused Scott's offer, stating he did not want to draw his sword against fellow Virginians. Shortly after taking over command, Lee named his force the Army of Northern Virginia.

After Seven Pines, McClellan pushed on, approaching Richmond from the east. On June 12, Lee's brilliant, dashing chief of cavalry, James Ewell ("Jeb") Stuart, decided to determine what "Little Mac" was up to: He and his cavalry rode completely around the Union army, taking some prisoners as well as learning that the Union left flank was unanchored.

On June 25, when McClellan was within seven miles of Richmond, Lee mounted a series of attacks known as "The Seven Days Campaign." The first engagement was fought on June 25 at "Oak Grove" (King's School House), followed by battles at *Mechanicsville* (June 26), *Gaines' Mill* (June 27), *Savage's Station* (June 29), and *White Oak Swamp* (June 30). The final battle at *Malvern Hill* on July 1 would not only be the last battle of the Seven Days but also the final conflict of McClellan's entire Peninsula Campaign.

BATTLE OF MALVERN HILL— JULY 1, 1862

In seven days, Lee had forced McClellan back about 30 miles and now the Union army occupied a strong defensive position on Malvern Hill.

Malvern Hill was a high, long, crescent-shaped plateau seven miles from Harrison's Landing on the James River, where the Union troops would board ships and return north. The 80,000 Federal troops that dug into the hilltop were under the immediate

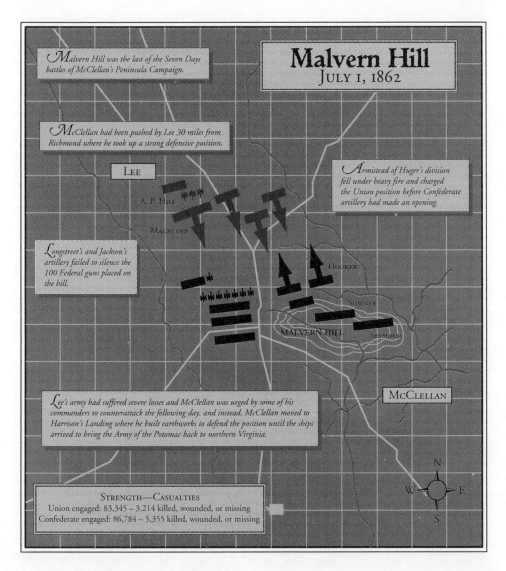

Malvern Hill was the last of the Seven Days battles of McClellan's Peninsula Campaign.

Malvern Hill
JULY 1, 1862

McClellan had been pushed by Lee 30 miles from Richmond where he took up a strong defensive position.

LEE

Armistead of Huger's division fell under heavy fire and charged the Union position before Confederate artillery had made an opening.

A. P. HILL

MAGRUDER

Longstreet's and Jackson's artillery failed to silence the 100 Federal guns placed on the hill.

HOOKER

SUMNER

MALVERN HILL

SEYMOUR

Lee's army had suffered severe losses and McClellan was urged by some of his commanders to counterattack the following day, and instead, McClellan moved to Harrison's Landing where he built earthworks to defend the position until the ships arrived to bring the Army of the Potomac back to northern Virginia.

McCLELLAN

N
W   E
S

STRENGTH—CASUALTIES
Union engaged: 83,345 – 3,214 killed, wounded, or missing
Confederate engaged: 86,784 – 5,355 killed, wounded, or missing

command of Brigadier Generals Edwin Sumner, Samuel Heintzelman, and Fitz-John Porter.

Lee, now joined by Jackson, also had about 80,000 men. His strategy was to place Major General James Longstreet with 60 cannon on a nearby hill on the Confederate right and Stonewall Jackson with more cannon on the Confederate left. By directing a crossfire at the Union line, these two forces would theoretically open a hole through which infantry under Generals

Benjamin Huger, John B. Magruder, and D. H. Hill would charge. The signal for this attack would be given by Brigadier General Lewis A. Armistead. Armistead was to observe the effect of the artillery bombardment on the Federals, and when he deemed that the Federal line had been broken, his men were to make a charge with a yell.

But little went right for the Confederates that day. First of all, Magruder's divisions received poor directions for reaching their position and did not get into the fight until it was well underway. The hill on which Longstreet set up his guns was more or less surrounded by swamps and woods, and only a third of his cannon actually got into position to fire. These were soon silenced by the Federals' more than 100 guns. Worst of all, Armistead's men came under heavy fire early, and in order to protect themselves they charged the Union lines long before the Confederate cannon had smashed the hoped-for hole in the Union front. This activated the rest of the Southern troops on the front line, and when they charged, they were torn apart by the entrenched Federal soldiers and cannon, which switched from solid shot to canister. Some of the Confederates got to within 20 yards of the Federal lines, but they could go no further. In a letter home after the battle, a Federal cannoneer wrote that it made him heartsick to see how the cannon "cut roads through the attackers, some places ten feet wide." Infantrymen were firing so rapidly that their gun barrels overheated.

By dark, Lee's army had failed to break the Union defense, and fighting stopped, not to resume the next day.

Malvern Hill was a bad day for Lee's army. The morning after the battle, as the sun came up and the mist lifted, the Federal troops could see and hear thousands of men lying on the battlefield. "A third of them dead or dying," Colonel William Averell wrote, "but enough of them alive to give the field a singular crawling effect."

The following day, the Army of the Potomac returned, undisturbed, to Harrison's Landing on the James River where they would shortly embark on the ships to bring them back north.

Malvern Hill had been a bloody battle, especially for the Confederate army, with 5,355 casualties compared to 3,214 Union casualties. In the course of the entire Seven Days, Union losses were 16,000 compared to 20,000 Confederate.

General Lee and his Army of Northern Virginia would continue achieving brilliant victories and defeats until the war ended on April 9, 1865, at Appomattox Court House.

The Army of the Potomac would eventually win battles, but under Grant and George Meade, not McClellan.

A few months after the *Battle of Antietam*, September 17, 1862, McClellan was removed as commander of the Army of the Potomac and he eventually resigned from the Union army.

In the election of 1864, the Democratic Party nominated McClellan for president, running on a peace platform he did not entirely support.

During the summer of 1864, the North had become horrified at the huge Union casualties Grant was producing as he attempted to defeat Lee and take Richmond. The war had become very unpopular and even Lincoln believed he would lose the election of 1864. Then, on September 3, everything changed, the North was electrified with the news from General Sherman who wired, "So Atlanta is ours, and fairly won."

The North saw victory and the end of the war in sight and reelected Lincoln.

Malvern Hill Battlefield is a part of the much larger Richmond National Battlefield Park, which includes other battlegrounds of the 1862 Peninsula Campaign, such as Seven Pines, Fair Oaks, and Harrison's Landing, as well the 1864 battles of Cold Harbor and Gaines' Mill.

SECOND BATTLE OF BULL RUN (MANASSAS)—AUGUST 28–30, 1862

One of Lincoln's few major mistakes in his conduct of the war was appointing Major

General John Pope commander of the newly created Army of Virginia.

Organized in June 1862 the army was made up of the several elements in the area, including Major Generals Nathaniel Banks's and Irvin McDowell's corps. It was a force of some 47,000 men. The army's function was to guard Washington, disrupt enemy communication lines, and help support McClellan's Peninsula Campaign by drawing troops from General Robert E. Lee's defense of Richmond.

Pope had done quite well in the western theater and had been promoted to major general for his handling of the advance and siege of Corinth, but as head of an eastern army he had many handicaps, not all of his own making.

Most of Pope's senior officers were easterners and resented serving under a westerner. More important, some of them

favored Major General George McClellan and may have intentionally contributed to Pope's downfall.

But Pope proved to be his own worst enemy. He divided the cavalry among his several corps so that he, personally, had no "eyes" to keep him informed on the strength and movement of enemy troops, especially Major General Thomas Jackson's fast-moving "foot cavalry."

He also made untactful remarks. Soon after assuming command, Pope issued a long, pompous address to his army which included the statement, "I have come to you from the West, where we have always seen the back of our enemies."

By early July, Lee was becoming quite certain that McClellan would not move on Richmond and sent Jackson north with 12,000 men to deal with Pope. After arriving in northern Virginia, Jackson realized

Camp of the 36th Pennsylvania in Virginia. When this and similar regiments took to the field the men would give up their spacious tents and often have no shelter at all from the elements. (Library of Congress)

his force was too small to take on Pope, so Lee sent him Brigadier General A. P. Hill with another 12,000 men.

Pope had crossed the Rappahanock River and was advancing on Culpepper. Jackson saw his chance to destroy Bank's corps who were in advance of the main Federal army. The resulting Battle of Cedar Mountain, between Cedar Creek and Robinson's River, gained precious little for either side except casualties—1,300 Union and 2,300 Confederate.

Lee saw that Jackson's force was still too small to handle Pope and ordered Major General James Longstreet with his wing of the Army of Northern Virginia north to reinforce him. By August 17, Jackson had joined up with Longstreet on the south side of the Rapidan River, so Lee now had an army of about 55,000 to oppose Pope's army of almost equal size.

In the meantime, McClellan had given up on his attack on Richmond and was preparing to return north by ship with his Army of the Potomac.

On August 22, Lee's chief of cavalry, Major General J.E.B. Stuart, captured Pope's personal baggage train and learned that in a few days Pope expected to have an army of 100,000.

Lee realized he would have to strike Pope at once, as Pope had now withdrawn behind the Rappahannock River.

Lee and Jackson worked out a plan to get Pope in a good position in order to attack him.

On August 25, the day after their meeting, Jackson moved north, around the Bull Run Mountain, and turned east at a small town located on the railroad running from Manassas through Throughfare Gap. By dark, Jackson had cut Pope's communication lines by capturing Manassas Junction. It contained quantities of Pope's supplies,

and what Jackson's hungry men could not eat or carry away, they burned.

Jackson's move gave Pope a wonderful chance to defeat Lee's divided force by dealing one at a time with Jackson and then Longstreet, but Pope did not have a cavalry force capable of telling him their exact positions.

In fact, Pope had lost all track of Jackson and by the time Pope received word of the raid on Manassas Junction, Jackson had moved five or so miles north along Sudley Road and had taken an excellent position near Sudley Springs on Stoney Ridge behind an unfinished railroad. Here Jackson waited for Lee, Longstreet, and especially, for Pope.

Jackson deliberately announced his presence by attacking one of Major General Irvin McDowell's divisions that appeared in the area.

Delighted to have finally found Jackson, Pope seemed to have forgotten all about Longstreet and concentrated his entire force to finish Jackson before Longstreet arrived. This was certainly feasible, as Pope had around 62,000 to Jackson's 20,000 men. But on the first day of battle on August 29, Pope ordered piecemeal frontal attacks on the strong Confederate position that got nowhere.

The fighting continued until dark, with no positive results on either side. Jackson withdrew from the more advanced positions he had occupied. Pope took this as a sign of retreat and planned to pursue Jackson in the morning. Pope did not know, of course, that in the morning he would be facing not only Jackson, but Lee and Longstreet as well.

On August 29, Longstreet had pushed aside one of McDowell's divisions to join with Lee and Jackson.

Lee had wanted Longstreet to join in the

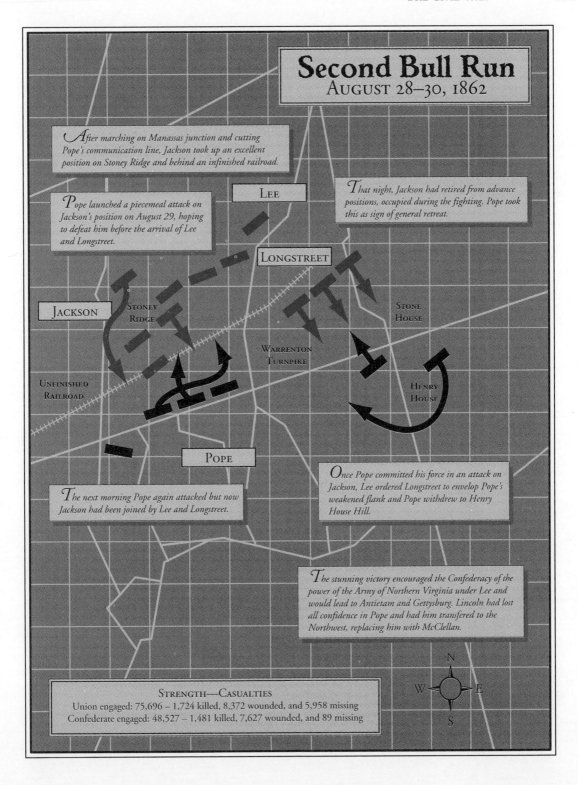

Second Bull Run
AUGUST 28–30, 1862

After marching on Manassas junction and cutting Pope's communication line, Jackson took up an excellent position on Stoney Ridge and behind an infinished railroad.

Pope launched a piecemeal attack on Jackson's position on August 29, hoping to defeat him before the arrival of Lee and Longstreet.

That night, Jackson had retired from advance positions, occupied during the fighting. Pope took this as sign of general retreat.

LEE

LONGSTREET

JACKSON

STONEY RIDGE

STONE HOUSE

WARRENTON TURNPIKE

UNFINISHED RAILROAD

HENRY HOUSE

POPE

Once Pope committed his force in an attack on Jackson, Lee ordered Longstreet to envelop Pope's weakened flank and Pope withdrew to Henry House Hill.

The next morning Pope again attacked but now Jackson had been joined by Lee and Longstreet.

The stunning victory encouraged the Confederacy of the power of the Army of Northern Virginia under Lee and would lead to Antietam and Gettysburg. Lincoln had lost all confidence in Pope and had him transfered to the Northwest, replacing him with McClellan.

N
W   E
S

STRENGTH—CASUALTIES
Union engaged: 75,696 – 1,724 killed, 8,372 wounded, and 5,958 missing
Confederate engaged: 48,527 – 1,481 killed, 7,627 wounded, and 89 missing

fighting on the 29th and if he had, it might have been the end of Pope's Army of Virginia. But Longstreet begged off until the next day.

When Pope began his pursuit on the morning of August 30, Lee waited until he had committed his forces against Jackson on his left and then ordered Longstreet to envelop Pope's weakened opposite flank.

Jackson and Longstreet with Confederate artillery were too much for Pope. His army was driven back to Henry House Hill. There was some fighting that continued into the following day, but by then the battle was about finished and by September 3, Pope had retreated to the protection of Washington, D.C.

Both armies suffered severe losses. Of the 75,696 Union troops engaged, casualties totaled over 16,000—1,724 killed, 8,372 wounded, and 5,958 missing. The far smaller Confederate army of 48,527 lost over 9,000—1,481 killed, 7,627 wounded, and 89 missing.

It had been a fierce battle and the ground would bear the scars of battle for many years.

The battle convinced the Confederacy of the power of the army led by Lee and would open the way for Lee's invasion of Maryland, which ended at Antietam.

On September 2, Pope was relieved of his command. The Army of Virginia was absorbed into McClellan's Army of the Potomac. Pope was made commander of the Department of the Northwest where he could fight Indians and be far, far away from the likes of Lee, Jackson, and Longstreet.

BATTLE OF HARPERS FERRY— SEPTEMBER 13–15, 1862

Just four days before the terrible battle of Antietam on September 17, a far smaller but important battle was fought at Harpers Ferry, in what is now West Virginia.

Strategically located on a point of land at the confluence of the Shenandoah and Potomac rivers, and west of Baltimore, the village was the site of a United States arsenal established in 1798, to manufacture a variety of weapons.

On October 16, 1859, John Brown, a militant abolitionist, raided Harpers Ferry to get weapons for his projected uprising of southern slaves. He was captured by a detachment of United States Marines commanded by Colonel Robert E. Lee, tried for murder, treason, and attempting to cause a slave insurrection, found guilty, and hung.

When Virginia joined the Confederacy, after the fall of Fort Sumter, the pro-Union western counties, including Harpers Ferry, seceded and established an independent government. They would later become West Virginia.

Because of the arsenal and its strategic position, both the Union and Confederates wanted Harpers Ferry. During the course of the war Harpers Ferry would change hands three times, always ending up in the Union.

On April 18, 1861, Harpers Ferry was occupied by the men of the Virginia Militia, sent to force the western counties to remain in the Confederacy.

On June 18, the militia abandoned the village at the approach of Major General George McClellan, who had been sent to clear Confederate forces from Virginia's western counties. But before leaving, the militia managed to send some of the arsenal's weapon manufacturing machinery to Richmond.

As Lee moved his army north into Maryland in the late summer of 1862, he believed that the 12,000 Federal troops stationed at Harpers Ferry under Colonel Dixon S.

Miles would be withdrawn northward. Instead, Dixon was ordered to "hold Harpers Ferry to the last extremity." Consequently, Lee realized that to maintain his supply and communication lines through the Shenandoah Valley as he invaded the North, he needed to neutralize the town and arsenal. He sent Stonewall Jackson to do the job.

Jackson knew Harpers Ferry and the country around it well because he had been commander of the Confederate units there in the spring of 1861. As soon as he arrived in the vicinity of the town, he divided his army of 25,000 men into three parts and directed them to seize command of three hills—Bolivar Heights, Maryland Heights, and Loudoun Heights—from which his artillery could bombard the Federal garrison.

Miles's outnumbered, inexperienced troops were no match for Jackson's men. Though they fought admirably, by September 13, the Confederates had taken their hilltop objectives. The next day, after hauling their cannon into position, they started raining shells on the Federals. Miles knew that he could not long withstand the fearsome firestorm that followed, and surrendered at 9:00 A.M. on September 15.

Casualties in the three-day battle were relatively light. Union dead and wounded came to 219, out of a force of 14,000, but over 12,000 were taken prisoner. Jackson lost 286 of his men and captured 73 pieces of artillery, 11,000 small arms, 200 wagons, and miscellaneous supplies.

Jackson waited at Harpers Ferry just long enough to establish a division under Major General A. P. Hill, then hustled the rest of his force north to rejoin Lee at Sharpsburg, Maryland.

Hill would not remain long at Harpers Ferry. On September 17, his division made a forced march to Antietam Creek, arriving just in time to save Lee's army.

BATTLE OF ANTIETAM— SEPTEMBER 17, 1862

Antietam Creek, east of Sharpsburg, Maryland, was the scene of the bloodiest one-day battle of the Civil War. The Union, which claimed a somewhat dubious victory, lost 12,410 out of 75,000 men. Confederate losses were 10,318 out of 51,000 men.

Dunker Church, the Corn Field, West Wood, East Wood, "Bloody Lane," and the Stone Bridge, later named "Burnside Bridge," where some of the heaviest fighting occurred, have become part of the nation's heritage.

The battle was precipitated by Lee's earlier victories in Virginia, culminating with Second Bull Run on August 29, 1862. This encouraged President Jefferson Davis to order a general offensive. Davis ordered Major General Kirby Smith to drive into eastern Tennessee, General Braxton Bragg into Kentucky, and General Robert E. Lee to move into Maryland.

Lee at first resisted this move because he lacked equipment and clothing for his men but finally agreed. The morale of the Army of Northern Virginia was very high and Lee's corps commanders were extremely capable, especially Major Generals Thomas "Stonewall" Jackson and James Longstreet. Lee wanted to shift the fighting out of his beloved Virginia and he and Davis believed that the appearance of his army in Maryland might persuade the state to join the Confederacy. And if Lee could win a major battle on northern soil it might encourage Britain and France to formally recognize the Confederate States of America.

Lee crossed the Potomac near Leesburg, and by September 7 had assembled his army of around 40,000 at Frederick, Maryland. At the urging of President Davis, Lee issued a proclamation to the people of Maryland, stating the Confederate States stood ready

JOHN BROWN

John Brown, a radical abolitionist, was born in Connecticut in 1800. A deeply religious man, he was soon convinced that all slaves must be set free. In 1855, he gave up running an underground railroad station in Ohio that sheltered runaway slaves on their journey to freedom in Canada, to join his four grown sons in Kansas.

Kansas at that time was called "Bleeding Kansas" because of the bitter fight between the abolitionist and slaveholding settlers. After a pro-slavery raid on Lawrence, and with his sons and two companions, Brown murdered five pro-slave men on the banks of the Pottawatami River.

In 1859, Brown decided to seize the U.S. arsenal at Harpers Ferry to procure arms and lead a slave insurrection. With 21 men, he took the arsenal in mid-October, occupied portions of Harpers Ferry, and kept some of the inhabitants prisoner. But that was all he accomplished.

The Virginia militia appeared and blocked Brown's escape from the town, and the following morning, Captain Robert E. Lee and Lieutenant J.E.B. Stuart arrived with a detachment of U.S. Marines and attacked Brown and his men, who were barricaded in the arsenal's firehouse. Brown was captured after ten of his men, including two of his sons, had been killed.

Brown was tried for treason, found guilty, and ordered to be hanged. His last speech before the court on November 2, 1859, remains a powerful document:

> I have, may it please the Court, a few words to say. In the first place, I deny everything but what I have all along admitted, the design on my part to free the slaves. I intended certainly to have made a clean thing of that matter, as I did last winter, when I went into Missouri and there took slaves without the snapping of a gun on either side, moved them through the country, and finally left them in Canada. I designed to have done the same thing again, on a larger scale. That was all I intended. I never did intend murder, or treason, or the destruction of property, or to excite or incite slaves to rebellion, or to make insurrection.
>
> This court acknowledges, as I suppose, the validity of the law of God. I see a book kissed here which I suppose to be the Bible, or at least the New Testament. That teaches me that all things whatsoever I would that men should do to me, I should do even so to them. It teaches me, further, to remember them that are in bonds, as bound with them. I endeavored to act up to that instruction. I say, I am yet too young to understand that God is any respecter of persons. I believe that to have interfered as I have done—as I have always freely admitted I have done—in behalf of His despised poor, was not wrong, but right. Now, if it is deemed necessary that I should forfeit my life for the furtherance of the ends of justice, and mingle my blood further with the blood of my children and with the blood of millions in this slave country whose rights are disregarded by wicked, cruel, and unjust enactments, I submit; so let it be done!

Seated on a coffin in the wagon that carried him to the gallows, Brown looked around at the surrounding countryside and remarked, "This is a beautiful country—." After his death, Brown became a martyr to the Northern abolitionists and a demon to the South.

THE BATTLE HYMN OF THE REPUBLIC

In the early months of the war, thousands of Union troops poured into Washington, D.C. As they marched, they would often sing words they had made up to a popular tune of the time, such as "John Brown's Body Lies A-molderin' in the Grave but His Soul Goes Marching On." They also sang to the same tune, "We'll Hang Old Jeff Davis on a Sour Apple Tree."

Mrs. Julia Ward Howe, living in Washington at the time, liked the tune to this song, written in 1852 by William Steffe, but felt that the words made up by the soldiers were not suitable for the noble cause that they were fighting for. She set to work writing a marching song that would be both religious and inspiring. In February 1862, *The Atlantic Monthly* published her verses, which she entitled "The Battle Hymn of The Republic."

Her verses, set to Steffe's tune, became an instant hit. "The Battle Hymn of The Republic" was more than a hymn; it became the North's battle cry. It remains as popular today as it was in the Civil War, and has practically become a second national anthem (with the added advantage that it is far easier to sing than the "Star-Spangled Banner").

THE BATTLE HYMN OF THE REPUBLIC

Mine eyes have seen the glory of the coming of the Lord:
He is trampling out the vintage where the grapes of wrath are stored;
He hath loosed the fatal lightning of His terrible swift sword;

His truth is marching on.

I have seen Him in the watch-fires of a hundred circling camps,
They have builded Him an altar in the evening dews and damps;
I can read His righteous sentence by the dim and flaring lamps:

His day is marching on.

I have read a fiery gospel writ in burnished rows of steel:
"As ye deal with my contemners, so with you my grace shall deal;
Let the Hero, born of woman, crush the serpent with his heel,

Since God is marching on."

He has sounded forth the trumpet that shall never call retreat;
He is sifting out the hearts of men before His judgment seat:
Oh, be swift, my soul, to answer Him! Be Jubilant, my feet!

Our God is marching on.

In the beauty of the lilies Christ was born across the sea,
With a glory in his bosom that transfigures you and me:
As he died to make men holy, let us die to make men free,

While God is marching on.

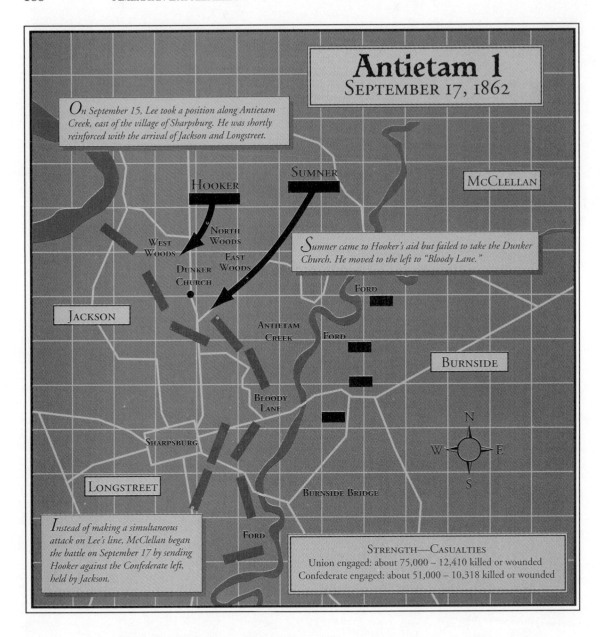

Antietam 1
SEPTEMBER 17, 1862

On September 15, Lee took a position along Antietam Creek, east of the village of Sharpsburg. He was shortly reinforced with the arrival of Jackson and Longstreet.

HOOKER

SUMNER

McCLELLAN

NORTH WOODS

WEST WOODS

EAST WOODS

DUNKER CHURCH

Sumner came to Hooker's aid but failed to take the Dunker Church. He moved to the left to "Bloody Lane."

FORD

JACKSON

ANTIETAM CREEK

FORD

BURNSIDE

BLOODY LANE

SHARPSBURG

N
W   E
S

LONGSTREET

BURNSIDE BRIDGE

Instead of making a simultaneous attack on Lee's line, McClellan began the battle on September 17 by sending Hooker against the Confederate left, held by Jackson.

FORD

STRENGTH—CASUALTIES
Union engaged: about 75,000 – 12,410 killed or wounded
Confederate engaged: about 51,000 – 10,318 killed or wounded

to help them drive out the Yankees. It did not have much effect.

Lincoln was aware of Lee's advance into Maryland and moved to stop it. He reluctantly retained McClellan in command and reinforced his Army of the Potomac with troops from Pope's Army of Virginia, bringing total Union strength to approximately 84,000.

Lincoln urged McClellan to move immediately to stop Lee's northern advance. McClellan did move, but slowly and cautiously as this was his habit. Once again, McClellan erred by relying on faulty

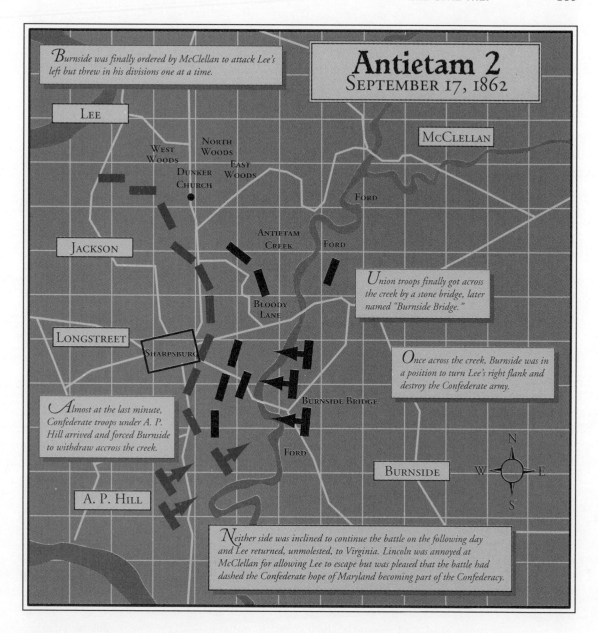

Antietam 2
SEPTEMBER 17, 1862

Burnside was finally ordered by McClellan to attack Lee's left but threw in his divisions one at a time.

LEE

NORTH WOODS

WEST WOODS

EAST WOODS

DUNKER CHURCH

McCLELLAN

FORD

JACKSON

ANTIETAM CREEK

FORD

Union troops finally got across the creek by a stone bridge, later named "Burnside Bridge."

BLOODY LANE

LONGSTREET

SHARPSBURG

Once across the creek, Burnside was in a position to turn Lee's right flank and destroy the Confederate army.

Almost at the last minute, Confederate troops under A. P. Hill arrived and forced Burnside to withdraw accross the creek.

BURNSIDE BRIDGE

A. P. HILL

FORD

BURNSIDE

Neither side was inclined to continue the battle on the following day and Lee returned, unmolested, to Virginia. Lincoln was annoyed at McClellan for allowing Lee to escape but was pleased that the battle had dashed the Confederate hope of Maryland becoming part of the Confederacy.

intelligence that reported Lee had an army of 120,000 "or more."

By September 9, Lee learned that elements of McClellan's army were advancing on him, but he continued his march north. Lee ordered Jackson, with 6 divisions, to take Harper's Ferry in order to remove the threat from the 12,000 Union troops stationed there and secure a line of communication west of the Shenandoahs. Jackson was also to get badly needed arms and cannon from the Harper's Ferry arsenal.

On September 13, Lee split his force again, sending Longstreet with 3 divisions

Confederate artillery was positioned near the little whitewashed Dunker Church at Antietam. Both sides fought to hold the church and the surrounding high ground. The original church was destroyed in a storm and rebuilt in 1962. (National Park Service)

to Hagerstown to fight with a Pennsylvania force of militia that never appeared.

On that same day, the unthinkable happened. A copy of Lee's orders to his commanders fell into McClellan's hands. It was wrapped around three cigars that a Union soldier found lying on the ground and passed on to his commander.

When McClellan saw Lee's orders, he telegraphed Lincoln declaring he would now dispose of Lee's army at once. But, again, he failed to deliver. For one thing, he talked too freely about the lucky find and a southern sympathizer heard about and got word to Lee; then his advance was further delayed by Confederate infantry and J.E.B. Stuart's cavalry.

Around noon on the fifteenth, Lee was moving north through the town of Sharpsburg when he got word that Jackson had taken Harpers Ferry and was on his return march. Lee ordered Longstreet back from Hagerstown.

Lee also learned that McClellan was close by and decided to stop him at Sharpsburg, in spite of the fact that, until Jackson and Longstreet arrived, he had only 19,000 men.

Sharpsburg was not an ideal place for Lee to make a stand, because the only escape route to Virginia was via Boteler's Ford on the Potomac. But Lee considered his position suitable for the defensive battle he intended to fight. The site selected was just east of Sharpsburg on rising ground behind Antietam Creek. The creek itself did not offer much protection, as it was crossed by four bridges and several fords, but the outcropping of rocks, wood lots, and fields of corn ready for harvest did offer good defensive positions.

McClellan had originally planned to attack on September 15, but wasted much time directing placement of the various batteries, bivouacs, and other chores that could easily have been handled by subordinates. His delay gave time for Jackson and Longstreet to join Lee, giving him now about 38,000 men.

Lee ordered Jackson to hold the left, Longstreet the right, and Anderson the center.

McClellan probably originally planned to attack both flanks of Lee's force simultaneously and then hit the center. But he apparently had a change of heart, for on the morning of the seventeenth McClellan began the action by only sending Hooker's corps against the Confederate left held by Jackson.

Major General Joseph Hooker's attack began with artillery fire that cleared the cornfield. Then the infantry advanced. One of its objectives was the Confederate artillery on the open ground right beyond the little white Dunker Church just off Hagerstown Pike.

Jackson and Stuart's artillery on Nicodemus Hill drove off Hooker's attack and Major General Joseph Mansfield came to Hooker's aid. Shortly afterward, Mansfield was killed and Hooker wounded. McClellan continued to fight in bits and pieces and ordered Major General Edwin Sumner's corps to attack. Sumner's troops did manage to reach the Dunker Church, now occupied by rebel infantry, but were forced back when Jackson sent in reinforcements.

Sumner moved his attack further left to a sunken lane, later to be called "Bloody Lane."

By this time, the ground where the earlier fighting occurred was already soaked in blood and covered with killed and wounded. In the first half hour of battle, Union casualties were already at 2,000.

On the Union right, Major General Ambrose Burnside had been waiting for several hours for word from McClellan to attack. When he finally did get the order, he, like McClellan, attacked piecemeal, throwing in one division at a time. But he eventually managed to fight his way across Antietam Creek by a bridge that has since borne his name. Burnside could have crossed the creek by one of the many fords and why he decided to waste so many men crossing the well-defended bridge is very hard to answer.

Lee's left and center were holding but now Burnside was across the creek in force, and threatening his right flank. Lee had no more men he could throw in to stop Burnside and his only hope of saving his army was the almost immediate arrival of Major General A. P. Hill's corps from Harpers Ferry.

In early afternoon, Lee was told that Hill was only an hour or so away. His men and officers fought to hold off Burnside from folding up the right flank. Just as Burnside was gaining his objective, Hill, with about half his corps, joined the fight. Hill's men were exhausted from the 17-mile forced march but they hit Burnside's flank, stopping his advance. Burnside called on McClellan to send reinforcements but none were forthcoming. This refusal struck many, including Lincoln, as most strange because at that very time, McClellan had 24,000 troops of Porter's and Franklin's corps that had been held in reserve throughout the battle.

Under pressure from Hill, Burnside was finally forced to withdraw across the creek. By that time, it was becoming too dark to fight so the battle ended.

Several of Lee's commanders suggested

George B. McClellan was called "The Young Napoleon" when he took over the Union army shortly after First Bull Run. He applied his organizational abilities to creating the Army of the Potomac but did not have the tactical ability to use the army with success. (National Archives)

that the army should withdraw that night but, having fought McClellan before, Lee was certain he would not renew the attack the next day. He was correct, for while McClellan did have enough troops to destroy Lee's shattered force, he made no move to do so. The following day McClellan did not prevent Lee's army from crossing the Potomac to return to Virginia.

Instead of pursuing Lee, McClellan wrote to his wife: "The spectacle yesterday was the grandest I could conceive; nothing could be more sublime. Those in whose judgement I rely tell me that I fought the battle splendidly and that it was a masterpiece of art."

Actually, the Confederate forces had once again proved their mettle, but while Antietam may not have been a Union victory, it was something of a defeat for the Confederacy. Davis's and Lee's ultimate aims to bring Maryland over to their side and enlist foreign support were not achieved.

Lincoln was disappointed over the outcome at Antietam, for McClellan had not only failed to destroy Lee's army but had allowed it to return to Virginia. But Lincoln did consider it a sufficient Union victory to issue his Emancipation Proclamation. Thus, what had first been a war to preserve the Union also became a war to free the slaves, and this greatly strengthened domestic and foreign support.

Throughout the fall, McClellan made no move against Lee and on November 7, Lincoln ordered McClellan to turn over his command to General Ambrose Burnside.

BATTLE OF CORINTH— OCTOBER 3–4, 1862

After the battle at Shiloh, General Beauregard marched south to Corinth and had his men dig trenches to defend this vital rail center from anticipated attack by Grant's Union forces.

But despite Lincoln saying to a visitor "I can't spare this man," Shiloh had tarnished Grant's military reputation and he was demoted to deputy commander under Major General Henry Halleck. In his memoirs, Grant later recalled that after this point, "I was nothing more than an observer."

If Grant had remained in command it is possible that he and Buell would have gone after Beauregard as soon as the troops caught their breath after Shiloh, but

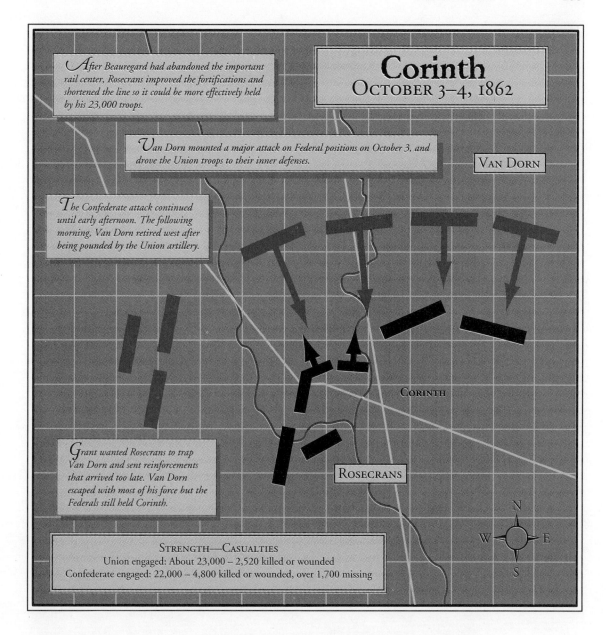

Corinth
OCTOBER 3–4, 1862

After Beauregard had abandoned the important rail center, Rosecrans improved the fortifications and shortened the line so it could be more effectively held by his 23,000 troops.

Van Dorn mounted a major attack on Federal positions on October 3, and drove the Union troops to their inner defenses.

VAN DORN

The Confederate attack continued until early afternoon. The following morning, Van Dorn retired west after being pounded by the Union artillery.

CORINTH

Grant wanted Rosecrans to trap Van Dorn and sent reinforcements that arrived too late. Van Dorn escaped with most of his force but the Federals still held Corinth.

ROSECRANS

N
W   E
S

STRENGTH—CASUALTIES
Union engaged: About 23,000 – 2,520 killed or wounded
Confederate engaged: 22,000 – 4,800 killed or wounded, over 1,700 missing

Halleck was no Grant. It was not until April 29 that the Union army left its bases around Pittsburg Landing to march on Corinth, arriving there in early May.

Halleck began a formal siege of the strong Confederate defenses and Beauregard soon became convinced that the city was untenable, as by this time Union forces had cut two of the railroad lines bringing supplies to his army. On May 30 he withdrew his army to the area around Tupelo.

Soon after the Federal army occupied Corinth, there was another major change

Major General Philip Sheridan, a highly aggressive Union leader, was eventually put in command of the Army of the Potomac's cavalry. It was this force, backed by infantry, that blocked Lee's path of retreat at Appomattox Courthouse. (National Archives)

of command, and Halleck's large force was split and dispatched to other parts of the country. Halleck went to Washington as general in chief of the Union armies. Grant, resuming command of the Army of the Tennessee, as well as western Tennessee and Kentucky, stayed at Corinth, where he was joined by Major General Rosecrans, commander of the Army of the Mississippi. Of the two, Grant was the senior.

Meanwhile, General Bragg had assumed command of the Confederate forces in the middle South, and while the Federals did little to follow up on their earlier advantage, he seized the initiative and set out to capture control of Tennessee and Kentucky. To further his operations, he sent troops under Major General Price and Van Dorn to

pin down Grant and Rosecrans at Corinth. Since they had given up several divisions to support the Union armies to the north and east, Bragg thought he could handle them with comparative ease.

On September 19, 1862, Price tangled with Rosecrans, at Iuka, Mississippi, then withdrew before he was caught in the trap that Grant had expected Rosecrans to set for him. Price then joined forces with Van Dorn, his senior officer, and on October 3, the two tried to drive the Federals out of Corinth.

The Yankees, however, were well entrenched. During the months following the capture of Corinth, they had not only strengthened the entrenchments that the Confederates had dug but had also added to them and created inner defenses consisting of batteries connected by breastworks. Nevertheless, when the Confederates, with about 22,000 men, hit the Federal outer defenses, the Northern troops, also numbering about 22,000, were forced slowly back toward their inner line close to the center of the town. But when the fighting resumed the next morning, the Confederates could go no farther. Artillery fire from the Federal right broke the back of the attack.

In the meantime, Grant, anticipating this outcome and hoping to trap the Confederates, had sent out a call for reinforcements from Jackson, Mississippi, and Bolivar, Tennessee. Reinforcements arrived too late, but by noon of October 4 the Confederates had begun retreating to the northeast.

Union casualties amounted to 2,520 out of 23,000 engaged. The Confederate army of 22,000 lost about 4,800 killed or wounded and had 1,700 listed as missing.

The Union occupation lost the Confederacy an important railroad center.

BATTLE OF PERRYVILLE— OCTOBER 8, 1862

At about the same time that Lee was driven out of Maryland and Van Dorn was repulsed at Corinth, Mississippi, General Bragg attempted to add Kentucky to the Southern cause, setting the stage for the battle of Perryville.

Prior to the battle in August, General Bragg and Major General Kirby Smith had moved into Kentucky along widely spaced parallel routes.

Marching from Knoxville, Tennessee, Smith was positioned in the eastern part of the state and Bragg had moved from Chattanooga to more or less the middle of Kentucky. At Frankfort on October 4, Bragg appointed Richard Hawkes as the state's Provisional Confederate Governor.

Further to the west in Kentucky, Union Major General Don Carlos Buell was keeping close tabs on the movements of Bragg and Smith. As if these two Confederate generals were not trouble enough to Buell, he was also having his own difficulties with officials in Washington, D.C., who blamed him for allowing Bragg to enter Tennessee. In fact, Buell had been replaced by Major General George Thomas, who gave up the job the day after his appointment, and Buell was reinstated.

Buell was anxious to keep Bragg and Smith from uniting, while Bragg was equally anxious to keep Buell from getting in their way. But when Bragg finally met up with Buell at Perryville, he did not realize that Buell outnumbered him more than two to one.

Military academicians call the battle that followed a "meeting engagement." This means that the fight started before either side had made a real plan for it.

At the time, that area of Kentucky was suffering from a severe drought, and the first shots were fired when Buell sent out men before daylight on October 8 to find water. The shooting escalated quickly, subsided for a time, then burst out again and was fierce throughout the rest of the day. Two Union brigadiers, James S. Jackson and William R. Terrill, were killed. Confederate Major General Leonidas Polk was almost captured when, toward evening, he ordered some troops to stop firing and then discovered that the soldiers he had given orders to were Federals, not Confederates. General Buell knew little of what was happening because his headquarters was out of earshot of most of the shooting.

$\mathscr{P}$ONTOON BRIDGES

At the time of the Civil War, most bridges in the South were made of wood and easily destroyed by either side to prevent enemy forces from advancing, or, in some cases, from retreating.

In order to cross a river where there was no bridge, Union forces relied on easily assembled pontoon bridges built of pontoon boats. These were flat-bottomed, 30-foot craft that were wider at the bow than the stern and still wider—6 feet—in between. They were transported to the site on four-wheeled wagons and loaded with the lumber necessary to complete the bridge. At the river, the boats were unloaded, tied to a cable that was made fast upstream, and floated across. When they were fastened end to end, stringers were laid from boat to boat and these were covered with wide planks laid at right angles to the boats. Army engineers could build a bridge up to 600 feet long in about five minutes.

That, of course, was assuming the engineers received enough pontoon boats on time, which was not the case before the Battle of Fredericksburg in 1862.

The 8th New York Regiment and other army engineers assembled pontoon bridges, built bridges, repaired damaged railroad lines, and did other construction work often while exposed to enemy attack. (National Archives)

The battle came to an end when a Confederate brigade attacked the division under Philip H. Sheridan, who had just been promoted to brigadier general. Sheridan's men stopped the Confederates, then chased them back into the streets of Perryville. From there they withdrew to the Southern lines.

Bragg knew by then that he was hopelessly outnumbered. He withdrew to Harrodsburg to join forces with Smith. Buell pursued with little enthusiasm and finally retired his army to Glasgow and Bowling Green.

As was true of so many battles in this war, action at Perryville was a very bloody affair. Union casualties were 3,696 of the 36,940 engaged. The Confederate lost 3,145 out of 16,000 engaged.

Buell had failed to destroy Bragg's and Smith's armies at Perryville but had forced them out of Kentucky and now, with no army to support it, the Provisional Confederate of Kentucky faded away, leaving the state in Union hands, where it would remain for the rest of the war.

BATTLE OF FREDERICKSBURG— DECEMBER 11–13, 1862

By the fall of 1862, Lincoln had given up all hope that McClellan would move against Lee and Richmond, and on November 7 replaced him as commander of the Army of the Potomac with Major General Ambrose E. Burnside, a corps commander who had done as well as any other at Antietam.

When Burnside took command, the Union army was slowly moving to a position to strike between the two wings of Lee's army.

Under considerable pressure from the White House to take immediate action, Burnside abandoned this plan and shifted his troops in order to cross the Rappahannock River at Fredericksburg and then move south against Richmond before Lieutenant General Thomas Jackson in the Shenandoah could join up with Lee. But Burnside would have to move quickly to catch Lee unsupported.

By November 17, the advance force under Major General Edwin Sumner was in Falmouth, more or less opposite Fredericksburg. Sumner wanted to ford the river, clean out the small enemy forces in Fredericksburg, and then take the high ground in back of it. But Burnside turned down the suggestion as he wanted to move his entire army across on pontoon bridges, which were to arrive that day. But because of some foul-up, the pontoons were not delivered for 11 days. By then Lee had figured out what Burnside was up to, and now, joined by Jackson and Lieutenant General James Longstreet, moved 73,000 veteran troops into a magnificent defensive position on the high ground in back of Fredericksburg.

When his tardy pontoon bridges finally arrived, Burnside planned to attack on December 11. Burnside organized his 120,000-man army into four grand divisions with the right under Major General Edwin Sumner, the center under Major General Joseph Hooker, the left under Major General William Franklin, and reserves under Major General Franz Sigel.

Before dawn of December 11 the Union engineers began assembling the pontoon bridges and by daylight came under heavy rifle fire from Brigadier General William Barksdale and his Mississippi Sharpshooters, hidden in the Frederickburg buildings.

Downstream, however, two of the three planned bridges were completed by 9:30

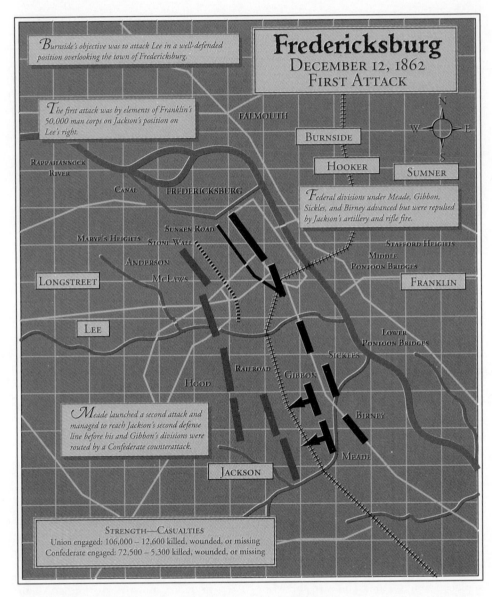

Burnside's objective was to attack Lee in a well-defended position overlooking the town of Fredericksburg.

Fredericksburg
DECEMBER 12, 1862
FIRST ATTACK

The first attack was by elements of Franklin's 50,000 man corps on Jackson's position on Lee's right.

FALMOUTH

BURNSIDE

HOOKER

SUMNER

RAPPAHANNOCK RIVER

CANAL   FREDERICKSBURG

Federal divisions under Meade, Gibbon, Sickles, and Birney advanced but were repulsed by Jackson's artillery and rifle fire.

SUNKEN ROAD

MARYE'S HEIGHTS   STONE WALL

STAFFORD HEIGHTS
MIDDLE PONTOON BRIDGES

ANDERSON

McLAWS

LONGSTREET

FRANKLIN

LEE

LOWER PONTOON BRIDGES

SICKLES

RAILROAD   GIBBON

HOOD

BIRNEY

Meade launched a second attack and managed to reach Jackson's second defense line before his and Gibbon's divisions were routed by a Confederate counterattack.

MEADE

JACKSON

STRENGTH—CASUALTIES
Union engaged: 106,000 – 12,600 killed, wounded, or missing
Confederate engaged: 72,500 – 5,300 killed, wounded, or missing

A.M. Instead of sending a force across to take out the sharpshooters, Burnside ordered his artillery to blast them out.

For over an hour, Federal artillery around Falmouth on Stafford Heights pounded Fredericksburg, and while it destroyed much of the town, it did little harm to the Mississippi riflemen who did not retire until late afternoon.

By nightfall the Union forces had occupied the burning town and had lost valuable time.

Lee had made no major effort to prevent Burnside from crossing the Rappahannock River as he had other plans for dealing with Burnside. Lee's army occupied the high ground just west of Fredericksburg and on his right was Jackson, now

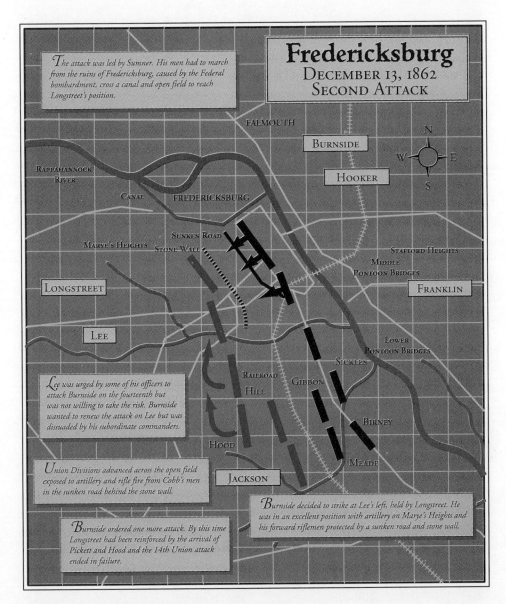

Fredericksburg
DECEMBER 13, 1862
SECOND ATTACK

The attack was led by Sumner. His men had to march from the ruins of Fredericksburg, caused by the Federal bombardment, cross a canal and open field to reach Longstreet's position.

FALMOUTH

BURNSIDE

HOOKER

RAPPAHANNOCK RIVER

CANAL   FREDERICKSBURG

SUNKEN ROAD
MARYE'S HEIGHTS   STONE WALL

STAFFORD HEIGHTS
MIDDLE
PONTOON BRIDGES

LONGSTREET

FRANKLIN

LEE

LOWER
PONTOON BRIDGES

SICKLES

Lee was urged by some of his officers to attack Burnside on the fourteenth but was not willing to take the risk. Burnside wanted to renew the attack on Lee but was dissuaded by his subordinate commanders.

RAILROAD
HILL   GIBBON

BIRNEY

HOOD

MEADE

Union Divisions advanced across the open field exposed to artillery and rifle fire from Cobb's men in the sunken road behind the stone wall.

JACKSON

Burnside decided to strike at Lee's left, held by Longstreet. He was in an excellent position with artillery on Marye's Heights and his forward riflemen protected by a sunken road and stone wall.

Burnside ordered one more attack. By this time Longstreet had been reinforced by the arrival of Pickett and Hood and the 14th Union attack ended in failure.

reinforced by Major Generals Jubal Early's and H. P. Hill's divisions.

Longstreet was on the left in a splendid defensive position. At Longstreet's back was his artillery on Marye's Heights and at his front was a sunken road and four-foot-high stone wall.

Lee had placed his artillery so effectively that one of his artillerymen remarked that

"a chicken could not live in the field when open on it."

On the morning of December 12, Burnside ordered Major General John Reynolds of Franklin's command to attack Johnson's position on Prospect Hill.

Reynolds picked Major General George Gordon Meade's division to lead the attack, which got underway at 8:30. It soon came under fire from Major General J.E.B. Stuart's artillery, placed more or less at right angles to Jackson's right so Stuart could fire lengthwise up the river valley. This was answered by the Union artillery across the river. But Jackson's cannon, concealed on the hill that was the Federal objective, were silent. He had given instructions that they were not to fire and thus reveal their positions no matter how badly the Northern artillery hit them.

But when Meade's advancing infantrymen were close enough, Jackson's gunners opened up. Slowly, the blue-clad soldiers fell back to safer ground.

Meade launched a second attack shortly after noon. His objective was a tongue of wooded land that jutted from the hill into the plain running beside the river. By luck, the Federals struck between two Confederate brigades and crashed on through to the Confederate second line of defense.

While Meade pushed ahead, Brigadier General John Gibbon was supposedly moving alongside. But the two units began to split apart, and the Confederates, discovering this, launched a counterattack on both. The result was a rout. Happily for the Yankees, it did not last long, because the Confederates were hit on the flank by yet another Federal division under Brigadier General David B. Birney. Despite Jackson's attempt to launch a late-afternoon counterattack, this just about ended the fighting on the Confederate right.

Burnside had planned to strike Longstreet at Marye's Heights after Franklin's divisions had rolled up Lee's right. As this was not accomplished, Burnside decided to send Sumner's division to strike at Longstreet anyway. And now the dreadful slaughter began.

On December 13, as Sumner's men started to form on the streets of Fredericksburg for the attack, they fell under fire from Confederate artillery. Union troops moved forward, crossing a canal and then crossing an open field toward the enemy's position.

Major General William French's, Major General Winfield Scott Hancock's, Brigadier General Oliver Howard's, and Brigadier General Samuel Sturgis's divisions rushed across the open ground only to be met by a blizzard of bullets from Brigadier General Thomas Cobb's riflemen positioned along the sunken road behind the stone wall.

Few Union soldiers managed to get within 150 yards of the wall and one regimental commander ordered a bayonet charge on the wall, believing this might be more effective than stopping to reload. The men got within fifty yards of the wall before the attack ended.

The 400-yard field in front of the wall was now covered with dead or wounded. Soldiers looked for protection from the deadly fire from the wall in depressions in the field or the dead bodies of their companions.

Around 3:30 P.M., Burnside ordered one more attack on the wall. By this time, Lee had moved Major General George Pickett's division and one brigade of Major General John Hood to Marye's Hill to help defend the position.

Burnside chose this moment to order Major General Joseph Hooker to attack with two divisions but this failed to accomplish anything except adding to the Union casualty list.

By now Burnside had ordered fourteen attacks on the wall. All there was to show for the attacks were almost 6,000 Union casualties. The Confederate defenders also suffered casualties, including General Cobb, who was killed.

Darkness ended the possibility of still another attack on the wall, and that night soldiers on both sides could hear the cries and moans of the wounded lying on the cold field.

There was a truce on December 14 so the dead could be buried and the wounded removed from the field.

That night, Burnside and his army recrossed the Rappahannock River and returned to their base outside Washington, D.C.

Fredericksburg had been the site of one of the war's most dreadful battles. A total of over 12,600 Union soldiers were either killed, wounded, or missing out of the 106,000 who took part in the fighting. Out of the 72,500 engaged, Confederate casualties were 5,300.

On January 25, 1863, Lincoln relieved Burnside, Sumner, and Franklin of command and appointed Major General Joseph Hooker to head the Army of the Potomac.

Lee's Army of Northern Virginia would spend the winter in their strong position outside Fredericksburg. They would remain until May 1 when they left to deal with Hooker at Chancellorsville.

Fredericksburg Battlefield is a unit of the Fredericksburg and Spotsylvania National Military Park.

Major General Ambrose E. Burnside was a competent Union corps commander. Burnside is best remembered for the short time he was commander of the Army of the Potomac and launched a series of futile and costly attacks on Lee's strong position outside Fredericksburg, Virginia. (National Archives)

BATTLE OF STONES RIVER— DECEMBER 31, 1862– JANUARY 2, 1863

Following his unsuccessful invasion of Kentucky (ending with the battle of Perryville on October 8), General Braxton Bragg withdrew his Confederate army to Tennessee. With 35,000 men he established a line on both sides of Stones River, Tennessee, northwest of his supply depot at Murfreesboro.

Pressed by Washington to pursue and attack Bragg's army, Major General William Rosecrans, with some 45,000 men, moved out of Nashville and headed south. Though harassed by Brigadier Joseph Wheeler's Confederate cavalry, he reached Stones River on December 30 and deployed his force in a line facing Bragg.

Rosecrans's plan of attack was to send Major General Thomas Crittenden's and Major General George Thomas's corps against Bragg's right, held by Major General John Breckinridge positioned on the east side of the river.

Bragg also planned to strike his enemy's right and he hit first.

Early on the morning of December 31, Major General William J. Hardee, supported by divisions of Lieutenant General Leonidas Polk, attacked Major General Alexander McCook's corps on the Union right.

The attack by 10,000 Confederates came as a total surprise to McCook, who understood that it would be the Union left who would be attacking and his three divisions,

James Ewell Brown ("Jeb") Stuart was perhaps the most famous cavalry commander of the Civil War. His daring exploits, including twice riding around the entire Union army and raiding Pope's headquarters just before the Second Battle of Bull Run, delighted the South and made him one of their favorite heroes. Stuart was only thirty-one when mortally wounded at Yellow Tavern on May 11, 1864. (National Archives)

around 14,000, were to protect the army's right flank, the nearby Nashville Pike, and the Nashville Chattanooga Railroad—Rosecrans's supply lines and also his only path of retreat.

One of McCook's divisions practically disintegrated under the force of the initial attack and another was only able to put up resistance for a short time before withdrawing.

But Brigadier General Philip Sheridan was a fighter and his 5,000-man division held on, giving better than they took.

Hardee now sent in two fresh divisions of Polk's corps to dislodge him. Sheridan repulsed the first, commanded by Major General Cheatham. Sheridan withdrew to get ammunition and then took a position near the Nashville Pike, alongside one of Thomas's divisions that had also been forced back.

By then the Union right had been driven back about three miles and the center had also given ground.

Sheridan's resistance provided Rosecrans, who had given up his idea of attacking, time to concentrate on saving his army by reinforcing the right and center by drawing men from Crittenden's corps.

By 10:00 A.M., Bragg thought that final victory would be his in short order and threw a whole series of attacks against the Federals. But by this time Rosecrans had established a strong line, somewhat in the shape of an open door hinge. Much of the fighting to follow was around the pivot of the hinge.

The terrain of the battle area was rather flat and dotted with rocks and clumps of trees. There was no high ground from which troop movements could readily be observed and was therefore unsuited for organized warfare, so the men fought each other as best they could.

Fighting was especially vicious around a cluster of trees called Round Forest. This place was later referred by soldiers of both sides as "Hell's Half Acre," with good reason.

Confederate forces made many attacks on this position that was near the center of the Union line. A Mississippi regiment tried to take it with half its men carrying sticks, for lack of rifles. Another regiment of the same state used their rifles as clubs because the recent rain made their rifles too wet to fire.

Despite the terrible casualties suffered as his men crossed an open field to attack the strong Union position at Round Forest, Bragg believed that with sufficient men he could take it and win the battle.

In the early afternoon he ordered Breckinridge, who had so far played no important role in the battle, to send his five brigades to join in the attack. But the four brigades that Breckinridge reluctantly

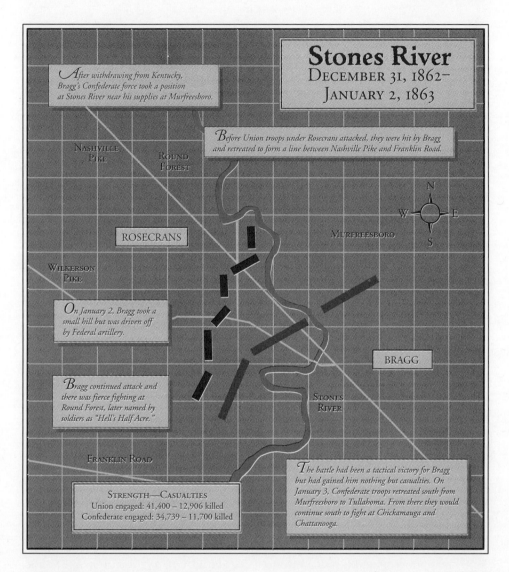

Stones River
DECEMBER 31, 1862–
JANUARY 2, 1863

After withdrawing from Kentucky, Bragg's Confederate force took a position at Stones River near his supplies at Murfreesboro.

Before Union troops under Rosecrans attacked, they were hit by Bragg and retreated to form a line between Nashville Pike and Franklin Road.

NASHVILLE PIKE

ROUND FOREST

N
W   E
S

ROSECRANS

MURFREESBORO

WILKERSON PIKE

On January 2, Bragg took a small hill but was driven off by Federal artillery.

BRAGG

Bragg continued attack and there was fierce fighting at Round Forest, later named by soldiers as "Hell's Half Acre."

STONES RIVER

FRANKLIN ROAD

STRENGTH—CASUALTIES
Union engaged: 41,400 – 12,906 killed
Confederate engaged: 34,739 – 11,700 killed

The battle had been a tactical victory for Bragg but had gained him nothing but casualties. On January 3, Confederate troops retreated south from Murfreesboro to Tullahoma. From there they would continue south to fight at Chickamauga and Chattanooga.

delivered were sent in piecemeal and were torn to pieces by Union artillery and rifle fire.

The Union defenders were also suffering from the repeated attack on their position, but their line held and late afternoon the firing stopped and the day's fighting was over.

There was no fighting on January 1, but the following day Bragg ordered Breckinridge to dislodge a Union force under Colonel Samuel Beatty that had crossed the river and occupied a hill threatening Polk's position.

Breckinridge's brigades, supported by artillery, attacked Beatty's position, and after fierce fighting drove them from the hilltop. But as the Confederate troops pursued them down the slope, they came under massive artillery fire from 58 of

Crittenden's guns. Beatty, then reinforced, retook the hill. The attempt to take and hold the hill resulted in 1,700 Confederate casualties.

Bragg now decided that he should desert the battlefield entirely. The river was rising and could isolate his forces. Furthermore, he had received captured papers showing that Rosecrans had been reinforced. So during the night of January 2, the Confederate army withdrew south to take up winter quarters 20 or so miles away at Tullahoma, Tennessee, leaving 2,000 wounded behind.

The battle had been one of the bloodiest of the war. In three days, Federal casualties were about 12,906 of the 41,400 troops engaged. Bragg lost around 11,700 of his smaller army of about 35,000.

It had been a fight that neither side could claim as a clear victory. But it cost the Confederacy men it could not readily replace and forced Bragg to give up more of Tennessee as he moved south toward Chattanooga, where he would clash again with Rosecrans.

BATTLE OF CHANCELLORSVILLE— MAY 1–3, 1863

Chancellorsville is often referred to as "Lee's Masterpiece," and is studied by the military as an example of how Lee's daring and brilliant tactics, and his quick response to errors made by his opponent, made it possible for him to defeat an army over twice the size of his.

After repulsing the Union army under Major General Ambrose Burnside on December 13, 1862, Lieutenant General Robert E. Lee took up winter quarters at his well-defended position outside Fredericksburg, Virginia.

On January 20, 1863, Burnside made another attempt to dislodge Lee. Prolonged rains had turned the Virginia roads into quagmires and by January 23, the advance, called even in official reports the "Mud March," was terminated.

Burnside's command over the Army of the Potomac was also terminated and on January 26, Major General Joseph Hooker assumed command of the Union army.

Hooker had earned the nickname "Fighting Joe" for his action during the battles of the Seven Days and did so well in subsequent battles that he was given command of the "Grand Division" at the battle of Fredericksburg.

In April 1863, Hooker had devised a good plan to deal with Lee. Major General George Stoneman would take his 10,000 cavalrymen across the Rappahannock, cut the Confederate communication lines, and trap Lee between his force and infantry that would also have crossed the river.

Stoneman's cavalry rode off on April 13, but was unable to ford the Rappahannock because it was swollen from heavy rains.

Hooker worked out another plan to defeat Lee's 60,000-man army by dividing his own 134,000-man force into three parts.

Hooker would command the major element of about 54,000 men, composed of three corps under Major Generals Henry Slocum, O. O. Howard, and George Meade, and cross the Rappahannock above Fredericksburg, swing west, and then south to Chancellorsville, striking Lee from his rear.

In the meantime, Major General John Sedgwick, with a force of 40,000 that included Major General John Reynold's corps, would cross the river at Fredericksburg to make Lee think Sedgwick planned to attack his front.

Major General Daniel Sickles's corps were in reserve to support Sedgwick, should

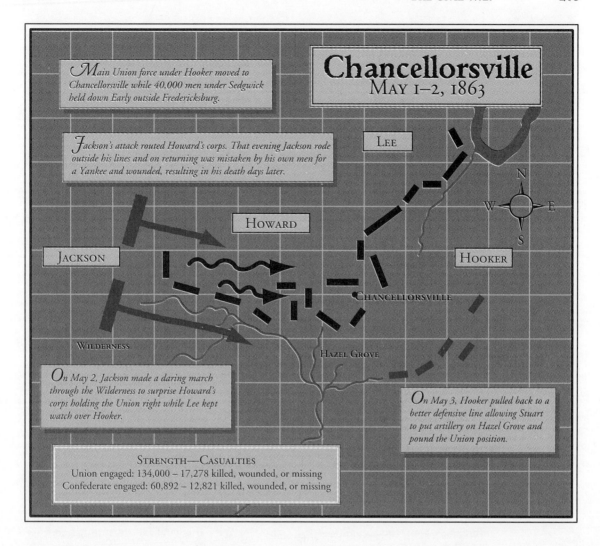

Main Union force under Hooker moved to Chancellorsville while 40,000 men under Sedgwick held down Early outside Fredericksburg.

Chancellorsville
MAY 1–2, 1863

Jackson's attack routed Howard's corps. That evening Jackson rode outside his lines and on returning was mistaken by his own men for a Yankee and wounded, resulting in his death days later.

LEE

HOWARD

JACKSON

HOOKER

CHANCELLORSVILLE

WILDERNESS

HAZEL GROVE

On May 2, Jackson made a daring march through the Wilderness to surprise Howard's corps holding the Union right while Lee kept watch over Hooker.

On May 3, Hooker pulled back to a better defensive line allowing Stuart to put artillery on Hazel Grove and pound the Union position.

STRENGTH—CASUALTIES
Union engaged: 134,000 – 17,278 killed, wounded, or missing
Confederate engaged: 60,892 – 12,821 killed, wounded, or missing

Lee attack and if not, to join with Hooker. Major General Darius Couch, Hooker's second in command, was to keep his corps in reserve to support the main force.

On April 30, Hooker had every reason to be pleased. Sedgwick was in position at Fredericksburg, the main force of 54,000 men was at the crossroads at Chancellorsville, threatening Lee's flanks and between him and his 6,500 cavalry, under Major General James Ewell Brown Stuart.

Some of Stoneman's cavalry had crossed the river and screened Hooker's movements from Stuart, so when he finally informed Lee of an impending attack, Hooker was already in position and had outmaneuvered Lee.

Lee acted immediately, splitting his forces, leaving Major General Jubal Early with 10,000 men to hold the fortified position at the base of Marye's Heights against Sedgwick, and Lee, with Lieutenant

General Thomas "Stonewall" Jackson and 50,000 men, would move to deal with Hooker at Chancellorsville.

Chancellorsville at that time was little more than a crossroads, as there was only one house. Other than the clearing at Hazel Grove, the surrounding terrain was called "The Wilderness." In fact, the early settlement in these parts was called "The Wilderness of Spotsylvania" because the land was so heavily wooded with one road from the crossroads running to nearby Spotsylvania Court House.

Two roads from Chancellorsville ran east to Salem Church and on to Fredericksburg. One was the Plank Road, the other a gravel turnpike that extended west past the Wilderness Church and Wilderness Tavern.

The wilderness surrounding the crossroads was a difficult site for a battle. The flat land had few high spots, much of it covered with trees, many heavily laced with vines that tore flesh and clothing.

Many of the so-called roads through the wilderness were nothing more than trails that meandered about, and one could easily lose sense of direction.

On May 1, advance units of Hooker's army had occupied the open ground of Hazel Grove. They went on to take a nearby ridge, on which stood small wooded Zoan Church, which was outside the Wilderness on the highest ground around. But before Union forces could secure the ridge, they were driven off by one of Jackson's divisions under Major General Richard Anderson.

Fighting continued that day but was limited to small skirmishes. Union forces, however, had the advantage of numbers and Meade found his corps unopposed on the Confederate flank. Slocum had stopped Anderson.

Then, when everything seemed to be going well, Hooker later admitted, he lost his nerve. He recalled the advance forces, and much to the chagrin and even anger of some of his subordinate commanders, established a defensive line.

Hooker may have been intimidated by the report from a Union observation balloon that Lee was bringing his entire army to Chancellorsville and that Lee would be shortly reinforced with troops under Lieutenant General James Longstreet and Major General John Hood. If this was correct, Hooker preferred that Lee attack his defensive position and suffer the same fate as Burnside at Fredericksburg.

Hooker was certain that Lee would attack and said "I have got Lee just where I want him; he must fight me on my own terms."

The center of Hooker's line was Chancellorsville. The left under Meade was well anchored by the river. But the right under Howard drifted away into the Wilderness beyond Wilderness Church.

That night, Lee and Jackson met to plan the next move. Scouts had informed them that Hooker's troops had considerable artillery behind field fortifications reinforced with felled trees.

The two generals were soon joined by Stuart, who cheerfully reported that Hooker's right was not anchored but "in the air."

With this vital fact in mind, Lee once again split his small army. Lee, with 17,000 men, would hold down Hooker's main force while Jackson with 26,000 would make a wide sweep through the Wilderness and strike the Union right.

Through his chaplain, Jackson found the son of Colonel Charles Wellford, living in nearby Catherine Furnace, who knew the Wilderness roads and trails and was willing to serve as guide.

Early on the morning of May 2, Jackson's force began a daring march that began by crossing Hooker's front.

Union Brigadier General David Birney's

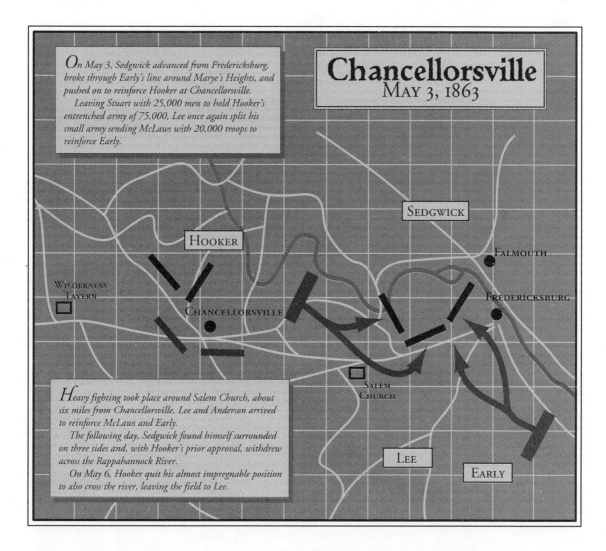

On May 3, Sedgwick advanced from Fredericksburg, broke through Early's line around Marye's Heights, and pushed on to reinforce Hooker at Chancellorsville.

Leaving Stuart with 25,000 men to hold Hooker's entrenched army of 75,000, Lee once again split his small army sending McLaws with 20,000 troops to reinforce Early.

Chancellorsville
MAY 3, 1863

SEDGWICK

HOOKER

FALMOUTH

WILDERNESS TAVERN

CHANCELLORSVILLE

FREDERICKSBURG

SALEM CHURCH

Heavy fighting took place around Salem Church, about six miles from Chancellorsville. Lee and Anderson arrived to reinforce McLaws and Early.

The following day, Sedgwick found himself surrounded on three sides and, with Hooker's prior approval, withdrew across the Rappahannock River.

On May 6, Hooker quit his almost impregnable position to also cross the river, leaving the field to Lee.

LEE

EARLY

division had occupied Hazel Grove and from this vantage point saw Jackson's column moving south.

When this was reported to Hooker, he first believed the Confederate forces were in retreat. By the time he realized this was not the case and ordered an attack, Jackson's column had disappeared into the wilderness.

It took Jackson's force six and a half hours to cover 12 miles through the Wilderness and it was not until 6:00 P.M. that they were in position to attack Howard's corps.

Howard was aware of enemy activity in the area but did not believe a force of any strength could move through the seemingly impenetrable Wilderness. His men had stacked their arms and were playing cards or lounging about when Jackson attacked.

Their first inkling of what was happening came when terrified deer, rabbits, and other wild animals came running out of the woods. Then came the sound of bugles and the bloodcurdling Rebel yell, and suddenly Confederates with smoking rifles appeared out of the dense woods.

Elements of Howard's corps broke and fled, a few grabbing up their rifles and firing a shot or two before running off, but by dark the Union ranks were stiffening and Jackson called off the attack and organized his now scattered forces for action the next day.

At about 8 P.M., Jackson, with some of his staff officers, rode beyond the Confederate line to reconnoiter the Union position. As the party was returning, a North Carolina detachment mistook them for enemy and fired, wounding Jackson in the left arm. In great pain, he was carried to a field hospital where doctors amputated his arm. On learning of this, Lee remarked, "General Jackson has lost his left arm, but I my right."

Stuart assumed Jackson's command. Jackson died eight days later of pneumonia.

On May 3, Hooker had the perfect chance to do great harm to the Confederate forces as they were spread out with Early at Fredericksburg facing Sedgwick, with Stuart to the west and Lee in between, on the Union center. Hooker not only did not attack but ordered Sickles to withdraw from Hazel Grove. Stuart occupied this desirable position with his 31 guns, which supported the infantry that now surged across the open field to strike the Union line.

One of Stuart's shells struck a house pillar that Hooker was leaning against, knocking him unconscious. When he came to, he summoned Couch, his second in command, but then refused to relinquish command. Instead, Hooker withdrew to a stronger position with both flanks solidly anchored by rivers.

After receiving a series of conflicting orders from Hooker, Sedgwick finally moved and forced Early to withdraw from his defensive position and in the direction of Chancellorsville.

Lee was worried that once Sedgwick had defeated Early, he could quickly come with 40,000 men to reinforce Hooker. So once again, Lee divided his small army, sending Major General Lafayette McLaws and 20,000 men to join up with Early.

Sedgwick and McLaws fought each other to a virtual standstill on ground around Salem Church. Hooker informed Sedgwick that he was anxious for Lee to return and attack Sedgwick in his entrenched position and gave Sedgwick permission to withdraw if he believed he was endangered.

With the arrival of Lee and Anderson, Sedgwick was surrounded on three sides and on the night of May 4, withdrew and recrossed the Rappahannock River.

Lee apparently had no desire to please Hooker by attacking his huge and well-entrenched army, and remained waiting for Hooker to make the next move.

After a council of war on the night of May 5, "Fighting Joe" Hooker overrode the opinions of his corps commanders and crossed the Rappahannock, leaving the battlefield of Chancellorsville to Lee.

It had been a hard battle for both sides. Of the approximately 134,000 Union troops engaged, about 17,278 were killed, wounded, or missing. The smaller Confederate army of 60,892 had 12,821 killed, wounded, or missing.

Lee paid a high price for his brilliant victory over a far superior size Union army. He not only lost thousands of veteran soldiers that he could never replace but he lost his best lieutenant, General Jackson. The two leaders had a unique relationship, working as a team, together planning how best to fight a battle.

Lee would sorely miss Jackson about two months later when his army would fight the Union army again at Gettysburg.

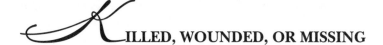ILLED, WOUNDED, OR MISSING

At the time of the Civil War there was no organized official method of informing a soldier's family that he had been killed, wounded, captured, or missing in action.

Casualty lists were sometimes compiled by local reporters and posted outside the newspaper office or town hall, but these were not always complete or accurate.

There were no "dog tags" at that time and soldiers would often pin some form of identification tag to their uniform in case they were killed or seriously wounded.

As regiments at that time were made up mostly of men from the same vicinity, it was often a fellow soldier who notified the soldier's family of his fate.

When Captain Oliver Wendell Holmes was wounded in the neck at Antietam, it was a fellow officer who first notified his family. By the time the family received a letter from Holmes, his father, Dr. Holmes, was already on his way south from Boston.

Dr. Holmes spent two weeks searching in Maryland and Pennsylvania for his wounded son and finally found him in Harrisburg.

In her famous diary, Mary Chestnut of South Carolina writes of how families attending services in a church in Richmond, where she was living at that time, learned of the Chancellorsville casualties.

"It was Sunday, and I was in Mrs. Randolph's pew. The battle of Chancellorsville was raging. And the rattling of the ammunition wagons, the tramp of the soldiers, the everlasting slamming of those iron gates of the Capitol Square just opposite the church, all made it hard to attend to the service.

Then began a scene calculated to make the stoutest heart quail.

The sexton quietly walking up to persons, members of whose family had been brought down wounded, dying, or dead, and the pale-faced people following the sexton out.

Finally, Mr. Minnegerode himself leaned across the chancel rail for a few minutes' whispered talk with the sexton. Then he disappeared, and the assistant clergyman went on with the communion which he was administering.

At the church door stood Mrs. Minnegerode, as tragically wretched and as wild looking as Mrs. Siddons. She managed to tell her husband "Your son is at the station—dead."

When the agonized parents reached the station, it was someone else—a mistake. Somebody's son, all the same. Pale and wan came Mr. Minnegerode back to his place within the altar rails. After the sacred communion was over, someone asked him what it all meant.

"Oh, it was not my son who was killed, but it came so near—it aches me yet."

MARY CHESTNUT'S CIVIL WAR
ed. C. Vann Woodward.
Copyright © 1983 Yale University Press.

At Gettysburg, Lee's lieutenants, A. P. Hill, Longstreet, and Ewell, unlike Jackson, seemed unable to achieve the objective that Lee had assigned, or to suggest a better one.

The battlefield at Chancellorsville is a unit of the Fredericksburg and Spotsylvania National Military Park that also includes Fredericksburg, Spotsylvania, and Wilderness battlefields.

BATTLE OF GETTYSBURG— JULY 1–3, 1863

On June 3, General Robert E. Lee's Army of Northern Virginia was preparing to leave its base at Fredericksburg, Virginia, to march north into Pennsylvania.

President Jefferson Davis and Lee had several sound reasons for this northern invasion, timed to capitalize on the momentum generated by the Confederate victory at Chancellorsville on May 3.

They believed that a similar-size victory on Northern soil would fuel the Northern peace movement and perhaps force Lincoln to end the war through negotiation.

The invasion would also force Major General Joseph Hooker's Union army to follow Lee north, thereby relieving the threat to Richmond, as well as preventing Union reinforcements, being sent west to aid in the attack on Vicksburg.

Finally, in Pennsylvania Lee's army could live off the land and obtain much-needed provisions no longer available in the South due to the Union blockade.

The first battle of the "Gettysburg Campaign" took place at Brandy Station, a few miles west of Fredericksburg, where Major General J.E.B. Stuart, Lee's chief of cavalry, prepared to cross the Rappahannock River and ride north to cover the right flank of Lieutenant General James Longstreet's corps, headed for Pennsylvania.

On June 9, a force of Major General Alfred Pleasonton's Union cavalry under Brigadier John Buford crossed the river at Beverly's Ford and took Stuart by surprise.

What followed was the biggest cavalry battle of the war, as 11,000 Union troopers plus infantry and 9,500 Confederate horsemen went after each other with saber, pistol, carbine, and musket.

Upon learning that other Union forces had crossed the river and occupied Brandy Station, Stuart called on Longstreet to send some infantry.

After an eleven-hour battle, Buford finally returned and recrossed the river. The battle at Brandy Station had established the Union cavalry as an effective force; no longer would Stuart's cavalry reign supreme.

Stuart went on to screen the move of Lee's army into Pennsylvania from Hooker. With this task completed, Stuart received Lee's permission to go off and cut Hooker's supply lines and capture provisions. Lee made an error here, as Stuart ended up making a long dramatic ride around Hooker's army and Lee did not see him again until July 1 near Gettysburg. In the meantime, Lee had to operate in unfamiliar territory without his "eyes."

Hooker was also having problems as he was not sure exactly what Lee was up to. In addition, Hooker was having difficulties with his superior, Major General Henry Halleck, the Union Army General in Chief, who wanted him to defend Har-pers Ferry, protect Washington, and find and defeat Lee.

This seemed like a tall order to Hooker, especially as he believed that Lee's army outnumbered his. Hooker became so upset that he finally requested to be relieved of command. Perhaps much to his surprise, his resignation was accepted.

For some weeks, Lincoln had been looking for someone to replace Hooker, and on June 28 he gave the command to Major General George G. Meade, a brave and conscientious leader who had commanded the Union V Corps at Chancellorsville.

Meade immediately moved his army north to get it between Lee and Washington and prepared to fight Lee whenever he had the opportunity.

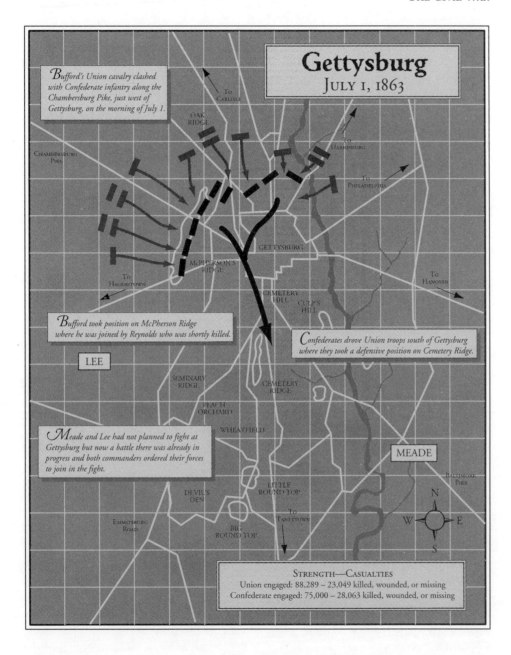

Gettysburg
JULY 1, 1863

Bufford's Union cavalry clashed with Confederate infantry along the Chambersburg Pike, just west of Gettysburg, on the morning of July 1.

To
CARLISLE

OAK
RIDGE

To
HARRISBURG

CHAMBERSBURG
PIKE

To
PHILADELPHIA

McPHERSON'S
RIDGE

GETTYSBURG

To
HAGERSTOWN

To
HANOVER

CEMETERY
HILL
CULP'S
HILL

Bufford took position on McPherson Ridge where he was joined by Reynolds who was shortly killed.

Confederates drove Union troops south of Gettysburg where they took a defensive position on Cemetery Ridge.

LEE

SEMINARY
RIDGE

CEMETERY
RIDGE

PEACH
ORCHARD

Meade and Lee had not planned to fight at Gettysburg but now a battle there was already in progress and both commanders ordered their forces to join in the fight.

WHEATFIELD

MEADE

BALTIMORE
PIKE

DEVIL'S
DEN

LITTLE
ROUND TOP

EMMITSBURG
ROAD

To
TANEYTOWN

N
W   E
S

BIG
ROUND TOP

STRENGTH—CASUALTIES
Union engaged: 88,289 – 23,049 killed, wounded, or missing
Confederate engaged: 75,000 – 28,063 killed, wounded, or missing

As Meade moved north, he learned that Lee was in Pennsylvania with forces in York, Chambersburg, Cashtown, and Carlisle. Roads from these towns were among the ten roads that converged at the small town of Gettysburg with a population of 2,400 and surrounded by farm and orchards.

Without Stuart's cavalry it was June 28 before Lee learned of Meade's appointment as commander and that he was moving toward Pennsylvania with a

90,000-man army. Lee immediately ordered his scattered army of 75,000 to concentrate in the Gettysburg-Cashtown area.

Meade, at Pike Creek, Maryland, was now aware of the importance of Gettysburg and ordered Major General John Reynolds to take his corps there.

On June 30, Reynolds's advance cavalry brigade under Buford clashed with Confederate infantry along the Chambersburg Pike, just outside the town.

After a brisk skirmish, Buford's dismounted cavalry took a position on nearby McPherson Ridge.

Early the following morning, Brigadier James J. Pettigrew, of Major General Henry Heth's division, arrived at Gettysburg to get shoes for the men that were reported to be available there.

Instead of shoes, he found Buford, and, not wishing to engage in an unauthorized battle, returned to Cashtown and reported his findings to Heth.

Heth immediately moved his division to Gettysburg and around 8:00 A.M., July 1, made contact with Buford's brigade on McPherson Ridge.

The battle at Gettysburg was under way. Heth's initial attack was stopped by Union artillery and musket fire, but Buford realized he would soon need help and sent messages to Meade and Reynolds.

Reynolds responded at once and on his arrival at Buford's position sent a message to Meade stating, "I will fight them inch by inch and if driven into town will barricade the streets and hold them as long as possible."

Reynolds and Buford, two very aggressive fighters, had committed Meade to fight at Gettysburg. Lee would have to do the same and now both commanders moved their entire armies to this quiet little town.

The fighting around McPherson Ridge was turning into a major battle with both sides receiving reinforcements, and soon some 40,000 men were engaged.

As Reynolds was urging his men forward to drive the Confederate troops out of McPherson Ridge, he turned his back and was killed by a musket ball. He was the first of the total of seven generals who would be killed at Gettysburg.

After Reynolds was killed the Confederate forces began to gain the upper hand. Lieutenant General Richard Ewell's and Lieutenant General A. P. Hill's corps had arrived to drive the Union troops off McPherson Ridge and through the streets of Gettysburg.

Major Generals O. O. Howard and Winfield Scott Hancock rallied the retreating Union troops and took a defensive position south of town on Cemetery Ridge and Culp's Hill.

The first day of the battle at Gettysburg had been a good one for Lee's army. After inflicting heavy casualties they had driven the Union army out of town, to a defensive position south of town.

By the evening of July 1, Meade and Lee had both arrived at Gettysburg and were concentrating their forces that by morning would number around 88,000 Union and 75,000 Confederate troops.

The morning of July 2 found Meade in an excellent defensive position. His three-mile-long line was roughly in the shape of an inverted fishhook with the "hook" at the line's northern end, curved around Cemetery Hill and Culp's Hill. The shank of the fishhook ran along Cemetery Ridge and the "eye" was anchored at the south by two small hills—Little Round Top and Round Top.

Lee took up a position on Seminary Ridge, named for the Lutheran Seminary that stands there today. The line was parallel to Cemetery Ridge and separated from it by about one mile of relatively

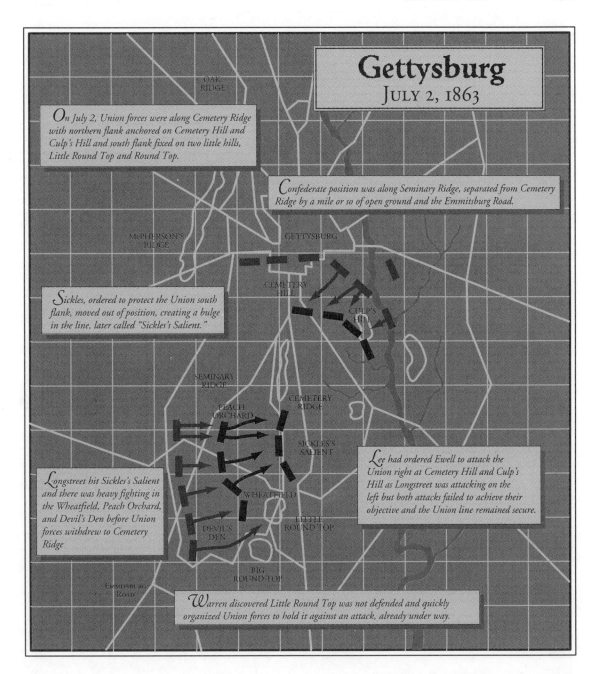

Gettysburg
JULY 2, 1863

On July 2, Union forces were along Cemetery Ridge with northern flank anchored on Cemetery Hill and Culp's Hill and south flank fixed on two little hills, Little Round Top and Round Top.

Confederate position was along Seminary Ridge, separated from Cemetery Ridge by a mile or so of open ground and the Emmitsburg Road.

Sickles, ordered to protect the Union south flank, moved out of position, creating a bulge in the line, later called "Sickles's Salient."

Longstreet hit Sickles's Salient and there was heavy fighting in the Wheatfield, Peach Orchard, and Devil's Den before Union forces withdrew to Cemetery Ridge

Lee had ordered Ewell to attack the Union right at Cemetery Hill and Culp's Hill as Longstreet was attacking on the left but both attacks failed to achieve their objective and the Union line remained secure.

Warren discovered Little Round Top was not defended and quickly organized Union forces to hold it against an attack, already under way.

OAK RIDGE

McPHERSON'S RIDGE

GETTYSBURG

CEMETERY HILL

CULP'S HILL

SEMINARY RIDGE

PEACH ORCHARD

CEMETERY RIDGE

SICKLES'S SALIENT

WHEATFIELD

LITTLE ROUND TOP

DEVIL'S DEN

BIG ROUND TOP

EMMITSBURG ROAD

---

flat, open ground and the Emmitsburg Road.

As Meade was deploying his forces to defend his position, Lee was planning how best to take it. Longstreet, who arrived with his corps around midnight, was opposed to an attack, believing that with Meade's strong position this was not the place to fight him.

Lee disregarded these objections and ordered Longstreet to lead the main attack on Meade's left and Ewell to attack the

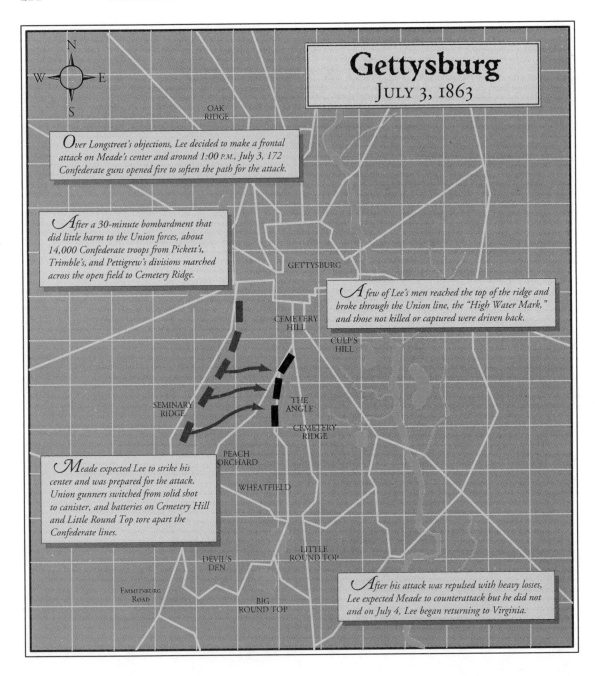

Over Longstreet's objections, Lee decided to make a frontal attack on Meade's center and around 1:00 P.M., July 3, 172 Confederate guns opened fire to soften the path for the attack.

After a 30-minute bombardment that did little harm to the Union forces, about 14,000 Confederate troops from Pickett's, Trimble's, and Pettigrew's divisions marched across the open field to Cemetery Ridge.

A few of Lee's men reached the top of the ridge and broke through the Union line, the "High Water Mark," and those not killed or captured were driven back.

Meade expected Lee to strike his center and was prepared for the attack. Union gunners switched from solid shot to canister, and batteries on Cemetery Hill and Little Round Top tore apart the Confederate lines.

After his attack was repulsed with heavy losses, Lee expected Meade to counterattack but he did not and on July 4, Lee began returning to Virginia.

Gettysburg
JULY 3, 1863

Union right at Cemetery Hill and Culp's Hill when he heard the sounds of Longstreet's artillery.

In the late morning of July 2, Major General Daniel Sickles made a serious blunder.

Meade had ordered him to hold the southern end of Cemetery Ridge and the two Round Tops. Sickles, however, had moved his corps to what he considered a more favorable position on higher ground, but closer to the Emmitsburg Road. This action created a bulge in the Union line, now called "Sickles's Salient."

Meade was upset when he found what Sickles had done, for it left the south end of the line in a dangerous position. Sickles told Meade he would withdraw to his original position. Meade said it was now too late as shells from Longstreet's guns were already falling on the salient. He urged Sickles to hold on as long as he could and Meade would try to reinforce him.

Brigadier General Gouverneur Warren, Meade's chief engineer, had accompanied him to Sickles's position and climbed up Little Round Top to get a better idea of the surrounding terrain.

To Warren's horror, he found that not only was this vital hill not defended, but Confederate troops were about to occupy it. Without authority, Warren ordered any Union troops to go and defend the hill.

Among the troops were Colonel Joshua Chamberlain's regiment, the 20th of Maine, who arrived at the top of the hill just as a regiment from Alabama appeared. Some very fierce fighting followed, and just as the men from Alabama were near the top, Chamberlain's men ran out of ammunition. He ordered a bayonet charge that drove the Confederates off the hill. For his action that day, Chamberlain received the Medal of Honor.

It was not until around 4:00 P.M. that Longstreet ordered two of his divisions commanded by Major General John Hood and Major General Lafayette McLaws, supported by Major General Richard Anderson's division of Lieutenant General A. P. Hill's corps, to attack Sickles.

Despite the fact that their position was such that they could be attacked on three sides, Sickles's men made the Confederates fight for every inch. This included the wheatfield, the apple and peach orchards, as well as Devil's Den—a massive mound of boulders that could well have been created by some evil spirit.

The fighting went on for about four hours. Both Sickles and Hood were wounded, and despite reinforcements the Union troops were being pushed back. The troops finally broke and fled toward Cemetery Ridge, followed by the enemy. It was then that Major General John Sedgwick's corps appeared and counterattacked to stop the Confederate advance.

Observing the now heavily reinforced Union line along Cemetery Ridge, Longstreet called off the attack.

During Longstreet's attack Ewell had gone after Cemetery and Culp's Hills. He had ordered his artillery to pave the way but the Federal guns on higher ground of Cemetery Hill had the advantage.

Ewell decided to attack anyway and Major General Edward Johnson's troops occupied a portion of Culp's Hill before being checked by the reinforced defenders.

Major General Jubal Early's attack on Cemetery Hill made good progress until his troops were finally driven off by artillery fire and reinforcements sent by Hancock.

The attack on the Union center by Anderson's division managed to reach the crest of the ridge before Meade sent reinforcements to drive them off.

One of the important advantages of Meade's relatively short line was that he could quickly move reinforcements where needed.

Despite his army's rather mediocre performance on the second day of the battle Lee planned to make another attack the following day, this time on the center of the Union line.

Meade expected such an attack because previous attacks on his flanks had failed. He

LINCOLN'S GETTYSBURG ADDRESS

On November 19, 1863, the Gettysburg National Cemetery, in which the Union soldiers who died at Gettysburg are buried, was dedicated. The principal speaker was Edward Everett, a former senator, governor, statesman, and Harvard president. He delivered an excellent two-hour oration that no one remembers. He was followed by President Abraham Lincoln, who spoke for only two minutes:

Fourscore and seven years ago our fathers brought forth on this continent a new nation, conceived in liberty and dedicated to the proposition that all men are created equal.

Now we are engaged in a great civil war, testing whether that nation or any nation so conceived and so dedicated can long endure. We are met on a great battle field of that war. We have come to dedicate a portion of that field as a final resting place for those who here gave their lives that that nation might live. It is altogether fitting and proper that we should do this.

But, in a larger sense, we can not dedicate—we can not consecrate—we can not hallow—this ground. The brave men, living and dead, who struggled here, have consecrated it, far above our poor power to add or detract. The world will little note, nor long remember, what we say here, but it can never forget what they did here. It is for us the living, rather, to be dedicated here to the unfinished work which they who have fought here have thus far so nobly advanced. It is rather for us to be here dedicated to task remaining before us–that from these honored dead we take increased devotion to the cause for which they gave the last full measure of devotion—that we here highly resolve that these dead shall not have died in vain—that this nation, under God, shall have a new birth of freedom—and that government of the people, by the people, for the people, shall not perish from the earth.

was so certain of Lee's intentions that he said to Brigadier General John Gibbons of Hancock's corps, "If Lee attacks tomorrow, it will be in your front."

Lee did intend to strike the Union center along Cemetery Ridge with about 14,000 men, including a fresh division of over 4,000 Virginians commanded by Major General George Pickett.

At the same time the center was attacked Ewell would make another attack on Cemetery and Culp's Hills and Stuart, who finally arrived on July 1, would attack the Union rear with his 10,000 cavalrymen.

Lee ordered Longstreet to command the attack on July 3 despite his stated belief that there were no 15,000 men who could cross the mile-wide open space under enemy fire.

So with considerable misgivings, Longstreet ordered Pickett to organize the 10 brigades for the attack.

Longstreet told his artillery chief, Colonel E. Porter Alexander, to position 172 guns to prepare the way for the infantry attack and further told Alexander that he should decide, based on his assessment of the effectiveness of the artillery fire, if the attack should be made. Alexander allowed he could not make such an assessment.

At 1:00 P.M. Alexander's guns opened fire. The focal point of the artillery and the coming charge was a clump of trees near the center of the Union line, later called the "Angle."

The Confederate artillerymen did not have the correct range and many of the

shells passed right over the heads of the Union soldiers, standing behind breast-works added to the top of an existing stone wall.

Union artillery returned fire and the earth was pounded by shells.

Around 1:35 P.M., Alexander saw what he believed was Union artillery withdrawing near the Angle. He also thought there might be slight slacking of Union fire. More important, his ammunition was almost gone. He notified Pickett that now was the time to attack and Pickett asked Longstreet for an order to attack. Longstreet, disgusted with the very concept of an attack, could not voice his consent but simply nodded his head indicating "Yes."

At 1:45 P.M. 14,000 or so Confederate troops began their advance on the Union line, now known as "Pickett's Charge."

Pickett, of course, did not command the charge, only his Virginia division, positioned on the right. Major General Isaac Trimble's brigades were at the center and Brigadier General James Johnson Pettigrew's on the left.

As if on parade, the ranks of Confederate troops in their tattered uniforms, many without shoes, advanced across the mile of open ground. When the ranks passed around an obstruction, they would come to a halt and re-form their line.

Union cannoners switched from shell to canister and on crossing the Emmitsburg

On July 2, 1863, Hood's artillery on this site poured shot on Union infantry attempting to hold "Sickles's Salient." (National Archives)

Road, the advancing columns fell under withering fire from Union guns on Cemetery Hill and Little Round Top, along with musket fire from the ridge.

Union fire tore great holes in the advancing lines and observers on each side were impressed by the bravery of Lee's soldiers and the care displayed in keeping their ranks aligned.

Some managed to reach the top of Cemetery Ridge and there was fierce fighting, much of it hand-to-hand, around the clump of trees and the Angle.

Brigadier General Lewis Armistead, cheering his men along with his cap on the point of his raised sword, penetrated the Union line but was almost instantly killed as he placed a hand on a cannon.

This was the high-water mark of the attack that had failed. The survivors returned to their original position, crossing ground littered with their dead and wounded.

Lee fully expected Meade to launch a counterattack. He directed Pickett to move his division to a defensive position. Pickett sadly replied, "General, I have no division now."

The two other attacks Lee had launched that day also failed.

Union cavalry under Major General David Gregg, which included a brigade commanded by Brigadier General George A. Custer, repulsed Stuart's cavalry attack on the Union rear.

Ewell's attack on Meade's northern flank failed.

Lee had failed to achieve a decisive victory on Northern soil. On the night of July 4, in a driving rainstorm, what remained of Lee's army left Gettysburg to cross the Potomac River and return to Virginia.

They found the Potomac's waters too high to cross. With their backs to the river, the weary, disheartened Confederates were in danger of being wiped out by the pursuing Federal army. But Meade did not push his forces to attack and on July 13 Lee's army returned to Virginia, where it would remain on the defensive for the rest of the war.

The three-day battle at Gettysburg had been a bloody one. Of the approximately 88,289 Union troops engaged, over 23,000 were listed killed, wounded, or missing. Lee's army of 75,000 lost around 28,063, over one third of his force.

Gettysburg is probably the most famous battle of the Civil War and the largest one ever fought on American soil. It has become one of the most important events in the nation's history and inspired President Abraham Lincoln to deliver his immortal "Gettysburg Address" when portions of the battlefield were dedicated as a National Cemetery on November 19, 1863.

On July 4, as Lee's army was retreating from Gettysburg, Major General U. S. Grant's Union forces captured Vicksburg, Mississippi. This had far greater strategic value than the victory at Gettysburg, because the fall of this city gave the Union control of the Mississippi River, cutting the Confederacy in half.

Lincoln was disgusted that Meade had allowed Lee to get away and fight for another two years. What Lincoln seemed to overlook was that unlike his other generals, McClellan, Pope, Burnside, and Hooker, Meade had whipped Lee decisively.

It would not be until March 1864 that Lincoln would find in Grant a general who would press Lee, until he was forced to surrender.

VICKSBURG CAMPAIGN— DECEMBER 1862 TO JULY 4, 1863

Control of the Mississippi River was of vital importance to the federal government as it would furnish an effective way to bring troops and supplies for the projected invasion of the South's western regions and also cut off Texas, Arkansas, and much of Louisiana from the rest of the Confederate states.

By the fall of 1862, the Union had cleared the river of all Confederate forces except for the two strongholds of Vicksburg in Mississippi and Port Hudson in Louisiana, some seventy-five miles north of New Orleans.

In October 1862, Major General Ulysses S. Grant was appointed commander of the Department of Tennessee and almost immediately moved to capture Vicksburg.

The city sits on a bluff on the eastern shore of the Mississippi River, overlooking a bend in the river. In 1862, its defense included artillery positioned along the river front and a maze of swamps and bayous to the north and south that would discourage attack from these directions.

Lieutenant General John Pemberton had 32,000 Confederate troops in the area to defend the city and his immediate superior, General Joseph E. Johnston, had another 6,000 men at the state's capital of Jackson, to the east of Vicksburg.

During the winter of 1862–63, Grant, on the west side of the river, launched a series of amphibious attacks on Vicksburg but these attacks, later to be called the "Bayou Expedition," failed to accomplish anything.

By the spring of 1863, Grant gave up trying to take Vicksburg from the side facing the river. On March 31, he moved his 41,000 army downriver, along its western shore, so as to cross it south of Vicksburg, cut its supply lines from Jackson, and then swing west and attack the east side of the city.

Grant crossed to the east side of the river on April 30. Pemberton failed to stop his advance on May 1 at Port Gibson, on May 12 at Raymond, and on May 14 at Jackson.

From Jackson, Grant headed due west along the Jackson-Vicksburg railroad line and again encountered Pemberton at Champion Hill, about halfway between Jackson and Vicksburg.

BATTLE OF CHAMPION HILL— MAY 16, 1863

Pemberton, ignoring Johnston's order to attack Grant west of Jackson, moved to cut his supply line at Raymond, then changed his mind and returned to Edwards Station, between Vicksburg and Champion Hill.

As Grant continued moving west, Pemberton realized he could not get north of the Jackson-Vicksburg railroad line before being attacked by Grant. He therefore decided to take a defensive position on Champion Hill, rising about 100 feet above the surrounding land that was heavily wooded and laced with numerous gullies.

Pemberton's three divisions formed a right-angle defense line on the hilltop. Major General C. L. Stevenson was on the left, facing north; Brigadier General John S. Bowen and Major General William W. Loring were more or less facing east. Bowen was in the center and Loring on the right.

When Federal Brigadier General Alvin P. Hovey's division discovered the Confederates, it promptly went on the attack. Driving straight up the hill through the woods, it took prisoners and guns to right and left. But it did not hold the hilltop for long. The Confederates regrouped and drove it back down. This pattern of events was repeated several times during the rest of the day.

Soon after Hovey's advance and retreat, Major General John A. Logan's division joined the battle on his right, and between them, they overwhelmed Stevenson. But then, just in the nick of time, Bowen shifted his division to the left to support Stevenson, and suddenly, the tide of battle changed. The Confederates drove the Federals back down the hill until they were less than a half mile from the Champion house, in which Grant had his headquarters.

In their retreat, the Federal soldiers encountered General Logan, who ordered them to pull themselves together and get back into the fight. "General," replied one of them, "the Rebels are awful thick up there." "Damn it!" exploded the general. "That's the place to kill them—where they are thick."

Once again the tide of battle shifted. Brigadier General Marcellus M. Crocker's Federal division arrived on the field and joined the battle. Now, it was the Confederates' turn to retreat. This left Pemberton with only one ace in the hole. He had called on Loring earlier to support Bowen and Stevenson in their successful attack, and Loring had refused on the ground that he expected the main Federal attack to develop to his east. Now Pemberton repeated his order. This time Loring acceded; however, he was not only late, he also took a roundabout route to the battle.

Grant had the same trouble with Major General John A. McClernand as Pemberton had with Loring. Ordered to shift his division northward to join the battle, McClernand at first refused. When he finally agreed, his lead division under Brigadier General Peter J. Osterhaus went into action against Bowen's exposed right flank. This new threat more or less coincided with the threat that Logan was making against Stevenson's left; Pemberton could now see the handwriting on the wall.

The Confederates were not only outnumbered, but they were also running out of ammunition. So at about 5:00 P.M., Pemberton ordered a retreat. The Federals pursued, but the Confederates were able to reach the Big Black River before nightfall.

The Confederates, with 22,000 troops, had lost 3,800. The Union, numbering 32,000 men, lost 2,400.

The battle of Champion Hill revealed an interesting side of General Grant. Just at the height of the action, he appeared behind the Federal line. One of his soldiers, S.H.M. Byers, later wrote that he heard a quiet though commanding voice telling a colonel to move his men a little to the left. "On looking around," Byers wrote,

I saw immediately behind us Grant, the commander in chief, mounted on a beautiful bay mare, and followed by perhaps half a dozen of his staff. For some reason, he dismounted, and most of his officers were sent off, bearing orders, probably, to other quarters of the field. It was Grant under fire. The rattling musketry increased on our front, and grew louder, too, on the left flank. Grant had led his horse to the left, and thus kept near the company to which I belonged.

He now stood leaning complacently against his favorite steed, smoking—as seemed habitual with him— the stump of a cigar. His was the only horse near the line, and must, naturally, have attracted some of the

enemy's fire. . . . I am sure everyone who recognized him wished him away; but there he stood—clear, calm, and immovable. I was close enough to see his features. Earnest they were; but sign of inward movement there was none. It was the same cool, calculating face I had seen before . . . the same careful, half-cynical face I afterward saw busied with affairs of state.

The Champion Hill Battlefield, near Bolton, Mississippi, is designated as a National Historic Landmark but is privately owned and has no official boundaries. Visitors can, however, see much of it from the roads that lace through the area.

SIEGE OF VICKSBURG— MAY 18–JULY 4, 1863

The day after Champion Hill, Grant attacked Pemberton at Big Black River Bridge and drove the Confederate troops into the fortifications at Vicksburg. As night fell on May 18, the Federals had taken up position along the city's outer fortifications. Eventually, there were more than 70,000 Union soldiers (versus 30,000 Confederates). Sherman was on the invading force's right; McPherson in the center; McClernand on the left. If Pemberton, in command of the defending force, had chosen to escape from the city, he could have done so easily enough because there were no Northern troops south of McClernand's corps; but Pemberton had no intention of deserting Vicksburg. As the siege wore on, and the Confederate position grew weaker and weaker, he was urged repeatedly by General Johnston, who was in Jackson, to escape before he was forced to surrender; but he steadfastly refused.

Pemberton wrote Jefferson Davis that he believed "it to be in my power to hold Vicksburg;" and from the start of Grant's campaign against the city, Pemberton's troops proved their commander right.

On May 19, Grant ordered an attack along the line of fortifications because he was confident that the Confederates were demoralized and would give up. Instead, they killed, wounded, or captured 900 Federals. Undeterred by this failure, Grant tried again on the twenty-second. This time, he lost 3,200 men without making any progress. Now, at last, he realized that he could not take the city by storm and settled down for a siege.

By bringing in additional troops, Grant tightened the noose around Vicksburg and shut off all possible escape routes. Half his troops, however, had to be kept ready to repulse an attack in case Johnston and his army should appear and attempt to lift the siege. Trenches were dug opposite the Confederate trenches; in some cases, the two forces were close enough to toss hand grenades back and forth. Several efforts were made by the Federals to burrow under the Southern lines and blow them up with mines, but none worked. Writing of one of these attempts, James C. Fitzpatrick, a Union newspaper correspondent, noted that "so terrible a spectacle is seldom witnessed. Dust, dirt, smoke, gabions, stockades, timber, gun-carriages, logs—in fact, everything connected with the fort—rose hundreds of feet into the air, as if vomited forth from a volcano."

Despite such failures, the outcome of the siege was inevitable. Time was on the Union's side. A constant bombardment drove the Southern troops and city residents underground. Their food supply dwindled and ran out. Rats ran rampant. Death was on every side. Dispatches from Johnston to Pemberton held out hope that he was coming to lift the siege; but he never

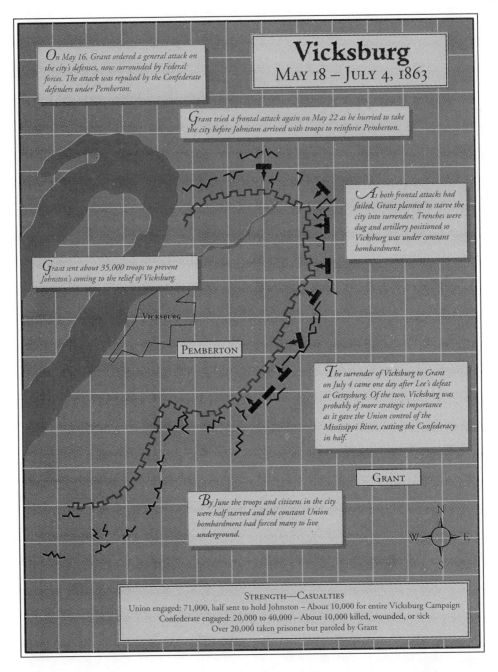

On May 16, Grant ordered a general attack on the city's defenses, now surrounded by Federal forces. The attack was repulsed by the Confederate defenders under Pemberton.

Vicksburg
MAY 18 – JULY 4, 1863

Grant tried a frontal attack again on May 22 as he hurried to take the city before Johnston arrived with troops to reinforce Pemberton.

As both frontal attacks had failed, Grant planned to starve the city into surrender. Trenches were dug and artillery positioned so Vicksburg was under constant bombardment.

Grant sent about 35,000 troops to prevent Johnston's coming to the relief of Vicksburg.

VICKSBURG

PEMBERTON

The surrender of Vicksburg to Grant on July 4 came one day after Lee's defeat at Gettysburg. Of the two, Vicksburg was probably of more strategic importance as it gave the Union control of the Mississippi River, cutting the Confederacy in half.

GRANT

By June the troops and citizens in the city were half starved and the constant Union bombardment had forced many to live underground.

N
W   E
S

STRENGTH—CASUALTIES
Union engaged: 71,000, half sent to hold Johnston – About 10,000 for entire Vicksburg Campaign
Confederate engaged: 20,000 to 40,000 – About 10,000 killed, wounded, or sick
Over 20,000 taken prisoner but paroled by Grant

appeared. Finally, on July 4, Pemberton surrendered.

Even while he was taking control of the city, once known as the Gibraltar of the West, Grant turned Sherman with an army of 50,000 loose to pursue Johnston. The latter withdrew into Jackson; he hoped Sherman would attack him there. Instead, Sherman began to encircle Jackson, and Johnston, fearing he would lose a force as big as that captured at Vicksburg, fled east-ward. Sherman pursued him for a few miles before Grant recalled him.

The 40,000 or so Union troops that were actively engaged in the siege and battles fought during the Vicksburg campaign suffered around 10,000 casualties. Of the 20,000 to 40,000 Confederates engaged, about 10,000 were casualties and 20,000 taken prisoner.

With the fall of Vicksburg, Port Hudson was untenable and surrendered on July 9. The Union now controlled the Mississippi River, prompting Lincoln to state, "The Father of Waters again goes unvexed to the sea."

Coming the day Lee began his retreat from Gettysburg, the loss of Vicksburg was another blow to the South. Not only was the Confederacy cut in half but it lost an army of around 40,000 and the path was now open for a Union advance on Chattanooga.

SIEGE OF PORT HUDSON— MAY 22–JULY 9, 1863

Port Hudson, on the east side of the Mississippi River about 13 miles north of Baton Rouge, Louisiana, was a Confederate bastion almost as formidable as Vicksburg. It rose on a steep bluff high above the river and was well surrounded by deep, steep-sided ravines that were dense with trees and vines. Gun batteries protected the fort on all sides. In March 1863, when Union Rear Admiral David Farragut tried to take a fleet of seven ships north to shut off the flow of supplies reaching the fort from the Red River country in Louisiana, only two safely survived the batteries. So, it was clear to the Union command that, if the Mississippi was to become a Union waterway, they had to remove this obstacle in addition to

Major General William Tecumseh Sherman is considered by many military authorities to be the first modern strategist to realize that in order to win a war it was essential to destroy the enemy's morale and ability to fight by bringing the war to the homefront. His famous "March through Georgia" was an example of this strategy. (National Archives)

conquering Vicksburg. No real effort to achieve this goal was made, however, until May 22, 1863, when Port Hudson was surrounded by Federal troops under Major General Nathaniel Banks, and a fleet under Farragut moved in to provide cannon support. In all, not counting navy men, about 30,000 Federals faced a garrison of 7,500.

Five days after taking positions around Port Hudson, Banks set in motion a grand assault against all points of the Confederate line. But because the attack was made

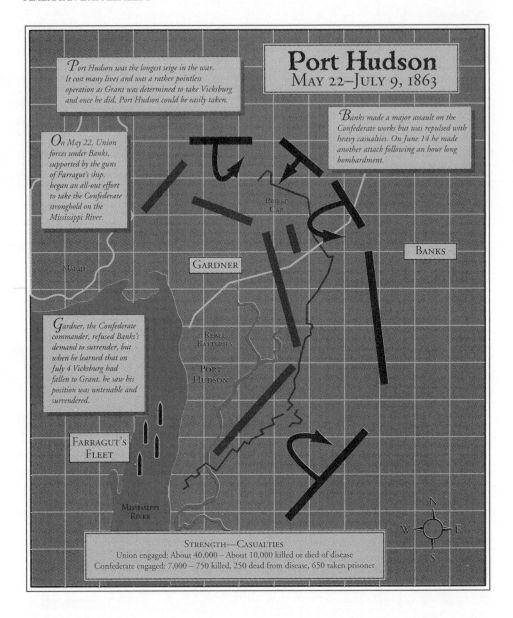

Port Hudson was the longest seige in the war. It cost many lives and was a rather pointless operation as Grant was determined to take Vicksburg and once he did, Port Hudson could be easily taken.

Port Hudson
MAY 22–JULY 9, 1863

On May 22, Union forces under Banks, supported by the guns of Farragut's ship, began an all-out effort to take the Confederate stronghold on the Mississippi River.

Banks made a major assault on the Confederate works but was repulsed with heavy casualties. On June 14 he made another attack following an hour long bombardment.

PRIEST CAP

MARSH

GARDNER

BANKS

Gardner, the Confederate commander, refused Banks's demand to surrender, but when he learned that on July 4 Vicksburg had fallen to Grant, he saw his position was untenable and surrendered.

REBEL BATTERIES

PORT HUDSON

FARRAGUT'S FLEET

MISSISSIPPI RIVER

N
W   E
S

STRENGTH—CASUALTIES
Union engaged: About 40,000 – About 10,000 killed or died of disease
Confederate engaged: 7,000 – 750 killed, 250 dead from disease, 650 taken prisoner

sporadically, the defenders were able to reposition themselves for each onslaught. About 2,000 Union soldiers were killed or wounded.

Another great assault was made by the Federals on June 14, following a day of extremely heavy cannon fire. This assault was centered at the Priest Cap, on the east side of the fortifications, but once again,

the attackers were repulsed with 1,800 casualties.

Realizing that he was not going to overcome Port Hudson by direct assault, Banks settled in for a siege, during which his men dug approach trenches and inched their cannon forward. The Confederates were totally cut off and were reduced to eating their mules and even rats.

Finally, on July 7, Major General Franklin Gardner, who commanded the Confederates, received word that Vicksburg had fallen. Without Vicksburg, Port Hudson was of little strategic value to the South, and on July 9, Gardner surrendered. The siege, which lasted 46 days, was the longest in American military history. Federal losses totaled almost 10,000 men. The Confederates lost 1,000. About half of the Federal casualties and a fourth of the Confederates were attributable to disease and heat stroke.

BATTLE OF CHICKAMAUGA— SEPTEMBER 19–20, 1863

The bloody battle at Stones River ended on January 3, 1863, with Major General William Rosecrans's Union Army of the Cumberland in possession of Murfreesboro and Confederate General Braxton Bragg and his Army of Tennessee in winter quarters at Tullahoma, some 20 miles to the south.

For almost six months the two forces sat tight and it would be another three months before they fought each other again, this time over the control of Chattanooga, Tennessee.

Chattanooga was vitally important to both sides as it was on the Western and Atlantic Railroad that was Bragg's supply line to Atlanta but could also serve the North as a gateway into the heart of the Confederacy.

On June 12, Rosecrans moved to cut off Bragg's retreat south to Chattanooga. But before he managed to do it, Bragg had left Tullahoma and was on his way to cross the Tennessee River and defend Chattanooga, some 55 miles away.

Rosecrans did not immediately pursue Bragg but remained at Murfreesboro for two months while he attempted to get reinforcements from Washington.

On August 16, Rosecrans finally headed for Chattanooga and with some masterful deception crossed the Tennessee River unopposed, and by September 4, had one force positioned below the town with the main force above it.

Rosecrans was informed, incorrectly, that Bragg was about to evacuate Chattanooga so he made a wide sweep to the left to get in back of Bragg and cut off his southward retreat. But because of the mountainous terrain, Rosecrans had to send Major General George Thomas's corps and Major General Alexander McCook's corps on different routes. This was not without risk for the army would be spread over a 40-mile front and the two corps could not support each other.

Bragg learned that Union forces under Major General Ambrose Burnside had taken Knoxville, 100 or so miles to the northeast, so now he was outflanked and under frontal attack. On September 8, Bragg abandoned Chattanooga without a fight and moved south toward Lafayette, Georgia, to concentrate his forces, planning to attack Rosecrans while his forces were still divided by the mountains. Bragg had also received word that Lieutenant General James Longstreet and his corps were on the way from Virginia and would arrive around September 18.

Rosecrans believed that Bragg's withdrawal was a full-scale retreat to Rome, Georgia, and made plans to pursue and crush him.

Early efforts by Confederate forces to wipe out Major General James Nealey's division near Lemore's Cove and Major General Thomas Crittenden's corps at McFarland's Gap were unsuccessful and convinced Bragg to organize a concentrated attack on the enemy. He had already received some reinforcements and would have a force of 65,000 to oppose Rosecrans's 70,000 or so.

Rosecrans was now becoming aware that it was he and not Bragg who was in danger. He immediately began assembling his scattered army to move north toward Chattanooga. Thomas's, McCook's, and Crittenden's corps gathered along the Lafayette-Rossville Road.

Confederate forces, also gathering in the area on the night of September 18, camped on the west shore of Chickamauga Creek.

Bragg may have intended to get his army between Rosecrans's army and Chattanooga but he failed to cut the north-south Lafayette-Rossville Road. Also, his orders to corps commanders were vague, specifying the objective to turn the enemy's left and sweep up Chickamauga Creek.

It is said that in Cherokee, "Chickamauga" is "River of Blood," and while the creek would not run red with blood in the next two days, the ground to the west would.

The valley of the Chickamauga was a terrible site for a battle. The terrain consisted of a few clearings but heavy woods and underbrush and a small pond that after the battle was referred to as "Bloody Pond."

The battle site did have some high ground but because of the thick woods it was not suitable for artillery or even observation. Snodgrass Hill was probably the only site for artillery.

The heavy woods also made it difficult for both sides, because visibility was often limited to 150 yards. Commanders could not see what was going on or even determine the exact location of their troops, or distinguish them from the enemy's.

As was true of many Civil War battles, Chickamauga would develop into a bloody, savage "Soldier's Battle" with soldiers firing away in hope that the target was the enemy and not one of their own.

The battle began on September 19, around 10:30 A.M. when Thomas, who was holding the Union left, sent Brigadier General John Brannan's brigade to destroy what was believed to be a single brigade. Brannan encountered Brigadier General Nathan Buford Forrest's dismounted cavalry, which was shortly reinforced by two Confederate divisions. Brannan called for help.

Each side poured in reinforcements but in the meantime, Bragg was building up strength on his right or northern flank. This forced Rosecrans to shift forces to support Thomas and each Confederate attack was blocked by stubborn Union resistance.

The fighting that day settled nothing but many believed the next day's fighting would settle a lot. During an uneasy night, both sides rearranged the location of their troops to better suit the enemy's force and the terrain.

Union soldiers built log breastworks while Bragg, with the arrival of Longstreet and the remaining two brigades of his corps, divided his army into two wings, Longstreet would be on the left and Lieutenant General Leonidas Polk on the right.

On the morning of September 20, Lieutenant General Harvey Hill's corps attacked Thomas's position.

Thomas's men were more than holding their own, even when Longstreet sent a division to support Hill. But matters would change when Rosecrans committed a fatal error.

Earlier in the battle, Thomas called on Brigadier General J. S. Negley for support, believing his division was being held in reserve. But through some foul-up, Negley was in the line. Even so, Negley sent men to Thomas and his position was taken over by Major General Charles Wood's division, which was in reserve.

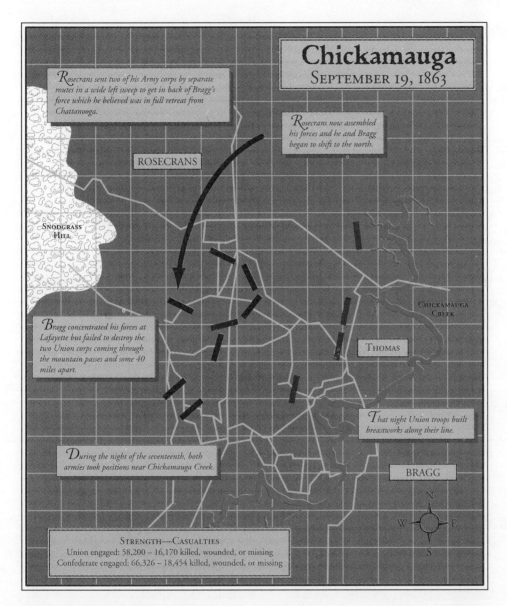

Chickamauga
SEPTEMBER 19, 1863

Rosecrans sent two of his Army corps by separate routes in a wide left sweep to get in back of Bragg's force which he believed was in full retreat from Chattanooga.

Rosecrans now assembled his forces and he and Bragg began to shift to the north.

ROSECRANS

SNODGRASS HILL

Bragg concentrated his forces at Lafayette but failed to destroy the two Union corps coming through the mountain passes and some 40 miles apart.

CHICKAMAUGA CREEK

THOMAS

That night Union troops built breastworks along their line.

During the night of the seventeenth, both armies took positions near Chickamauga Creek.

BRAGG

N W E S

STRENGTH—CASUALTIES
Union engaged: 58,200 – 16,170 killed, wounded, or missing
Confederate engaged: 66,326 – 18,454 killed, wounded, or missing

Rosecrans was unable to see the exact location of his command and believed there was a gap in his line. He therefore ordered Wood to close up to Major General Joseph Reynolds on the right. After questioning this order, Wood moved to the right.

This movement did create a gap in the Union line and Longstreet took full advantage of it. He ordered Major General John Hood to drive through it with three divisions.

Major Generals Philip Sheridan and Jefferson Columbus Davis's divisions were shattered and the entire Union right was rolled back. The Union line was cut in half as Confederate troops poured through the gap and kept going for about one mile.

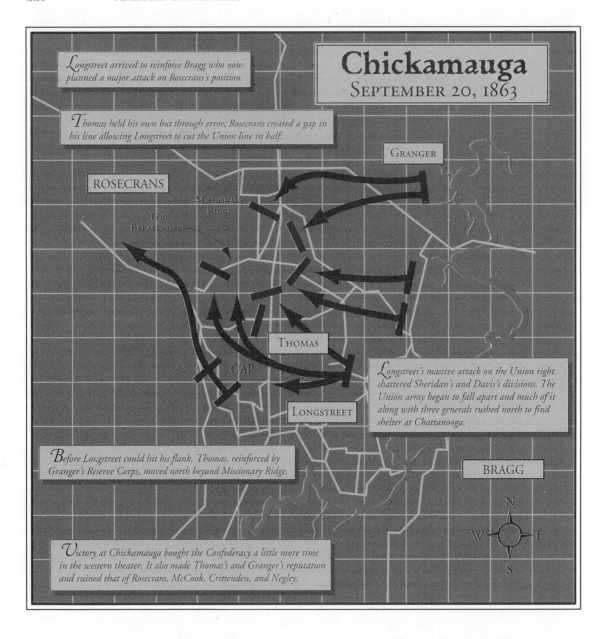

Longstreet arrived to reinforce Bragg who now planned a major attack on Rosecrans's position.

Thomas held his own but through error, Rosecrans created a gap in his line allowing Longstreet to cut the Union line in half.

Chickamauga
SEPTEMBER 20, 1863

GRANGER

ROSECRANS

MISSIONARY RIDGE

LOG BREASTWORKS

THOMAS

GAP

LONGSTREET

Longstreet's massive attack on the Union right shattered Sheridan's and Davis's divisions. The Union army began to fall apart and much of it along with three generals rushed north to find shelter at Chattanooga.

Before Longstreet could hit his flank, Thomas, reinforced by Granger's Reserve Corps, moved north beyond Missionary Ridge.

BRAGG

Victory at Chickamauga bought the Confederacy a little more time in the western theater. It also made Thomas's and Granger's reputation and ruined that of Rosecrans, McCook, Crittenden, and Negley.

Many of the Union troops panicked and rushed toward Chattanooga as the scene became a tangle of men, artillery, baggage wagons, ambulances, and other equipment.

Rosecrans, McCook, and Crittenden, whose corps were also routed, tried to rally their troops and then left for Chattanooga

to arrange for its defense. Bragg had been well to the rear during the battle.

Longstreet was gloating over the fact that the Yankees had run off but he was wrong. Thomas and his corps were very much around in a defensive position on Snodgrass Hill.

Longstreet tried to push them off but the artillery and rifle fire was too much for his now exhausted troops to handle. He asked Bragg for reinforcements but none were sent.

Thomas held on and just as he was to be outflanked was rescued by the arrival of a division of Major General Gordon Granger's corps that had been held in reserve.

About sundown, Thomas was ordered by Rosecrans to withdraw to beyond Missionary Ridge. As he moved north, he fortified McFarland's Gap, closing off the Confederate pursuit.

Thomas managed to gather most of the army together and get them to Chattanooga. His action that day would give him a title, "Rock of Chickamauga," that still endures.

Chickamauga produced very heavy casualties. Of the 58,200 Union troops engaged, 16,170 were listed as killed, wounded, or missing. The somewhat larger Confederate army of 66,326 had casualties totaling 18,454.

The two-day battle turned out to be a bad time for many of the generals involved. Rosecrans, McCook, Crittenden, and Negley would soon be relieved of command. Bragg, who did not appear to get along with any of his officers, fired Polk along with several other general officers.

Chickamauga National Battlefield is a unit of Chickamauga and Chattanooga National Military Park at Fort Oglethorpe, Georgia.

BATTLE OF CHATTANOOGA— NOVEMBER 24–25, 1863

The day after the battle at Chickamauga, Major General William Rosecrans's defeated army took up a defensive position in Chattanooga.

General Braxton Bragg first planned to attack the Union force of 40,000 but discovered their defenses were too much for his 36,000 Confederate army. Instead, he decided to starve out Rosecrans by occupying the mountains, ridges, and hills south of the town so that the forces in Chattanooga would be hemmed in between the mountains and the Tennessee River.

In mid-October, Major General U. S. Grant was put in command of the Military Division of the Mississippi that included almost all of Union forces between the Alleghenies and Mississippi River.

Grant considered Chattanooga to be among his top priorities and arrived there October 23. He had already replaced Rosecrans with Major General George Thomas and transferred Major Generals Alexander McCook and Thomas Crittenden to other forces, giving their corps to Major General Gordon Granger, who, with Thomas, had saved the Union army after Chickamauga.

The first thing Grant had to attend to was establishing a safe supply line to bring food to a half-starved army. The present supply line came overland by way of Stevenson, north of the river and 60 miles from Chattanooga. This route was subject to constant attack by Brigadier General Joseph "Fighting Joe" Wheeler and his Confederate cavalry, and Grant was shocked to learn that it took 10 days for a wagon to cover the route and had resulted in the loss of 10,000 horses and mules to date.

Brigadier General William Smith, Rosecrans's chief engineer, had worked out an alternate route by moving supplies by water from Bridgeport. The one problem with this plan was that Confederate artillery on Racoon and Lookout Mountains controlled that portion of the river, but

Smith had figured out a way to solve this problem and on October 24, Grant gave the order to go ahead with it.

Major General Joseph Hooker crossed the river at Bridgeport and moved east to hold Wauhatchie and continued east to Brown's Ferry.

During the night, the Confederates launched counterattacks on Wauhatchie and other points to cut the line to Bridgeport but failed to accomplish anything.

Now there was a secure supply line between Bridgeport and Chattanooga called by hungry Union troops "The Cracker Line."

In the meantime, the Confederates were having troubles. Bragg, who apparently did not get along with any of his subordinates, found a way to get rid of Lieutenant General James Longstreet by sending him and 12,000 troops to retake Nashville from Major General Ambrose Burnside.

But while Bragg was getting rid of a capable general and 12,000 men, Grant's forces were increasing. The Army of the Potomac had sent two corps and on November 13, Major General William T. Sherman arrived at Bridgeport with the Army of the Tennessee, increasing the total Union force at Chattanooga to 70,000 to oppose Bragg's 50,000.

Grant was now ready to attack and planned it so Bragg could not readily reinforce any portion of his line. Sherman, with the major force, was to cross the Tennessee River and push Bragg's right flank toward Tunnel Hill and link up there with Thomas coming east from Chattanooga. Hooker was to go into Lookout Creek Valley to hold down Bragg's left.

The attack was to begin November 21, but heavy rain delayed Sherman getting across the river. The delay confused Bragg, who now believed Sherman was on his way

to reinforce Burnside at Nashville. Bragg was about to send Longstreet two more divisions, but changed his mind on learning of Thomas's attack on his center.

Around 2:00 P.M. on November 23, Thomas had marched out of Chattanooga and seized the Confederate line along Orchard Knob and Indian Hill. Thomas wanted to press the attack to prevent Bragg's shifting troops to the right to reinforce the troops opposing Sherman. Grant approved the plan and ordered Hooker to create a show of force against the enemy on Lookout Mountain. But when Hooker began his move, about 4:00 P.M. on November 24, he discovered the weakness of the Confederate position and decided on a full-scale attack in what would be called "The Battle Above the Clouds."

Dense fog and rain hid most of the action from the Confederates on the surrounding hills as well as from Federal troops on the plains, but by nightfall it appeared as if another Confederate position had been taken. In the morning all around could see the Stars and Stripes flying on the top of the mountain.

Sherman, however, was not making much progress on the major attack on Tunnel Hill at the north end of the Confederate line along Missionary Ridge. Part of his problem was the difficult terrain, the other, stiff resistance by Confederate troops under Major General William Hardee.

After the "Battle of the Clouds," Bragg concentrated his forces on holding Tunnel Hill as it was key to the northern tip of his line along Missionary Ridge. He ordered Major General John Breckinridge to take three divisions and hold the left and gave Hardee four divisions to hold the right.

Breckinridge spread out his force in order to defend much of the ridge, allowing

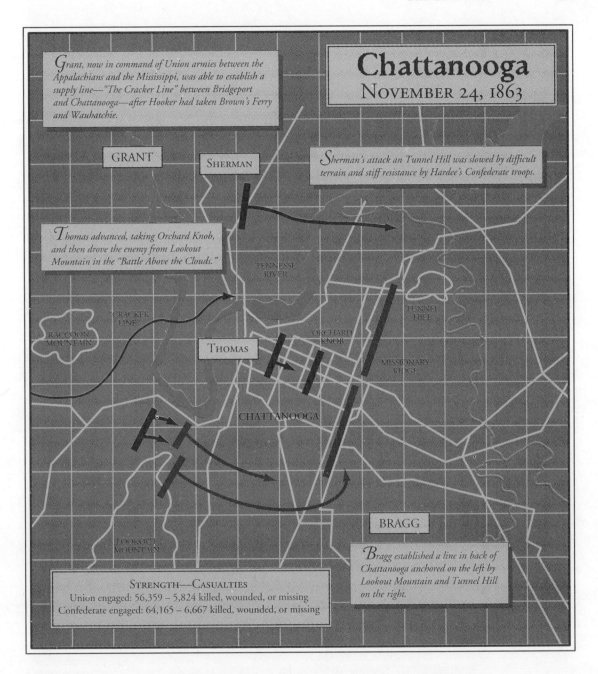

Grant, now in command of Union armies between the Appalachians and the Mississippi, was able to establish a supply line—"The Cracker Line" between Bridgeport and Chattanooga—after Hooker had taken Brown's Ferry and Wauhatchie.

Chattanooga
NOVEMBER 24, 1863

Sherman's attack an Tunnel Hill was slowed by difficult terrain and stiff resistance by Hardee's Confederate troops.

GRANT

SHERMAN

Thomas advanced, taking Orchard Knob, and then drove the enemy from Lookout Mountain in the "Battle Above the Clouds."

TENNESSE RIVER

"CRACKER LINE"

TUNNEL HILL

RACCOON MOUNTAIN

THOMAS

ORCHARD KNOB

MISSIONARY RIDGE

CHATTANOOGA

BRAGG

Bragg established a line in back of Chattanooga anchored on the left by Lookout Mountain and Tunnel Hill on the right.

LOOKOUT MOUNTAIN

STRENGTH—CASUALTIES
Union engaged: 56,359 – 5,824 killed, wounded, or missing
Confederate engaged: 64,165 – 6,667 killed, wounded, or missing

Hardee to concentrate his force around Tunnel Hill.

Grant had moved his headquarters to Orchard Knob on November 24 and launched the final attack. Sherman, with the major force, would continue to attack Bragg's right to join with Thomas at Tunnel Hill and Hooker would strike the left end of the enemy's line along the ridge.

By November 24, Sherman was still not

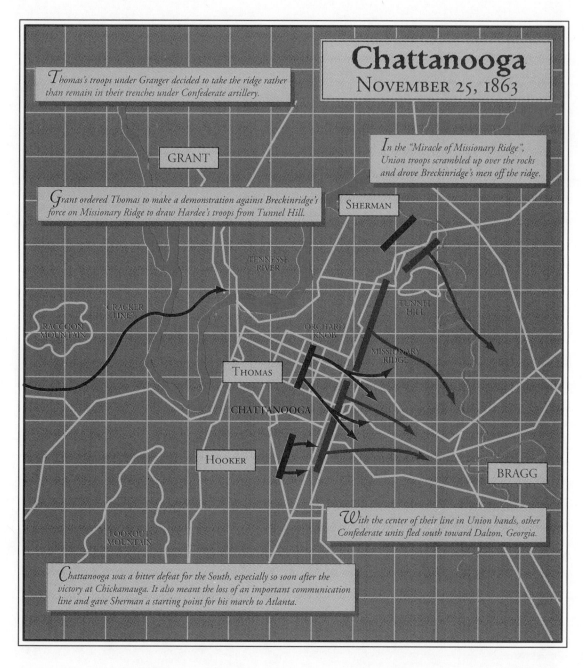

Chattanooga
NOVEMBER 25, 1863

Thomas's troops under Granger decided to take the ridge rather than remain in their trenches under Confederate artillery.

GRANT

In the "Miracle of Missionary Ridge", Union troops scrambled up over the rocks and drove Breckinridge's men off the ridge.

Grant ordered Thomas to make a demonstration against Breckinridge's force on Missionary Ridge to draw Hardee's troops from Tunnel Hill.

SHERMAN

TENNESSE RIVER

"CRACKER LINE"

RACCOON MOUNTAIN

TUNNEL HILL

ORCHARD KNOB

MISSIONARY RIDGE

THOMAS

CHATTANOOGA

HOOKER

BRAGG

With the center of their line in Union hands, other Confederate units fled south toward Dalton, Georgia.

LOOKOUT MOUNTAIN

Chattanooga was a bitter defeat for the South, especially so soon after the victory at Chickamauga. It also meant the loss of an important communication line and gave Sherman a starting point for his march to Atlanta.

making much progress against Hardee so Grant ordered Thomas to make a demonstration in order to force Bragg to take troops from Hardee and reinforce Breckinridge.

Major General Gordon Granger, who commanded Thomas's center corps, instructed his divisional commanders to make an attack on the enemy rifle pits at the base of the ridge. Around 4:00 P.M. the Union troops advanced and easily took the rifle pits. Now they were within range of Confederate guns along the ridge. Granger's troops could either remain to be chewed up by enemy artillery, retreat from the recently hard-won rifle pits, or go ahead and silence the guns. They all apparently decided to go up the sides of the ridge and take the guns.

The story goes that before the attack divisional commander, Major General Philip Sheridan, took out his flask and raised to toast the enemy on the ridge. They answered with a cannon shot that landed near him and splattered his uniform with mud. "For that," Sheridan shouted, "I'll take that gun."

Led by divisional, brigade, and regimental officers, the men left from the rifle pits and madly scrambled up the rocky and tree-covered ridge.

When Grant saw his troops advancing up the ridge under enemy fire he asked Thomas, "Who ordered the men up the ridge!" Thomas answered that he had not and did not know who had. Grant, much annoyed, said, "Someone will suffer for it, if it turns out badly."

But this "Soldiers Battle" did not turn out at all badly and, in fact, would be known as the "Miracle of Missionary Ridge," for by the time the Union soldiers finally reached the top, the defenders had fled.

Sheridan not only got the gun that fired the round that soiled his uniform but 35 additional guns.

Late that afternoon, Hardee rode up to see how Breckinridge was getting along only to find that he and his entire corps had disappeared.

There are several reasons for the poor performance by defenders of the ridge. For several days they had seen one Union victory after another so their morale was pretty

low. And because there were few soldiers for the large area to defend, men were spaced 7 to 8 feet apart. A Confederate soldier felt he was almost alone as he faced the oncoming Yankee soldiers.

As Missionary Ridge was being attacked, Hooker was rolling up the Confederate left. Sherman was still getting nowhere but by now it did not matter. The siege of Chattanooga was over and Bragg's disorganized army was retreating to Dalton, Georgia, some 25 miles to the south. Soon after he resigned his commission.

Casualties in the 3-day battle were relatively light. Grant lost a total of 5,824 out of the 56,359 engaged. Confederate losses of the 64,165 engaged totaled 6,667.

The loss of Chattanooga was a severe blow to the already tottering Confederacy as it opened the road for a Union advance into its heartlands. The high number of Confederates missing after the battle, some 4,146, was a strong signal that the South was becoming tired and discouraged fighting the war.

Within about five months, Sherman would leave Chattanooga bound for Atlanta, Georgia, and then on to Savannah.

Chattanooga Battlefield includes battlefields of Lookout Mountain, Orchard Knob, Missionary Ridge, and Wauhatchie. It is a unit of the Chickamauga and Chattanooga National Military Park.

THE BATTLE OF THE WILDERNESS—MAY 5–6, 1864

Grant was put in command of all Federal armies and given the rank of lieutenant general on March 2, 1864. He quickly appointed Sherman to succeed him as commander of the Military Division of the Mississippi and retained Meade in command of the Army of the Potomac.

Confederate troops atop Missionary Ridge felt secure because they did not believe Union troops could advance over such difficult terrain. But Grant's soldiers found a way, resulting in victory called the "Miracle of Missionary Ridge." (National Park Service)

Grant's basic strategy for winning the war was not just to defeat the Confederates in battle but to destroy the Confederate armies. To achieve this objective he determined that, instead of allowing each campaign to be followed by a period of inactivity, as had been the Federal habit in the past, he would maintain continuous pressure on the Confederates, never giving them a chance to rest and regroup. One of Meade's staff officers said, "Grant wears an expression as if he had determined to drive his head through a brick wall and was about to do it."

As Grant was very familiar with Sherman's qualities as a leader and fighter, he left Sherman to handle military affairs in the west while Grant would remain with Meade to make certain that Lee's army would never escape as it had after Antietam and Gettysburg.

In spring of 1864, Lee's Army of Northern Virginia was in a strong position, where it had spent the winter, along the south bank of the Rapidan River, which flows into the Rappahannock River north of Chancellorsville.

Grant planned to get around Lee's right and get between him and Richmond so Lee would have to fight to defend his capital. On May 4, the 118,000 Army of the Potomac was crossing the Rapidan on pontoon bridges via Germanna, Ely's, and other fords, to take on Lee's 62,000-man army.

Separating the two armies was the Wilderness, an almost impenetrable expanse of densely packed second-growth trees and underbrush lying to the east of Chancellorsville where Lee had defeated Hooker's huge Union army a year ago.

Grant and Meade fully expected to have crossed this dreadful patch of earth and to reach the open ground to the west by May 5, before Lee was aware they were across the Rapidan.

But Lee was not easily fooled and had received reports of the Union army's movements. He organized his forces to attack Grant and Meade in the Wilderness, where the terrain could favor his smaller mobile force, and where the enemy's superior artillery would be unable to play a major role.

His plan was to strike the Union left as it entered the Wilderness. He ordered

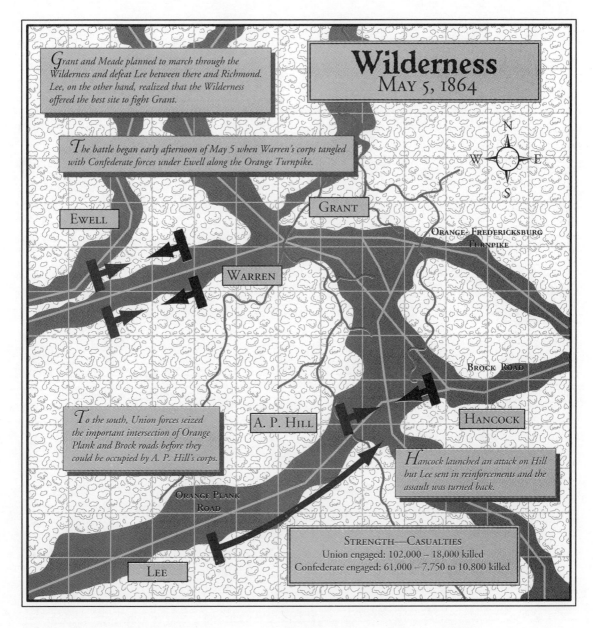

*G*rant and Meade planned to march through the Wilderness and defeat Lee between there and Richmond. Lee, on the other hand, realized that the Wilderness offered the best site to fight Grant.

*T*he battle began early afternoon of May 5 when Warren's corps tangled with Confederate forces under Ewell along the Orange Turnpike.

Wilderness
MAY 5, 1864

EWELL

GRANT

WARREN

ORANGE—FREDERICKSBURG TURNPIKE

BROCK ROAD

*T*o the south, Union forces seized the important intersection of Orange Plank and Brock roads before they could be occupied by A. P. Hill's corps.

A. P. HILL

HANCOCK

*H*ancock launched an attack on Hill but Lee sent in reinforcements and the assault was turned back.

ORANGE PLANK ROAD

STRENGTH—CASUALTIES
Union engaged: 102,000 – 18,000 killed
Confederate engaged: 61,000 – 7,750 to 10,800 killed

LEE

Lieutenant General Richard Ewell to march his corps east along the Orange Turnpike that cut through the middle of the Wilderness and for Lieutenant General A. P. Hill's corps to move in the same direction along the Orange Plank Road, running roughly parallel and to the south of Ewell's route.

Lee also directed Lieutenant General James Longstreet, whose corps was twenty miles to the west at Gordonsville, to come to the Wilderness.

Union hopes of reaching open ground beyond the Wilderness by May 5 were dashed early that morning when advanced units of

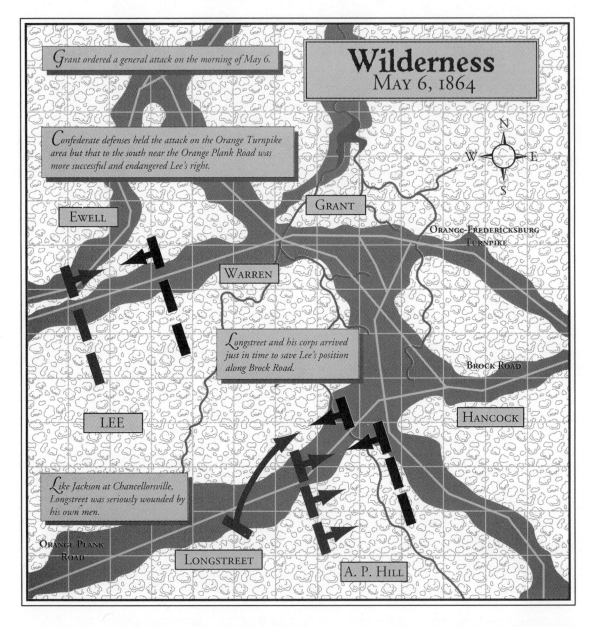

Grant ordered a general attack on the morning of May 6.

Confederate defenses held the attack on the Orange Turnpike area but that to the south near the Orange Plank Road was more successful and endangered Lee's right.

GRANT

EWELL

ORANGE-FREDERICKSBURG TURNPIKE

WARREN

Longstreet and his corps arrived just in time to save Lee's position along Brock Road.

BROCK ROAD

HANCOCK

LEE

Like Jackson at Chancellorsville, Longstreet was seriously wounded by his own men.

ORANGE PLANK ROAD

LONGSTREET

A. P. HILL

Wilderness
MAY 6, 1864

Major General G. K. Warren's V Corps reported the presence of Ewell's corps.

By early afternoon there was fierce fighting along the Orange Turnpike as Warren tried to stop Ewell's advance and drive him back. Soon, the fighting spread southward and became more and more intense as Warren's troops battled to hold their initial gains. Even with the arrival of divisions of Major General John Sedgwick's VI Corps, Warren's men were unable to advance and by dark the battle had become a stalemate with both forces digging in for the night.

To the south, Federal cavalry had earlier taken the vital intersection of the Orange Plank Road and it was soon secured by one of Sedgwick's divisions. Later in the afternoon Major General Winfield S. Hancock's Second Corps arrived and launched a series of fierce attacks on Hill's position. Lee reinforced Hill with reserves and Hancock's attacks hurt but did not defeat Hill.

By nightfall, when the day's fighting ended, the entrenched battle lines extended for five miles through the Wilderness west of the Germanna and Block Roads.

Lee's north, held by Ewell, was secure but Hill's command at the south was badly disorganized. That night Lee sent Longstreet a message ordering him to make a forced march in order to arrive at the Wilderness by early next morning.

Grant and Meade resumed their attack the following morning and while their troops were unable to make any advance against Ewell's defended position, the strike against Hill at the south by Hancock's corps and supported by other divisions made substantial gains. Just as it appeared they might completely smash Hill's corps and destroy Lee's right flank, Longstreet's corps arrived at the scene after a 42-mile march.

Lee sent him around the Union left flank in hope of rolling it up. His attack took Hancock's men by surprise and drove their first line beyond their entrenchments.

Lee became so excited he tried to lead Brigadier General John Greg's Texas-Arkansas brigade in a counterattack across the open fields of the Tapp Farm but was firmly sent to the rear by the call from the brigade, "Lee to the rear."

Longstreet should have also retired to the rear for, like Stonewall Jackson, he was wounded by one of his own men. Fortunately, the wound was not too serious and he was back in action in a few months.

Longstreet's attack, however, was so vicious that Federal troops were thrown back to entrenchments they had previously prepared.

In early evening, Confederates attacked both flanks of the Union line. Brigadier General John B. Gordon's Confederate brigade hit the right flank and took 600 prisoners but had to retire on getting no support from Ewell. This attack ended the fighting at the Wilderness as Grant realized he would gain nothing but grief attacking the dug-in enemy.

On May 7, he ordered Meade to move the army south to the road center at Spotsylvania.

In a war of so many frightful battles the Wilderness was one of the worst. In addition to the claustrophobic nature of fighting hand-to-hand in the dense vegetation was the horror of forest and brush fires which incinerated some of the men who had been wounded too badly to escape the flames and filled the air with the odor of roasted human flesh.

In the two-day battle, Union casualties were 18,000 out of the 102,000 engaged. Confederate casualties were between 7,750 and 10,800 of the 61,000 or so engaged.

Despite heavy casualties, Grant not only did not withdraw but rather moved southward, sliding past Lee's flank and continuing to fight a series of bloody battles until the Army of Northern Virginia had neither the manpower nor will to go on fighting.

The Wilderness Battlefield is a unit of the Fredericksburg and Spotsylvania National Military Park that also includes battlefields at Fredericksburg, Chancellorsville, and Spotsylvania.

BATTLE OF SPOTSYLVANIA COURT HOUSE—MAY 8–21, 1864

When Grant and Meade started moving their army south from the Wilderness, their troops cheered. Although many of their comrades had fallen in the Wilderness, this was the first time that the Union army had moved ahead against the enemy after a battle in Virginia. The move was in keeping with Grant's determination to never give Lee's army a chance to pull itself together after a fight.

The Union army's objective was Spotsylvania Court House, about fifteen miles south of the Wilderness and of strategic importance as its crossroads included the shortest road to Richmond and offered Grant the possibility of enveloping Lee's flank to get between his army and Richmond.

Scouts told Lee that the nearby Union pontoon bridge at Germanna Ford on the Rapidan had been removed, eliminating any possibility of Union forces' withdrawing from the region. Stuart had reported Federal activity to the south.

From these facts, Lee immediately grasped what Grant was up to and ordered his army to move southward.

The night of May 7–8 found both armies racing by separate routes to be the first to occupy Spotsylvania Court House. Lee won the race.

Meade blamed the failure of the Union troops to reach their objective before Lee on Sheridan's 10,000 cavalry division that hogged the Brock Road (now State Route 613) slowing the infantry's march.

Sheridan, famous for his short temper, told Meade he was only following his orders and a heated debate followed. Grant smoothed his brilliant cavalry commander's wounded pride by sending him to ride off and threaten Richmond. This turned out to be a mistake on Grant's part, for in the coming battle he, like Lee at Gettysburg, would have no cavalry to tell him of the enemy's movements.

On the morning of May 8, advance columns of the two armies made contact at Spindle Farm on Brock Road, just north of Spotsylvania. Although reinforced by soldiers arriving from the Wilderness, the Union advance was stopped and by the morning of May 9, Confederate troops were at Spotsylvania Court House establishing a defense line north between the Po and Ny rivers to block a Union advance southward.

Lee, a West Point–trained military engineer, laid out a very formidable six-mile-long line, roughly in the shape of an inverted V, that ran north from the village and then turned west across Brock Road.

At about the center of the line was a bulge, a salient, also in the shape of an inverted V, some three-quarters of a mile deep and a half-mile wide at its base, known by its shape as "The Mule Shoe Salient."

Mule Shoe and the entire line were protected with trenches, breastworks of earth and logs, and abatis of logs, fence rails, and what other materials were handy, and by artillery.

Union forces took a position running roughly parallel to the Rebel line and so close to it that artillerymen were often exposed to Confederate sniper fire.

Major General John Sedgwick, in fact, was mortally wounded by such fire on May 9, as he was directing placement of Union artillery and only a minute or so after telling his gun crews trying to dodge the occasional Minié bullets that whizzed over their heads, "Don't duck, they couldn't hit an elephant at this distance."

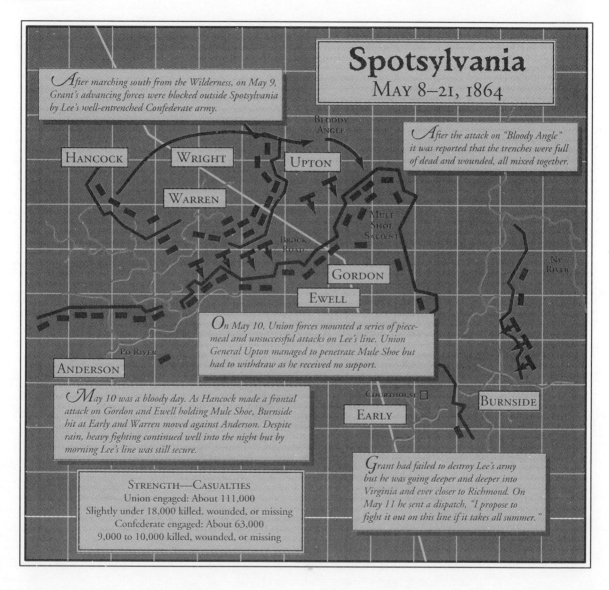

Spotsylvania
MAY 8–21, 1864

After marching south from the Wilderness, on May 9, Grant's advancing forces were blocked outside Spotsylvania by Lee's well-entrenched Confederate army.

BLOODY ANGLE

After the attack on "Bloody Angle" it was reported that the trenches were full of dead and wounded, all mixed together.

HANCOCK   WRIGHT   UPTON

WARREN

MULE SHOE SALIENT

NY RIVER

BROCK ROAD

GORDON

EWELL

On May 10, Union forces mounted a series of piecemeal and unsuccessful attacks on Lee's line. Union General Upton managed to penetrate Mule Shoe but had to withdraw as he received no support.

PO RIVER

ANDERSON

COURTHOUSE

EARLY

BURNSIDE

May 10 was a bloody day. As Hancock made a frontal attack on Gordon and Ewell holding Mule Shoe, Burnside hit at Early and Warren moved against Anderson. Despite rain, heavy fighting continued well into the night but by morning Lee's line was still secure.

Grant had failed to destroy Lee's army but he was going deeper and deeper into Virginia and ever closer to Richmond. On May 11 he sent a dispatch, "I propose to fight it out on this line if it takes all summer."

STRENGTH—CASUALTIES
Union engaged: About 111,000
Slightly under 18,000 killed, wounded, or missing
Confederate engaged: About 63,000
9,000 to 10,000 killed, wounded, or missing

On May 10, Grant and Meade began to probe Lee's line by launching attacks from Laurel Hill on Major General Richard Anderson's corps on the Confederate left. These piecemeal attacks were not successful.

Major General Horatio Wright, now in command of Sedgwick's corps, and Major General Emory Upton believed that Mule Shoe could be taken by a sudden and well-organized attack.

In late afternoon of the tenth, after Union artillery had pounded Lieutenant General Richard Ewell's men, who held Mule Shoe, Upton hit the salient with twelve regiments and penetrated the defense line. The attack was not supported and Upton was forced to withdraw.

The attack convinced Grant and Meade that Mule Shoe was the weak spot in Lee's line and could be taken with a concentrated attack planned for the morning of May 12.

Major General Winfield Scott Hancock's corps were to hit the tip of the salient and Wright its northwest face. Major General Ambrose Burnside was to attack the east side of the main line held by Major General Jubal A. Early and Major General Gouverneur K. Warren's V Corps would strike at Anderson's position.

The fighting, which would continue for the next twenty-three hours, began at 4:30 on the morning of May 12. Hancock, with 20,000 men, struck the point of the salient and within fifteen minutes had penetrated Ewell's line, taking around 3,000 prisoners. Hancock's advance down the length of the salient was finally checked by Brigadier General John Gordon who was holding the neck of the Mule Shoe salient.

Lee, sensing potential disaster, rode over to assist Gordon in a counterattack but, as was the case at the battle of the Wilderness, was forced to return by the cries of his soldiers, "General Lee to the rear. General Lee to the rear."

Gordon failed to drive Hancock out of the salient and fighting continued.

Some of the most ferocious fighting of the entire war was on Wright's front at a kink in the line soon to be called "Bloody Angle."

Musket fire was so intense that the breastwork's logs and fence rails were shattered by the hail of Minié balls, and trees as much as twenty-two inches in diameter were felled as hundreds upon hundreds of musket balls whittled away their trunks. Muskets soon became so fouled with powder they could not be fired, so the stocks were turned into clubs to smash the skulls of the enemy. Men fought hand-to-hand with whatever weapon was handy, be it a bayonet, sword, or knife.

Confederate gunners hauled their pieces to the top of the breastworks and fired canister to mow down the advancing Union troops.

Fighting continued into the night despite a fierce rain. But around midnight the two armies were fought out. By then Hancock had been forced out of most of Mule Shoe and the Confederate troops retired behind Gordon's defensive line at the neck of the salient.

While Hancock and Wright were involved in Mule Shoe, Burnside and Warren launched unsuccessful attacks on other sections of the line.

On May 18, Grant again tried to crack Lee's line but with no luck. The following day, Ewell took his corps, now down to 6,000 men, to swing around the Union right to see if Grant was moving and, if so, in which direction. After crossing the Ny River, Elwell ran into Union Brigadier General Tyler with his command of heavy artillerymen retrained to fight as infantry. In the ensuing battle at Harris Farm, Tyler lost 1,500 and Ewell 900.

This engagement ended the battle at Spotsylvania Court House as Grant concluded it was a waste of men to continue attacks against such strong defenses. Instead, Grant would once again try to slide around Lee's flank.

It had been another dreadful battle of the Civil War. In all 18,000 of the Union army's 111,000, not all engaged, were casualties. The far smaller Confederate army of 63,000 lost around 9,500.

This was not a good battle for Lee for he not only failed to keep Grant out of central Virginia but had to fight without his great commanders, who might have helped him achieve a decisive victory. Jackson was dead. Longstreet had not yet recovered from his wounds and A. P. Hill was sick.

Then, as the fighting raged round Mule Shoe, Lee learned that Stuart, whom he had sent to check Sheridan around Richmond, had been killed on May 11 in cavalry fight at Yellow Tavern. Of Stuart's death Lee remarked, "I can scarcely think of him without weeping."

The battle had been no great victory for Grant, as he failed to destroy Lee's army or even defeat it. But Grant was not to be stopped in his attack on Lee's army and on May 19 had sent the following dispatch to Washington: "I purpose to fight it out on this line if it takes all summer."

It would take more than a summer to finish Lee, and in the meanwhile Grant slipped around Lee's left to meet up with him a few days later at the North Anna River.

The Spotsylvania Court House Battlefield is a unit of the Fredericksburg and Spotsylvania National Military Park that also includes the battlefields at Fredericksburg, Chancellorsville, and Wilderness.

BATTLE OF NEW MARKET— MAY 15, 1864

The battle of New Market was the first in the 1864 Union campaign to secure control of the Shenandoah Valley and destroy the farms that supplied the Southern armies with much of their food and fodder. The battle, however, ended in a Northern defeat. The Federals, numbering almost 9,000 men, suffered a 10 percent loss in casualties. The Confederates also lost 10 percent of their 5,300 men, but they succeeded in derailing the Union campaign for a number of months.

New Market, Virginia, was a tiny village of no military importance except that the Valley Turnpike, which ran up and down the Shenandoah Valley, was here intersected by the only road for miles that ran east over the Blue Ridge Mountains toward Fredericksburg. The Confederates wanted to keep this road open; the Northerners wanted it closed.

The Union army under Major General Franz Sigel had been heading south toward New Market for about a week. The Confederates, under Major General John C. Breckinridge, aided by Brigadier General John D. Imboden, had moved north to meet it. On the way, Breckinridge's badly outnumbered troops were reinforced by 247 14- to 18-year-old cadets from the Virginia Military Institute in Lexington. This was the first time in the war that the institute's student body had been tapped for active duty.

By dawn on the day of battle, the Confederates had established their line on Shirley Hill, just south of New Market. The Northerners occupied the town and Bushong's Hill to the north. When Sigel refused to attack, as Breckinridge hoped he would, the latter went on the defensive and soon pushed the advance soldiers of the Northern army out of the town and back to the base of Bushong's Hill. In the meantime, Imboden's cavalry skirted around the Federal left flank, crossed Smith's Creek and opened fire on the Federal cavalry on the west side of the creek. This had little effect on the battle's outcome but did force the Northern cavalry to retreat northward.

At Bushong's Hill, the initial Rebel drive sputtered out. As they started to fall slowly back, a large hole opened in their center. Sigel should have taken advantage of this,

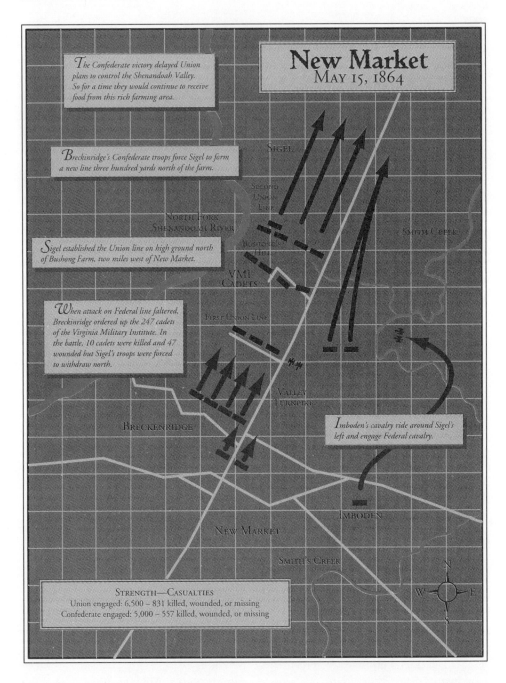

New Market
MAY 15, 1864

The Confederate victory delayed Union plans to control the Shenandoah Valley. So for a time they would continue to receive food from this rich farming area.

Breckinridge's Confederate troops force Sigel to form a new line three hundred yards north of the farm.

SIGEL

SECOND UNION LINE

NORTH FORK SHENANDOAH RIVER

SMITH CREEK

BUSHONG'S HILL

Sigel established the Union line on high ground north of Bushong Farm, two miles west of New Market.

VMI CADETS

FIRST UNION LINE

When attack on Federal line faltered, Breckinridge ordered up the 247 cadets of the Virginia Military Institute. In the battle, 10 cadets were killed and 47 wounded but Sigel's troops were forced to withdraw north.

VALLEY TURNPIKE

BRECKENRIDGE

Imboden's cavalry ride around Sigel's left and engage Federal cavalry.

IMBODEN

NEW MARKET

SMITH'S CREEK

N W E S

STRENGTH—CASUALTIES
Union engaged: 6,500 – 831 killed, wounded, or missing
Confederate engaged: 5,000 – 557 killed, wounded, or missing

but he was a cautious man and neglected to do so. This gave Breckinridge time to regroup and go back on the offensive.

The weather was miserable. It had been raining since the previous day, and the low ground at the foot of Bushong's Hill had become a quagmire. But Breckinridge was not deterred. Though he acted reluctantly, he threw the cadets into the center of his line and gave the order to attack just as

1,500 Federals came storming down the hill. The bloodiest fight of the battle ensued. The Confederates held their ground; then, buoyed by this success, renewed their charge. Many of the men, especially the cadets, lost their shoes in the sticky mud. But they were not to be stopped. They reached the top of the hill and the Federal troops withdrew to the north. A small skirmish followed two miles farther on at Rudes's Hill, but the Northerners' ammunition was running as low as their morale, and they broke off the battle, retreated across the Shenandoah River, and destroyed the bridge.

The Federal campaign in the Shenandoah Valley was resumed several weeks later, but neither Sigel nor Breckinridge was in command. The latter, with 2,500 troops, had joined Lee east of the Blue Ridge. Sigel was relieved of his command and replaced in the valley by Major General David Hunter. Why Sigel lost at New Market is unclear. Some believe that because he was German-born he gave orders on Bushong's Hill in German and no one understood him. But it is more likely that he was just another of the North's many poor commanders. During the entire war, the only battle he won was that at Pea Ridge, Arkansas.

Of the 6,500 Union troops engaged, 831 were casualties. Confederate casualties of the 5,000 engaged totaled 577, including 57 Virginia Military Institute cadets, 10 of whom were killed, and 47 wounded.

BATTLE OF COLD HARBOR— MAY 31–JUNE 3, 1864

Cold Harbor, so near Richmond that its inhabitants could hear the thunder of musket rifle and artillery fire, was Lee's last great victory. In little more than half an hour on the morning of June 3, 7,000 Union soldiers were killed or wounded in an unwise attack and Grant's advance toward Richmond was halted.

The battle at Cold Harbor followed closely on the heels of the bruising fights at the Wilderness, Spotsylvania Court House, and at the North Anna River.

The battle at the North Anna River of May 23 to 26 occurred as a result of Grant's decision to send Meade's Army of the Potomac southward to turn Lee's right and get between him and Richmond.

Lee guessed Grant's intentions and moved to block his army's southward advance. During the night of May 21, both armies were marching south, on more or less parallel routes, heading for the railroad center of Hanover Junction on the south side of the North Anna River.

It was here that Grant planned to get around Lee's right, while Lee expected to be joined at Hanover Junction by Major General John Breckinridge's corps and believed the steep banks of the river would be a good place to stop Grant.

As he was marching south on the shorter interior route, Lee's troops only had to march twenty miles to reach Hanover Junction on the following day, one day before Union troops began arriving on May 23.

By the time Union forces arrived at the North Anna River, most of Lee's 53,000 men were entrenched on the south side.

Federal troops crossed the river via the several bridges and fords and in the afternoon attacked Confederate forces and were beaten back. But these attacks convinced Lee that his present line could not withstand an attack by Grant and Meade's entire army of 68,000. That night Lee set his men to building a new defense line. In

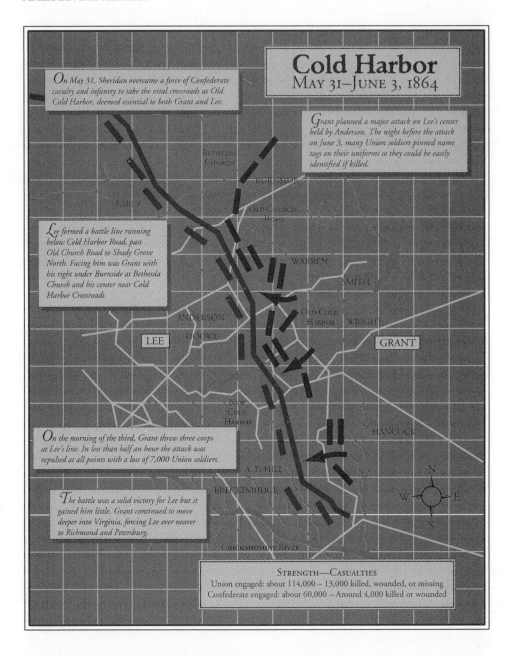

Cold Harbor
MAY 31–JUNE 3, 1864

On May 31, Sheridan overcame a force of Confederate cavalry and infantry to take the vital crossroads at Old Cold Harbor, deemed essential to both Grant and Lee.

Grant planned a major attack on Lee's center held by Anderson. The night before the attack on June 3, many Union soldiers pinned name tags on their uniforms so they could be easily identified if killed.

Lee formed a battle line running below Cold Harbor Road, past Old Church Road to Shady Grove North. Facing him was Grant with his right under Burnside at Bethesda Church and his center near Cold Harbor Crossroads.

On the morning of the third, Grant threw three corps at Lee's line. In less than half an hour the attack was repulsed at all points with a loss of 7,000 Union soldiers.

The battle was a solid victory for Lee but it gained him little. Grant continued to move deeper into Virginia, forcing Lee ever nearer to Richmond and Petersburg.

BETHESDA CHURCH

BURNSIDE

EARLY

OLD CHURCH ROAD

WARREN

SMITH

ANDERSON

OLD COLD HARBOR   WRIGHT

HOOKE

LEE

GRANT

NEW COLD HARBOR

HANCOCK

A. P. HILL

BRECKINRIDGE

CHICKAHOMINY RIVER

N
W   E
S

STRENGTH—CASUALTIES
Union engaged: about 114,000 – 13,000 killed, wounded, or missing
Confederate engaged: about 60,000 – Around 4,000 killed or wounded

the shape of an inverted V with the point facing the river and the sides or flanks turned back, the new line was intended to present Grant with two unsatisfactory choices: If he attacked just one side of the V, Lee could quickly move men to reinforce

this point; if Grant attacked both sides simultaneously he would have to split his forces and each would be totally separated and unable to support the other.

On the morning of May 24, Grant learned that Confederate troops on Lee's left, outside the entrenched line, had retired and, assuming it indicated Lee's entire army had withdrawn, ordered a general attack on both flanks.

Lee, of course, had not withdrawn and the attacking forces were mowed down by heavy crossfire and failed to penetrate the line. Confederate defenses were so strong that Grant not only called off the attack but had his men dig entrenchments in case Lee launched a counterattack.

After some skirmishes on the night of May 26–27, Grant crossed to the river's north shore and marched downstream.

The battle at the North Anna River had been a vicious fight with the Union suffering 2,623 casualties and the Confederates 2,517.

During the weeks in May, as Grant was moving from the north toward Richmond, Major General Benjamin Butler with "The Army of the James" was sailing up the James River to strike the confederate capital from the south.

Butler, a smarter politician than a general, disembarked his troops at Bermuda Hundred and began a slow march toward Richmond which ended on May 16 at Drewry's Bluff, where he was stopped by a Confederate force under Lieutenant General P.G.T. Beauregard, who not only whipped Butler and drove him back to Bermuda Hundred, but dug entrenchments to hold him there. As Grant put it, Butler's army "was now as completely shut off from further operations directed against Richmond as if it had been in a bottle strongly corked."

Grant figured Butler did not need a lot of company in his "bottle" at Bermuda Hundred and ordered Brigadier General William Smith to bring his corps north.

Lee was desperate for reinforcements and, despite Beauregard's objections,

Photograph of General Robert E. Lee taken shortly after his surrender at Appomattox. It is interesting to speculate whether the Civil War would have lasted four years if Lee, a man of great dignity and military ability, had accepted General Scott's offer in 1861 to command the Union armies. (National Archives)

finally got Major General Robert Hoke's division. Smith and Hoke would arrive in time for the opening round of battle at Cold Harbor.

After leaving his position at the North Anna River on May 27, Grant moved about twenty miles downriver for another try to get around Lee's right and found him entrenched behind Totopotomoy Creek, eighteen miles south of the North Anna River and ten miles north of Richmond.

At Totopotomoy Creek there were a couple of days of heavy skirmishing and by the end of May both forces continued moving southward.

The Union goal was the vital crossroads at Old Cold Harbor, where one road ran to Richmond and another northwest toward Lee's army. Old Cold Harbor is located between Totopotomoy Creek and the Chickahominy River, about eight miles north of Richmond.

The general area was relatively unoccupied other than the two taverns, New Cold Harbor and Old Cold Harbor, about one mile apart and, to their north, Bethesda Church on Old Church Road.

On May 31, Major General Philip Sheridan's cavalry division occupied the crossroads at Old Cold Harbor after driving off the Confederate cavalry commanded by General Lee's nephew, Major General Fitzhugh Lee.

Both Grant and Lee rushed forces to this point of contact and the first to arrive were Lieutenant General Richard Anderson's Confederate First Corps and Hoke's division.

When the Confederates showed up, Sheridan felt threatened and withdrew from Old Cold Harbor but was ordered by Meade to return and hold the crossroads until he could be relieved. Between his artillery and his dismounted trooper's repeating rifles, Sheridan, the aggressive pint-size general, held off Anderson and Hoke until relieved by Major General Horatio Wright's Sixth Corps.

On the afternoon of June 1, Anderson was joined by Smith and his Eighteenth Corps that had just arrived from Bermuda Hundred and around 6:00 P.M. they launched an attack on Anderson's position.

The Union troops managed to penetrate the line but before they could enlarge the breach reinforcements arrived to plug it. That ended the fighting for the day.

Grant and Lee had decided to continue to fight in this area and on the night of June 1–2 both armies were gathering their strength and preparing for a major battle.

Lee's seven-mile-long line extended southward from Totopotomoy Creek to the Chickahominy River. Facing Lee was Grant's five-mile-long line that ran from the Bethesda Church region southward past Old Cold Harbor.

Grant and Meade were sure that Lee's worn and half-starved army of 59,000 was whipped, and that was an attack of sufficient force that would drive it across the Chickahominy where it could be destroyed.

With a total force of somewhere between 108,000 and 114,000 soldiers, the two Union generals decided to attack Lee's line on June 2 with three corps totaling around 50,000. Orders went out to Major Generals Winfield S. Hancock and G. K. Warren to come at once to be on hand for the attack.

Warren and his Fifth Corps showed up in plenty of time but Hancock's Second Corps seemed to have lost its way and had to march all night before it reached its designated position at 7:30 A.M. The men were so exhausted that Meade postponed the scheduled morning attack until 2:00 P.M. to give Hancock's men a chance to rest.

Grant, however, believed the men needed more than just a few hours rest because for the past month they had been either fighting or marching and ordered Meade to order the attack at 4:30 A.M. the following day.

This delay gave Lee extra hours to perfect his defense and by the morning of June 3, his men had built an intricate system of straight and zigzag trenches and breastworks with gun emplacements to enfilade advancing enemy troops from several different points.

Grant, for unexplained reasons, ordered

General Grant leans over the back of the bench to study the map held by Meade at this informal council of war held in the sprint of 1864 near Massaponax Church and Spotsylvania Court House. (National Archives)

the attack on the main portion of Lee's line held by around 30,000 men rather than a concentrated attack on single point in the line.

Hancock's corps was to strike at Lee's left held by Lieutenant General A. P. Hill and Major General John Breckinridge, and Wright and Smith would hit the Confederate center held by Anderson and Hoke. To the north of Lee's line, Major General Ambrose Burnside and Warren at Bethesda Church would hold Lieutenant General Richard Early on Lee's left and support Smith's attack on Anderson.

Union soldiers apparently took a dim view of attacking the formidable Confederate line, for the night before the attack many wrote identification tags and pinned them to their uniforms in case they were killed or badly wounded.

Those who made identification tags were wise because the attack was a Union disaster. Later in his memoirs, Grant would write, "I have always regretted that the last assault was ever made."

As each of the three Union corps began their advance at daylight June 3, they fell under intense frontal and crossfire from the well-placed Confederate artillery and riflemen. As each corps moved forward along diverging lines, the farther each advanced, the more of its flanks were exposed to crossfire.

Lines of Union troops fell like rows of dominoes as they were enfiladed by artillery and rifle fire.

Within minutes after the attack began, the ground in front of the Confederate line was covered with mounds of Union dead and wounded, prompting one Confederate general later to remark, "It was not war, it was murder."

Within a little over half an hour the Union attack had been smashed and the three corps had suffered 7,000 casualties.

After withdrawing across the ground littered with their dead and wounded comrades, the survivors formed an entrenched line, at some points only fifty yards or so from the Confederate entrenchment.

For the next nine days neither side moved and even the wounded between the lines were left to suffer in the heat. Finally, on June 7, Grant asked for a truce so his men could go to the aid of the wounded who had managed to survive.

Cold Harbor was a slaughter pen for Grant's army with 13,000 casualties from June 1 to 3. Confederate losses over the same period came to over 4,000 but only 1,200 occurred on June 1.

Since the May 5 battle of the Wilderness, total Union casualties amounted to around 50,000 and Confederate 32,000. Grant could always replace his losses because of the North's huge reservoir of manpower but the South now had few men to send to Lee.

Cold Harbor checked Grant's advance on Richmond, and as he no longer had space to maneuver around Lee, he swung east and then south toward the railroad center of Petersburg which he concluded was "the key to Richmond."

Cold Harbor changed the course of warfare in the East from one of maneuver to one of siege and demonstrated that well-trained troops in good entrenchments and supported by artillery were almost impregnable against frontal attacks. This fact seemed to have been lost to the generals directing operations on the Western Front in the First World War.

Cold Harbor Battlefield is a unit of the much larger Richmond National Battlefield Park that includes Drewry's Bluff that led to General Butler's Union force being "bottled up" as well as many sites of the 1862 Peninsula Campaign.

BATTLE OF BRICE'S CROSS ROADS—JUNE 10, 1864

As Major General William T. Sherman and his army of 100,000 advanced southward on Atlanta, he was concerned with the safety of his main supply line, a single-track railroad running between Nashville and Chattanooga, threatened by Major General Bedford Forrest and his 3,500 Confederate cavalry.

In May 1864, Sherman ordered Major General Samuel Sturgis to find Forrest and eliminate him and his brigade. On June 2, Sturgis left his base at Memphis with 4,800 infantry and artillery and 3,000 cavalry under Brigadier General Benjamin Grierson and moved into northern Mississippi where he believed he could find Forrest.

Unfortunately for Sturgis, Forrest figured out what he was up to and decided to intercept him in the area around Brice's Cross Roads. Grierson's cavalry, however, arrived there first on the stifling hot morning of June 10 and easily drove off the small Confederate patrol.

Then, one of Forrest's brigade arrived and, although they were outnumbered, the dismounted cavalrymen held their own until the arrival of Forrest with another brigade.

Forrest ordered a concentrated attack to smash Grierson's line before Sturgis's infantry arrived and by early afternoon his dismounted cavalry and artillery had pushed back the Union line.

About this time, Sturgis's infantry arrived after an exhausting five-mile forced march in the intense heat. As soon as the men took a position they fell under heavy attack by Forrest's men firing from the shelter of the underbrush.

By mid-afternoon, Sturgis's line had been forced back to the crossroads and both flanks were threatened. Sturgis planned a careful withdrawal but his plan fell apart when the road of retreat was blocked by an overturned wagon on the bridge crossing the Tishomingo Creek.

The Union soldiers, anxious to escape the deadly Confederate fire, began to cross the creek by the fords located above and below the wagon-blocked bridge. The retreat soon turned into a rout as soldiers fled to the north, abandoning their equipment in their haste to escape.

For the next three days, Forrest chased Sturgis's shattered army until it finally reached the safety of Memphis.

The battle at Brice's Cross Roads had cost the Union 2,612 casualties out of the 8,100 engaged. Forrest claimed he lost 493 men out of the 3,500 engaged.

In their haste to escape, Sturgis's men abandoned 225 wagons, 18 pieces of artillery, and thousands of hand weapons.

The battle had been another stunning victory for Forrest, a natural military genius with little education or military training, who had condensed volumes on military tactics to seven words, "Get there first with the most men."

The small battlefield of Brice's Cross Roads where Confederate General Nathan B. Forrest's cavalry defeated Union forces on June 10, 1864. (National Park Service)

RISON CAMPS

"There is so much filth about the camp that it is terribly trying to live here. With sunken eyes, blackened countenances from pitch pine smoke, rags and disease, the men look sickening. The air reeks with nastiness."

JOHN RANSOM,
Michigan Cavalry
Prisoner at Andersonville

Andersonville, officially called Camp Sumter, is the most infamous of all Civil War prison camps—in the North and the South. Within 14 months, over 45,000 Union soldiers were confined to the Confederate stockade prison in Americus, Georgia: 12,912 of them would not leave it alive.

Andersonville opened in February 1864 and was enlarged in June so that the 15-foot-high pine log stockade walls enclosed an area of over 26 acres. In the shape of a parallelogram, the stockade walls were 1,620 feet long and 779 feet wide. Sentry boxes, which the prisoners called "pigeon roosts," were spaced every 30 yards along the four walls. Nineteen feet inside the walls was the "deadline"; any prisoner crossing it would be shot. A branch of the Sweetwater Creek, called Stockade Branch, flowed through the camp to supply the prisoners with drinking water.

By 1864, the Confederacy was short of everything except the will to keep fighting the Yankees. There was not enough food, clothing, tents, and medicine for the army, let alone for war prisoners, so little was spared for Andersonville. Half-starved prisoners were clothed in rags and exposed to the elements. Without medicine, doctors who attended the sick in the camp hospital could do little. A prisoner either got well on his own or died, which too often was the case. While it would have been possible to improve sanitation facilities, little effort was made and conditions remained horrible.

At the end of the war, the commandant of Andersonville, Captain Henry Wirz, was arrested by Union forces. Tried and found guilty of "murder in violation of the laws of war," he was hanged.

In the summer of 1865, Clara Barton, who had been active during the war in getting medical supplies to the Union armies, came to Andersonville with some soldiers and laborers to identify and mark the graves of dead prisoners.

Only enlisted men were sent to Andersonville. Many Union officers were sent to Libby Prison in Richmond, Virginia. Formerly a warehouse, Libby was also grim, as were all Civil War prison camps. Of the 18,000 prisoners housed at Florence, South Carolina, 12,912 died and at the Union prison of Camp Douglas, 4,454 out of 30,000 Confederates met death. On the whole, however, there were fewer deaths at Northern prisons, such as Point Lookout in Maryland, because the Union did have a better supply of medical supplies, clothing, and blankets.

Until early 1863, prisoners were not a major problem for either side because a prisoner could be exchanged or paroled on condition that he would not fight again. But in late 1863, these arrangements began to break down and prisoners had to be held for long periods.

When Ulysses S. Grant assumed command of all Union forces in March 1864, he put an end to any exchange or parole of prisoners. This was a harsh measure and soon Andersonville, Libby, and other prison camps became packed with Union soldiers. But this edict probably speeded up the end of the war. The Confederacy had a very limited manpower reserve and could not readily replace a captured soldier. The Union, however, had a huge manpower reservoir, including thousands of black soldiers anxious to fight.

Captured prisoners of each side could only wait until the war was over for their release. But when it ended, it was too late for many. Out of 211,400

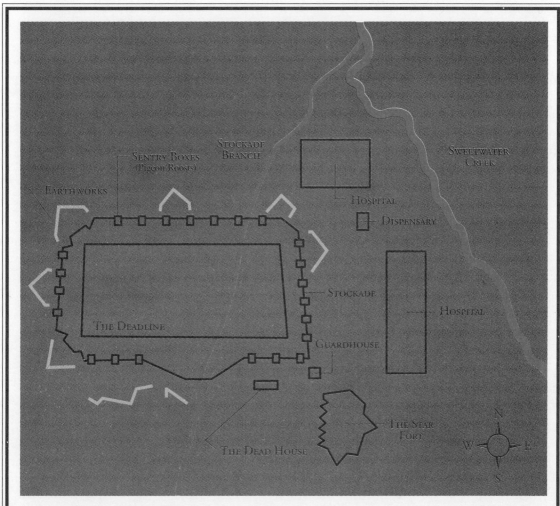

A schematic plan of the Andersonville prison.

Prisoners were held in the pen that originally contained sixteen and a half acres. The pen was enlarged in June 1864 to include twenty-six and a half acres.

Outside the stockade were Star Fort and seven smaller earthworks around the stockade's perimeter. Armed with artillery, these strongholds were intended to put down a major prisoner disturbance and defend against potential attack by Union cavalry. The "Dead House" was where the bodies of dead prisoners were put until they were loaded into a wagon and hauled to the prisoners' cemetery.

captured Union soldiers, 30,208 would die as prisoners. Out of 462,000 captured, 25,976 Confederate soldiers died in prison camps, which includes those who surrendered at the end of the war.

Civil War prison camps were generally terrible places but probably no more so than in other wars. During the Revolutionary War, for example, many captured Americans ended up on British prison ships. As British officers at that time were not famous for their consideration of their own soldiers and sailors, it's not hard to imagine how they treated American rebel captives. A few captured British soldiers and dangerous Loyalists ended up at Newgate Prison in Connecticut, to sleep in the stone underground galleries of an abandoned copper mine. Today Old Newgate Prison, near Bradley Airport, is open to visitors, who are likely to feel claustrophobic after visiting the galleries.

At the end of the Civil War, Andersonville passed through several hands, including the Women's Relief Corps, until it was made a National Historic Site, administered by the National Park Service.

It is located ten miles northeast of Americus, Georgia, on GA 49. This 475-acre park includes the site of the prison, a Visitors Center, exhibits of the prison camp, relief maps and a slide presentation. The park also includes the Andersonville National Cemetery where some 16,000 veterans are buried. This National Historic Site will shortly include a museum dedicated to American P.O.W.s from the Revolution to Somalia to be completed in 1996.

Bird's-eye view of the Union's Hammond General Hospital and prisoner of war camp at Point Lookout, Maryland. The hospital layout provided patients with good natural light and fresh air. The captured Confederate soldiers lived in a nearby tent city. Small insert in upper left shows headquarters of the area's commanding general. This splendid lithograph was made by Edward Saches of Baltimore and first published in 1864 by George Everett of Point Lookout. (Library of Congress)

Sturgis's defeat did not discourage Sherman's efforts to eliminate Forrest. Shortly after the battle Sherman wrote,

"Forrest had licked Sturgis fair and square and now I will put him up against A. J. Smith and Mower, and let them try their hand."

BATTLE OF KENNESAW MOUNTAIN—JUNE 27, 1864

In spring of 1864, Lieutenant General Ulysses S. Grant, commander of all Union armies, ordered a concentrated attack by all forces and directed Major General William T. Sherman to move on the Confederate army in Georgia and "break it up and go into the interior of the enemy's country as far as you can, inflicting all the damage you can on their war resources."

The start of Sherman's march into Georgia coincided with the beginning of Grant's campaign against Richmond. With his army of approximately 110,000 men and 254 pieces of artillery, Sherman left Chattanooga and fought his first battle of the campaign against a Confederate force of 65,000 men at Rocky Face Ridge, near Dalton, Georgia. The Confederate army was now under the command of General Johnston, who had little use for his commander in chief, Jefferson Davis.

During the weeks that followed, Davis kept urging Johnston to attack Sherman, but Johnston, knowing what he was up against, insisted on remaining on the defensive. He apparently hoped to wear Sherman down and then seize the offensive.

At Rocky Face Ridge, Resaca, Adairsville, Cassville, and the Dallas-New Hope Church-Pickett's mill area, Sherman used the same tactics. He attacked Johnston head-on with part of his army, while sending another part on a flanking move that would presumably cut off Johnston's path of retreat. Although the Confederates in every case escaped entrapment, Sherman's strategy was effective in driving them steadily southward toward Atlanta.

By June 19, Johnston had established a defensive line along the crest of Kennesaw Mountain, a high ridge with rock slopes, about three miles from Marietta, Georgia.

The Confederate position had been prepared before the battle. It consisted of a maze of trenches with cannon placed so that, no matter from which angle the attackers approached, they would be covered. Starting with Major General Joseph Wheeler's cavalry at the north, just beyond Kennesaw Mountain, the Confederate line formed a gentle curve around Marietta, Georgia, about three miles west. South of Wheeler were Generals William W. Loring, Patrick R. Cleburne, Benjamin F. Cheatham, and John Bell Hood, who was just north of Peter Kolb's farm. Facing them were Major General McPherson's three corps to the north, Major General Thomas's large army in the center, and Major General John McAllister Schofield's small force on the south.

Schofield moved to get around the Confederate left flank, and on June 22 was stopped near Kolb's Farm by Hood, who had moved to the left in anticipation of such a maneuver.

After failing to turn Johnston's left, Sherman pounded his line with artillery and launched infantry attacks on various points. Little was gained for if the Union soldiers did manage to take a position, the Confederates simply withdrew to a previously prepared defense.

Sherman was bound and determined to destroy Johnston's army, which he believed was exhausted and ripe for annihilation and on June 27 ordered a frontal attack on the entire line, with a major two-pronged assault on the Confederate center after artillery had prepared the way.

Around 8 A.M. 5,500 men of Thomas's corps crossed the swampy, heavily wooded terrain to take the mountain spur which today is called Pigeon Hill. Before they reached the hill, heavy enemy fire forced them to take shelter among the rocks and trees. They were shortly driven back as the Confederate soldiers on nearby Little Kennesaw Mountain rolled huge rocks down on them.

An hour or so after the futile assault on Pigeon Hill, the second prong of the attack, consisting of 8,000 men, moved south of the Dallas Road to hit Cleburne's and Cheatham's divisions, two of Johnston's best. After heavy action that ended in hand-to-hand fighting, the attack was repulsed with heavy Union casualties. The attack marked the end of the one-day battle.

The battle cost Sherman 3,000 casualties out of his 110,000-man army while the far smaller Confederate army of 65,000 lost about 1,000 men.

The fighting ended the day it started, and the two sides spent the next five days glaring at each other. Then on July 2, McPherson's army, accompanied by Major General George Stoneman's cavalry, easily circled around the Confederate left, forcing Johnston once again to withdraw toward Atlanta—this time to previously prepared positions at the Chattahoochee River. Here Sherman, reverting to his old successful tactics, sneaked around Johnston's flank and forced him to withdraw to the outskirts of Atlanta.

Shortly after this, on July 18, Johnston was relieved of his command and replaced by Hood. Then a series of battles around Atlanta followed, which resulted in the city's fall on September 2. The next day, Sherman wired Washington: "Atlanta is ours. . . . Since May 5, we have been in one constant battle or skirmish, and need rest."

But he did not rest a long time. On November 16, after burning Atlanta, he resumed his march to the sea. Of this, one Union soldier wrote: "Destroyed all we could not eat, stole their niggers, burned their cotton and gins, spilled their sorghum, burned and twisted their R. Roads and raised Hell generally." Mrs. Louise Cornwell of Hillsboro, Georgia, wrote: "The sky was red from flames of burning houses." An old woman at Conyers told the Yankee invaders: "I've run away from you six times, clear across the south, starting back in Kentucky. I don't care where you go next, I'm done running. I'm going to let you go first, maybe I'll follow."

BATTLE OF TUPELO— JULY 14–15, 1864

Despite the Union army's defeat at Brice's Cross Roads on July 10, 1863, General Sherman remained determined to crush General Forrest, who was threatening Sherman's supply line, so essential to the Union advance on Atlanta. For this reason, he ordered the commander of the Federal District of West Tennessee "to go out and follow Forrest to the death, if it costs 10,000 lives and breaks the Treasury. There will never be peace in Tennessee 'til Forrest is dead."

To carry out Sherman's order Major General Andrew Jackson Smith, with 14,000 men, was sent from Memphis to LaGrange, Tennessee, and then southward to meet Forrest. They finally clashed on July 14 at Harrisburg, one mile west of Tupelo, Mississippi. The Federals were under the direct command of Brigadier General James A. Mower, Brigadier General Benjamin H. Grierson, Colonel David Moore, and Colonel Edward Bouton leading the First Brigade of U.S. Colored Troops. The Confederates, with 9,500 men, were under the direct command of Brigadier General Philip D. Roddey, Colonel Edward

Crossland, Brigadier General James R. Chalmers, Brigadier General Abraham Buford, and Brigadier General Hyland B. Lyon.

The Federals were well entrenched; Forrest later said their line was impregnable. Perhaps because he was suffering acutely from boils, Forrest did not coordinate the Confederate movements as he usually did. In any case, from the Confederates' opening attack at 7 A.M. things went badly for them.

Fighting that day ended shortly after noon, but that night, as the Federals exposed themselves by burning Harrisburg, they were shelled by the Confederate artillery and subjected to direct attack by Forrest and his horsemen. Neither attack fazed them; they returned the fire with good effect.

The next morning, as the Federals began to pull back toward LaGrange, the Confederates kept snapping at their heels, and a small but real fight broke out along Old Town Creek. But the Confederates were driven off with comparative ease. The North, however, failed to dispose of Forrest as Sherman had ordered. Even when they shot him in the right foot, they did not stop him, because despite his pain, he commandeered a buggy and stayed right with his men. Southern casualties, totaling about 1,300 men, were roughly double those of the Union.

SIEGE OF PETERSBURG—JUNE 15, 1864–APRIL 1, 1865

When he was defeated at Cold Harbor, Virginia, Grant gave up the idea of capturing Richmond immediately and moved his army farther south to Petersburg, Virginia, where the railroads into Richmond

converged. But his initial efforts to capture that city failed despite the fact that Lee did not know the whereabouts of the Federals after Cold Harbor. On June 15, when they suddenly reappeared outside Petersburg, they bulled their way through the city's outer defenses. But repeated attempts over the next three days to get all the way into the city were to no avail.

Having failed in their attempt for a major victory, the Federals laid siege to the city. They constructed elaborate field fortifications according to the best principles taught at West Point. They even built a railroad to bring supplied from their base at City Point on the James River.

On June 21, Grant made the first of numerous moves to cut the rail lines leading into Petersburg from the South. It failed when Lieutenant General A. P. Hill's Confederate corps got between the two corps Grant had sent out on the mission and whipped them so badly that they were able to take 1,700 prisoners. Another Federal force sent out at the same time did better. It ripped up miles of track on two railroads and returned happily to base only to hear that the Rebels promptly relaid the track and had trains running a few days later. Grant renewed his railroad-disrupting efforts in August with somewhat more success. The Weldon line was cut and held in the vicinity of Globe Tavern, a few miles south of Petersburg. But later in the month, when troops under Major General Hancock set out to destroy the tracks below Globe Tavern, they got into a bloody fight at Reams Station with Lieutenant General Hill and lost 2,700 men.

While such basic military moves were in progress, a variety of ideas for bringing a sudden end to the siege kept flowing into Grant's headquarters. One was especially intriguing. A Pennsylvania regiment

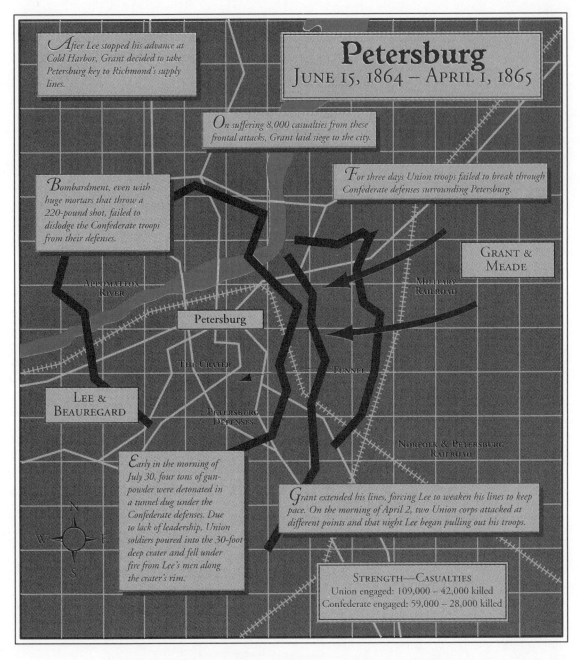

Petersburg
JUNE 15, 1864 – APRIL 1, 1865

After Lee stopped his advance at Cold Harbor, Grant decided to take Petersburg key to Richmond's supply lines.

On suffering 8,000 casualties from these frontal attacks, Grant laid siege to the city.

For three days Union troops failed to break through Confederate defenses surrounding Petersburg.

Bombardment, even with huge mortars that throw a 220-pound shot, failed to dislodge the Confederate troops from their defenses.

GRANT & MEADE

APPOMATTOX RIVER

MILITARY RAILROAD

Petersburg

THE CRATER

TUNNEL

LEE & BEAUREGARD

PETERSBURG DEFENSES

NORFOLK & PETERSBURG RAILROAD

Early in the morning of July 30, four tons of gunpowder were detonated in a tunnel dug under the Confederate defenses. Due to lack of leadership, Union soldiers poured into the 30-foot deep crater and fell under fire from Lee's men along the crater's rim.

Grant extended his lines, forcing Lee to weaken his lines to keep pace. On the morning of April 2, two Union corps attacked at different points and that night Lee began pulling out his troops.

N W E S

STRENGTH—CASUALTIES
Union engaged: 109,000 – 42,000 killed
Confederate engaged: 59,000 – 28,000 killed

made up largely of coal miners suggested tunneling under the Confederate positions around Petersburg and blowing a hole in the fortifications with a mighty charge of gunpowder. This was approved, and by July 23, the tunnel was completed. Now, the following well-developed plan of action was put into effect.

• Hancock was sent across the Appomattox River to attack the Confederates and persuade Lee to

No. 361.—RAILROAD MORTAR AT PETERSBURG, VA.,
July 25, 1864.

weaken the defenses at Petersburg by bringing reinforcements from the city.

- Troop movements were initiated to conceal the point from which the real attack on Petersburg was to be made.

- The division of black soldiers selected to spearhead the attack when the gunpowder went off was given special instructions by Burnside about bypassing the crater created by the explosion, flanking nearby Confederate defenses, and seizing the hill behind the Confederates' front line.

- The powder charge was to be set off July 30.

Then, almost at the last moment, for no clear reason, General Meade insisted that the charge should be led, not by blacks, but by men who had served in the ranks for a longer time and were more experienced.

Trouble started when the sputtering fuse burned out inside the tunnel and a trembling volunteer had to crawl in to relight it. The explosion that followed at 4:45 A.M. was, in Yankee eyes, magnificent. It produced a crater about 170 feet long, 60 feet wide, and 30 feet deep. Men, guns, cannon, and

Called the "Dictator," this 13-inch mortar weighing 17,000 pounds had to be carried on reinforced railroad tracks in order to pound Confederate positions at Petersburg. (National Archives)

WILLIE PEGRAM: BOY ARTILLERIST

William Johnson Pegram was a famous Confederate artillery commander and probably one of the best. At the age of 20, he joined the Southern army soon after the war started and was killed three years later in the Battle of Five Forks, shortly before the war ended. He was an unlikely looking hero—small, slender, quiet, and so nearsighted that he had to squint through thick glasses. But he was a fearless, magnetic leader who constantly exposed himself, on horseback, to enemy fire. Several top commanders urged Lee to promote him to a brigadier general of infantry, but Lee prized him too highly in the artillery to transfer him from that service. As a lieutenant in the Purcell Battery, Pegram fought with great distinction in all the battles of the Seven Days Campaign. At the end of the campaign, he had lost all his officers and 60 of his 80 men. After that, he was in all the major battles fought by Lee. He was wounded once but stuck with his men through the rest of the fight. At another time, when he was home on furlough, he became seriously ill. But, when he learned that Lee was marching into Pennsylvania, he rode 90 miles in an ambulance to rejoin his unit and fight at Gettysburg. During the defense of Petersburg, when the Confederates were being driven back in the battle at Peebles' Farm, he grabbed a battle flag, placed his horse 50 years ahead of the retreating confederate line and let a counterattack. He was promoted frequently and finally was made a colonel. As he led his men in his last battle, one of his 19-year-old subordinates observed that "he looked like the god of war."

rubble were blown high into the air. Now it was time for the selected men to go charging through the great gap in the Confederate defenses, fall upon the dazed defenders, and overcome those believed to be hidden on the hill.

But the attack did not perform as expected. Lacking proper instructions or a senior officer to take charge, the Union soldiers crowded into the crater instead of continuing the attack. This mass of men made an ideal target for Confederate artillery and riflemen that quickly took up positions around the crater's rim.

The Union black division was finally sent forward just in time to be struck by a savage Confederate counterattack. The great experiment ended in a giant fiasco, resulting in 4,000 Union casualties.

The conventional methods of waging war that came next were more successful.

But it was quite a while before Grant realized the results he desired.

More attacks on rail lines and major highways were made. There were numerous skirmishes and a number of sizable battles. Fort Stedman, almost in the center of the Union forward lines, fell to Lee and was retaken soon after. Inch by inch Grant extended his trenches south and west, thus forcing Lee to weaken his own lines by keeping pace. Finally, at 4:30 A.M. on April 2, 9 1/2 months after Grant reached Petersburg, the Federal army charged through the Confederate defenses. The fighting was over by nightfall. Later that night, Lee informed President Davis that he was pulling all troops out of Petersburg and Richmond. He had lost 28,000 men, including Lieutenant General Hill, and had only 30,000 left. Grant lost 59,000 men, but he had started the campaign with 109,000.

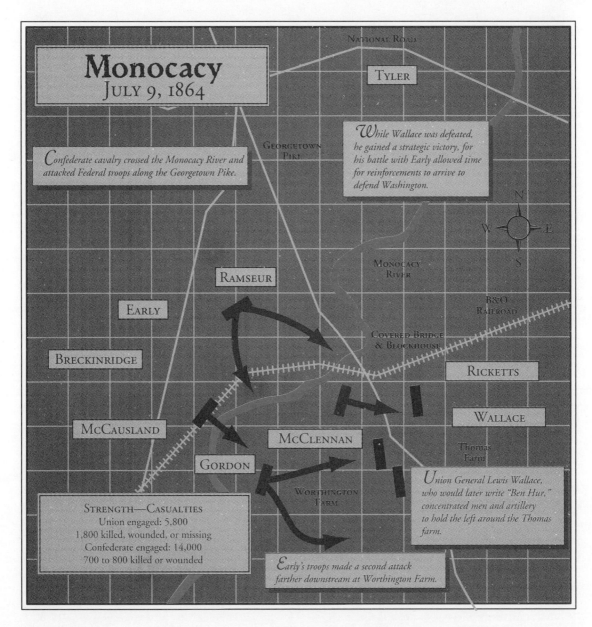

Monocacy
JULY 9, 1864

NATIONAL ROAD

TYLER

GEORGETOWN
PIKE

While Wallace was defeated, he gained a strategic victory, for his battle with Early allowed time for reinforcements to arrive to defend Washington.

Confederate cavalry crossed the Monocacy River and attacked Federal troops along the Georgetown Pike.

MONOCACY
RIVER

N
W E
S

RAMSEUR

EARLY

B&O
RAILROAD

BRECKINRIDGE

COVERED BRIDGE
& BLOCKHOUSE

RICKETTS

WALLACE

McCAUSLAND

McCLENNAN

Thomas
Farm

GORDON

Union General Lewis Wallace, who would later write "Ben Hur," concentrated men and artillery to hold the left around the Thomas farm.

WORTHINGTON
FARM

STRENGTH—CASUALTIES
Union engaged: 5,800
1,800 killed, wounded, or missing
Confederate engaged: 14,000
700 to 800 killed or wounded

Early's troops made a second attack farther downstream at Worthington Farm.

BATTLE OF MONOCACY— JULY 9, 1864

During the Civil War, the confederates made several threats to attack Washington. This final attempt resulted in a battle near the Monocacy River in Maryland.

Having momentarily driven most of the Federal troops out of the Shenandoah Valley, Confederate Lieutenant General Early, with 14,000 men, turned toward Washington. The only Northern soldiers in his path were 5,800 men commanded by Major General Lewis Wallace. Wallace did

TRENCH WARFARE

Union troops in trenches at Petersburg. In the course of the long siege at Petersburg both sides built elaborate trenches and earthworks, forerunners of those constructed on the Western Front in First World War. (National Archives)

The early Civil War battles—like battles in previous wars—were fought by two armies standing and advancing in more or less parallel lines, firing at each other until they were close enough to use the bayonet. But improved rifle and artillery fire soon began to change battle tactics to provide the smallest target for the enemy. Armies tended to form battle lines farther apart to keep out of range, and it was now firepower rather than shock attacks that would often be the deciding factor. Consequently, troops began to shelter themselves in trenches.

The character of a trench depended on the soil, time to dig it, and the availability of tools.

In relatively sandy or other easy-to-dig soil, a shallow trench could be dug with a bayonet, metal dish, or drinking cup and sometimes with hands. The excavated soil was piled on top of the trench to form a breastwork and its height could be increased by adding fence rails, tree trunks, or stone.

Deeper and more elaborate trenches were dug when there was time and there were shovels and picks on hand. These would often include artillery positions and were shaped to enfilade the attacking force with artillery and musket fire.

General Robert E. Lee, a West Point-trained military engineer, with his much smaller army and lacking the huge reservoir of manpower of the Union forces, used his training and talents to develop trench warfare to its fullest extent.

He was, for instance, well entrenched before the battles of Fredericksburg, at Spotsylvania, North Anna River, and Cold Harbor. Major General Ambrose and later Lieutenant General U. S. Grant were unable to penetrate Lee's entrenched lines and only succeeded in suffering terrible casualties.

At Fredericksburg, Lee's entrenchments eventually extended almost twenty-two miles. Some were in parallel double lines and interconnected so that, if the first was overrun, its soldiers could fall back to the second and continue to fight.

At Spotsylvania and North Anna River his men dug V-shaped trenches to force the enemy to split his force in order to attack both sides of the V.

Lee's straight and zigzag interconnected trenches at Cold Harbor were such an effective entrenchment that 7,000 Union soldiers were killed and wounded in the attack lasting a little over half an hour.

During the siege of Petersburg in 1864, the Confederate defenders and the union attackers constructed elaborate earthen defense and attack positions comparable to those used in the First World War.

---

not think he had much chance against Early, but he hoped at least to slow him down enough to give Grant an opportunity to detach men from his Army of the Potomac and get them back to Washington in time to send Early packing.

As it turned out, even though the reinforcements arrived in Washington, they were not needed because Early, the winner of the battle of Monocacy, allowed the opportunity to invade Washington slip through his fingers.

Wallace had decided the best place to stop Early's advance on either Washington or Baltimore was the Monocacy River, not far from Monocacy Junction, where the Georgetown Pike to Washington, the National Road to Baltimore, and the Baltimore and Ohio Railroad crossed the river by three separate bridges.

A rather makeshift force of 2,500 formed into a brigade under Brigadier General Erastus Tyler Wallace established a line along the east shore of the river and positioned artillery to cover the three bridges and numerous fords.

Around 1 A.M. of July 9, Brigadier General James B. Ricketts arrived with an experienced brigade to bring Wallace's force to about 5,800. Tyler was sent north to hold the National Road Hill and Ricketts would defend the other two.

The battle began around 6:30 A.M. July 9, as Early's advance column under Major General Stephen Ramseur drove back some of Wallace's troops from the west side of the river but soon fell under heavy fire from Union guns.

About noon, while Early and Ramseur were planning what to do next, Brigadier General John McCausland's Confederate cavalry crossed the river by a ford. Ricketts immediately responded to this attack by moving men across the fields of the Thomas farm and toward those of the Worthington house. They would shortly beat off McClausland's dismounted cavalry which was moving through the cornfields.

Wallace became certain that Early would make another attack on his left and moved troops and artillery to stop it. He also set fire to the Georgetown Pike covered

BATTLE TACTICS

Columbiads, such as these at Confederate-held Fort Pickens, Pensacola Bay, Florida, had been adopted in 1860 by the United States as the standard gun for coastal defenses. (National Archives)

Civil War battle tactics were eventually determined by devastating firepower of the .58 caliber Springfield rifled musket, the standard weapon of the Union and confederate infantry.

Before the introduction of the rifled musket, troops relied on the smooth-bore musket with an effective range of 50 to 100 yards. Massed troops could advance on the enemy, get off a shot or two, and then go in with the bayonet. The rifled musket, on the other hand, had an effective range of around 350 yards and an experienced sniper or

sharpshooter could hit a target at 700 yards. The rifled musket got off more shots a minute than the smooth-bore, and the later introduction of the breach-loading and repeating rifle would further increase rate of fire.

Increased firepower often favored the defending force, especially if the troops were protected by some form of breastworks and the flanks anchored by a river, ravine, or other natural or manmade barrier. Attacking a well-defended position was uphill work, especially if the advancing enemy line was *infladed*,

Artillery going into Action on south bank of Rappahannock River — June 4, 1863.

Federal artillery going into action on the south bank of the Rappahannock River, June 4, 1863.

Such field guns were hauled into position attached to two-wheel horse-drawn limbers, which carried one case of ammunition. With the gun in firing position the limber was disconnected and withdrawn to the rear but ready to advance and move the gun if required. Caissons were also two-wheel vehicles drawn by limbers and carried two cases of additional ammunition. (Library of Congress)

swept by artillery and rifle fire. Two of the war's great battles, Fredericksburg and Gettysburg, were won by the army with an excellent defensive position.

To defeat a force in a well-defended position, the attacking army might attempt a *turning movement*, swinging far around to avoid the enemy's position and by threatening some vital point to the rear, force him to leave his position and fight elsewhere.

After Spotsylvania Court House, Grant attempted a series of turning movements designed to place his army between Lee and Richmond and force him to attack the far larger Union army.

An *envelopment* is an attack directed at turning the enemy's flank and reach his rear. A *double envelopment* is when both flanks are struck simultaneously.

At Antietam, McClellan had the opportunity to envelop both of Lee's flanks but would not commit enough men to pull off the maneuver.

It was virtually impossible to envelop a flank if it was well anchored and properly defended. Burnside learned this at Fredericksburg and Lee at Gettysburg.

As the Civil War dragged on and battle casualties began to number in the tens of thousands, many commanders saw that a tightly formed body of advancing troops was cut to pieces long before it reached the enemy line. A new approach called for troops to advance in open ranks with men far enough apart so as not to provide a large target but close enough to support each other and present a show of force. And now, instead of advancing in the open, troops took protection from any cover they found along the way.

An infantry attack was often preceded by an artillery bombardment to weaken the enemy. (This, however, did not work for Lee on the last day at Gettysburg. For over an hour, 142 Confederate guns pounded the Union lines but because of poor aim, most of the shells overshot the target.) If properly organized, the main attack would begin with an advance of skirmishers followed by successive lines of troops to force an opening in the enemy's line. Once this was accomplished, additional troops were sent in to enlarge the breakthrough.

While many infantry carried bayonets, the swords did not appear to be important weapons for defense or attack. Many soldiers used bayonets as entrenching tools, as a spit for broiling meat and a holder for candles.

Despite the fame that has adhered to such commanders as Stuart, Hampton, Buford, Custer, and Sheridan, the cavalry did not play a major role in any of the large battles of the war. A man on a horse made too perfect a target for a rifle bullet. Cavalry was used primarily for reconnaissance, raids, cutting enemy supply lines, defense, and occasionally fighting isolated forces or with enemy cavalry.

Brandy Station, Virginia, was the scene of the first and greatest true cavalry battles of the war on June 9, 1863.

During the last great battle of the war at Petersburg, Virginia, the tactics on both sides degenerated into the brutal trench warfare that would be a hallmark of the Western Front in World War I.

bridge so it would no longer have to be defended.

At 3:30 P.M. Confederate forces struck at Tyler on the National Road while Major General John Gordon's division attacked Ricketts at the Worthington farm.

Heavy fighting followed as Rickett's men put up stiff resistance in the cornfields and in the farm buildings of the Thomas farm. Eventually they were driven back to a position along the Georgetown Pike which provided some protection from enemy fire, and fighting continued at close quarter.

Wallace saw that despite their courage his heavily outnumbered army had no chance of stopping Early's advance and so, rather than risking the destruction of his small army, around 4:30 P.M., ordered his men to break off action and withdraw.

The small union force of 5,800 suffered over 1,800 casualties while the Confederate army of 14,000 lost only around 800.

Early, normally an aggressive fighter, did not pursue Wallace or even advance the 45 miles to Washington. His rather bizarre explanation for allowing Wallace to escape was that he did not wish to burden himself by taking more prisoners.

Wallace and his little army had spared Washington from attack, an event that would have been a humiliating disaster for the Union. For this reason the relatively minor battle at the Monocacy River can be considered one of the most important of the war.

BATTLE OF MOBILE BAY— AUGUST 5–23, 1864

Grant and rear admiral Farragut had long requested permission to attack the city of Mobile, Alabama, but for one reason or another had been turned down. After Grant

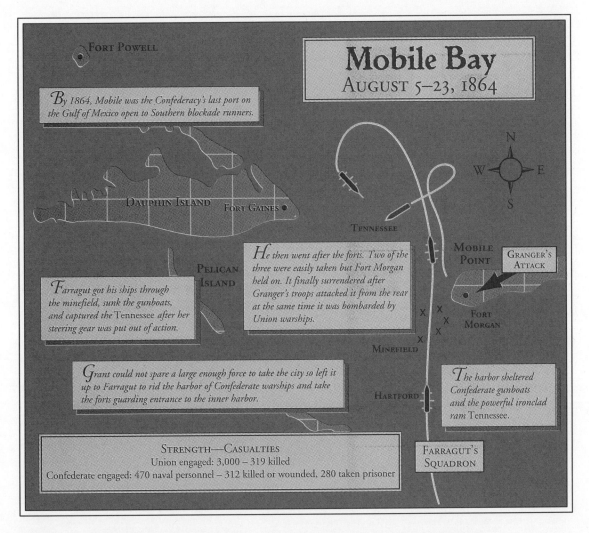

Mobile Bay
AUGUST 5–23, 1864

FORT POWELL

By 1864, Mobile was the Confederacy's last port on the Gulf of Mexico open to Southern blockade runners.

DAUPHIN ISLAND   FORT GAINES

TENNESSEE

MOBILE POINT

GRANGER'S ATTACK

PELICAN ISLAND

He then went after the forts. Two of the three were easily taken but Fort Morgan held on. It finally surrendered after Granger's troops attacked it from the rear at the same time it was bombarded by Union warships.

FORT MORGAN

Farragut got his ships through the minefield, sunk the gunboats, and captured the Tennessee *after her steering gear was put out of action.*

MINEFIELD

Grant could not spare a large enough force to take the city so left it up to Farragut to rid the harbor of Confederate warships and take the forts guarding entrance to the inner harbor.

HARTFORD

The harbor sheltered Confederate gunboats and the powerful ironclad ram Tennessee.

FARRAGUT'S SQUADRON

STRENGTH—CASUALTIES
Union engaged: 3,000 – 319 killed
Confederate engaged: 470 naval personnel – 312 killed or wounded, 280 taken prisoner

assumed command of all Union forces, however, he considered a move against the city one of his priorities. Farragut was delighted to go along with this and promptly began shifting his fleet into position to attack the forts that guarded Mobile Bay and the huge new Confederate ram, *Tennessee.* But Grant was able to send only a small force of 2,400 soldiers under Major General R. S. Granger, so the battle of Mobile Bay was primarily a naval engagement.

The attack began on August 5. Farragut's squadron consisted of seven large ships each with a gunboat tied to the port side, four monitors in a parallel column, four gunboats stationed off Fort Powell, and six more gunboats stationed off Fort Morgan. At the head of the main column of large ships was the *Brooklyn.*

The ships started firing on Fort Morgan as they approached the entrance to Mobile Bay, but the fort was slow to reply. In about an hour, however, a general battle was in full sway. So as to better see the action through the smoke, Farragut was lashed in the rigging of his flagship, the *Hartford.*

About two hours after the start of the attack, the *Tennessee* came down the bay toward the attackers with three gunboats behind. Attempting to stop it, the leading union gunboat, *Tecumseh*, accidentally strayed into a Confederate minefield, where it struck a mine and sank with five-sixths of the crew within two minutes.

Soon after this, the *Brooklyn*, noticing suspicious objects in the water ahead, went into reverse to avoid them; whereupon Farragut decided to put the *Hartford* at the head of the attack. Warned that mines (then called torpedoes) lay ahead, he is supposed to have exclaimed: "Damn the torpedoes! Full speed ahead!"

The ships passed through the minefield safely even though they were under heavy fire from Fort Morgan, the *Tennessee*, and the latter's three gunboats. Only one ship was seriously damaged. Federal attempts to put the *Tennessee* out of action, however, were unsuccessful. Although the gunboats had been silenced, it launched a ramming attack on Farragut's fleet. The Federal ships answered by trying to retaliate. Four attempts were made and all failed. In two cases, the Federals received more damage than their target.

Shelling of the big ship was only slightly more fruitful until—probably through luck—shots from the Northern monitors carried away the exposed chains connecting the *Tennessee*'s tiller to its rudder. Once this happened, it was no longer capable of being steered, and it surrendered. That was about four hours after the start of the battle.

With the Confederate ships out of the way, only the forts prevented easy access to Mobile Bay, and Farragut wasted no time in going after them. Fort Powell was the first to fall. After the garrison had fled, it was blown up.

Fort Gaines fell two days later after a bombardment to which it did not make a strong reply.

Now only Fort Morgan remained, and the commander, Brigadier General R. L. Page, had no intention of giving in. The Federal answer was to land Granger's army troops behind the fort and to inaugurate a slow bombardment from the ships, while the soldiers moved up for an assault. Finally, on August 22, an all-out bombardment began. It was so ferocious and set so much of the fort on fire, threatening to ignite the powder magazine, that Page raised the white flag the next day.

So ended the battle of Mobile Bay. The city of Mobile, however, was not occupied until April 11, 1865, for several reasons: (1) the city was no longer of great importance—by taking possession of the lower bay, the Federals had made it impossible for Southern blockade runners to get through; (2) the city was protected by additional forts plus a ship that had been sunk across the main channel to the city; and (3) other operations seemed of greater importance to the Federal command and government.

BATTLE OF FORT FISHER— JANUARY 6–15, 1865

Wilmington, North Carolina, on the Cape Fear River, was the last major seaport through which the Confederacy could bring supplies for its war effort. Gideon Welles, Lincoln's secretary of the navy, had been agitating to attack and close the port for a long time. But it was not until late in the war that he succeeded in convincing anyone that, if Wilmington was taken, Richmond would probably fall for lack of supplies. Once Grant accepted Welles's argument, progress was made toward

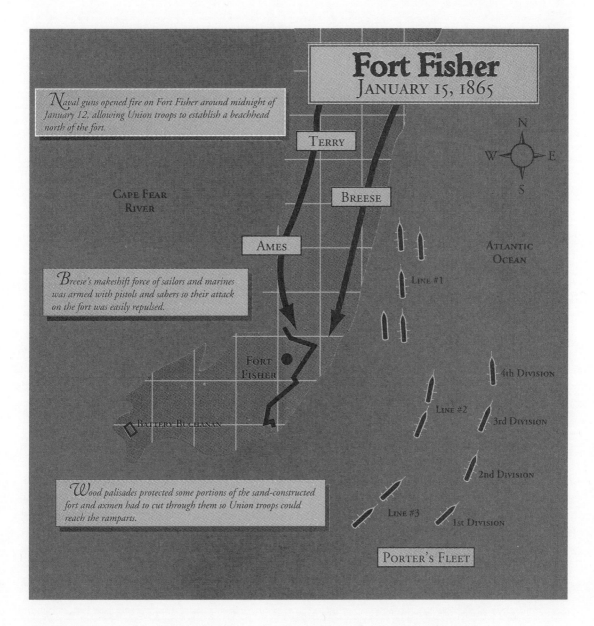

Fort Fisher
JANUARY 15, 1865

Naval guns opened fire on Fort Fisher around midnight of January 12, allowing Union troops to establish a beachhead north of the fort.

TERRY

CAPE FEAR
RIVER

BREESE

AMES

Breese's makeshift force of sailors and marines was armed with pistols and sabers so their attack on the fort was easily repulsed.

ATLANTIC
OCEAN

LINE #1

FORT
FISHER

4th DIVISION

BATTERY BUCHANAN

LINE #2

3rd DIVISION

2nd DIVISION

Wood palisades protected some portions of the sand-constructed fort and axmen had to cut through them so Union troops could reach the ramparts.

LINE #3

1st DIVISION

PORTER'S FLEET

carrying out the attack. A formidable fleet was assembled under Rear Admiral David D. Porter, and a land force of 6,500 men was shipped out under Major General Benjamin Butler.

Fort Fisher was not expected to be an easy target. Built at the tip of Cape Fear, it was a mile long and had sand walls more than 25 feet thick. It mounted 47 large cannon and was manned by 1,500 soldiers under Colonel William Lamb. To avoid making a direct attack on the fort, Butler thought of blowing it up with a ship loaded with 235 tons of gunpowder. During the night of December 23, the vessel was run ashore near the northeast corner of the fort and exploded. Nothing happened. The occupants of the fort hardly heard the blast.

The next day, the battle fleet pounded the fort, and on Christmas morning, foot soldiers were put ashore to make an attack. Instead, they made a reconnaissance of the fort and were discouraged about the prospects. Butler decided the case was hopeless and pulled the troops out.

Porter was furious, as was Grant. He fired Butler and ordered Major General A. J. Terry to take over.

On January 13, as Terry positioned his men north of the fort, Porter, with an enlarged fleet of 44 ships, began bombarding it. Porter had noticed that the December attack had little effect because many of the shots were fired at the fort's flagpole. This time he ordered the ships' gunners to take their time and aim at specific targets. As a result, when the firing finally stopped on the afternoon of January 15 to allow the ground troops to attack, much of the fort had been reduced to rubble, and more than half of its cannon had been knocked out. In all, the Federal navy fired more than 1,500,000 pounds of ordnance at the Fort.

The ground assault on the fifteenth was made by two columns. A force of 2,000 sailors and marines led by Navy Captain K. R. Breese moved to attack the northeast corner of the fort. Assuming that this was the main Federal attack, The Confederates concentrated their defenses against it. This attack was repulsed but it provided the opportunity for Terry's main force of 4,000 men under Brigadier General Adelbert Ames to break through the fort's northwest corner defenses.

An intense fight within the fort followed, but in the end Confederate resistance was broken. Around ten that night, the 400 soldiers at Battery Buchanan surrendered and Fort Fisher was in Union hands.

Of the almost 8,000 Union forces engaged, 955 were casualties and over 2,000 Confederates taken prisoner.

Wilmington fell when more Federal troops were available. It then became a Federal base, and as Lee had predicted, his armies in Virginia could not continue fighting for long without it. In fact, the war ended at Appomattox Courthouse less than three months after the fall of Fort Fisher.

BATTLE OF SAYLER'S CREEK— APRIL 6, 1865

As he retreated from Richmond and Petersburg, General Robert E. Lee intended to move westward, then southward to join General Joseph Johnston's army in North Carolina. Lee first objective was Rice Depot, about three miles from the Appomattox River where he expected to find supplies for his half-starved men.

Lee's column was headed by Lieutenant General James Longstreet's corps, followed by Lieutenant General Anderson's smaller corps, Lieutenant General Richard Ewell's corps, and finally the wagon train with Lieutenant General John Gordon's corps as rear guard. Altogether there were about 24,000 men.

The column was closely followed by Major General Philip Sheridan and his cavalry, Major General Horatio Wright's Sixth Corps, and Major General Andrew Humphrey's Second Corps.

On the morning of April 6, Brigadier General George A. Custer's cavalry hit at a gap in the Confederate column and cut Longstreet off from the remainder of the column.

Learning that Humphrey was attacking Gordon, Ewell ordered the wagon train to take a different road and then, with 3,000

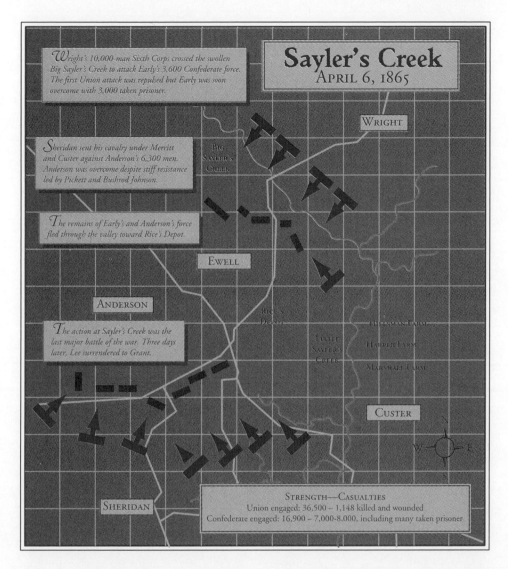

Sayler's Creek
APRIL 6, 1865

Wright's 10,000-man Sixth Corps crossed the swollen Big Sayler's Creek to attack Early's 3,600 Confederate force. The first Union attack was repulsed but Early was soon overcome with 3,000 taken prisoner.

Sheridan sent his cavalry under Merritt and Custer against Anderson's 6,300 men. Anderson was overcome despite stiff resistance led by Pickett and Bushrod Johnson.

The remains of Early's and Anderson's force fled through the valley toward Rice's Depot.

The action at Sayler's Creek was the last major battle of the war. Three days later, Lee surrendered to Grant.

WRIGHT

BIG SAYLER'S CREEK

EWELL

ANDERSON

RICE'S DEPOT

HILLSMAN FARM

LITTLE SAYLER'S CREEK

HARPER FARM

MARSHALL FARM

CUSTER

N
W E
S

SHERIDAN

STRENGTH—CASUALTIES
Union engaged: 36,500 – 1,148 killed and wounded
Confederate engaged: 16,900 – 7,000-8,000, including many taken prisoner

men, took up a defensive position on the southwest side of Sayler's Creek.

The 10,000 Federal troops moved in for the kill.

In his desperate plight, Lee split his army, sending the infantry along one road and the slower wagon train along another. In the resulting confusion, the rear guard followed the wagons. In hard pursuit, the Federal Second Corps under Major General Andrew A. Humphrey tailed the wag-

ons, while Major General Sheridan's cavalry and Major General Horatio G. Wright's Sixth Corps moved on the heels of the Confederate infantry. Along Sayler's Creek, in Virginia, on April 6, the Northerners closed in for the kill.

The battle was actually three separate engagements. Wright struck Lieutenant General Ewell at the Hillsman Farm. But when the Federals crossed the swollen creek, the Confederates drove them back and counterattacked. It was a futile gesture: they lost many men, and when the Union troopers attacked a second time, Ewell's force was overwhelmed. In all, it lost 3,400 men, including six generals.

Sheridan struck Lieutenant General Richard Anderson's corps at a crossroads bounded by the Harper and Marshall farms. Anderson's men fought stubbornly but vainly. Major General George A. Custer's cavalry played an active and well-publicized role in the fight.

The third fight, between Humphreys and the rear guard under Lieutenant General John B. Gordon that defended the Confederate supply train, was waged at Lockett Farm. The infantrymen took shelter behind the wagons, which became bogged down as they tried to cross the creek, then fought determinedly. But when the Federals threatened a flanking attack, the Confederates were forced into the open and overwhelmed.

In the fighting, Gordon lost about 1,700 men but managed to rally the survivors and retreat to safety for the night. When other fragments of his army appeared, Lee exclaimed, "My God! Has the army dissolved?"

The battle had been a disaster for Lee. He had lost between 7,000 and 8,000 men, one third of the once proud and mighty Army of Northern Virginia. Union casualties were a little over 1,100 but with only 166 killed out of a force of around 36,500.

Sayler's Creek was the last major battle of the war. Three days later Lee surrendered to Grant at Appomattox Courthouse.

SURRENDER AT APPOMATTOX COURTHOUSE—APRIL 9, 1865

Finally the Civil War, or War Between the States, as it is sometimes called in the South, came to end. It had lasted almost four terrible, bloody years. No war is U.S. history killed or wounded so many men.

Even after his serious losses at Sayler's Creek, Lee still hoped to escape with what remained of his army by crossing to the north side of the Appomattox River, burning all bridges behind him, and marching to Lynchburg, Virginia. He made a good effort in this direction, but no matter how fast he moved, the Northerners clung hard on his heels.

On April 7, a little north of Farmville, the Confederates fended off a Federal attack and continued the march toward Appomattox Courthouse. By the time they arrived, around 9 P.M. on April 8, Sheridan's cavalry was already there.

The day before at Appomattox Station, Custer's cavalry had captured the railroad trains that were to bring 80,000 rations to the exhausted, hungry Confederate troops. And now, Lee found his route of retreat ahead was blocked by Sheridan's cavalry and infantry with Grant and Meade advancing on his rear.

On the morning of Palm Sunday, April 9, Lee's Army of Northern Virginia made what would be its final attack as it attempted to break through Sheridan's line of cavalry. Sheridan did withdraw, but only to let an infantry corps join the fight.

Lee knew that this marked the end and called off the fighting. "There is nothing left for me to do but to go see General Grant," he said, "and I would rather die a thousand deaths."

Grant had sent a note through the lines to Lee on April 7, suggesting he surrender to stop further bloodshed. Lee rejected the idea but kept the door open by asking what terms Grant would demand. Grant replied on April 8, stating his great desire for peace and asking Lee's army give up their arms and return to their homes. In reply, Lee

Wilmer McLean farmhouse as it appeared on April 9, 1865, when Lee met with Grant in the parlor to surrender his Army of Northern Virginia. In 1893 the McLean house was dismantled and taken to Washington, D.C., as a war museum.

suggested they meet and discuss the matter but Grant declined to talk unless to discuss surrender.

Directly after stopping action on the morning of April 9, Lee sent a note to Grant, stating he was now prepared to surrender.

The assembly took place in a parlor of the Wilmer McLean house about 60 yards from the Appomattox Courthouse around 8:30 A.M. on April 9. Lee was attired in his best formal uniform, with a sword at his side. He was accompanied into the McLean parlor by only one aide. Grant wore a private's uniform, the stars on his shoulder the only sign of his rank. He carried no sidearms. Colonel Amos Webster, one of his staff, recalled: "Grant, covered with mud in an old faded uniform, looked like a fly on a shoulder of beef." He was accompanied by a number of his commanders.

After a few minutes of strained conversation, Grant put down on paper the terms of surrender. They were generous. Lee's men were to lay down their arms and once accepting parole would return to their homes. Officers could retain their sidearms and their horses.

On reading the terms, Lee told Grant that in the Confederate army, many enlisted men in the cavalry and artillery furnished their own horses and did the terms cover this situation? Grant said they did not, but would instruct officers accepting paroles to allow any man who owned his horse to take it to help him get a crop in the coming summer.

The most far-reaching of Grant's terms stated that once a soldier or officer accepted parole, he could return home, "not to be disturbed by United States authority as long as they observed their parole and the laws in force where they reside."

These 23 words meant that no Confederate soldiers would be paraded through cities as prisoners of war and none of their officers tried for treason. The concept of these terms were included in the surrender of other Confederate forces.

And so the Civil War would not generate into a "civil war" with the south and border states the scenes of years and years of guerrilla fighting.

Grant may have exceeded his authority by including this overall pardon in the surrender terms but he, like Lincoln, was anxious to heal the wounds of war. And as Grant now commanded one of the most formidable armies in the world, he could write whatever surrender terms he saw fit.

After accepting the terms, Lee mounted his famous horse Traveler and rode away to tell his troops the news.

Grant arranged to send rations to the desperately hungry Army of Northern Virginia, now down to approximately 27,000 men. Grant also discouraged his army celebrating their victory.

The war in the East was over. Directly after the surrender, a number of Union officers rode over to the Confederate camp to visit with fellow officers they had known as friends and comrades in the days before the Civil War.

When the Union troops heard that surrender papers had been signed, a soldier later wrote, "The air is black with hats and boots, coats, knapsacks, shirts and cartridge boxes, blankets and shelter tents, canteens and haversacks. They fall on each others' neck and laugh and cry by turns. Huge lumbering, bearded men embrace and kiss like schoolgirls, then dance and sing and shout, stand on their heads and play at leapfrog. All the time, the deep-mouthed cannon give their harmless thunders, and at each hollow boom the vast concourse rings out its joy."

But the war actually continued until April 18, when Confederate general Johnston and Union general Sherman signed a similar agreement in the farmhouse of James Bennett near Durham Station, North Carolina. The Federal government insisted that the agreement had to be renegotiated, so the war in the Southeast did not officially end until April 26.

There were some pockets of resistance even after this. The last official battle was fought at Palmito Ranch, Texas, on May 12 and 13, and the Confederacy did not end until the Confederate flag in Galveston, Texas, was hauled down on June 2.

Appomattox Courthouse National Historical Park is on VA Route 24 fifteen miles east of Lynchburg, Virginia.

MAJOR CIVIL WAR COMMANDERS—UNION

ANDERSON, ROBERT—1805–1871

Background: Kentucky. West Point, 1825. Major 1st U.S. Artillery.

In command of Fort Sumter at the time it was attacked by Conferedate artillery. After surrendering the fort, Anderson was made a brigadier general and a brevet major general when he resigned from the army for reasons of health.

BANKS, NATHANIEL P.—1816–1894

Background: Massachusetts. Former U.S. Congressman and Governor of Massachusetts.

Appointed major general because of his ability to rally support for the war, he fought in Virginia at Kernstown, Cedar Mountain, and Second Bull Run. After he was sent south, his attacks on Port Hudson were repulsed. It was not until the fall of Vicksburg that Port Hudson surrendered.

Banks resigned from the army and made a successful run for Congress.

BUELL, DON CARLOS—1818–1894

Background: Ohio. West Point, 1841. Fought in Seminole War and War with Mexico.

As a brigadier general he helped McClellan organize the Army of the Potomac. Appointed major general, he was given command of an army operating in Eastern Tennessee and joined up with Grant on the second day of Shiloh. Later, he defeated Bragg at Perryville, but because he failed to pursue the Confederate army, he was relieved of command. Never given another command, Buell resigned his commission in June 1864.

BUFORD, JOHN—1826–1863

Background: Kentucky. West Point, 1848. U.S. Cavalry. Served in Utah against the Mormons.

Fought at First and Second Bull Run, Fredericksburg, and Brandy Station. Moving into Pennsylvania ahead of Meade's army, Major General Buford and his brigade of cavalry ran into a Confederate force just outside Gettysburg and fired the opening shots of the great battle.

Buford died on December 16, 1863, at the age of 37 as a result of typhoid fever, exposure, and exhaustion.

BURNSIDE, AMBROSE E.—1824–1881

Background: Indiana. West Point, 1847. Stationed in Mexico, wounded fighting Apaches in U.S. Southwest.

Fought at First Bull Run and promoted a major general after leading a successful expedition against the coast of North Carolina. At Antietam he commanded corps and later replaced McClellan as commander of the Army of the Potomac. Burnside's one battle, Fredericksburg, was a Union disaster. Replaced by Hooker, Burnside was sent west to secure Knoxville, Tennessee. On his return, he led his corps at the Wilderness, Spotsylvania, North Anna River, Cold Harbor, and the Siege of Petersburg. He was held responsible for the disaster following the explosion of the mine at Petersburg and sent on leave but never recalled.

After the war Burnside served as governor of Rhode Island and later as one of its U.S. Senators.

Because of his luxuriant whiskers, men and barbers began referring to these facial hairs as "burnsides" and later on as "sideburns."

BUTLER, BENJAMIN F.—1818–1893

Background: New Hampshire. Successful criminal lawyer and Massachusetts politician.

For securing Baltimore Butler was made a major general. He was defeated at Big Bethel, the first land battle of the war, June 10,

1861, but made a successful attack on Cape Hatteras.

In 1864, Butler was defeated south of Richmond at Drewry's Bluff and his army bottled up at Bermuda Hundred. After his dismal failure at Fort Fisher and Petersburg Butler was removed from command and resigned his commission on November 3, 1865. The following year he was elected to Congress and, now as a Radical Republican, was a leader in the attempt to remove President Andrew Jackson from office.

Butler was hated by the South for determining that runaway slaves who reached Union-held territory were considered contraband and not returned to their owner. Even worse was his in famous "Woman's Order," which he issued while military governor of New Orleans in 1862, in reaction to the women of the city who displayed visible hostility toward their Yankee conquerors. The order stated that any woman who by word, movement, or gesture showed contempt for Union officers and soldiers would be "treated as women of the town plying her avocation."

BUTTERFIELD, DANIEL—1831–1901

Background: New York. Businessman, active in the militia. Led first Federal regiment to set foot in Virginia.

Butterfield fought in the First Bull Run campaign. As brigadier general he was wounded at Gaines' Mill and again at Second Bull Run, Antietam, and Fredericksburg. He was wounded at Gettysburg and headed west to join Hooker at Chattanooga. Butterfield took part in the beginning of Sherman's Atlanta campaign and fought at Resaca, Dallas, New Hope Church, and Kennesaw Mountain.

In 1892, Butterfield was awarded the Medal of Honor for gallantry at Gaines' Mill.

At Harrison's Landing, on the Richmond peninsula, Butterfield wrote a new "lights out" bugle call which is now called "Taps."

CHAMBERLAIN, JOSHUA LAWRENCE—1828–1914

Background: Maine. Professor, Bowdoin College.

Joining the 20th of Maine regiment as lieutenant colonel, Chamberlain was at Antietam, Fredericksburg (wounded), and Chancellorsville. He was awarded the Congressional Medal of Honor for action at Gettysburg where he received his second wound. He resumed command in May 1864, led his regiment at Cold Harbor, was wounded at Petersburg. Grant promoted Chamberlain brigadier general before he was taken to the field hospital.

Chamberlain returned to siege of Petersburg and was wounded for the fourth time. Brevetted a major general in March 1865, he was given the honor of commanding the troops that formally accepted the surrender of Lee's army at Appomattox. Chamberlain believed that this occasion offered the opportunity to help reunite the nation, so as the defeated Confederate soldiers began to pass by, the Union troops moved their rifles to the marching salute. Confederate General Gordon drew his sword in reply and then ordered his men to return the salute.

After the war, Chamberlain served as governor of Maine and president of Bowdoin College.

CURTIS, SAMUEL RYAN—1805–1866

Background: New York. West Point, 1831. Served in Mexican War. Resigned seat in U.S. Congress to become colonel of the 2nd Iowa.

As brigadier general Curtis led forces operating in Missouri and Tennessee. His defeat of the Confederate army at Perryville earned him the rank of major general. Curtis helped stop Price's 1864 invasion of Missouri. At the end of the war he was sent west to serve as an Indian commissioner and examiner of Union Pacific Railroad.

CUSTER, GEORGE ARMSTRONG—1839–1876

Background: Ohio. West Point, 1861. Graduated last in his class.

Commissioned a second lieutenant in 1861. By June of 1863 Custer was a brigadier general at age 23. By age 25 he was promoted to major general.

Custer's battles include First Bull Run, the Peninsula Campaign, Antietam, Chancellorsville, Gettysburg, and Yellow Tavern, where J.E.B. Stuart was mortally wounded. Custer went on to fight at Winchester, Cedar Creek, Five Forks, and harass Lee's army as it moved toward Appomattox Courthouse.

Custer remained in the army after the war as lieutenant colonel fighting the western Plains Indians. He and his five troops of the U.S. Seventh Cavalry were killed on June 25, 1876, by Indians near the Little Bighorn River.

FRÉMONT, JOHN CHARLES—1813–1890

Background: Georgia. As a second lieutenant in the Army Typographical Corps spent seven years as an explorer, earning the nickname "The Pathfinder." Played a key role securing California for the Union during the Mexican War. U.S. Senator from California and as the first Republican Party candidate for president lost to James Buchanan in the 1856 election.

Appointed major general in July 1861, in command of Western Department. He failed to send men to Lyon who was shortly defeated at Wilson's Creek and angered Lincoln by establishing martial law in Missouri and freeing the slaves of all who resisted the government.

Sent east in 1862 Freemont's corps were defeated at Cross Keys. When his corps became part of Pope's Army of Virginia, Freemont refused to serve under him and resigned.

Freemont would later serve as Arizona's territorial governor.

GRANT, ULYSSES S.—1822–1885

Background: Ohio. West Point, 1843. After fighting in the Mexican War he was stationed on the West Coast. He resigned his commission on July 31, 1854, after failing to raise money to have his wife join him

and amid rumors of his heavy drinking. At the outbreak of the Civil War he was a clerk in a family leather store.

Grant's offer of his services was turned down by the War Department and McClellan, but with the help of a local Congressman Grant was given command of an Illinois regiment and his second military career began. By February 1862, he was a major general and establishing a battle record that would eventually include Fort Henry and Donelson, Shiloh, Champion Hill, Vicksburg, Chattanooga, the Wilderness, Spotsylvania, North Anna River, Cold Harbor, and Petersburg.

After a brilliant war career, Grant went on to become a mediocre U.S. President. The memoirs he wrote as he was dying of throat cancer are outstanding.

HALLECK, HENRY WAGNER—1815–1872

Background: New York. West Point, 1839, and Mexican War. Taught at West Point. Wrote books on military affairs earning him the nickname "Old Brains." Left the army as captain in 1854. General Winfield Scott recommended him for an important position at the start of the Civil War. As major general Halleck was put in command of Department of Missouri and after Grant took forts Henry and Donelson, in command of all forces in the West.

Halleck was a good organizer but a poor field commander. In his only campaign he moved so slowly on Corinth that the Confederate force had ample time to withdraw.

When Grant was put in command of all Union forces in March 1864, Halleck became Chief of Staff headquarters in Washington, D.C.

After the war, Halleck remained in the army.

HANCOCK, WINFIELD SCOTT—1824–1886

Background: Pennsylvania. West Point, 1844. Served on the frontier, Seminole War, and Mexican War.

Hancock's brigade fought effectively during the Peninsula Campaign. At Antietam he was appointed commander of a division.

As a major general, Hancock fought at

Fredericksburg and Chancellorsville. When General Reynolds was killed on the first day of Gettysburg, Meade gave Hancock Reynolds's wing of the army and left it up to him to decide if Gettysburg was the place to fight Lee.

Hancock held the center of Meade's line along Cemetery Hill where he was wounded. He recovered to fight in the Wilderness, to lead the attack on the Mule Shoe salient at Spotsylvania, and fight at North Anna River. His command suffered losses at Cold Harbor. He deferred command at Petersburg because he lacked knowledge of the situation.

In 1866 Hancock was appointed major general in the regular army. In the 1880 presidential election he was narrowly defeated by the Republican candidate, James Garfield.

HOOKER, JOSEPH—1814–1879

Background: Massachusetts. West Point, 1837. Seminole War, the frontier, and War with Mexico. Resigned from army in 1853 and moved to California. Because he had managed to antagonize both General Winfield Scott and Colonel Halleck, he was not able to get a command until after he had written to President Lincoln.

Hooker fought in the Peninsula Campaign and the Seven Days, where he earned the rank of major general. Transferred to Pope's Army of Virginia, he was at the second battle at Bull run and commanded a corps at Antietam, where he was wounded. Under Burnside he commanded the Grand Division at Fredericksburg. After this disastrous Union defeat, Hooker took over from Burnside only to be defeated by Lee at Chancellorsville.

He remained in command when Lee began his invasion of Pennsylvania but resigned on June 28, 1863.

After the Union defeat at Chickamauga, Hooker was sent to Chattanooga with two corps. In the forthcoming battle, his troops captured Lookout Mountain. During the Atlanta campaign, Hooker asked to be relieved of his command after being passed over for a high command. He spent the remainder of the war in the middle west.

HOWARD, OLIVER OTIS—1830–1909

Background: Maine. West Point, 1854.

Commanded a brigade at First Bull Run. As a brigadier general fought in the Peninsula Campaign where he was wounded at Seven Pines and lost his right arm. At Antietam Howard took over John Sedgwick's division, which he continued to lead at Fredericksburg. As a major general, Howard held the Union right at Chancellorsville.

At Gettysburg he took over command when Reynolds was killed. He was later replaced by Hancock on Meade's order.

He was sent west and fought at Chattanooga. In the Atlanta campaign, Sherman made him commander of the Army of Tennessee, Sherman's right wing on his march to Savannah.

In 1893, Howard received the Congressional Medal of Honor for his actions at Seven Pines. He retired from the army as a major general of the regular army.

HUNT, HENRY JACKSON—1819–1889

Background: Michigan. West Point, 1839. Wounded in War with Mexico.

Was a major in the Union artillery, Hunt's battery broke the Confederate pursuit of the retreating soldiers. As a colonel he commanded the Federal guns at Gaines's Mill and Malvern Hill. As brigadier general he saw action at Antietam. At Fredericksburg he assembled 147 guns to open the battle that probably prevented Lee from counterattacking.

At Gettysburg, Hunt's artillery mowed down the ranks of the Confederate troops attacking in "Pickett's Charge."

Promoted major general for his role at Gettysburg; Grant put him in charge of the siege operations at Petersburg.

Hunt remained in the army until his retirement in 1883.

McCLELLAN, GEORGE BRINTON—1826–1885

Background: Pennsylvania. West Point, 1846. Served with distinction in War with Mexico. As captain of cavalry he was sent to study European armies. He developed the "McClellan Saddle" that was in use until the U.S. Army gave up cavalry. He resigned his commission in 1857. He was president of the Illinois Central Railroad where he became acquainted with their lawyer, Abraham Lincoln.

When the war began McClellan was 39 and soon a major general of the regular army. Before First Bull Run he received praise for clearing Confederate forces out of what would later become West Virginia.

After Bull Run he was given command of the armies around Washington and later replaced General Winfield Scott as commander in chief of the Army. He applied his talents to the organization and training of the Army of the Potomac.

Hailed at the beginning of the war as the "Young Napoleon" McClellan was never able to achieve a decisive victory despite his large and well-equipped army. His Peninsula Campaign to take Richmond ended in failure and encouraged Halleck to give Pope the next major command.

After Pope was defeated at Second Bull Run, McClellan was again in control but failed to use his army. He was finally forced to use it when Lee invaded Maryland.

Lincoln finally gave up on McClellan when he did not pursue and destroy Lee's army after Antietam, and gave the command to Burnside.

On giving up his command on November 9, 1862, McClellan returned home. As the Democratic nominee he ran against Lincoln in the election of 1864.

McCLERNAND, JOHN ALEXANDER—1812–1900

Background: Kentucky. Lawyer, politician, and Illinois congressman. In 1832 served two months as private in Black Hawk War.

As a politically appointed brigadier general and later a major general he saw action at Forts Henry and Donelson, Shiloh, Champion Hill, and Vicksburg. Far better at recruiting troops than leading them, McClernand disliked taking orders from West Pointers. He supplied the press with self-congratulatory articles describing his imagined victories. Grant tired of this during the siege of Vicksburg and relieved him of command.

McDOWELL, IRVIN—1818–1885

Background: West Point, 1838. Educated in France before attending West Point. Served on the frontier and War with Mexico.

As brigadier general he was given command of troops south of the Potomac that fought at First Bull Fun. After his defeat, McDowell was given command of a division and was major general of a corps that saw action at Cedar Mountain. Criticized for his performance at Second Bull run, McDowell demanded a court of inquiry that cleared him. He served for a time as commander of the Department of the Pacific and retired in 1882.

McPHERSON, JAMES BIRDSEYE—1828–1864

Background: Ohio. West Point, 1853. Graduated head of his class, taught engineering at the academy, and later engaged in military engineering projects.

As colonel and later brigadier general, McPherson was Grant's engineering officer at Fort Henry and Fort Donelson.

Promoted to major general, he commanded one wing of Grant's army during the Vicksburg Campaign. In command of the Army of Tennessee, with Sherman on his drive to Atlanta.

Just outside Atlanta, McPherson's West Point classmate John Hood led a Confederate force to crush the Army of Tennessee and McPherson was killed. He was 35 years old.

MEADE, GEORGE GORDON—1815–1872

Background: Born in Spain. West Point, 1835. Served a year in the artillery before resigning to become a civil engineer. Reentered the army in 1842 and served in War with Mexico.

A brigadier general of Volunteers, Meade was wounded during the Peninsula Campaign. He commanded a brigade at Second Bull Run, a division at Antietam, and a corps at Chancellorsville.

On June 28, 1863, he replaced Hooker as commander of the Army of the Potomac and joined with him in taking on Lee at the Wilderness, Spotsylvania Court House, North Anna River, Cold Harbor, and Petersburg, finally driving the Confederate army to Appomattox Courthouse.

Seven years after the war ended, Meade died of pneumonia.

POPE, JOHN—1822–1892

Background: Kentucky. West Point, 1842. Served in Mexican War.

Appointed brigadier general in June 1861. Performed well on upper Mississippi River at New Madrid, Island Number Ten, and Corinth.

Promoted to major general in June of 1862, Lincoln appointed him commander of the newly formed Army of Virginia.

Bombastic and highly critical of his eastern officers, Pope and his army took a terrible beating at Second Bull Run where he faced a far smaller Confederate army but one led by Lee, Jackson, and Longstreet.

On September 2, Pope was relieved of his command and his army was absorbed into McClellan's Army of the Potomac.

Pope remained on active duty and commanded the Department of the Northwest.

PORTER, FITZ-JOHN—1822–1901

Background: New Hampshire. West Point, 1845. Served in War with Mexico and wounded at Chapultepec and during operations against the Mormons where he served as Albert Sidney Johnston's adjutant.

Attained the rank of brigadier general soon after the start of the war and worked with McClellan in training the Army of the Potomac.

Porter's skilled performance during the Seven Days campaign earned him the rank of major general.

He was ordered to join Pope's new Army of Virginia and this was where his military career ended. At Second Bull Run, Porter failed to attack as ordered because he believed the order was based on faulty information.

For this action, Pope relieved him from command, "Charging him with disobedience and misconduct in the face of the enemy."

Porter spent the next sixteen years trying to overturn the conviction which he believed unjust. In 1878, a new board reexamined the evidence and recommended the sentence be remitted.

Four years later President Chester A. Arthur took action and in 1886, a special act of Congress restored Porter to rank of colonel effective May 1861, but without back pay.

REYNOLDS, JOHN FULTON—1820–1863

Background: Pennsylvania. West Point, 1841. Mexican War, saw action in the western frontier and at the start of Civil War was commandant of cadets at West Point.

Reynolds was captured during the Seven Days and exchanged on August 13, 1862, in time to fight at Second Bull Run. Sent to Pennsylvania to raise a militia at the time of Lee's invasion of Maryland, he missed Antietam. As a major general he commanded a corps at Fredericksburg, Chancellorsville, and Gettysburg, where he was killed by a sniper on the first day of the battle.

Reynolds had been considered to succeed Hooker but for political considerations the job was given to Meade.

ROSECRANS, WILLIAM STARKE—1819–1898

Background: Ohio. West Point, 1842. Resigned from army in 1854 and reentered it at start of Civil War.

Appointed a brigadier general on June 16, 1861, and commanded the Army of Occupation, West Virginia, until he was superseded by Freemont. Sent west at his own request, "Old Rosy" as his soldiers called him, was given command of the Army of the Mississippi, under Grant.

As major general he replaced Buell as head of the Army of Ohio which was renamed Army of the Cumberland. He defeated Bragg at Stones River (Murfreesboro) but allowed Bragg to leisurely withdraw to Chattanooga.

Rosecrans was soundly defeated by Bragg at Chickamauga and removed from command.

He resigned from the army in 1867 to serve as Minister to Mexico.

SEDGWICK, JOHN—1813–1864

Background: Connecticut. West Point, 1837. Served in Seminole Wars, War with Mexico, and in the West fighting against the Mormons and Indians.

Wounded during the Seven Days, he was wounded again, as major general, at Antietam where his division was attacked on three sides.

At Chancellorsville he broke through the Confederate line but was stopped at Salem Church.

His corps were held in reserve at Gettysburg but they saw plenty of action at the Wilderness and Spotsylvania, where Sedgwick was killed by a sniper while directing the placement of artillery.

SHERIDAN, PHILIP HENRY—1831–1888

Background: New York. West Point, 1853. Suspended for a year at West Point for threatening a fellow cadet with a bayonet and attacking him with his fists.

In early months of war served in various staff positions. Appointed colonel of cavalry regiment in May 1863, and brigadier general in July. He commanded a division at Perryville and achieved rank of major general for action at Stones River.

Fought at Chickamauga and distinguished himself at Chattanooga. Selected by Grant to command the cavalry corps of the Army of the Potomac. He played a minor role at the Wilderness and Spotsylvania.

In the 1864–65 Shenandoah Valley Campaign,

Sheridan defeated Confederate forces under Early at Winchester, Fishers Hill, Cedar Creek, and Waynesboro and destroyed crops that the Confederate army depended upon.

He rejoined Grant at Petersburg, fought at Sayler's Creek at Five Forks, and later blocked Lee's retreat at Appomattox.

After the war he was appointed military governor of Texas and Louisiana but was so severe he was recalled after six months. In 1869, he was made lieutenant general and in 1884, succeeded Sherman as commander in chief of the army. He became a full general in 1888, the year of his death.

SHERMAN, WILLIAM TECUMSEH—1820–1891

Background: Ohio. West Point, 1840. Served in California during War with Mexico. Resigned in 1853, and became a banker and later a lawyer. At outbreak of war was superintendent of a military school in Louisiana.

Commissioned colonel, Sherman fought at First Bull Run and one month later was made brigadier general. Sent to Kentucky, he was stationed at Paducah during the Fort Henry and Donelson campaign, charged with sending reinforcements to Grant. It was then the two men began their long association.

Sherman commanded a division at Shiloh where he was wounded. Appointed major general on May 1, 1862, he commanded a corps at Vicksburg. As commander of the Department of the Tennessee he joined Grant at the battle of Chattanooga.

When Grant was appointed commander in chief of all Union forces in 1864, Sherman took over command of the Military Division of the Mississippi responsible for all military operations in the West.

In May 1864, Sherman began his march on Atlanta that resulted in a series of battles at Rocky Face, Resaca, New Hope Church, Dallas, Kennesaw Mountain, culminating in the siege of Atlanta.

The fall of Atlanta and Sherman's capture of Savannah ensured Lincoln's reelection in 1864.

Sherman was a very complex man and some of the press stated he was crazy. His march through Georgia destroyed a huge amount of property and the South hated him. But the terms of surrender he offered to General Johnson were so generous that officials at Washington would not approve them and required they be revised to conform with the same terms offered and accepted by Lee at Appomattox.

Sherman became a lieutenant general on July 25, 1866, and a full general on March 4, 1869, and succeeding Grant as commander in chief of the army.

SLOCUM, HENRY WARNER—1826–1894

Background: New York. West Point, 1852. Resigned from army 1856 to practice law.

As colonel of a New York regiment he was wounded at First Bull Run. Promoted to brigadier general he fought in battles of the Seven Days. As major general he led his corps at Second Bull Run and Antietam. Arriving too late to take part in Fredericksburg, Slocum commanded three corps at the start of the battle of Chancellorsville and the Union right wing on Culp's Hill at Gettysburg.

After the defeat at Chickamauga, Slocum and O. O. Howard were ordered west to join with Hooker at Chattanooga. Slocum had been highly critical of Hooker's behavior at Chancellorsville and resigned rather than serve under him again. The problem was temporarily solved by giving Slocum command of Vicksburg. The final solution came about when Hooker resigned rather than serve under his junior, O. O. Howard, who had been appointed commander of the Army of Tennessee.

Slocum took over Hooker's corps and in November 1864, was in command of the Army of Georgia that marched with Sherman to the sea.

After the war, Slocum served in Congress and was active in clearing Fitz-John Porter's name.

THOMAS, GEORGE HENRY—1816–1870

Background: Virginia. West Point, 1840. Brevetted captain and then major for action in War with Mexico, he was wounded by an arrow on the western frontier fighting alongside Lee, Hardee, Hood, and Van Dorn.

Although a Virginian, when the Civil War began he would remain in the Union army.

Appointed brigadier general on August 3, 1861, Thomas commanded a division at Shiloh and at the advance on Corinth. He was second in command of the Army of the Ohio at the battle of Perryville.

On April 25, 1862, he was promoted to major general and fought at Stones River and Chickamauga. At Chattanooga his new command, the Army of the Department of the Cumberland, took Lookout Mountain and Missionary Ridge and eventually joined in the Atlanta campaign.

Called "Pap Thomas" by his soldiers, Thomas is known to many as "The Rock of Chickamauga," earned for holding his position against tremendous odds.

Thomas remained in the army until his death and was given the Thanks of Congress.

WALLACE, LEWIS—1827–1905

Background: Indiana. A newspaper reporter and lawyer before serving in War with Mexico. Active in militia.

Named colonel of the 11th Indiana regiment in April 1861, he was promoted to brigadier general in September of that year and major general in May 1862.

At Fort Donelson he commanded a division. Due to contradictory orders he did not get his division to Shiloh until the first day's fighting was over. While he performed well on the second day of battle, he nevertheless became the scapegoat for this near disaster and was relieved of his command.

After serving on military boards, Wallace was given command of a small force to stop Early's advance on Washington. His little army was finally defeated at Monocacy, Maryland, but Early gave up his advance.

At the close of the war, Wallace served on courts that tried Lincoln's assassins and convicted Henry Wirtz, commandant of Andersonville Prison.

In 1878, Wallace was appointed governor of New Mexico where he wrote *Ben Hur* and *A Tale of the Christ.*

WARREN, GOUVERNEUR KEMBLE—1830–1882

Background: New York. West Point, 1850. As a typographical engineer he worked on canal and railroad projects until the early part of the war.

As colonel, Warren was wounded at Gaines' Mill. He fought at Malvern Hill, Second Bull Run, and Fredericksburg. Promoted to brigadier general, he was named Chief Typographical Engineer for the Army of the Potomac in June 1863.

On the second day of Gettysburg Warren, now a major general, secured the Union left by gathering troops to hold Little Round Top.

Warren commanded the 5th Corps at the Wilderness, Spotsylvania, North Anna River, Cold Harbor, and during the siege of Petersburg. Unfortunately for Warren, there was now a rift between him and Grant, Meade, and Sheridan, chief of cavalry.

After Petersburg Union forces pursued Lee who was moving west. Warren was put under Sheridan who relieved him of command during the battle of Five Forks because Sheridan thought his attack was poorly coordinated.

Warren remained in the army and was a lieutenant colonel of engineers at his death in 1882.

After repeated requests and fourteen years after the war, a court of inquiry exonerated Warren of Sheridan's charges. But he had been professionally ruined and left instructions that he was not to be buried in uniform.

There is a statue honoring Warren at battlefield of Gettysburg.

MAJOR CIVIL WAR COMMANDERS—CONFEDERATE

ANDERSON, RICHARD HERON—1821–1879

Background: South Carolina. West Point, 1842. Served in Mexican War and on Kansas border. Captain of 2nd Dragoon. Resigned on March 3, 1861, to join Confederate forces.

As colonel he served at bombardment of Fort Sumter. As brigadier general he fought at Williamsburg, Seven Pines, and the Seven Days battles.

Promoted major general, he joined Lee at Second Bull Run and was wounded at Antietam. Recovered in time to fight at Fredericksburg.

Anderson played a key role at Chancellorsville and was with A. P. Hill's corps at Gettysburg. At the Wilderness he took over the wounded Longstreet corps and won the "race" to Spotsylvania Court House. He led the corps at North Anna River, Cold Harbor, and Petersburg. On May 31, 1864, he was promoted to lieutenant general. Sent to reinforce Early in the Shenandoah but was shortly recalled. Upon Longstreet's return "Dick" Anderson was given another corps that was all but destroyed at Sayler's Creek the day before Appomattox.

The war left Anderson impoverished as it did other Confederate officers.

BEAUREGARD, PIERRE GUSTAVE TOUTANT—1818–1893

Backrgound: Louisiana. West Point, 1838. Served in Mexican War as engineering officer on General Scott's staff. Wounded at Chapultepec. For a short time was superintendent of West Point.

As brigadier general in the Confederate army he commanded the bombardment of Fort Sumter. At First Bull Run he was second in command under J. E. Johnson.

Promoted to general in early 1862, he was sent west and assumed command at the battle at Shiloh when his immediate superior, General A. S. Johnson, was killed.

When Beauregard went on sick leave in June of 1862, he turned over his command, temporarily he thought, to Bragg. But President Davis relieved Beauregard for going on sick leave without permission.

Assigned in the east to command coastal defenses, Beauregard defeated Butler at Drewry's Bluff and "bottled" his army of Bermuda Hundred.

Beauregard fought in the siege of Petersburg and commanded a division under J. E. Johnson in North Carolina.

After the war, Beauregard turned down the high rank offered to him by several foreign countries. He later received criticism for being supervisor of the Louisiana Lottery.

BRAGG, BRAXTON—1817–1876

Background: North Carolina. West Point, 1837. Served in Seminole War, on the frontier, and Mexican War. Resigned from U.S. Army in 1856.

After commanding Southern coastal defenses Bragg, now a major general, was sent west to serve under General Johnson organizing an army at Corinth, Mississippi.

Bragg commanded the Confederate right at Shiloh and, after Johnston's death and Beauregard's departure on sick leave, Bragg was given command of the Army of Tennessee with rank of full general.

His invasion of Kentucky was not a success. He allowed only a portion of his force to fight at Perryville and failed to achieve victory at Stones River.

Retreating south to Chattanooga, Bragg defeated Rosecrans at Chickamauga but then did nothing as Grant built up a powerful army at Chattanooga. After his defeat in the mountains around Chattanooga, he was replaced by J. E. Johnson. Bragg returned to Richmond and served as military advisor to President Davis and later went with him to Georgia where he was captured. After being paroled, Bragg became a civil engineer.

Bragg was irritable and had disputes with many of his subordinate commanders. He did not get along with himself for, as the story goes, he had a written argument with himself while serving both as company commander and quartermaster.

BRECKINRIDGE, JOHN CABELL—1821–1875

Background: Kentucky. Served as major in War with Mexico but saw no action. Elected to Congress and became Buchanan's vice president. Ran for president in 1860 on the Southern Democrat Party ticket. At outbreak of war he fled Kentucky fearing he would be arrested as traitor to the U.S.

Made brigadier general in Confederate army and commanded the reserve corps at Shiloh. Promoted to major general, he served with J. E. Johnston at Vicksburg and commanded a division at Chickamauga and Chattanooga.

Transferred east, Breckinridge fought at Cold Harbor and at Monocacy.

On February 4, 1865, he was appointed Secretary of War by President Davis. At War's end he traveled to Cuba and then to Europe before returning to Kentucky to practice law.

EARLY, JUBAL ANDERSON—1816–1894

Background: Virginia. West Point, 1837. Fought in Seminole War and Mexican War. After resigning from army in 1838, he became a lawyer and state legislator. He voted against Virginia's secession but nevertheless followed it out of the Union.

As a colonel, Early fought at First Bull Run and as a brigadier general saw action during the Peninsula campaign, where he was wounded. He recovered in time to lead his command at Second Bull Run, Cedar Mountain, Antietam, and Fredericksburg.

Promoted to major general in April of 1863, he led his division at Chancellorsville, Gettysburg, the Wilderness, and North Anna River.

In May 1864, Early succeeded Ewell as commander of Ewell's Second Corps and as a lieutenant general led it at Cold Harbor.

He was then sent north to attack Washington. This project ended at the Monocacy River in Maryland.

In the Shenandoah Valley campaign, Early was so badly outgeneraled by Sheridan that Lee, responding to public criticism, relieved him of command.

At end of war, Early went to Mexico and Canada and eventually returned to practice law in Virginia.

EWELL, RICHARD STODDERT—1817–1872

Background: Virginia. West Point, 1840. Served in the dragoons on the frontier, Mexican War, and against Indians, before resigning as captain in U.S. Army in May 1861.

Appointed brigadier general in June 1861, Ewell led a brigade at First Bull Run. By January 1862, he was promoted to major general.

He commanded one of Jackson's divisions during the Shenandoah Valley campaign. He fought at Winchester and Cross Keys and followed Jackson south to fight in the Peninsula Campaign and the Seven Days battles.

After fighting at Cedar Mountain, he lost a leg at Second Bull Run.

Promoted to lieutenant general in May 1863, Ewell commanded Jackson's old corps at Gettysburg, the Wilderness, and Spotsylvania, where one of his divisions was practically destroyed at the Mule Shoe salient.

Ewell fought his last major battle at North Anna River. Because of illness, he was removed from his command and given another command in Richmond. He was taken prisoner at Sayler's Creek and not paroled until the following August, after which he retired to a farm in Tennessee.

Ewell was a disappointment to the Confederacy because he was unable to fill Jackson's shoes. Many reasons are given for his failures as a commander. One of the most important is that for almost two decades Ewell was a company commander in the regular army and lacked Jackson's ability to immediately adjust to changing battlefield conditions.

FORREST, NATHAN BEDFORD—1821–1877

Background: Tennessee. With only six months' formal education he rose from poverty to wealth by trading in cotton, real estate, livestock, and slaves.

He enlisted in the Confederate army as a private on June 14, 1861. By October of that year Forrest was a commissioned lieutenant colonel commanding a mounted brigade he raised at his own expanse.

After escaping from Fort Donelson with his command and other units, Forrest covered the retreat from Shiloh and was promoted brigadier general during the siege of Corinth.

He made successful raids into Tennessee and captured the Union supply base of Murfreesboro.

After commanding a corps at Chickamauga, Forrest was promoted major general. In April 1864, his command took part in the Fort Pillow "Massacre" where many black and white Union soldiers were killed after surrendering.

He defeated Sturgis at Brice's Cross Roads and suffered heavy losses at Tupelo. He joined with Hood to take part in another Tennessee campaign. In the closing months of the war, Forrest was promoted to lieutenant general and finally met defeat at Selma, Alabama.

By the end of the war, Forrest had lost his fortune. He became a planter and went into railroading. He also became involved with the Ku Klux Klan.

Forrest was a natural military genius and many would agree with A. E. Johnson that if Forrest had education and military training he would have been the central leader of the Civil War.

GORDON, JOHN BROWN—1832–1904

Background: Georgia. Graduated University of Georgia. Lawyer and superintendent of coal mine.

Entered Civil War as captain of the "Racoon Roughs," a company of mountaineer volunteers.

Named colonel of an Alabama regiment, he fought in the Peninsula campaign and at Seven Pines. Severely wounded in the head at Antietam, Gordon later said that a hole in his hat prevented him drowning in his own blood.

He was promoted brigadier general in May 1863, and led a Georgia brigade at Chancellorsville, Gettysburg, and the Wilderness. He earned the stars of major general at Spotsylvania where he repulsed the Union attack on the neck of Mule Shoe salient.

Gordon saw action at Cold Harbor, Petersburg, the Shenandoah Valley, Monocacy, Fisher Hill, and Cedar Creek. Returning to Petersburg, he planned the attack on Fort Stedman. At Appomattox his troops made the last charge of Lee's army.

After the war, he went into politics and served as a senator and governor of Georgia.

HARDEE, WILLIAM JOSEPH—1815–1873

Background: Georgia. West Point, 1838. Fought in Seminole War, studied in France, returned to fight in War with Mexico.

Returned to West Point as instructor and commandant of cadets. Wrote several textbooks, including *Hardee's Tactics*, which was widely used by both sides in the Civil War.

Hardee entered the Confederate army as a colonel and was promoted to brigadier general in June of 1861 and to major general in October of the same year.

He commanded a corps at Shiloh where he was wounded. He participated in the defense of Corinth, Mississippi. At Perryville Gordon commanded Bragg's left. As a lieutenant general he commanded a corps at Stones River and at Chattanooga he held off Sherman's attack on the Confederate right.

Hardee apparently did not like Hood, so when Hood took over from Joseph E. Johntson during Sherman's Atlanta campaign, Hardee accepted transfer to the Atlantic coast. Realizing he could not hold off Sherman, Hardee evacuated Savannah and left Charleston to join with J. E. Johnston in North Carolina where they surrendered to Sherman on April 26, 1865.

Called "Old Reliable," Hardee is considered by many to be among the best of Confederate corps commanders. After the war he had a plantation in Alabama.

HILL, AMBROSE POWELL—1825–1865

Background: Virginia. West Point, 1847. Served in Seminole War, at a garrison in Mexico, and on the frontier. Resigned U.S. Army on March 1, 1861.

As a colonel Hill commanded reserves at First Bull Run. He was promoted to brigadier general in February 1862. He led his brigade at the battle of Williamsburg. Promoted to major general in May 1862, he led his divisions in the battle of the Seven Days. Sent north to join Jackson, A. P. Hill served at Cedar Mountain, Second Bull Run, Harpers Ferry, Antietam, and Chancellorsville, where he succeeded Jackson.

In May 1863, Hill was appointed lieutenant and led his corps at Gettysburg where his performance was mediocre, due perhaps to illness. Hill was so sick at the Wilderness that Lee had to direct his corps. Hill was on sick leave during the battle at Spotsylvania Court House, rejoining his corps in time to lead them at North Anna River, Cold Harbor, and Petersburg. In March 1865, he was again on sick leave. On his return he was shot and killed by Union soldiers on April 2, 1865.

Hill, who had been a splendid divisional

commander, did not do well commanding a corps. This may be because of his health or because the responsibility of commanding so many thousands of men was too much for him.

HILL, DANIEL HARVEY—1821–1889

Background: South Carolina. West Point, 1842. Served in Mexican War. Resigned army in 1849 to become a teacher. In 1861, he was superintendent of North Carolina Military Institute.

He led a regiment at Big Bethel, Virginia— the first land battle of the war, fought on June 10.

Appointed brigadier general in July 1861, and major general in March 1862, he led a division at Yorktown, Seven Pines, the Seven Days, Antietam, and Fredericksburg.

Hill was promoted to lieutenant general in July 1863, and went west to join Bragg and lead a corps at Chickamauga. Immediately after the battle Hill sent word to President Davis criticizing Bragg for not following up on the victory, allowing the Union army to withdraw to Chattanooga. Davis supported Bragg and not only removed Hill from his command but did not send his appointment to lieutenant general to the Senate for confirmation.

Reverting to the rank of major general, Hill was a volunteer on Beauregard's staff at Drewry's Bluff and Petersburg.

At the end of the war he was in North Carolina, serving as divisional commander in Joseph E. Johnston's army.

After surrendering, Hill returned to education and writing.

HOOD, JOHN BELL—1831–1879

Background: Kentucky. West Point, 1853. Served on frontier and was wounded fighting Indians. Resigned from U.S. Army in April 1861.

Given command of the "Texas Brigade" and the rank of brigadier general, he led them at Gaines' Mill, Second Bull Run, and Antietam.

Promoted to major general in October 1862, he commanded one of Longstreet's divisions at Fredericksburg and Gettysburg, where he was seriously wounded. He lost a leg at Chickamauga.

As lieutenant general he commanded a corps under Joseph Johnston in the Atlanta campaign. On July 17, with Sherman at the outskirts of Atlanta, he replaced Johnston as head of the Army of Tennessee and was given the temporary rank of general. Hood launched a series of disastrous attacks that failed to stop Sherman.

After evacuating Atlanta, Hood concentrated on Sherman's supply lines and moved north trying to draw him out of Georgia. Hood's army was all but destroyed in an attack on Nashville and he was relieved of command at his own request, reverting in rank to lieutenant general. He surrendered at Natchez on May 31, 1865.

After the war Hood settled in New Orleans where he, along with his wife and eldest daughter, died of yellow fever in 1879.

Hood's military career is another example of the common error of continually promoting a competent officer until he reaches a position that is beyond his capabilities.

JACKSON, THOMAS JONATHAN—1824–1863

Background: Virginia. West Point, 1846. Served in Mexican War. Resigned from U.S. Army in 1851 to teach at the Virginia Military Institute. Commanded a company of cadets at the hanging of John Brown.

In the early months of the war, Jackson organized a Confederate brigade at Harpers Ferry. At First Bull Run Jackson earned the nickname "Stonewall" and his brigade was later officially named "The Stonewall Brigade."

Promoted to major general in the fall of 1861, Jackson was in command in the Shenandoah Valley where in March 1862, a portion of his command was defeated at Kernstown. In May, Jackson stopped Freemont's advance on McDowell and launched a brilliant campaign that kept several larger Union forces off balance, achieving victories at Front Royal, Winchester, Cross Keys, and Port Republic.

Joining Lee in the defense of Richmond, Jackson was sent north to deal with the Union forces under Pope. Jackson had difficulties at Cedar Mountain but later displayed great ability in setting up Pope for a major defeat at Second Bull Run.

Preparing to invade Maryland, Lee ordered Jackson to secure Harpers Ferry. Once this was accomplished, Jackson joined Lee at Antietam.

Raised to the rank of lieutenant general in October 1862, Jackson held the Confederate right at Fredericksburg and repulsed repeated attacks.

At Chancellorsville, Jackson executed his and Lee's audacious plan to turn Hooker's flank. After the day's success, Jackson was mortally wounded by one of his own men. Jackson was a brilliant tactician and his fast-moving "foot cavalry" often appeared where the enemy least expected.

He and Lee formed a perfect team. Jackson knew exactly what Lee expected and Lee allowed him the independence to execute the plan in the manner he thought best.

JOHNSTON, ALBERT SIDNEY—1803–1862

Background: Kentucky. West Point, 1826. Served in Black Hawk War, resigned from U.S. Army in 1834. Moved to Texas and enlisted as a private in the Texas army in 1836. Promoted to brigadier general, he was army commander and then Secretary of War in the Republic of Texas. Resigned these posts in 1840 and later fought in the Mexican War and against the Mormons in Utah.

At the start of the Civil War, General Scott offered Johnston second command of Union forces but he accepted Davis's offer as full general in the Confederate army.

Johnston was given command of the Western Department, where, after he seized Bowling Green, Kentucky, his subordinate generals were defeated at Forts Henry and Donelson.

Johnston organized an army at Corinth, Mississippi, and moved on Grant's army at Pittsburg Landing. The two forces clashed around Shiloh

Church and in the fighting Johnston was shot in the leg and bled to death before realizing the wound was serious.

Davis considered Johnston to be ablest military man living in the South or the North. And even though he did not distinguish himself in the Civil War, many Southerners living today would probably agree with Davis.

JOHNSTON, JOSEPH EGGLESTON—1807–1891

Background: Virginia. West Point, 1829. Served at Black Hawk, in the Seminole Wars, and in the Mexican War, where he was wounded five times. Also served on the frontier and Kansas.

After resigning from the U.S. Army on April 22, 1861, he entered the Confederate army, and in May 1861 was named brigadier general.

Assigned in command at Harpers Ferry, he fooled the Union forces in the region and moved to reinforce Beauregard who was advancing on Manassas.

As senior commander, Johnston let Beauregard take over at First Bull Run because he was more familiar with the terrain than Johnston.

Johnston was given command of the troops defending Richmond and was appointed full general. He was wounded twice at Seven Pines and was relieved of his command by General Robert Lee.

On returning to duty, Johnston was put in command in the west over Bragg and Pemberton, but had few troops under his immediate control. The result was a series of Confederate defeats at Stones River, Vicksburg, and Chattanooga.

In December 1863, Johnston took command of Bragg's Army of Tennessee and in the following spring and summer used his talents to delay Sherman's advance on Atlanta.

On July 17, 1864, Johnston was relieved by Hood who, in a series of fruitless assaults on Union positions, practically destroyed the Confederate army. Johnston surrendered to Sherman on April 26.

After the war Johnston was in business and served a term in Congress. For a time he was a railroad commissioner. He died of pneumonia.

LEE, ROBERT EDWARD—1807–1870

Background: Virginia. West Point, 1829. Served on engineering projects before joining General Scott's staff in the Mexican War. Superintendent of the Military Academy at West Point in 1851–55. He served with the U.S. cavalry in Texas. In 1859 he took a force of marines to Harpers Ferry and arrested John Brown. On April 18, 1861, General Scott offered Lee command of the Union forces, which he refused. Two days later Lee took command of Virginia's troops.

Lee's first campaign to drive Federal troops out of portions of West Virginia ended in failure at Cheat Mountain, September 10 to 15, 1861.

He was recalled to Virginia and served as military advisor to Davis until June 1, 1862, when he succeeded General J. E. Johnston, wounded at Seven Pines, to command a force soon to be called the Army of Northern Virginia.

For almost three years General Lee and his army prevented Federal troops from capturing Richmond and defeated large and well-supplied Union armies led by Pope, Burnside, and Hooker. He achieved success by his ability to determine the enemy's strength, movement, and his ability to maintain the initiative. He also had outstanding lieutenants: Jackson, Stuart, and Longstreet.

Lee's two attempts to invade the North, however, ended in failure at Antietam and at Gettysburg, where he was unable to destroy the Union Army of the Potomac.

The initiative passed to the Union and Grant, with superior men and materials and competent leadership, would hammer at Lee's army until it was forced to surrender.

After the war, Lee accepted the presidency of Washington College at Lexington, Virginia, later to be renamed Washington and Lee University, and where he is buried.

LONGSTREET, JAMES—1821–1904

Background: South Carolina. West Point, 1842. Wounded during Mexican War. Served on frontier against Indians. Resigned from the U.S. Army June 1, 1861. Appointed brigadier general in Confederate army on June 17.

He commanded a brigade at First Bull Run and was promoted to major general in October. He led a division in the Peninsula Campaign and saw action at Yorktown, Seven Pines, and the Seven Days, where he commanded a wing of Lee's army.

At Second Bull Run, Longstreet commanded a slashing attack on Pope's Union forces and later fought at Antietam and Fredericksburg.

As a lieutenant general he opposed Lee's decision to attack Meade's army at Gettysburg, which may explain Longstreet's delay in mounting an attack on the Union left during the second day of battle, and his reluctance to follow the frontal attack ordered by Lee on the third and last day of the battle.

Sent west, Longstreet's wing of Bragg's army all but crushed Union forces at Chickamauga. Because Longstreet was critical of Bragg for now following through and destroying Rosecrans's army, he was sent to lay siege to Burnside at Knoxville.

Rejoining Lee, Longstreet was wounded at the Wilderness and did not return to command until Petersburg.

He remained with Lee for the remainder of the war and through the surrender at Appomattox.

Lee referred to Longstreet as his "Old War Horse"; others referred to him as "Old Pete."

After the war Longstreet went into business. When Grant became president, Longstreet was named Minister to Turkey.

Because some consider him responsible for the defeat at Gettysburg, not to mention the fact that he was critical of Lee, and became a Republican, Longstreet has never been a great Southern hero.

MORGAN, JOHN HUNT—1825–1864

Background: Alabama. As a volunteer he saw action in the Mexican War. He went into business in Lexington, Kentucky, and in 1857, raised a militia group named the Kentucky Rifles.

In September 1861, Morgan was a captain in the Confederate army with command of a squadron of cavalry.

As colonel, he led cavalry at Shiloh and commanded a brigade at Corinth. Appointed brigadier general he commanded a cavalry division operating in Kentucky and Tennessee.

In July 1863, Morgan violated Bragg's instructions and crossed the Ohio River into Indiana and Ohio. On July 26, he and much of his command were captured at New Lisbon, Ohio, and sent to the Ohio State Penitentiary at Columbus.

Morgan escaped on November 26, and was given command in eastern Tennessee and then in southwestern Virginia. On September 4, 1864, he was surprised and killed by Union troops at Greenville, Tennessee.

PEMBERTON, JOHN CLIFFORD—1814–1881

Background: Pennsylvania. West Point, 1837. Served in Mexican War, Seminole War, in the west fighting Indians and Mormons. At the start of the Civil War, General Scott offered to promote Pemberton from captain to colonel but Pemberton refused and went to fight for his wife's state of Virginia.

In October of 1862, after various commands along the Atlantic coast and around Richmond, he was promoted to lieutenant general in command of the Department of Mississippi and charged with protecting Vicksburg and Port Hudson.

When Grant crossed the Mississippi River in May 1863, Pemberton tried to stop him at Port Gibson, Raymond, Jackson, Champion Hill, and Black River Bridge, but was driven back to Vicksburg. Pemberton surrendered Vicksburg on the Fourth of July, 1863.

Between selecting Independence Day to surrender and his Northern birth, Pemberton was accused by press and public as a traitor. Davis found that Pemberton was no longer acceptable to the soldiers. Pemberton offered to resign and serve as a private but Davis recommissioned him as a lieutenant colonel of artillery.

After the war Pemberton lived on a Virginia farm.

PICKETT, GEORGE EDWARD—1825–1875

Background: Virginia. West Point, 1846. Ranked at the bottom of his 59-man class. Served in Mexican War and fought Indians on the frontier.

Entered Confederate army as a colonel. After promotion to brigadier general he led the "Gamecock Brigade" at Williamsburg, Seven Pines, and Gaines's Mill, where he was wounded. Achieved the rank of major general in October 1862 after Antietam. His command held the center at Fredericksburg and was part of Longstreet's corps at Gettysburg.

Pickett's division was shattered in the frontal attack on the Union position at Gettysburg and he was sent to recruit fresh troops in Virginia and North Carolina.

When Longstreet went west, Pickett directed the attack on New Bern and fought at Drewry's Bluff. Pickett rejoined Lee at Cold Harbor and went on to Petersburg. He was defeated by Sheridan at Five Forks and was all but destroyed at Sayler's Creek.

On April 1, 1865, Pickett rejoined Longstreet and surrendered with him at Appomattox.

After the war, Pickett was offered several positions in foreign countries and at home. He declined these to go into the insurance business.

Forever associated with "Pickett's Charge," Pickett never forgave Lee for wrecking his Virginia division at Gettysburg.

POLK, LEONIDAS—1806–1864

Background: North Carolina. West Point, 1827. Resigned six months after graduating in order to study for the Episcopal ministry. He was Bishop of Louisiana when he was persuaded by his friend, Jefferson Davis, to accept appointment as major general, more as a symbol than a military commander.

Ordered to fortify and defend the Mississippi River, Polk occupied Columbus, Kentucky, ending that state's neutrality.

He defeated Grant at Belmont, Missouri, in November 1861, and commanded the Confederate right at Shiloh. He was second in command to Bragg at Perryville. As a lieutenant general Polk fought at Stones River.

Polk commanded the Confederate right on the second day of Chickamauga. Because he failed to attack as ordered, Bragg relieved him of his command and began court martial proceedings. There was already bad blood between Polk and Bragg as Polk had urged Davis to replace Bragg.

Davis reinstated Polk and sent him to Mississippi. With a corps he joined Joseph E. Johnston in northern Georgia. Polk was killed by a shell from a Parrott gun on June 14, 1864, at Pine Mountain. Davis considered the loss of Polk on a par with the death of Jackson but few agreed with this. Polk was a fine gentleman and churchman but no great military commander.

STUART, JAMES EWELL BROWN—1833–1864

Background: Virginia. West Point, 1854. Fought Indians on the frontier and was wounded in the Kansas border war. He carried orders to Lee to proceed to Harpers Ferry and crush John Brown's raid.

He entered the Confederate army as a captain of cavalry in May 1861. Stuart fought at First Bull Run. As a brigadier general he led his troopers on a ride around McClellan's entire army and fought in the Seven Days. As a major general he commanded all of Confederate cavalry at Second Bull Run, Antietam, and Fredericksburg. After Jackson was mortally wounded at Chancellorsville, Stuart took command of his corps for the remainder of the battle.

At the start of the Gettysburg campaign, Stuart was taken by surprise at Brandy Station and had to have Longstreet send infantry to help drive off Buford's Union cavalry.

Immediately afterward, Stuart went off on a ride around Hooker's Union army and did not arrive until the second day of Gettysburg. On the third day, Union cavalry prevented Stuart from getting behind the Union rear.

Stuart went on to fight at the Wilderness and Spotsylvania. He was mortally wounded on May 11, 1864, during a clash with Sheridan's cavalry at Yellow Tavern outside Richmond.

Known as "Jeb," Stuart was probably the most famous cavalryman of the war. With his flowing beard, colorful uniform that included a cloak and plumed hat, he represented the South's ideal of the mounted "Cavalier"—brave, good-humored, religious, and a magnificent cavalry leader.

WHEELER, JOSEPH—1836–1906

Background: Georgia. West Point, 1859. Served on frontier fighting Indians. Resigned on April 22, 1861, to enter Confederate army.

As a colonel Wheeler led a regiment at Shiloh and at Corinth. Promoted to major general, he commanded the cavalry of Bragg's Army of Mississippi, led a mounted brigade at Perryville, and a division at Stones River. He commanded a cavalry corps at Chickamauga. Assigned to the Army of Tennessee, Wheeler led a series of raids on supply trains heading for Rosecrans's army at Chattanooga.

After the battle at Chattanooga, Wheeler moved south to interrupt supplies intended for Sherman's advance on Atlanta. After the fall of Atlanta, Hood went north to invade Tennessee, leaving Wheeler and his small force to deal with Sherman.

Wheeler was eventually captured in Georgia in May 1865.

After the war, "Fighting Joe" Wheeler was a congressman from Atlanta. He rejoined the U.S. Army to fight as a major general in the Spanish-American War. He retired from the regular army as brigadier general. Because of his service in the Spanish-American War, he is one of the few Confederates buried at Arlington National Cemetery.

MAJOR CONFLICTS OF THE CIVIL WAR

BOMBARDMENT OF FORT SUMTER, SOUTH CAROLINA—APRIL 12–14, 1861

The war began early of the morning of April 12 when Confederate shore batteries opened fire on the Union fort in Charleston harbor.

BIG BETHEL, VIRGINIA—JUNE 10, 1861

Fought in the Hampton-Yorktown area; the Confederates defeated a far larger Union army in this first land battle of the war.

FIRST BULL RUN (FIRST MANASSAS)—JULY 21, 1861

The first major battle of the war ended in major defeat of McDowell's Union army at the hands of Confederate forces commanded by Beauregard.

BATTLE OF WILSON'S CREEK, MISSOURI—AUGUST 10, 1861

The defeat of pro-Union forces in the first battle west of the Mississippi River allowed pro-Confederates to remain active in Missouri.

BATTLE OF FORT DONELSON, TENNESSEE—FEBRUARY 12–16, 1862

Surrender of the fort to Grant, following the surrender of nearby Fort Henry, would lead to the South being forced out of Kentucky and Tennessee.

BATTLE OF PEA RIDGE, ARKANSAS—MARCH 7–8, 1862

The Union victory ended any serious threat of Confederate control of Missouri.

BATTLE AT GLORIETA PASS, NEW MEXICO—MARCH 26–28, 1862

In the only battle in the Far West, the Confederate defeat ended the South's hope of acquiring New Mexico and access to the gold and silver mines of California and Colorado.

BATTLE OF SHILOH (PITTSBURG LANDING), TENNESSEE—APRIL 6–7, 1862

Although neither side could claim a decisive victory in this dreadful battle, Confederate forces withdrew, leaving the road open for a Union advance on the railroad center at Corinth, Mississippi.

ATTACK ON FORT PULASKI, GEORGIA—APRIL 10–12, 1862

Fall of this important Confederate fort cut the Port of Savannah off from the sea and further strengthened the Union blockade of the South.

BATTLE OF McDOWELL, VIRGINIA—MAY 8, 1862

Thomas "Stonewall" Jackson and his small Confederate army won the first battle in the famous "Shenandoah Valley Campaign" of 1862.

BATTLE OF CROSS KEYS, VIRGINIA—JUNE 8, 1862

Jackson prevented two Union armies, joining together in an attempt to destroy his far smaller force.

BATTLE OF PORT REPUBLIC, VIRGINIA—JUNE 9, 1862

After victory in this hard-fought battle, Jackson joined Lee to defend Richmond against McClellan's huge Union army.

BATTLE AT GAINES' MILL, VIRGINIA—JUNE 27, 1862

General Lee's first victory and the first in a series of battles around Richmond known as the "Seven Days."

MALVERN HILL, VIRGINIA—JULY 1, 1862

Lee's army suffered heavy casualties in an unsuccessful effort to break the Union line during this final battle of the Seven Days. McClellan had become discouraged trying to take Richmond and moved his army north.

BATTLE OF CEDAR MOUNTAIN, VIRGINIA—AUGUST 9, 1862

Jackson, sent north by Lee to deal with the threat posed by Pope and the newly created Army of Virginia, ran into considerable difficulty in defeating a Union force of 12,000 with his 20,000-man army.

SECOND BULL RUN (SECOND MANASSAS), VIRGINIA—AUGUST 28–30, 1862

Pope's Army of Virginia was soundly whipped by a smaller Confederate army led by Lee, Jackson, and Longstreet.

HARPERS FERRY, WEST VIRGINIA—SEPTEMBER 13–15, 1862

Sent north by Lee to secure his supply line for the invasion of Maryland, Jackson had no difficulty occupying strategically important Harpers Ferry.

BATTLE OF ANTIETAM (SHARPSBURG), MARYLAND—SEPTEMBER 17, 1862

The bloodiest one-day battle of the war was just enough of a Union victory for Lincoln to issue his Emancipation Proclamation and force Lee to return to Virginia.

BATTLE OF CORINTH, MISSISSIPPI—OCTOBER 3–4, 1862

Confederate forces were repulsed in their efforts to retake this vital railroad center that they had only recently abandoned.

BATTLE OF PERRYVILLE, KENTUCKY—OCTOBER 8, 1862

Union victory forced the Confederates out of Kentucky.

BATTLE OF FREDERICKSBURG, VIRGINIA—DECEMBER 11–13, 1862

His army suffered 12,000 casualties as Union General Burnside ordered repeated attacks on Lee's well-fortified position.

BATTLE AT STONES RIVER (MURFREESBORO), TENNESSEE—DECEMBER 31, 1862, TO JANUARY 1, 1863

The Union army considered this bloody battle a victory as it eventually forced Confederate General Bragg to give up portions of Tennessee.

BATTLE OF CHANCELLORSVILLE, VIRGINIA—MAY 1–3, 1863

Lee displayed great military talent by defeating Hooker's army, twice the size of the Confederate force. The great victory was marred, however, by the loss of Jackson, accidentally wounded by his own men.

BRANDY STATION, VIRGINIA—JUNE 9, 1863

The biggest battle of the war lasted eleven hours and involved 20,000 troops. Buford finally withdrew his Union troops, but the battle proved that Federal cavalry was a force to be reckoned with.

BATTLE OF GETTYSBURG, PENNSYLVANIA—JULY 1–3, 1863

There were over 50,000 casualties in this famous three-day battle that concluded with the Union repulse of "Pickett's Charge," followed by Lee's army retreating to Virginia.

BATTLE OF CHAMPION HILL, MISSISSIPPI—MAY 16, 1863

The last of the series of battles which included Port Gibson, Raymond, and Jackson that Grant fought and won to reach the east side of Vicksburg.

SIEGE OF VICKSBURG, MISSISSIPPI—MAY 18–JULY 4, 1863

Surrounded by Grant's large Union army and exposed to constant Union bombardment, this vital Confederate fortified city controlling the Mississippi River was finally forced to surrender. On the same day, Lee began his retreat from Gettysburg.

PORT HUDSON, LOUISIANA— MAY 22–JULY 9, 1863

After weeks of siege, this last Confederate bastion on the Mississippi River surrendered as its commander believed the fall of Vicksburg had made it untenable. The entire Mississippi River was now under Federal control.

BATTLE OF CHICKAMAUGA, GEORGIA— SEPTEMBER 18–20, 1863

The Confederate army under Bragg smashed Rosecrans's Union forces, sending them reeling back to seek security in nearby Chattanooga.

BATTLE OF CHATTANOOGA, TENNESSEE— NOVEMBER 23–25, 1863

Grant, now in command of all Union armies in the region, organized a successful attack on Bragg's forces positioned in the hills south of Chattanooga.

BATTLE OF THE WILDERNESS, VIRGINIA— MAY 5–6, 1863

Appointed commander of all Union forces, Grant remained in the east, determined to destroy Lee's Army of Northern Virginia. Despite heavy Union casualties, Grant failed to seriously harm Lee at the Wilderness and moved south to get between Lee and Richmond.

BATTLE OF SPOTSYLVANIA COURT HOUSE, VIRGINIA—MAY 8–21, 1864

By the time Grant reached this location, about twenty miles south of the Wilderness, Lee had arrived and his army was in a well-fortified position. After launching a number of unsuccessful and costly attacks, Grant decided to continue moving south to force Lee out of his fortified position.

BATTLE OF THE NORTH ANNA RIVER, VIRGINIA—MAY 23–26, 1864

When Grant's huge, slow-moving army reached the north side of the river, he found Lee already entrenched on the south shore. After an attack on Lee's cleverly designed "V"-shaped line had been repulsed with heavy casualties, Grant moved along the river's north back to circle around Lee's flank.

BATTLE OF NEW MARKET, VIRGINIA— MAY 15, 1864

This relatively small battle resulted in the defeat of the Union forces participating in the campaign to gain control of the Shenandoah Valley. It is best remembered by the 247 cadets of the Virginia Military Institute who marched from Lexington to reinforce the outnumbered Confederate force.

BATTLE OF COLD HARBOR, VIRGINIA— MAY 31–JUNE 3, 1864

Fought about eight miles north of Richmond, this would be Lee's last great victory. Grant ordered 50,000 men to attack Lee's magnificently designed defenses and in half an hour Grant lost 7,000 men.

BATTLE OF BRICE'S CROSS ROADS, MISSISSIPPI—JUNE 10, 1864

Sherman, advancing on Atlanta, thought his supply line was threatened by General Forrest's cavalry. Sherman sent Sturgis out to deal with Forrest. Forrest defeated Sturgis's army and chased it back to its base at Memphis.

BATTLE OF KENNESAW MOUNTAIN, GEORGIA—JUNE 27, 1864

Failing to stop Sherman's advance through northern Georgia, Johnson took a strong position along the ridge of Kennesaw Mountain north of Atlanta. Unable to dislodge the Confederate troops, Sherman circled around the mountain and finally took Atlanta on the second of September.

BATTLE OF TUPELO, MISSISSIPPI—
JULY 14–15, 1864

Sherman's second attempt to eliminate Forrest turned out better than the first. While the battle ended with the Confederates holding the field, they had lost 1,326 men out of a small force of 3,400 and no longer posed a threat to the Union supply line.

SIEGE OF PETERSBURG, VIRGINIA—
JUNE 15, 1864, TO APRIL 1, 1865

After Cold Harbor, Grant swung east, then south to take Petersburg and cut the supply line to Richmond. Petersburg, however, was well defended and did not fall until after a long siege.

BATTLE OF MONOCACY, MARYLAND—
JULY 9, 1864

General Early's Confederate force of 14,000 men moved north threaten or even capture Washington, D.C. At the Monocacy River, some 40 miles from Washington, they encountered a Union force of 5,800 under General Wallace. Early finally drove off Wallace's force but by this time had lost interest in going on to Washington and returned to Virginia.

BATTLE OF MOBILE BAY, ALABAMA—
AUGUST 5–23, 1864

Primarily a U.S. Navy affair. Rear Admiral Farragut first cleared the harbor by destroying the powerful Confederate ram *Tennessee,* and then bombarded the three harbor forts until they surrendered.

BATTLE OF FORT FISHER, NORTH
CAROLINA—JANUARY 6–15, 1865

Constructed of sand, Fort Fisher protected the last major Confederate port at Wilmington. Federal warships' cannon blasted the fort's sand defenses so that the infantry was able to move forward and take it.

BATTLE AT FIVE FORKS, VIRGINIA—
APRIL 1, 1865

Returning to the Petersburg area after his successful Shenandoah campaign, Sheridan moved on the Confederate right to drive them from their Petersburg defenses.

As this maneuver threatened Five Forks, key to Lee's supply line, Pickett was sent to check the Federal advance, making a stand at Five Forks but finally forced to withdraw.

Sheridan and Custer came out of the fight with their reputations enhanced. But as he was tardy bringing up his corps, Union General Warren was relieved of his command. Pickett arrived late for the battle because he was attending a shad bake, much to Lee's annoyance.

SAYLER'S (SAILOR'S) CREEK, VIRGINIA—
APRIL 6, 1865

This was the last major battle of the war. The powerful Union army hit the retreating Confederate army along Sayler's Creek. When the fighting had finished, Lee had lost almost one-third of his 30,000 army. Three days later, on April 9, Lee would surrender the remains of Army of Northern Virginia at Appottamox Courthouse.

Wars with Native Americans

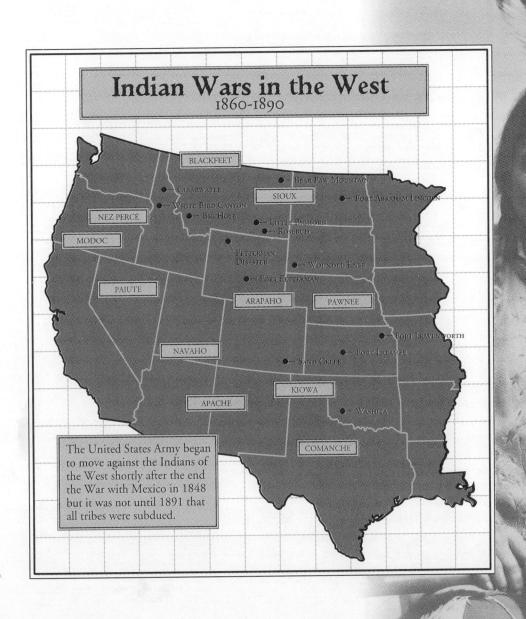

Indian Wars in the West
1860-1890

BLACKFEET

Bear Paw Mountain

Clearwater

SIOUX

Fort Abraham Lincoln

White Bird Canyon

Big Hole

NEZ PERCÉ

Little Bighorn

Rosebud

MODOC

Fetterman
Disaster

Wounded Knee

Fort Fetterman

PAIUTE

ARAPAHO

PAWNEE

Fort Leavenworth

NAVAHO

Fort Laramie

Sand Creek

KIOWA

APACHE

Washita

COMANCHE

The United States Army began
to move against the Indians of
the West shortly after the end
the War with Mexico in 1848
but it was not until 1891 that
all tribes were subdued.

The despair of all Native Americans who had fought for and lost their ancestral lands and traditional way of life is eloquently expressed in the message Chief Joseph of the Nez Percés sent to Colonel Nelson Miles after surrendering to him at Bear Paw Mountain, Montana, on October 5, 1877.

Tell General Howard I know his heart. What he told me before I have in my heart. I am tired of fighting. Our chiefs are killed. Looking Glass is dead. Too-hul-hul-sote is dead. The old men are all dead. It is cold and we have no blankets. The little children are freezing to death. My people, some of them, have run away to the hills, and have no blankets, no food; no one knows where they are—perhaps freezing to death. I want to have time to look for my children and see how many I can find. Maybe I shall find them among the dead. Hear me, my chiefs. I am tired; my heart is sick and sad. From where the sun now stands I will fight no more forever.

War between the Native Americans and the European settlers of the "new" world began shortly after the founding of Jamestown, Virginia, in 1607. Fighting between these two cultures continued for almost 300 years; the so-called Indian Wars officially ended in early 1891, a few weeks after the massacre at Wounded Knee, South Dakota. During the intervening years, about 22 major and many more minor wars were fought as the Native Americans attempted to protect their land and culture from the aggressive and land-hungry Americans.

Many of these wars were brief because the Indians could not hold out long against the better-organized and -armed white invaders. But a few wars dragged on for years, with many small battles. The Apache wars, for example, lasted for about 25 years, and war with the Sioux went on for over 20 years.

It is not known how many individual battles were fought during the Indian Wars, but they number in the hundreds. Only a few of these battle sites exist today, and these are primarily found in the West where the more recent wars occurred.

The National Park Service includes only around 20 Indian War battle sites at National Parks or Historic Sites. All the rest have vanished. Okeechobee Battlefield in Florida, for example, where Zachary Taylor's force defeated a band of Seminoles and Mikasauki on Christmas Day 1837, is today privately held grazing land.

It may be that the Indian War battles had too few casualties to attract lasting interest. Perhaps only a few today would remember the battle of Little Bighorn, where 225 men of the Seventh Cavalry were killed, if one of them had not been the famous "Boy General," Lieutenant Colonel George Armstrong Custer. Two hundred twenty-five casualties pales in comparison to the first day of fighting at Antietam, where 23,000 Union and Confederate soldiers fell. There is no accurate record of the thousands of men, women, and children, of both races, who were killed during the Indian Wars. It was, however, the Native Americans who suffered the most from their association with the Europeans.

It has been estimated by some authorities that in 1600 there were as many as 10 million Native Americans living in North America. By 1890, there were about 250,000. Only a relatively few Native Americans were killed in battle. Tens of thousands, however, died from diseases introduced by the Europeans to which the Native Americans had never before been exposed; Smallpox, measles, chicken pox, typhus, tuberculosis, and venereal disease spread rapidly.

Some whites employed an early form of germ warfare to destroy Native Americans. In 1762, General Jeffrey Amherst, in his attempt to put down Pontiac's Rebellion, authorized issuing to the Indians blankets infected with smallpox.

Many more Native Americans died of cold, hunger, and exposure as they were driven off their lands. Many others died on the long treks the government forced them to make from their homeland to some far distant reservation.

War with the Native Americans preceded the westward expansion of the ever-growing population of the United States. Prior to the American Revolution, most of the fighting took place in the East but at the end of the war, large numbers of settlers moved west and warfare extended into the midwest and southward into Alabama and Georgia. After the United States gained California and adjoining areas from Mexico in 1848, expansion into this territory resulted in warfare as well. The opening of western lands after the Civil War attracted thousands of settlers and miners, triggering more conflicts with the Plains Indians in the last era of the Indian Wars.

When the wars were over in 1891, European Americans had all the land they wanted—the entire country—and most of the Native Americans were forced onto reservations.

BATTLE OF THE WABASH, INDIANA—NOVEMBER 4, 1790

By the end of the Revolutionary War in 1783, the Indians of the northeast had been pretty much subdued, but within three years, the new nation would be at war again with the Indians of the Northwest Territory. This large area, today often referred to as "The Old Northwest," would in time become the states of Ohio, Indiana, Illinois, Wisconsin, and portions of Minnesota.

By the terms of the 1783 Treaty of Paris, the British agreed to vacate posts along the northern border of present-day Ohio and Indiana, but they not only refused to leave these bases, they also gave arms and encouragement to the Indians, primarily the Shawnee and Miami, to conduct raids on American settlements. In 1787, Congress passed the Northwest Ordinance, federalizing the territory, and Arthur St. Clair was appointed governor.

Under pressure from settlers to halt the Indian raids. in 1790 St. Clair sent Brigadier General Josiah Harmar with 1,500 militia to intimidate the combative tribes. Harmar marched north from Fort Washington (Cincinnati), and near present-day Fort Wayne, his scouting element was attacked by the Miami under Chief Little Turtle. Harmar was later attacked and defeated by Chief Blue Jacket's Shawnees, ending the campaign. Instead of their being intimidated, the victory over Harmar made the tribes even bolder.

Appointed major general, St. Clair was commissioned to take an army up the Maumee River and build a fort to contain the Indians. Though President George Washington warned St. Clair of the danger of an ambush, St. Clair did not heed Washington's warning and had not even sent out scouts or posted sentries.

Little Turtle and Blue Jacket found St. Clair's 2,300 poorly trained militia camped at a particularly vulnerable site by the Wabash River about 100 miles from Cincinnati. At dawn on November 4, the Indians attacked and the untrained militia fell apart.

In the three-hour battle, over half of St. Clair's army was destroyed—637 killed and

WARS WITH NATIVE AMERICANS FROM THE ATLANTIC TO THE PACIFIC, FROM MONTANA TO TEXAS

1622–1644
POWHATAN WARS
Virginia, Jamestown Region
Colonists v. Tidewater tribes under
Opechancanough
Period of Pocahontas and Capt. John Smith

1636–1637
PEQUOT WARS
Connecticut and Massachusetts
Colonists v. Pequots

1675–1676
KING PHILIP'S WAR
New England
Colonists and Militia v. Wampanoags, Narragansets,
and Nipmucs under King Philip (Metacom)

1711–1713
TUSCARORA WARS
North and South Carolina
Colonists and Militia v. Tuscaroras, who would later
go north to join Iroquois Confederation

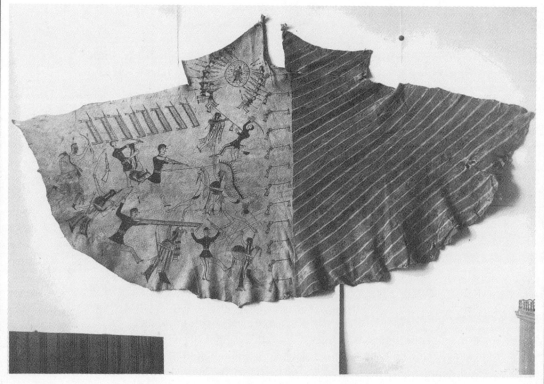

Portion of teepee hide, photographed about 1895, depicting a battle between Kiowas and U.S. soldiers. (National Archives)

1763–1764
PONTIAC'S REBELLION
Great Lakes region (Old Northwest)
British Army and Militia v. Pontiac's Ottawas, Hurons, and Potoawatomis

1773–1774
LORD DUNSMORE'S WAR
Western Virginia and Ohio
Virginia Militia v. Shawnees, Mongos, Delawares, and Wyandots

1779
WAR AGAINST THE IROQUOIS
Western New York and Western Pennsylvania
Continental Army and Militia v. Iroquois Confederation

1786–1794
LITTLE TURTLE'S WAR
U.S. Army and Militia v. Miamis and Shawnees
Ends with Battle of Fallen Timbers, August 20, 1794

1809–1811
TECUMSEH'S REBELLION
Indiana and adjoining areas (Old Northwest)
U.S. Army and Militia under William Henry Harrison v. Tecumseh's Shawnees and members of neighboring tribes
Ends with battle of Tippecanoe, November 7, 1811

1813–1814
CREEK WARS
Alabama and Georgia
U.S. Army, Volunteers, and Militia under General Andrew Jackson v. Red Stick Creeks
Ends with Battle of Horseshoe Bend, March 27, 1814

1816–1818
FIRST SEMINOLE WAR
Florida
U.S. Army and Militia under General Andrew Jackson v. Seminoles

After defeating Seminoles, Jackson went on to take Pensacola, prompting Spain to cede all Florida to the United States.

1832
BLACK HAWK WAR
Illinois and Wisconsin (Old Northwest)
U.S. Army, Volunteers, and Militia v. Black Hawk's Sauk, Fox, and neighboring tribes
Colonel Zachary Taylor, Captain Abraham Lincoln, and Lieutenant Jefferson Davis participated in this war.

1858
COEUR D'ALENE WAR
Washington and Idaho
U.S. Army v. Coeur D'Alenes, Spokanes, Palouses, Northern Paiutes, and Yakimas

1860
PAIUTE WAR (PYRAMID LAKE WAR)
Western Nevada
Nevada Volunteers and U.S. Regulars v. Southern Paiutes

1860–1863
APACHE WARS
Arizona, New Mexico, and Texas
U.S. Army v. Apaches under Cochise and Mangas Colorado
At end, over 6,000 Apaches were on reservations, but many eventually left and resumed their traditional way of life.

1863–1866
NAVAJO WARS
New Mexico and Southwest
U.S. Army under Kit Carson v. Navajo
At end of war, 8,000 Navajos surrendered with most sent to reservations.

1868–1869
SOUTHERN PLAINS INDIAN WARS
(SHERIDAN'S CAMPAIGN)
Colorado, Oklahoma, and Texas
U.S. Army v. Arapahos, Comanches, Kiowas, Sioux, and Southern Cheyennes
Sheridan's strategy of attacking the Indians in winter resulted in the battle/massacre at Washita River on November 27, 1868.

1876–1877
SIOUX WAR
Montana, North and South Dakota, and Wyoming
U.S. Army v. Sioux and Northern Cheyenne
The Indians achieved a smashing victory at the Battle of the Little Bighorn on July 25, 1876, but would lose the war.

1876–1877
FLIGHT OF THE NEZ PERCÉS—THE NEZ PERCÉ INDIAN WAR OF 1877
Idaho, Montana, and Wyoming
U.S. Army and Volunteers v. Nez Percé

The 1,700-mile trek made by 800 Nez Percé to escape the U.S. Army involved four battles including Big Hole on August 9 and 10, 1877.

1879–1886
APACHE WARS
Arizona, New Mexico, Texas, and the Republic of Mexico
U.S. Army with Apache Scouts v. Apaches led by Victorio, then by Geronimo
General George Crook failed to catch Geronimo but his replacement, Gen. Nelson Miles, did, and Geronimo surrendered to him on September 4, 1886.

1890
MASSACRE AT WOUNDED KNEE
South Dakota
U.S. Army v. 350 or so Sioux, including women and children
On December 29, the Army's Hotchkiss cannons opened fire, killing a large number of the Indians. On January 15, 1891, warfare between the whites and the Indians officially ended.

271 wounded. Only about 500 of the original 1,400-man army managed to escape. The Indians, on the other hand, lost only 21 killed and 40 wounded.

BATTLE OF FALLEN TIMBERS, OHIO—AUGUST 20, 1794

Humiliated by Harmar's and St. Clair's defeats, the government sought to build an army that would effectively fight the Indians. President Washington named Major General Anthony Wayne, who had served under him during the Revolution and was known as a tough imaginative fighting leader, to recruit and head this new army.

While the government was trying to effect a treaty with the Indians, Wayne was busy in Pittsburgh recruiting and training his army, which he named "The Legion of the United States." (At that time, a "legion" often referred to a force consisting of infantry, riflemen, artillery, and dragoons, or cavalry.)

In the spring of 1793, Wayne took his well-trained army of 2,000 to Cincinnati to await the outcome of negotiations with the Indians. With the failure of these talks, Wayne moved north and wintered at the fort he had built at Greenville, Ohio. In early 1794, Wayne continued north, heading for Fort Miami (Toledo) which the British had recently built on American soil.

With about 1,500 men, Blue Jacket planned to ambush Wayne before he reached Fort Miami. The site he selected was in a ravine just opposite the rapids on the Maumee River, only about five miles from the fort. Known as "Fallen Timbers," the ravine was covered with trees blown over by a windstorm and was a perfect place to lay an ambush.

The Indians took up their positions among the fallen trees and branches on August 17. Expecting Wayne to reach the site that day, they had not brought food. Wayne, however, was delayed by rain and did not arrive until the twentieth. By that time, some of the Indians had gone off in search of food, and others were weak from hunger.

Wayne's advance guard of mounted volunteers first made contact with the Indians and were forced to retreat to the main force. Wayne then formed his battle line, extending from the river to the thick wood on the left, and struck at the Indians with bayonets. The Indians were driven into the open where the mounted troops and infantry musket fire soon drove them back for two miles. The short battle left hundreds of Indians dead but cost the lives of only 38 of Wayne's army.

The surviving Indians retreated to Fort Miami but were refused admission because the British commander had been ordered to avoid any entanglement with Wayne. Wayne did not pursue the Indians into Canada but destroyed their villages and crops on the American side of the border.

The following year, 1,100 chiefs and warriors came to Fort Greenville and agreed to a treaty that ceded to the United States a huge tract of land that included present-day Ohio and much of Indiana.

Battlefield of Fallen Timbers is jointly administered by the Ohio Historical Society and Toledo

GENERAL   HARRISON

Metro Parks. The principal feature is a monument and a statue honoring Anthony Wayne. The battle site is close to Fort Meigs and Maumee and the site of Fort Miami.

BATTLE OF TIPPECANOE, INDIANA—NOVEMBER 7, 1811

The huge amount of land ceded by the Indians under the 1796 Treaty of Greenville whetted the U.S. appetite for more western territory, and between 1795 and 1809 it managed to acquire almost 15 million more acres of the Indian territory.

Tecumseh, the great Shawnee chief, was appalled at the loss of Indian land. A visionary, orator, and strategist who had learned history and literature from his white friend

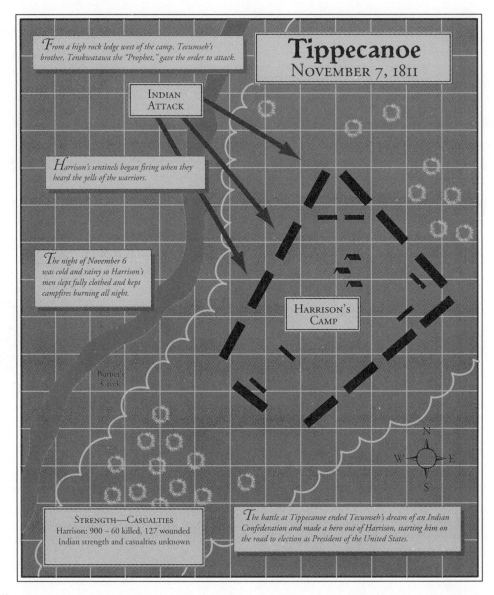

From a high rock ledge west of the camp, Tecumseh's brother, Tenskwatawa the "Prophet," gave the order to attack.

Tippecanoe
NOVEMBER 7, 1811

INDIAN ATTACK

Harrison's sentinels began firing when they heard the yells of the warriors.

The night of November 6 was cold and rainy so Harrison's men slept fully clothed and kept campfires burning all night.

HARRISON'S CAMP

Burnet's Creek

N W E S

STRENGTH—CASUALTIES
Harrison: 900 – 60 killed, 127 wounded
Indian strength and casualties unknown

The battle at Tippecanoe ended Tecumseh's dream of an Indian Confederation and made a hero out of Harrison, starting him on the road to election as President of the United States.

Rebecca Galloway, Tecumseh now became convinced that the Indian tribes must form a confederation to stop westward advance of the whites. He also believed that the Indians must return to their old ways and customs and cease association with the whites.

To promote these concepts among the neighboring tribes, he enlisted the aid of his brother, Tenskwatawa, a mystic who

claimed to have talked to the Great Spirit and became known as the "Prophet." The two brothers approached many tribes, with Tecumseh supplying the practical reasons for not giving up land, and the Prophet preaching the evils of liquor and encouraging a return to the traditional ways.

In 1808, they founded the settlement of Tippecanoe—later called "Prophet's

Town"—on a site where the Tippecanoe Creek flows into the Wabash River, as a place where all Indians could come and be free of the influences of the whites.

There was now growing tension between Tecumseh and William Henry Harrison, governor of Indiana Territory. Harrison had employed liquor and deceit to obtain Indian lands and on September 30, 1809, concluded a treaty with the Delawares, Miamis, and Kickapoos, along with other tribes, for 3,000,000 acres that would deprive Tecumseh of his favorite hunting grounds and bring the boundary of the whites within 50 miles of Tippecanoe. Tecumseh went to Vincennes to protest to Harrison, who told him he would refer the matter to President James Madison.

In the spring of 1811, Harrison warned Tecumseh about attacks on settlements and friendly Indians. Tecumseh assured Harrison of his friendship, but also brought up the matter of the 3 million acres. Soon after this meeting, Tecumseh went south to encourage the Creeks, Choctaws, and Chickasaws to join the confederation, leaving his brother at Tippecanoe.

As Tecumseh was apparently not going to be bound by the treaty ceding the 3 million acres, Harrison received approval from the War Department to collect about 1,000 men and force a confrontation. Under the pretext that he wanted the Prophet to surrender any Indians that had engaged in raids, Harrison marched from Vincennes with 900 men, including 270 dragoons. On the night of November 6, he encamped on a bluff about one mile from Tippecanoe and met a group of Indians, who requested a parley. The next day, they assured Harrison they planned no hostile acts.

Just before dawn on the seventh, the camp was awakened by a shot from one of

When Tecumseh's imaginative effort to form an Indian confederation ended at Tippecanoe, the great Shawnee chief joined with the British in Canada to fight the Americans in the War of 1812. He was killed in the October 5, 1813, Battle of the Thames. (Courtesy of Tippecanoe County Historical Association, Lafayette, Indiana)

the many sentinels Harrison had posted. In minutes the Indians, who had crawled through the tall grass around the camp, attacked. Hitting the camp from two directions, they caused some confusion among the American ranks, but Harrison was able to rally his men, and after a short bloody fight, the Indians withdrew and the battle was over. About 60 of Harrison's men were killed, and 127 were wounded. Indian casualties were probably about the same.

When Harrison's army entered the Indian village, they found it deserted, but before setting it on fire, they found firearms made in Britain, reinforcing the belief of the "war hawks" that the British were responsible for the Indian attacks on American settlers.

On his return from the south, Tecumseh saw his vision of an Indian confederation evaporate in the smoke of the village at Tippecanoe. On the eve of the War of 1812, he went to Canada, where the British greeted him warmly. He established good relations with British General Isaac Brock and took part in the capture of Detroit and siege of Forts Meigs and Stephenson before he was killed by Harrison's troops at the battle on the Thames, on October 5, 1813.

The battle at Tippecanoe ended Tenskwatawa's role as Prophet. Before ordering the Indians to attack he told them he had charmed the white man's bullets so they would not harm the Indians. Observing the battle from a safe distance, he could see that the charm did not work.

For his part, Harrison's victory made him the "hero of the west." Nearly thirty years later, the campaign slogan "Tippecanoe and Tyler Too" contributed to his successful run for president (with running mate John Tyler.)

Tippecanoe Battlefield State Memorial is administered by the Tippecanoe County Historical Association. An Interpretive Center contains a museum, a series of exhibits, and an audiovisual presentation.

BATTLE OF HORSESHOE BEND, ALABAMA—MARCH 27, 1814

At the time of the battle of Tippecanoe in November 1811, Tecumseh was in Alabama and Georgia encouraging the Creeks to join his Indian confederation.

The Creeks were then divided into two factions: the Upper Creeks and the Lower Creeks. The warlike Upper Creeks of the uplands, called "Red Sticks" because of the color of their war clubs, were in favor of Tecumseh's plan to drive the whites off Indian land. The more peaceful Lower Creeks, "White Sticks," believed in cooperating with the whites.

The Red Sticks became very agitated when Tecumseh returned to their region in 1812 with the news that Indians and British had gained a great victory by taking the American base at Detroit. But what really drove them to take up their war clubs against white settlers and White Stick Creeks was word that Little Warrior, a Red Stick leader, had been captured and later executed by the White Sticks.

Little Warrior had led some Red Sticks to Canada where they had taken part in the massacre of American soldiers along the River Raisin (near present-day Monroe, Michigan). On the way south to their homeland, Little Warrior's band had killed a number of white settlers. Big Warrior, a White Stick Chief, learned of these activities, and, anxious to maintain good relations with the whites, arrested and later executed Little Warrior. This act prompted the Red Sticks to take up their clubs to make war on white settlers and White Sticks.

On August 30, 1813, about 1,000 Red Sticks led by the mixed-blood Red Eagle (William Weatherford), with firearms obtained from the Spanish at Pensacola, Florida, attacked Fort Mins on the Alabama River north of Mobile. Many settlers had come to the fort for protection against raids, and they joined soldiers in its defense. The fort was eventually taken by the Red Sticks who set its buildings on fire with flaming arrows. When the Red Sticks had finished, some 400 men, women, and children had been either killed by war clubs or burned to death in the fires. Only about 36 whites escaped. The massacre at Fort Mins quickly

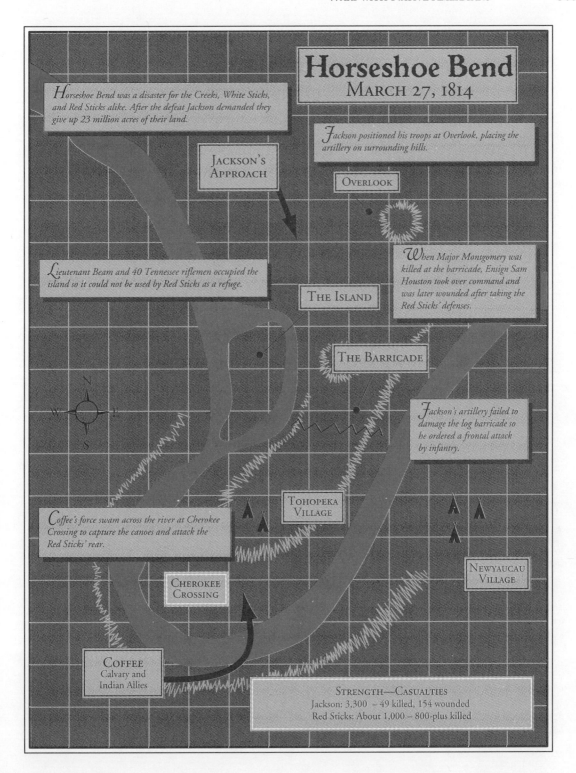

Horseshoe Bend
MARCH 27, 1814

Horseshoe Bend was a disaster for the Creeks, White Sticks, and Red Sticks alike. After the defeat Jackson demanded they give up 23 million acres of their land.

Jackson positioned his troops at Overlook, placing the artillery on surrounding hills.

JACKSON'S APPROACH

OVERLOOK

When Major Montgomery was killed at the barricade, Ensign Sam Houston took over command and was later wounded after taking the Red Sticks' defenses.

Lieutenant Beam and 40 Tennessee riflemen occupied the island so it could not be used by Red Sticks as a refuge.

THE ISLAND

THE BARRICADE

Jackson's artillery failed to damage the log barricade so he ordered a frontal attack by infantry.

N
W   E
S

TOHOPEKA VILLAGE

Coffee's force swam across the river at Cherokee Crossing to capture the canoes and attack the Red Sticks' rear.

NEWYAUCAU VILLAGE

CHEROKEE CROSSING

COFFEE
Calvary and Indian Allies

STRENGTH—CASUALTIES
Jackson: 3,300 – 49 killed, 154 wounded
Red Sticks: About 1,000 – 800-plus killed

$\mathcal{S}$AND CREEK MASSACRE—NOVEMBER 29, 1864

In the spring of 1864, as General William Tecumseh Sherman's army was marching on Atlanta, circumstances in Colorado would end in perhaps one of the most horrible massacres in American military history.

In 1864, Colorado was a great mining area, and Governor John Evans demanded the Southern Cheyennes and Arapahos give up their mineral-rich hunting grounds in exchange for a reservation. When they refused, he ordered Colonel John Chivington, military commander of the territory, to force them to comply.

A former minister, Chivington hated all Indians and believed the best way to deal with them was simply to eradicate them, including their babies and children. Chivington's militia set about killing and burning villages of the relatively peaceful Southern Cheyennes, who were soon joined in a defensive war by neighboring Arapahos, Sioux, and Comanches.

Chivington reinforced his militia by forming the Third Colorado Cavalry, about 100 mostly rough hard-drinking men from mining camps. After a summer of small skirmishes and raids, representatives of the Cheyennes and Arapahos met with Evans and

Sand Creek, in eastern Colorado, is the site of a massacre of over 200 of Chief Black Kettle's Cheyennes, two-thirds of them women and children. Black Kettle believed he had approval from authorities to camp at Sand Creek and even flew an American flag and a white flag by his teepee to indicate peaceful intentions. But none of this mattered to Colonel John Chivington and his Third Colorado Cavalry who, on the morning of November 26, 1864, rode into the camp and killed. (Depiction of Massacre, Robert Lindneux, 1936, from Colorado Historical Society)

Chivington at Camp Weld, near Denver. The Indians were warned that if they wanted peace they must turn in their weapons and camp near a fort, where they were to report regularly. Complying with the order, Chief Black Kettle of the Cheyenne decided to lead his band of 600 or so Cheyennes and a few Arapahos to Fort Lyon and was directed to camp at Sand Creek, some 40 miles away.

On November 29, Chivington arrived at Black Kettle's camp with about 700 troops, including the infamous Third Colorado Cavalry and four howitzers. Black Kettle's followers were naturally frightened by the appearance of these troops as the howitzers were being positioned to fire into the camp, but the chief assured them that he had complied with the directives from Evans and Chivington. As an extra precaution he raised both an American and a white flag above his teepee.

But Black Kettle's compliance did not prevent Chivington from engaging in his favorite pastime of killing Indians. Before he ordered the attack, he had told his men to take no prisoners.

The attack began with rifle and howitzer fire on the panic-stricken Indians. A few warriors found protection and returned fire but the cavalry quickly swept into the camp. Chivington's men—some of whom had been drinking—set about committing outrageous atrocities. The men used their knives to gut women, and rifle butts to knock the brains out of babies, children, and adults, who were then scalped. Dead warriors were castrated.

Chivington later proudly reported his men had killed over 500 Indians at Sand Creek. Others stated the figure was nearer 200. In either case, about two-thirds of those killed were women and children. Black Kettle escaped, but death would shortly catch up with him at Washita in November 1868.

The Massacre at Sand Creek created a considerable uproar, especially in the East where this type of behavior by American soldiers was condemned. A Congressional investigation of the affair denounced Chivington an forced him to resign.

For their part, Sand Creek strengthened the Southern Plains tribes' resolve to fight for their land, and warfare continued in the area until Sheridan's winter campaign of 1868.

A marker now indicates the site of the Sand Creek Massacre in Cheyenne County, some 140 miles east of Pueblo, Colorado. The nearest community ironically is "Chivington."

---

prompted the Tennessee legislature to authorize funds to raise and equip an army of 3,500, to be commanded by Major General Andrew Jackson.

On November 3, 1813, Jackson's advance cavalry, under his friend Colonel John Coffee, accompanied by Davy Crockett, defeated a band of Red Sticks at Tallasahatchee near the Tallapoosa River in Alabama. Coffee lost only five men, with 14 wounded, but 186 Red Sticks were killed. Later that month, Jackson went to the rescue of the White Stick fort at Talladega with a force of militia, killing 290 Red Sticks with his own loss of 25 killed and 85 wounded.

Jackson might have used the moment to end the conflict with the Red Sticks, but his army was disintegrating as enlistment periods expired. But by February 1814, he had a force of almost 5,000 that included 600 of the Thirty-Ninth U.S. Infantry and set out to destroy every Red Stick village in his path, fighting battles at Emuckfaw and Enotachopco Creek.

In March, Jackson learned that around 900 Red Stick warriors and 300 women and children were camped at Horseshoe Bend on the Tallapoosa River. With an army of 2,000 militia, the Thirty-Ninth Contingent, U.S. Infantry, John Coffee's 700 cavalry and artillery, and 600 White Stick and Cherokee allies, he marched south from Fort Williams on the Coosa River, cutting a 52-mile trail through the forest. On March 26, three days after leaving Fort Williams, the army camped about six miles from Horseshoe Bend.

The Red Stick Creeks were positioned on a 100-acre grass- and shrub-covered peninsula formed by the bend in the river. They had built the log village of Tohopeka and across the river the village of Newyaucau, which they destroyed with Jackson's arrival. To defend their position, the Indians had built a zigzag log barrier, five to eight feet high across the neck of the peninsula, and had beached their canoes along the shore ready for escape.

Around 10 A.M. Jackson marched from his camp to Overlook highpoint and positioned his troops and artillery on the surrounding hills. He sent Lieutenant Jesse Bean with 40 Tennessee militia to occupy a 15-acre island to prevent the Red Sticks from using it as a refuge and ordered Coffee to take his cavalry and Cherokees across the river to the rear of the barricade.

Jackson was impressed with the design and strength of the barricade and the placement of portholes that exposed a frontal infantry attack to cross fire. He moved his artillery to within 80 to 300 yards from it and at around 10:30 A.M. began a bombardment.

Coffee and his men swam over to the peninsula at Cherokee Crossing, captured the canoes, burned Tohopeka, where the women and children had taken shelter, and then attacked the defenders from the rear.

After bombarding the barricade for about two hours with a three-pounder and six-pounder, cannon, which produced little damage, Jackson ordered Major Lemuel Montgomery's Thirty-Ninth Infantry into a frontal attack. The Thirty-Ninth had almost reached the barricade when Montgomery was shot and killed. The Thirty-Ninth faltered, but young Ensign

Sam Houston rallied them with drawn sword and let the men in fierce fighting on the barricade.

The Red Sticks fought bravely, but their war clubs were no match for the bayonets, and gradually, they fell back. By late afternoon, the single remaining band left had taken a defensive position in a ravine. Houston volunteered to lead the attack on this position and was wounded. The battle turned into a massacre as Jackson's troops killed Indian men, women, and children. Many warriors jumped into the river in an effort to escape and were killed by riflemen along the shore and on the island. By dark at least 800 of the 1,000 Red Sticks had been killed. Five hundred fifty bodies lay on the peninsula; the remainder were killed in the river. Jackson lost 49 men, and 154 were wounded, many mortally. His Cherokee allies lost 18 men, and 36 were wounded.

A few days after the battle, Red Eagle entered Jackson's headquarters to surrender, but the general, who had admired his courage in battle, let him go free.

The Treaty of Horseshoe Bend imposed by Jackson was intended to punish the Red Sticks, but as most of them had fled the region, the harsh terms of the accord fell on the friendly White Sticks instead. In compensation for the cost of the war against the Red Sticks, the White Sticks were forced to cede about 23 million acres of their land.

Horseshoe Bend would be the last major battle of the Indian Wars east of the Mississippi River.

About a year after becoming president in 1829, Jackson signed the Indian Removal Act requiring all tribes east of the river to move to Oklahoma territory, opening that huge territory to settlement and eventually statehood.

Horseshoe Bend Military Park is administered by the National Park Service.

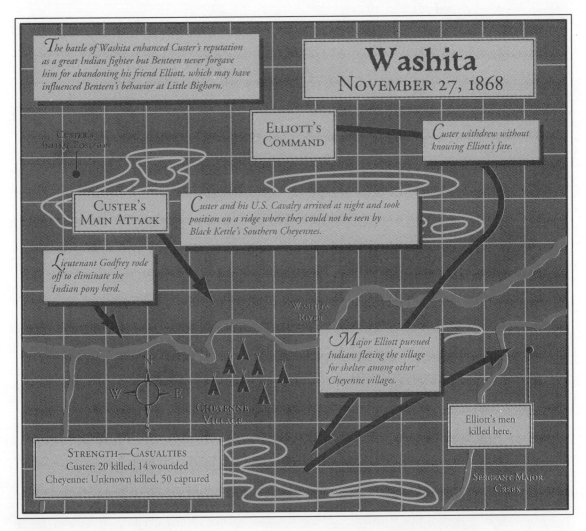

The battle of Washita enhanced Custer's reputation as a great Indian fighter but Benteen never forgave him for abandoning his friend Elliott, which may have influenced Benteen's behavior at Little Bighorn.

Washita
NOVEMBER 27, 1868

CUSTER'S INDIAN POSITION

ELLIOTT'S COMMAND

Custer withdrew without knowing Elliott's fate.

CUSTER'S MAIN ATTACK

Custer and his U.S. Cavalry arrived at night and took position on a ridge where they could not be seen by Black Kettle's Southern Cheyennes.

Lieutenant Godfrey rode off to eliminate the Indian pony herd.

WASHITA RIVER

Major Elliott pursued Indians fleeing the village for shelter among other Cheyenne villages.

N
W E
S

CHEYENNE VILLAGE

Elliott's men killed here.

STRENGTH—CASUALTIES
Custer: 20 killed, 14 wounded
Cheyenne: Unknown killed, 50 captured

SERGEANT MAJOR CREEK

BATTLE OF THE WASHITA, OKLAHOMA—NOVEMBER 26, 1868

During the spring and summer of 1868, the Southern Plains ran red with blood. Small bands of Cheyenne, Arapaho, Comanche, and Kiowa warriors swept through the inadequate defenses of settlements in Kansas, Colorado, Texas, and New Mexico.

Lieutenant General Philip Sheridan, in command of the Division of Missouri, had learned from his own experience that the seasons set the pattern for Indian warfare; war parties were active in spring and summer when the ponies were well nourished on plains grass, but in winter, the horse herds were half starved. Blizzards forced the Indians into sheltered areas such as river valleys. This was when they were most vulnerable to attack. Sheridan proposed using this winter hiatus, and sent Lieutenant Colonel George Armstrong Custer to test this new tactic.

At dawn on a bitter cold November day, Custer galloped down from the ridge with

THE BUFFALO SOLDIERS

In 1869, four black regiments, the Twenty-Fourth and Twenty-Fifth Infantry and the Ninth and Tenth Cavalry were sent to the western frontier to garrison posts and suppress hostile Indians, guard the mail, and protect settlers moving west and railroad workers. The Indians called these black troopers "Buffalo Soldiers."

There are several explanations given for the origin of this name. One is that the Indians noted that, while the white soldiers ate beef from cattle, the segregated blacks were given buffalo meat. Others

The Buffalo Soldiers Monument at Fort Leavenworth, Kansas, was dedicated July 15, 1992, to honor all blacks who had fought for the United States. (United States Army)

claim it was because the kinky hair of many black soldiers resembled the coat of a buffalo. Another theory is that Indians found that the black soldiers fought with the same force as cornered buffalo.

On reaching the western frontier, the black regiments were broken up into battalions or companies, and the units were scattered about to different posts, always commanded by white officers. (The practice of white commanding officers continued until the integration of the army in 1952. General John J. Pershing, of World War I fame, commanded the black Tenth Cavalry in his younger years. Because of this command, he was called "Black Jack" Pershing by many of his fellow officers.)

The Buffalo Soldiers had a miserable life on the frontier. They were given rejected horses and were ill-treated by the people they protected, local townspeople, settlers, and even cowboys. But the harsh treatment did not prevent them from being fine soldiers and they earned 18 Medals of Honor.

On July 25, 1992, at Fort Leavenworth, Kansas, a 12-foot-high bronze statue of a black cavalryman, pulling on the reins of his horse, was dedicated as the Buffalo Soldier Monument. It was also meant to honor the many blacks who that had over the years fought for the United States.

General Colin L. Powell, then Chairman of the Joint Chiefs of Staff, addressed the several thousands who attended the dedication. Also on hand that day was Commander Carlton G. Philpot, a Navy historian, at that time teaching at Fort Leavenworth Command and General Staff College, and who had led the effort to raise the money to pay for the statue.

The first black to die for the American cause was the slave Crispus Attucks, killed during the Boston Massacre on March 5, 1770.

Relatively few blacks were able to fight in the Revolutionary War because the government's policy was to accept only free blacks. But blacks did fight at Lexington and Concord and Bunker Hill.

At the battle of Lake Erie, September 10, 1813, Commodore Oliver Hazard Perry had 100 or more blacks among his ships' crews. Perry was at first upset at receiving the untrained blacks but began a rigorous training program. And after the battle, Perry wrote of them, "Men who were immediately under my observation evinced the greatest gallantry and I have no doubts that all others conducted themselves as American seamen."

The Emancipation Proclamation that went into effect January 1, 1863, opened the door for blacks to join the military. Soon after January 1, the governor of Massachusetts raised the Fifty-Fourth Massachusetts Colored Volunteer Infantry Regiment. In May, the War Department created a Bureau of Colored Troops to handle the recruitment and organization of black regiments. By the end of the war, there were approximately 122,000 black troops on active duty but less than 100 black officers.

During the Civil War, black regiments fought at Port Hudson, Millekins Bend, Fort Wagner, and at Chapin's Farm, where 13 black noncommissioned officers received the Medal of Honor.

About a year after the end of the Civil War, the number of black soldiers were reduced to around 15,000. The Twenty-Fourth and Twenty-Fifth Infantry and the Ninth and Tenth Cavalry regiments, created during the Civil War, were sent to the western frontier and remained as units through World War I.

---

800 troopers of his Seventh U.S. Cavalry and smashed into Chief Black Kettle's Southern Cheyenne village on the banks of the Washita River, in what today is the Oklahoma Panhandle.

The attack came as a complete surprise to Black Kettle and his sleeping followers. There were not aware that Custer was in the area, for he and his troops had arrived the night before after riding 70 miles, much through deep snow. In addition, Black Kettle never expected to be attacked because he had not made war against the Americans and was considered by many a "good" Indian. Now his sleeping people were awakened by the sounds of galloping horses and rifle shots, as the troopers rode among the village's 50 or so dwellings.

Half-asleep warriors attempted to defend themselves and their families and were quickly cut down by saber and rifle. The troopers laid waste to the village and set fire to blankets, clothing, food, and anything else of use to the Indians. Lieutenant Edward S. Godfrey's platoon had been ordered to capture or kill the tribes' pony herd.

Major Joel Elliott rode off with a small force in pursuit of a group of Indians fleeing from the village.

It did not take long for Custer's men to destroy the Cheyenne village; when they were done, more than 100 Indians had been killed, including Black Kettle. Accounts differ as to the fate of the women and children. Custer reported none were killed and 50 taken captive. Others claim that Black Kettle's wife, along with many other women, children, and old men, was killed, which, considering the nature of the attack, seems possible. Custer lost 5 men and 14 were wounded.

When Godfrey returned, he reported to Custer that he had been attacked by Indians from other villages coming to Black Kettle's aid and had to fight a slow withdrawing action until he joined the main command. Elliott had not returned, and Custer assumed that he, too, had run across Indians and would fight his way back. When he failed to appear, search parties were sent out, but found no sign of him or his command.

TREATIES WITH THE INDIANS

The treaties between the United States and the Native Americans were "designed to produce a settlement" but the settlement was always in the government's favor and usually included land—lots of it. During the Colonial period there were dozens of minor treaties signed with local tribes, these were of short duration, usually in effect just long enough to give whites time to organize a force to drive the Indians away or kill them off.

The agreement signed at Fort Greenville in 1794, a year after the Battle at Fallen Timber, was one of the first major treaties. In it, the Shawnees, Miamis, and other tribes ceded to the government a vast amount of land comprising much of present-day Ohio and Indiana.

In September 1809, William Henry Harrison, the governor of Indiana Territory, used whiskey and deceit to persuade Indian chiefs to cede 3 million acres—land that by Indian tradition they had no right to give away. Included in this land giveaway

The Fort Laramie treaty of 1868 promised the Indians much but delivered little. The delegation pictured met after the treaty was signed but before 1876. Chief Red Cloud is third from left with Red Dog and Little Wound to his far right and American Horse and Red Shirt to his far left. Standing is John Bridgeman, an interpreter.

were the favorite hunting grounds of the leader Tecumseh and the residual enmity would lead to the Battle of Tippecanoe in 1811 and Tecumseh joining the British in the War of 1812. After General Andrew Jackson defeated the Creeks at Horseshoe Bend in March 1814, he imposed a treaty on the Creek Nation in which they gave up around 23 million acres.

The nineteenth century would witness many more exchanges of "peace" for land. In 1830, the government bribed a minority of Choctaw leaders to sign the Treaty of Dancing Rabbit Creek, ceding all Choctaw land in Mississippi.

In the treaty of 1832 ending the Black Hawk War, in which Abraham Lincoln served, the Sacs and Foxes gave up a strip of their land of about 6 million acres along the Mississippi River in present-day Iowa; for a promise never to return, the Indians received $660,000 or around ten dollars an acre.

By 1868, the government had tired of fighting the Northern Plains Sioux and Cheyennes over land and by the terms of the Treaty of Laramie created a huge reservation of millions of acres that included much of present day western South Dakotas. But when gold was discovered in the Black Hills area of the reservation, the government failed to keep out white miners and the end result was a conflict that culminated in the battle at the Little Bighorn.

The U.S. government would break its agreement again in 1863, with the Nez Percé Indians of the Oregon, Washington, and Idaho area. In 1855 Nez Percé had signed a treaty establishing a reservation that included much of their original lands, but in 1863 the government, under pressure from white settlers, drew up a new treaty reducing the size of the reservation by three-fourths its original size. This act would lead to the Battle at Big Hole and the forced surrender of the Nez Percé at Bear Paw Mountain in October 1877.

The century ended as it began, and by 1889 the government had broken another treaty and had reduced food rations for the Indians living on North and South Dakota reservations. As many dispirited Indians joined the religious movement known as the Ghost Dance, apprehension on the part of whites would lead to the December 28, 1890, massacre at Wounded Knee. After this incident, there was no need for further treaties; the government had taken all the land it could and the unarmed Indians were forced by the U.S. Army to abandon their homelands for reservations.

Unsure of the number of Indian villages nearby, and concerned for the safety of his relatively small force and his seventy-mile-long supply line, Custer called off further search for Elliott, still believing he would return.

When the frozen and mutilated bodies of Elliott and his 14 men were eventually found, the number killed at the Battle of Washita was brought to 20.

Many officers of the Seventh including Captain Fred Benteen, who had been a friend of Elliott since they served together in the Civil War, believe Custer had abandoned Elliott.

The conflict at Washita established Custer's reputation as one of the great Indian fighters, and the Seventh Cavalry was believed to be the finest in the army. And, it proved the value of Sheridan's winter strategy campaign; the Plains Indians now realized they would have no security in their winter villages, and by spring of 1869, all the southern tribes had been forced onto reservations.

Washita Battlefield is owned by the Oklahoma Historical Society. There is an observatory tower where one can see some of the important sites of the battle. There are also maps and photographs that explain the battle.

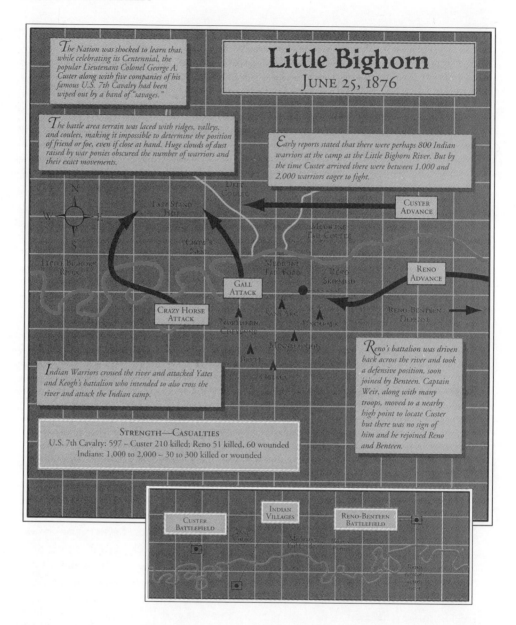

Little Bighorn
JUNE 25, 1876

The Nation was shocked to learn that, while celebrating its Centennial, the popular Lieutenant Colonel George A. Custer along with five companies of his famous U.S. 7th Cavalry had been wiped out by a band of "savages."

The battle area terrain was laced with ridges, valleys, and coulees, making it impossible to determine the position of friend or foe, even if close at hand. Huge clouds of dust raised by war ponies obscured the number of warriors and their exact movements.

Early reports stated that there were perhaps 800 Indian warriors at the camp at the Little Bighorn River. But by the time Custer arrived there were between 1,000 and 2,000 warriors eager to fight.

CUSTER ADVANCE

RENO ADVANCE

RENO SKIRMISH

GALL ATTACK

CRAZY HORSE ATTACK

RENO-BENTEEN DEFENSE

Reno's battalion was driven back across the river and took a defensive position, soon joined by Benteen. Captain Weir, along with many troops, moved to a nearby high point to locate Custer but there was no sign of him and he rejoined Reno and Benteen.

Indian Warriors crossed the river and attacked Yates and Keogh's battalion who intended to also cross the river and attack the Indian camp.

STRENGTH—CASUALTIES
U.S. 7th Cavalry: 597 – Custer 210 killed; Reno 51 killed, 60 wounded
Indians: 1,000 to 2,000 – 30 to 300 killed or wounded

CUSTER BATTLEFIELD

INDIAN VILLAGES

RENO-BENTEEN BATTLEFIELD

BATTLE OF THE LITTLE BIGHORN, MONTANA— JUNE 25, 1876

By 1868, the U.S. government had decided it would be cheaper to feed than fight the Indians and by the terms of a treaty signed at Fort Laramie, Wyoming, designated mil-lions of acres, including the Black Hills, as "The Great Sioux Reservation." The treaty promised the Indians that the government would protect them from "all depredation of people of the United States."

Many Indians, such as the Hunkpapa, Oglala, Uncapapa, and Minneconjou Sioux, along with the Northern Cheyenne,

joined with Sitting Bull in refusing to relocate to the reservation.

In 1874, Custer went into the Black Hills, a sacred site to the Indians, to establish an army fort to patrol the area and confirmed the presence of gold. Miners poured into the hills, and the army made only feeble efforts to keep them out. The government offered to buy or rent the Black Hills from the Indians but the offer was refused. Believing the government had broken the treaty, large numbers of Indians left to join those who had shunned the reservation.

In December 1875, all Indians were told to return to the reservation by January 31, 1876, or be treated as "hostiles"; the order

was generally ignored and in the spring, under the leadership of Sitting Bull, the Indians moved north to their traditional hunting and grazing lands in the Powder River area in present-day Montana.

Lieutenant General Sheridan decided to send three columns into southeastern Montana, where the Indians had gathered, to force them back to the reservation. Brigadier General George Cook was to move north from Fort Fetterman, Montana, with about 1,000 soldiers; Colonel John Gibbon would come east by way of the Yellowstone River with the "Montana Column" of 450 infantry, cavalry, and Indian scouts; and Brigadier General Alfred Terry would move

Major General William T. Sherman (to the right of the white-bearded man) presided with United States commissioners at the signing of a treaty with Chief Red Cloud at Fort Laramie, Wyoming Territory, on April 2, 1868. (National Archives)

*G*EORGE ARMSTRONG CUSTER (1839–1876)

As a most effective leader of Union cavalry, George Armstrong Custer achieved glory and the rank of major general during the Civil War. At the end of the war he remained in the army as a lieutenant colonel and became a famous Indian fighter. He met disaster along the Little Bighorn River in 1876. (Library of Congress)

Americans have been intrigued with the Battle of the Little Bighorn from the time unconfirmed reports about the conflict were first published in the *New York Herald* on July 6, 1876. The battle has since become the subject of numerous novels, historical accounts, and films, and at least 900 artists have depicted the scene. Since 1896, the Anheuser-Busch Brewing Company has printed and sold a million copies of Adams-Becker's fanciful lithograph *Custer's Last Stand.*

To many, the Battle of the Little Bighorn is immediately identified with George Armstrong

Custer, one of the best-known and respected military leaders of his day. From his early campaigns with the Army of the Potomac during the Civil War, Custer achieved so many military successes that his critics, as well as his friends, began to believe that his victories must be due to luck as well as ability. Many observers, including Custer, began to refer to "Custer's Luck."

It was Custer's good fortune that he graduated from West Point, with a dismal record, at the start of the Civil War, when the demand for officers was high. It was luck that after the First Battle of Bull Run, he was transferred to General George McClellan's staff and went on to become, at age 23, a major general, the youngest man ever to hold this rank in the army. The "Boy General" had the courage and dash needed to lead cavalry and fought so well at Gettysburg and at other battles that he earned the sobriquets "The Mural of the American Army" and "Beau Sabreur."

Shortly after the end of the Civil War, Custer was appointed a lieutenant colonel in command of the newly organized U.S. Seventh Cavalry. Though his attack on Black Kettle's camp on the Washita River was controversial, his luck held; he was now considered a great Indian fighter and his regiment became known as the "Incomparable Seventh Cavalry." His mentor, General Philip H. Sheridan, chose Custer to head the "Dakota Column" in the impending campaign against the Sioux in the Black Hills.

Custer loved to be in the public eye, and through interviews and newspaper articles he had written, he became embroiled in the impeachment of W. W. Belknap, President Ulysses S. Grant's secretary of war. Belknap was accused of profiting from the sale of reservation trading posts, and Grant's brother, Orvil, was also implicated.

Because he talked so much with the press, Custer was summoned to Washington to testify. Highly annoyed, Grant ordered Custer to remain in the capital until the proceedings were over, in spite of Custer's desire to return to Fort Abraham Lincoln in the Dakota Territory to prepare for the campaign. Sheridan interceded for him, and Grant relented, allowing Custer to return to the fort. But the president also insisted that while Custer could accompany his regiment, General Alfred Terry would be given overall command of the Dakota Column. Custer returned to his post, convinced that once in the field he would slip away from Terry and use the Seventh regiment as he saw fit.

Sheridan advised Custer to avoid the press, but with his love of publicity, Custer ignored the warning. When he rode into battle at the Little Bighorn on June 25, 1876, he was accompanied by Mark Kellogg, a reporter for the *Bismarck Herald*, who would be killed in the conflict.

After Custer's death, much of the Custer mythology was created through the writings of his wife. Elizabeth Bacon Custer. Besides her personal devotion to her husband, she had great admiration for his abilities and his leadership and had accompanied him to his stations whenever possible; she was lodged at Fort Abraham Lincoln when the steamer *Far West* arrived with the news of her husband's death.

Custer's role at Little Bighorn—and his character—remain a subject of debate. Some consider him a hero and military genius, felled by an error in judgment. Others believe he was a supreme egotist of unlimited ambitions with a boundless desire for personal fame. Whichever characterization is closer to the truth, one thing is for certain: On the afternoon of June 25, 1876, "Custer's Luck" ran out.

west with the "Dakota Column" from Fort Lincoln, near present-day Bismarck, North Dakota, and join with Gibbon. The principal element of Terry's command was Custer's Seventh Cavalry—about 600 troopers. In addition, Terry had two companies of infantry and a detachment to serve the three Gatling guns.

On June 1, Crook was attacked on the upper Rosebud River by Crazy Horse and a large force of Sioux and Cheyenne. After a six-hour battle, Crazy Horse withdrew, but Crook's army had been so weakened in the "Battle of the Rosebud" that he returned to Fort Fetterman and left the campaign. On June 21, Terry joined Gibbon on the Yellowstone near the mouth of the Rosebud River, where scouts told them that the Sioux had gathered to the south along the Little Bighorn River, in an area that the Indians called the "Greasy Grass."

That evening, Terry, Gibbon, and Custer met on the Yellowstone supply steamer *Far West* to plan the campaign. Custer and his regiment were to proceed south to the Bighorn Valley, and Terry and Gibbon would block the Indians' escape from the north.

On June 22, Custer headed south with a regiment consisting of 31 officers, 566 troopers, 39 white and Indian scouts, and a number of civilian packers and herders. Terry offered him the Gatling guns but he refused them, since they would be difficult to move over rough terrain. Although Terry gave Custer detailed written orders, he left to Custer's judgment the decision whether to engage the Indians or simply to prevent their escape to the south and drive them northward.

On June 24, Custer reached the lower Bighorn region. The surrounding land was laced with winding ridges, valleys, and coulees that obscured the view of both friend and foe. Clouds of dust raised by horses made it impossible to judge the number of the enemy, which might be anywhere from 20 to 200.

Custer was not sure how many warriors were present, but his primary concern was to locate the village and attack before the Indians escaped. Like most army officers of that time, he believed that no matter how great their number, the warriors would flee when faced by the U.S. army.

Custer had planned to attack on June 26, the day that Terry and Gibbon were to reach the mouth of the Little Bighorn River. The Indians would be caught between two giant pincers: Custer on the south; Terry and Gibbon on the north.

On the night of the twenty-fourth, Lieutenant Charles Varnum, in command of the Indian and white scouts, climbed to the top of the "Crow's Nest," a hill from which nearly every site in the valley could be seen. In the early morning of the twenty-fifth, Varnum and his Crow scouts saw rising smoke, giving them the approximate location of the village. That same morning, some of the soldiers had seen parties of warriors.

Realizing that he had been spotted by the Indians, Custer decided to attack on the twenty-fifth, for to wait even one day would give the Indians time to dismantle their village and escape. He divided his regiment into three battalions, giving three companies of 140 officers and men to Major Marcus Reno and three companies of 125 men to Captain Frederick Benteen. Custer kept the largest force for himself: five companies with about 225 men. He subdivided this force into two battalions with Companies E and F under Captain George Yates and Companies C, I, and L under Captain Myles Keogh.

When the entire regiment reached what is now Reno Hill, Custer ordered Benteen to wheel left and move southwest to determine if there were Indian forces in that area. Early in the afternoon, clouds of dust beyond a bluff indicated the location of the village, and Custer ordered Reno to attack it, telling him he would be "supported."

Reno crossed the Little Bighorn at what is today's Reno Creek and moved down the valley to hit the village on the upriver side. His battalion fell under heavy attack by a large force of warriors and had to make a fighting retreat, crossing to the other side of the river and taking a defensive position on a bluff. In this action, Reno lost 40, 13 wounded, and, apparently, his self-confidence.

Custer continued his advance on the village along the far side of the river. Scouts told him that the Indians had not scattered under Reno's attack. Custer saw enough of the village to suspect the large number of warriors he might face, and he decided to bring Benteen's battalion into the fight along with additional ammunition. His adjutant, William W. Cooke, handed Trumpeter John Martin a message to deliver: "Benteen. Come on. Big Village. Be Quick. Bring packs. W. W. Cooke. P. bring pacs [ammunition]." Martin rode off to deliver the message and was the last soldier to see Custer and his command alive.

Custer's battalion had to cross the Little Bighorn to reach the village, and as they made their descent to the river, the Indians poured across it and attacked.

Early estimates by scouts told Terry and Custer that there were around 800 warriors at the village but as more and more Indians, including warriors from the Sans Arc and Brule Sioux, had come to join with Sitting Bull. Custer was soon in a fight with between 1,000 and 2,000 warriors led by great war chiefs—Crazy Horse, Gall, Rain-in-the-Face, Low Dog, and Two Moon.

Just what happened on that June afternoon has been reconstructed from battlefield finds and the testimony of Indians; none of Custer's command survived.

Apparently, Yates's battalion came down Medicine Trail Coulee to cross the river but was stopped at the far shore by Gall and his warriors. Yates was forced to retreat from the river and fought his way to the southern end of a crest, now called Battle Ridge. It is not known if Keogh's battalion was to follow Yates into the village or strike it from another point, but in any event, he, too, was attacked by Gall and eventually joined Yates on a hill (later named after Lieutenant John Calhoun, commander of L Company).

By now, Indians had crossed the river below Medicine Trail Coulee and attacked the forces on Calhoun Hill. Yates moved north on the ridge in search of a better defensive position but was finally forced to look for shelter on the western slopes. Keogh's command had lost its horses and carbine ammunition and was forced to fight with pistols. Crazy Horse appeared with a large force that had crossed the river to sweep in a wide curve up Battle Ridge to hit Yates and Keogh.

On what is now called Custer's Hill, Companies E and F and the survivors of other companies made a final stand under Custer's headquarters' banner. Some of the soldiers left this position either to attempt a counterattack or escape. The 40 or so men who remained, slaughtered their horses for breastworks, and continued fighting until all had been killed.

Trumpeter Martin, his horse wounded by a bullet, finally found Benteen, who immediately moved toward the Little Bighorn River to see the last of Reno's men retreating. He fought his way to Reno who exclaimed: "For God's sake, Benteen, halt your command and help me. I've lost half my men."

No one knew where Custer was positioned but Captain Thomas Weir believed the distant firing should be investigated and decided to ride along a bluff to get a better view. His company followed him, and was shortly joined by other troops who gathered on a high hill, now called Weir Point. They were soon attacked by Indians and the companies eventually had to fight their way back to Reno's position on the bluff. Hundreds of warriors attacked the bluff, and the defenders endured a continuous and destructive fire from all sides. The attack did not end until darkness and began again at dawn the following day. The cavalrymen had made good use of the darkness, scooping out shallow entrenchments and using empty ammunition boxes, saddles, dead horses, and mules to make barricades. Dr. Henry Porter had laid the wounded out in a shallow depression and surrounded it with horses and mules to protect his patients.

There were few mounted charges from either side because of the nature of the terrain. Both soldiers and Indians rode to the scene of action and then fought dismounted. The Indians dispersed and fired from concealed positions behind hills, sagebrush, and troughs in the terrain; the army soldiers fought in groups that were difficult to conceal.

Custer's cavalry were armed with carbines and pistols. None carried sabers, which had been left behind at the beginning of the campaign.

The Indians used a variety of weapons—rifles, old muskets, and carbine they had taken from Reno's dead. Some warriors used bows and arrows, and these were most effective, since they made no sound to indicate where they were coming from, and the arrow could be aimed to descend on soldiers behind breastworks or in other defensive positions.

By early afternoon of the second day, the enemy fire began to slacken and that evening the entire Indian encampment made its way southwest toward the Bighorn Mountains.

The next morning Terry and Gibbon arrived to find half the Seventh Cavalry dead or wounded. No one knows when Custer fell. Some Indians claim it was early in the battle at the mouth of Medicine Trail Coulee and that his body was later moved to another position. Others believe he was with Keogh's battalion and was killed later in the fighting. The battle wiped out five companies of Custer's Seventh Cavalry— 210 men. Among them were five of Custer's relatives: his brothers, George, Thomas, and Boston; a nephew, Harry Reed; and his brother-in-law James Calhoun. Besides the 210 lost with Custer, another 51 had been killed and 60 wounded in Reno's retreat and the defense of the bluff. The exact number of Indian casualties is unknown but estimates range from 30 to 300.

On the morning of June 28, Reno's men rode to the Custer battlefield to bury the dead.

The Little Bighorn Battlefield National Monument is administered by the National Park Service and includes the Custer Battlefield, with a visitor center, and the Reno-Benteen Battlefield.

PURSUIT OF THE NEZ PERCÉ— OREGON, IDAHO, WYOMING, AND MONTANA

In spring, summer, and fall of 1877, about 800 Nez Percé Indians traveled over 1,500 miles through rugged terrain, across the Bitterroot Mountains and the recently established Yellowstone Park, to escape the pursuing U.S. army. In the course of the journey, the Indians engaged the army four times: at White Bird Canyon, Clearwater, Big Hole, and Bear Paw Mountain.

The Nez Percés were peaceful people living on grazing lands where the states of Oregon, Idaho, and Washington meet. In 1855, they agreed to a treaty with the government, establishing a reservation that included much of their original lands. But by 1863, settlers, stockmen, ranchers, and miners convinced the government to negotiate a new treaty, reducing the reservation to one-fourth its original size. The Indians living within the diminished reservation signed the treaty, but those living outside it refused to sign.

The so-called non-treaty Nez Percés led by Chief Joseph, remained on their homeland in the Wallowa River Valley.

In 1877, when the Indian Bureau ordered them to move onto the reservation, Chief Joseph met with General Oliver O. Howard at the reservation headquarters to state his people's case. Howard, however, had been directed to support the Indian Bureau and ordered all non-treaty Nez Percés to return to the reservation within 30 days.

The non-treaty Indians complied and had nearly all moved back onto the reservation by Howard's deadline, when on June 15, three young warriors killed four white settlers in revenge for the cheating and killing of older members of their families. Fearing retaliation by Howard, Chief Joseph, and 800 non-treaty Indians, including 125 warriors, fled north to White Bird, about 16 miles away, taking their belongings and as much livestock as they could gather together in such a short time.

When Howard heard of the killing and the escape of Chief Joseph's band, he ordered Captain David Perry to force the Nez Percés to return.

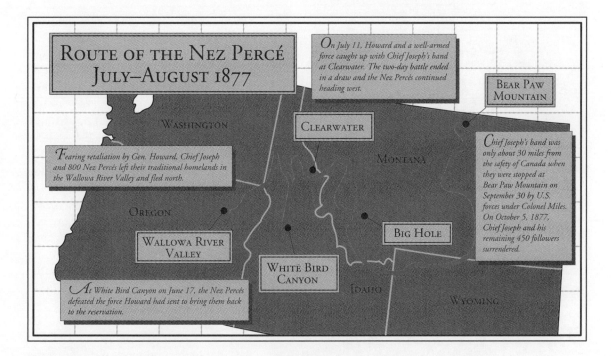

ROUTE OF THE NEZ PERCÉ
JULY–AUGUST 1877

On July 11, Howard and a well-armed force caught up with Chief Joseph's band at Clearwater. The two-day battle ended in a draw and the Nez Percés continued heading west.

BEAR PAW MOUNTAIN

WASHINGTON

CLEARWATER

MONTANA

Chief Joseph's band was only about 30 miles from the safety of Canada when they were stopped at Bear Paw Mountain on September 30 by U.S. forces under Colonel Miles. On October 5, 1877, Chief Joseph and his remaining 450 followers surrendered.

Fearing retaliation by Gen. Howard, Chief Joseph and 800 Nez Percés left their traditional homelands in the Wallowa River Valley and fled north.

OREGON

WALLOWA RIVER VALLEY

BIG HOLE

WHITE BIRD CANYON

IDAHO

WYOMING

At White Bird Canyon on June 17, the Nez Percés defeated the force Howard had sent to bring them back to the reservation.

With 100 cavalrymen and reinforced by volunteers, Perry made a forced march to intercept the Nez Percés before they reached the Salmon River, catching up with them on June 17 at White Bird Canyon. When Chief Joseph sent a delegation under a flag of truce to discuss a peaceful settlement, they were fired on by some of Perry's volunteers. The resulting battle was a disaster for Perry's command. The warriors poured deadly accurate fire on both his flanks, forcing him to retreat. He left 34 killed—one-third of his force.

On June 22, Captain Stephen Whipple and a small force attacked Chief Looking Glass's Nez Percé village near Clearwater, driving the formerly neutral Looking Glass to Chief Joseph's aid, bringing him 40 additional warriors.

On July 11, Howard, with 400 troops and artillery, was able to reach the rear of Chief Joseph's force near the Clearwater River undetected. But Howard lost the element of surprise by opening the battle with his artillery, and his force was attacked on three sides. The battle lasted for two days, with neither side able to claim victory. The Indians finally withdrew, but Howard believed his troops were too exhausted to pursue.

It was now obvious to the non-treaty Nez Percés that they could not escape the army in Idaho Territory. Following Looking Glass's advice that they leave their homeland, they headed east to join the Crows in Montana Territory. By early August, the Indians reached the Bitterroot Valley in Montana. Here they felt safe from Howard but were not aware that they were now being pursued by Colonel John Gibbon.

On August 7, they arrived at the Big Hole Valley, Montana. On the western side of the valley, where Ruby Creek joined Trail Creek to form the north fork of the Big Hole River, the steep slopes of (Battle Mountain) merged with a marsh and willows. But the east bank of the valley was flat and grassy,

Chief Looking Glass and several others wanted to go on fighting when under siege by the U.S. Army at Bear Paw Mountain. Chief Joseph and others favored surrender. After a council meeting, Looking Glass was killed by a stray bullet. (National Archives)

way around the base of the mountain and through the swamp until they were in earshot of the Indian camp. Gibbon's plan was to attack with three columns: two hitting the enemy's right and left flank and one assaulting the center. He held one detachment in reserve and ordered the artillery not to open fire until the battle was under way.

In the early morning, an Indian who had gone to check the horses was fired on by soldiers among the willows, and the attack began prematurely as the soldiers opened fire on the sleeping camp—but not for long. Now awake, the warriors found sniping positions, and their accurate fire drove the troops out of the camp and to the other side of the river.

The soldiers dug in along the river's shore, where they were pinned down all that day, that night, and most of the following day by the sniper fire of 60 warriors on the opposite side. Gibbon's artillery finally arrived, and the howitzers were placed on a hillside above the siege area. But before the cannon could be fired, the Nez Percés captured them and rolled them down the hill. Under protection of warrior fire along the shore, Chief Joseph and his band moved southward, shortly followed by those from the river bank.

It had been a hard battle for Gibbon but a devastating one for the Nez Percés. Out of their tiny band, 40 women, children, and old people were killed along with 40 warriors. Gibbon lost 30 soldiers and civilians, with 39 wounded.

The Indians headed east toward Yellowstone Park in the hope that they would find shelter among the Crows. But upon learning that the Crows were allied with Howard's force, they decided to go north into Canada to join Sitting Bull.

and it was there the Indians made their camp.

Now the tribe's war chief, Looking Glass, believed they were free of the army, and for the first time since leaving Clearwater, the people set up their teepees and engaged in ceremonial games and dances. Looking Glass was so certain of their safety that he did not post scouts or sentries.

On the night of August 8, Gibbon and 15 officers, 146 men of the U.S. Seventh Infantry, and 45 volunteers worked their

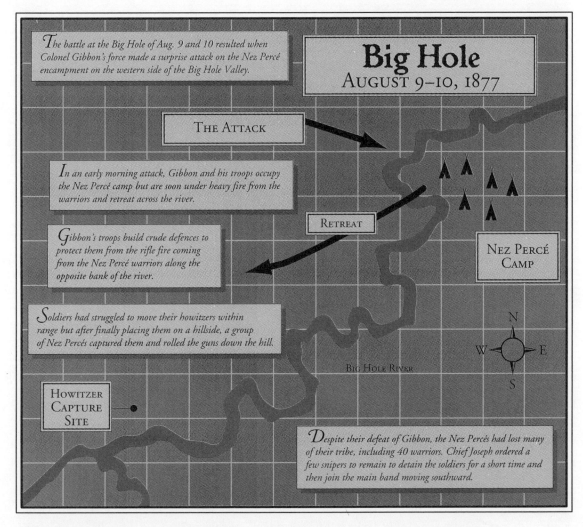

The battle at the Big Hole of Aug. 9 and 10 resulted when Colonel Gibbon's force made a surprise attack on the Nez Percé encampment on the western side of the Big Hole Valley.

Big Hole
AUGUST 9–10, 1877

THE ATTACK

In an early morning attack, Gibbon and his troops occupy the Nez Percé camp but are soon under heavy fire from the warriors and retreat across the river.

RETREAT

NEZ PERCÉ CAMP

Gibbon's troops build crude defences to protect them from the rifle fire coming from the Nez Percé warriors along the opposite bank of the river.

Soldiers had struggled to move their howitzers within range but after finally placing them on a hillside, a group of Nez Percés captured them and rolled the guns down the hill.

BIG HOLE RIVER

HOWITZER CAPTURE SITE

Despite their defeat of Gibbon, the Nez Percés had lost many of their tribe, including 40 warriors. Chief Joseph ordered a few snipers to remain to detain the soldiers for a short time and then join the main band moving southward.

On September 30, in the Bear Paw Mountains of Montana, just 30 to 40 miles from the Canadian border, the Nez Percés were surprised by Colonel Nelson Miles with about 400 men and artillery and Gatling guns. The Indians managed to take up a defensive position and killed a number of soldiers before Miles withdrew to lay siege to the camp. After five days of intermittent fighting and peace negotiations, the exhausted Nez Percés finally agreed on October 5 to surrender to Miles, and return to the reservation.

Of the 800 Nez Percés who had started the 1,700-mile journey, there were only 480 left to surrender. Many had been killed in battle, some had escaped into the hills, and 50 women and 100 warriors under White Bird managed to reach Canada.

Big Hole National Battlefield is administered by the National Park Service. The battlefield includes a visitor center with an audiovisual program as well as exhibits. Trails to tour the battlefield begin at the parking area. Hikers may follow part of all of the 1,270-mile Nez Percé War Trail.

THE GHOST DANCE

"The leaders beat time and sang as the people danced, going round to the left in a sidewise step. They danced without rest, on and on, and they got out of breath but still they kept going as long as possible. Occasionally, someone thoroughly exhausted and dizzy fell unconscious into the center and lay there "dead." Quickly those on each side of him closed the gap and went right on. After a while, many lay about in that condition. They were now "dead" and seeing their dear ones. As each one came to, she, or he, slowly sat up and looked about, bewildered, and then began wailing inconsolably. . . .

The visions varied at the start, but they ended the same way, like a chorus describing a great encampment of all the Dakotas who had ever died, where all were related and therefore understood each other, where the buffalo came eagerly to feed them,

and there was no sorrow but only joy, where relatives thronged out with happy laughter to greet the newcomer. That was the best of all!

Waking to the drab and wretched present after such a glowing vision, it was little wonder that they wailed as if their poor hearts would break in two with disillusionment. But at least they had seen! The people went on and on and could not stop, day or night, hoping perhaps to get a vision of their own dead, or at least to hear of the visions of others. They preferred that to rest or food or sleep. And so I suppose the authorities did think they were crazy—but they weren't. They were only terribly unhappy."

ANONYMOUS PINE RIDGE SIOUX
Native American Testimony

THE GHOST DANCE

Many Americans viewed the battle at the Little Bighorn during the summer of 1876 as a "public humiliation" and the U.S. army believed it now had the nation's support to avenge the death of Custer and pursue hostile Plains Indians to force them onto reservations.

A few weeks after Little Bighorn, troops from Fort Laramie, Wyoming, defeated about 1,000 Cheyennes on their way to join Sitting Bull and Crazy Horse. On November 25, a force of U.S. cavalry smashed the Northern Cheyenne camp of Dull Knife, and in January 1877, Crazy Horse and his Sioux warriors were defeated at the Battle of Wolf Mountain.

Seeing no alternative, Sitting Bull led his Hunkpapas into Canada, and remained

there until 1881, when he returned to the Standing Rock Reservation.

In late 1877, Crazy Horse surrendered, and his 1,000 or so Sioux were sent to the Pine Ridge Reservation in southwestern South Dakota. Other Indians were relocated to the Rosebud Reservation in South Dakota or Standing Rock in North Dakota. Even after he had surrendered, Crazy Horse was still considered dangerous, and on September 5, 1877, while resisting imprisonment, he was fatally wounded.

Being confined to reservations was a horrible life for a nomadic people who for generations had moved across the western plains to hunt buffalo and find suitable sites for their villages.

By the late summer of 1889, the Indians living on the several Dakota reservations were discouraged, confused, and frustrated.

In return for ceding some 9 million acres of their land, they had been promised adequate rations, and they soon learned these would be reduced. Many believed that short rations, coupled with the harshness of reservation life, would lead to widespread hunger, sickness, and death.

In their despair, the Indians found hope in rumors about a messiah in the far west who had come to help the Indians. The source of the rumors was a Paiute shaman, Wovoka, also called Jack Wilson, living on a reservation in western Nevada. In January 1889, Wovoka had a great vision that formed the basis for a religious movement that became known as the "Ghost Dance." In the fall of 1889, a delegation of Sioux slipped off Pine Ridge Reservation to investigate these rumors and learn more about the new messiah.

They returned to Pine Ridge with the news that the Son of God was truly on earth

and had come to benefit the Indians, not the whites. The delegation had adopted Wovoka's message to fit the particular needs of the Sioux living on reservations. The message prophesied that the whites would vanish, and Indians could return to their homelands. Their dead ancestors would return, assuring them of enough warriors to regain control of their land. Vast herds of buffalo would return, enabling the Sioux to renew their spiritual bond with an animal that had provided them with meat, shelter, clothing, warm robes, fuel for cooking, and heat for their teepees. To achieve these prophesies, the Indians had to engage in the Ghost Dance and wear a special garment. Ghost shirts and dresses were prepared and decorated in accordance with strict rituals.

It has been estimated that only about 40 percent of the Indians at Pine Ridge and 30 percent of those at Rosebud took part

Photograph of Pine Ridge Reservation taken on November 28, 1890. Shortly before, Indian agent Daniel F. Royner had telegraphed Washington: "Indians are dancing in the snow and are wild and crazy. We need protection and we need it now." (National Archives)

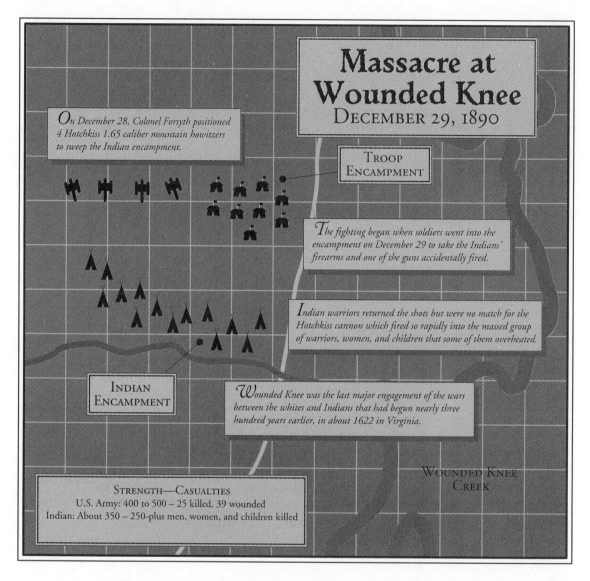

Massacre at Wounded Knee
DECEMBER 29, 1890

On December 28, Colonel Forsyth positioned 4 Hotchkiss 1.65 caliber mountain howitzers to sweep the Indian encampment.

TROOP
ENCAMPMENT

The fighting began when soldiers went into the encampment on December 29 to take the Indians' firearms and one of the guns accidentally fired.

Indian warriors returned the shots but were no match for the Hotchkiss cannon which fired so rapidly into the massed group of warriors, women, and children that some of them overheated.

INDIAN
ENCAMPMENT

Wounded Knee was the last major engagement of the wars between the whites and Indians that had begun nearly three hundred years earlier, in about 1622 in Virginia.

WOUNDED KNEE
CREEK

STRENGTH—CASUALTIES
U.S. Army: 400 to 500 – 25 killed, 39 wounded
Indian: About 350 – 250-plus men, women, and children killed

in the Ghost Dances. But this was enough to alarm the reservation agents and white settlers in the area. Many whites determined that the dances were a prelude to a general uprising, in spite of the Ghost Dancers' retreat from situations with potential for conflict.

Fear of an uprising grew to almost epidemic proportions as more converts joined the Ghost Dance, and newspapers pub-

lished unverified stories about Indian "depravations." On several occasions, reservation agents sent their police to stop the dances. Special Agent Royner reported that the matter was beyond control of the police and called for troops to prevent an outbreak, which he believed was imminent.

President Benjamin Harrison also concluded that an outbreak at Pine Ridge was forthcoming, and on November 13 ordered

Sitting Bull, chief of the Hunkpapa Sioux, was one of his people's most revered leaders. From bitter experience he had learned not to trust U.S. officials and eventually organized the large force of warriors that crushed Custer along the Little Bighorn. Greatly admired by Indians, he was feared and often ridiculed by whites. Many newspapermen of that day found it most amusing to refer to him as "Slightly Recumbent Gentlemen Cow." (Library of Congress)

Big Foot, chief of the Minneconjou Sioux, was on his way to Pine Ridge to persuade those in the Stronghold to surrender when he was captured and taken to Wounded Knee. There, he and over 250 of his followers were killed by the United States Army. (National Archives)

MASSACRE AT WOUNDED KNEE, SOUTH DAKOTA—DECEMBER 29, 1890

On November 20, Brigadier General John Brooke arrived with 400 soldiers at Pine Ridge and was joined three days later by a regiment of the U.S. Seventh Cavalry.

With the arrival of the army, the Indians began to divide into factions, and the agents were ordered to segregate the "well-disposed" from the "ill-disposed"—the Ghost Dancers. The latter group of some 3,500 gathered at the northwest corner of the reservation on a site called the Stronghold and sent word to Sitting Bull to join them.

Sitting Bull at Standing Rock Reservation had become a convert to the Ghost Dance, and the army considered him dangerous. He was arrested by Indian police before he could leave for Pine Ridge and in the scuffle he was killed along with seven of his warriors. Six of the Indian police were also killed. The army now turned its attention to Chief Big Foot on the Cheyenne River Reservation, whom they considered as dangerous as Sitting Bull, and ordered his arrest. Big Foot had been asked by several of the chiefs at Pine Ridge to come to "help make peace" with the U.S. army and offered him 100 horses for his aid.

Miles had closed the trail between Cheyenne River and Pine Ridge Reservation to prevent Big Foot and his followers from reaching Pine Ridge, but Big Foot managed to slip through. On learning that Big Foot had left the reservation, Miles ordered Major Samuel Whiteside to go from his recently established camp by Wounded Knee Creek to find and capture him.

Secretary of War Redfield Proctor to ready troops. The following day, Major General Nelson Miles, commander of the Division of the Missouri, was ordered to take whatever action necessary to restore order on the reservations and set up his headquarters at Rapid City, South Dakota.

On December 28, Whiteside, with four troops of the Seventh and two pieces of artillery, located Big Foot's band near Porcupine Creek, about 30 miles east of Pine Ridge. The Indians put up no resistance, since Big Foot had pneumonia. He was placed in a wagon, and his group was ordered by Whiteside to camp near his base at Wounded Knee Creek.

On Sunday evening, December 28, Colonel James W. Forsyth arrived at Whiteside's camp to take command and ordered the four Hotchkiss cannon he had brought positioned around the camp.

The following morning, he ordered his soldiers into Big Foot's camp to gather up all firearms. Some of the Indians advocated resistance, but Big Foot knew this would be suicidal; there were about 500 soldiers but only 350 Indians, mostly women and children.

Some Indians surrendered older weapons but kept the newer ones hidden, and the soldiers began to search the camp for concealed guns. One soldier attempted to take a gun from a deaf Indian named Black Coyote, and in the struggle, the rifle went off. Immediately, other rifles opened fire, and soon there was fighting at close quarters. The Indians now ran for cover, and the Hotchkiss artillery opened fire. At a range of only 300 to 400 yards, the artillery cut down the fleeing Indians—men, women, and children.

Ghost dancers photographed on August 9, 1890. They were members of Big Foot's band of Minneconjou Sioux and many of them, if not all, were killed on December 29 at the Massacre at Wounded Knee. (National Archives)

It took less than an hour to destroy Big Foot's little band. By the time the guns were silent, 250 or so Indian men, women, and children had been killed. Army casualties were 25 killed and 39 wounded. In late afternoon, the army left the site, still occupied by a few surviving Indians.

A blizzard on December 1 prevented an Indian rescue party from reaching Wounded Knee until January 1, 1891, where, they found eleven wounded alive. Two days later a party of civilians with a military escort came to bury the dead in a mass grave. There were 146 bodies, but many of the other dead had been removed from the site by relatives.

Miles did not approve of Forsyth's behavior at Wounded Knee and immediately removed him from command and demanded a court of inquiry look into his actions. The court met and acquitted Forsyth of any wrongdoing.

Following the massacre at Wounded Knee, there were a few skirmishes between the Indians and the army, which ended when Kicking Bear surrendered his rifle to Miles.

On January 18, 1891, Miles pronounced the end of the Sioux campaign, bringing the American Indian Wars that began in Virginia in 1622 to a close.

All America's previous wars had dramatic endings: Wolfe and Montcalm both mortally wounded outside Quebec on the Plains of Abraham; American and French regulars drawn up to receive the surrender of Cornwallis's British army at Yorktown; thousands of scarlet-uniformed British regulars marching into the artillery and rifle fire coming from Jackson's men defending New Orleans; General Winfield Scott and his escort riding as conquerors into Mexico City; and Generals Grant and Lee sitting in the parlor of the Wilmer

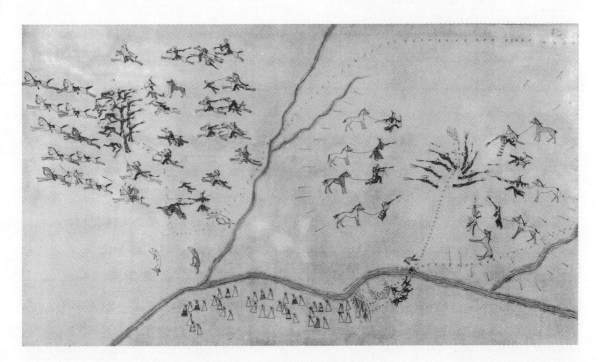

McLean farmhouse at Appomattox Court-house while Grant wrote the terms of surrender as Union officers stood in the background, observers to this momentous event.

But the Indian Wars did not end in high drama or with military pageantry. It ended by a little creek in South Dakota, with a detachment of United States soldiers firing carbine and artillery into a few hundred Indians, killing women and children along with warriors.

It was a sad ending to a long sad war. It was a sad day for Big Foot's people, a sad day for Native Americans, a sad day for all Americans.

On May 28, 1903, the Indian survivors of the massacre, erected and dedicated a granite monument at the site of the mass grave at Wounded Knee. In 1992 the site became a National Historic Landmark.

The Wounded Knee National Historic Land-mark, commonly known as the Wounded Knee Massacre Site, is located on the Pine Ridge In-dian Reservation in southwestern South Dakota. The site includes important natural features that played roles in the events in the massacre, includ-ing the hill where Forsyth positioned his artillery.

Battle at the Little Bighorn as depicted by White Bird, an Indian warrior who was engaged in the battle. (West Point Museum)

Attack on Pearl Harbor —December 7, 1941

Pearl Harbor
DECEMBER 7, 1941

When the Japanese war planes first appeared, many Americans on the island believed they were either their own forces coming back from patrol or reinforcements from the mainland.

Surprised U.S. sailors fired on the enemy planes with whatever weapons they could muster.

UTAH (Training Ship)

ARIZONA
TENNESSEE
NEVADA
FORD ISLAND
MARYLAND
W VIRGINIA
OKLAHOMA

Seven United States battleships were at anchor and the USS Pennsylvania was in dry dock when the Japanese aircraft attacked.

CALIFORNIA

PENNSYLVANIA

U.S. NAVAL STATION

CASUALTIES
U.S. Navy – 2001 killed, 710 wounded
U.S. Army and Marines – 340 killed, 433 wounded
U.S. Civilians – 54 killed, 35 wounded
Japanese – 64 killed, wounded–unknown

The day after the attack on Pearl Harbor, the United States declared war with Japan and entered the Second World War.

With the ending of the Plains Indians War in January 1891, there were no battles on U.S. territory for the next half century. Battles fought by Americans during the Spanish-American War (1898) and in World War I took place either at sea or on foreign soil.

Then, a few minutes before 8 A.M. on December 7, 1941, without warning, around 189 Japanese bombers, torpedo, and fighter planes from the six carriers only 230 miles away, attacked Pearl Harbor on the Hawaiian Island of Oahu, home port of the U.S. navy's mighty Pacific Fleet. On that Sunday morning, there were some 130 warships anchored in the harbor or along-side docks. Among them were the fleet's eight battleships: *Arizona, California, Maryland, Nevada, Oklahoma, Pennsylvania, Tennessee,* and *West Virginia.* Seven of these "battlewagons" were lined up along "Battleship Row"; *Pennsylvania* was in the nearby dry dock. Cruisers and destroyers rode at anchor about the harbor. The two Navy carriers, *Enterprise* and *Lexington,* were at sea, escorted by cruisers and destroyers.

About 15 minutes after the attack began, a 1,760-pound Japanese bomb smashed through *Arizona*'s deck into the ammunition magazine. The explosion sent the ship to the bottom of the harbor, taking to her watery grave 1,177 of the crew. *Oklahoma,* hit by several torpedoes, rolled over and sank with 400 of the crew trapped in the inverted hull. *California* and *West Virginia* were hit so many times by bombs and torpedoes that they sank at their moorings. *Maryland, Pennsylvania,* and *Tennessee* were seriously damaged, and *Utah*, now a training ship, was so damaged she capsized with 50 of the crew. It was only the *Nevada* that, while hurt, managed to make a break for open water. But after receiving additional hits, it was forced to beach so as not to be sunk and block entrance to the harbor.

For the military personnel—sailors, marines, and soldiers—who manned the ships at Pearl Harbor and the many U.S. military installations on the island of Oahu, December 7 started out as a typical peaceful Sunday. Some had obtained leave to visit Honolulu; others planned to attend church, perhaps play some golf or just take it easy. On board ships, many sailors were sitting down to a late Sunday breakfast.

When planes first appeared, many believed they were B-17s expected from the mainland. Then the planes dove down and the quiet of that Sunday morning was shattered by the explosion of bombs and torpedoes as they hit the navy's ships again and again.

Sailors rushed to defend their ships, often having to get tools to smash the locks so they could reach the ammunition for their guns. Even so, five minutes after the attack began, the antiaircraft cannon poured fire at the attacking planes. Marines and soldiers used any weapons they could get their hands on to fire on the enemy aircraft.

Other U.S. military installations on Oahu, including Shoefield Barracks and the airfields of Hickham, Wheeler, Bellows, Ewa, and Kaneohe were also attacked.

There was a brief lull in the onslaught, and then around 8:40 A.M. a second wave of enemy planes attacked Pearl Harbor. *Nevada* was so badly damaged that she was forced aground. Several smaller ships were sunk, and the dry dock was damaged. Planes also struck the airfields, all but eliminating U.S. ability to retaliate. A handful of U.S. fighter planes did manage to get off the ground and reported shooting down 12 enemy planes.

At 10:00 A.M. the second wave of Japanese flew back to their carriers. The attack was finally over.

In two hours, Japan had achieved its objective of immobilizing the U.S. Pacific Fleet. All eight battleships had been sunk or seriously damaged, along with ten cruisers, destroyers, and auxiliary ships. Most of the aircraft had been put out of action: 164 planes were destroyed, 159 badly damaged.

The attack on Pearl Harbor is commonly referred to as a "surprise attack," but actually it was not the attack that was the surprise, but the manner in which it was made.

Relations between the United States and Japan had been deteriorating since the Japanese invasion of Manchuria in 1931. Since then, Japan had embarked on an expansion policy, taking more of China and moving into southeast Asia. Japan was convinced that to survive it must acquire new territory to supply it with oil and other raw materials. The United States responded firmly, demanding that Japan get out of China and cease its expansion policy. The U.S. government attempted to use economic measures, such as freezing U.S. credit and placing an embargo on oil, to force Japan to make concessions.

But the summer of 1941, the United States and Japan had both taken a position from which there could be no retreat. In late November 1941, Washington informed the commanders at Pearl Harbor and Oahu, Rear Admiral Husband Kimmel and Major General Walter Short, that war with Japan could begin at any moment.

Many military authorities of that time believed that in the event of war, Japan would strike Pearl Harbor to destroy the Pacific Fleet, either with submarines or an invasion force. Few believed that the Japanese had the technical ability to assemble a large force and sail, undetected, halfway across the Pacific with bombs and torpedoes capable of going through the 15-inch armor of U.S. battleships. Since an air attack seemed out of the question, because of the belief that the Japanese lacked the technical ability to send their air force to Pearl Harbor, Kimmel arranged his ships against a submarine attack on the harbor. (At 6:40 A.M. on December 7, the USS *Ward* did see and destroy a midget enemy submarine at the entrance to the harbor.) Short concentrated the U.S. Air Force fighters on the airport runways, where they could be easily protected from an enemy infantry attack or sabotage from residents of Oahu of Japanese ancestry.

The United States suffered great casualties that Sunday, especially the Navy, which lost 2,001 killed and 710 wounded. Army and Marine forces had 340 killed and 433 wounded. Fifty-four civilians were killed that day and another 35 wounded.

But the Japanese attack had been only a partial success. While Pearl Harbor took a dreadful beating, the shipyards, fuel storage area, and submarine base suffered only minor damage. The lost and damaged aircraft were shortly replaced, and within months, all but three of the battleships returned to sea duty. The carriers *Enterprise* and *Lexington* had not been scratched.

The attack on Pearl Harbor immediately unified the American people, who had been divided between those who believed the United States should take a more active role in the defeat of the Axis powers and those who felt complete neutrality a more prudent course.

Kemmel and Short ruined their military careers by underestimating Japan's technical military abilities. But they were not alone. Most Americans at that time believed the Japanese only capable of making cheap toys and trinkets.

In the summer of 1942, a young U.S. Air Force captain inspected a captured Japanese Zero fighter that had been shipped to the United States for study. After looking over this plane that had earned the respect of the U.S. combat pilots, the captain's only comment was, "Piece of junk! Doesn't even have an ashtray in the cockpit." It would take four years of war to reverse this popular opinion of the enemy.

On December 8, 1941, the United States declared war on Japan, as the public took up the war cry, "Remember Pearl Harbor!"

Japan's allies, Germany and Italy, declared war on the United States on December 11, 1941. About four years later, all three nations suffered a crushing defeat at the hands of America and its allies.

Dedicated in 1962, the USS Arizona *Memorial, the 184-foot-long structure spanning the midportion of the sunken battleship, consists of three main sections: the entry and assembly rooms, a central area designed for observation and ceremonies, and a shrine room, where the names of those killed on the* Arizona *are listed on the marble wall.*

The visitor center and USS Arizona *are located on Pearl Harbor Naval Base; the National Park Service maintains these facilities. Visitors first go to the center to view a 20-minute film on the battle and then take a navy shuttle boat to the memorial.*

APPENDIX I

GUIDE TO AMERICAN BATTLEFIELDS AND MILITARY MUSEUMS

CHAPTER ONE

FORT NECESSITY

The fort is located about 11 miles east of Uniontown, Pennsylvania, on U.S. 40. The Battlefield Superintendent's address is Route 2, Box 528, Farmington, PA 15437.

FORT WILLIAM HENRY

It is open to the public (for a charge) seven days a week from May to mid-October. The fort is located near Lake George Village, which is at the foot of the lake, just off Route 87. For more information, call (518) 668-5471.

FORT TICONDEROGA

It is open daily to the public, at a charge, from mid-May through mid-October. It is located in northeastern New York, 18 miles east on Route 74 from Exit 28 on I-87 or a half mile west of Fort Ti ferry from Shoreman, Vermont. For more information, call (518) 585-2821.

CROWN POINT

It provides guided tours from mid-May to late October. It is about 12 miles north of Fort Ticonderoga on New York State Route 9N. For more information, call (518) 598-3666.

OLD FORT NIAGARA

It is open daily throughout the year except on major holidays. There is an admission fee applied to maintenance. The fort is only about 20 minutes from Niagara Falls. Fore more information, call (716) 745-7611 or write to: Old Niagara Association, Inc., Box 169, Youngstown, NY 14174.

CHAPTER TWO

LEXINGTON-CONCORD

For more information, contact the Park Superintendent, Box 160, Concord, MA 01742.

BUNKER HILL MONUMENT

It is located about .5 mile or so from the center of Boston on Route 1 off I-93.

PRINCETON BATTLE FIELD

Princeton Battle Field State Park is located on the southern end of Princeton in New Jersey on Route 583. A visitor center is scheduled to be built.

HUBBARDTON BATTLEFIELD

It is open from mid-May through mid-October, Wednesday–Sunday, 9:30 A.M. to 5:30 P.M. It is located in East Hubbardton, 7 miles north of U.S. Route 4, from Castleton. For more information about the battle site, write to: Vermont Division for Historic Preservation, Montpelier, VT 05602.

BENNINGTON BATTLEFIELD

It is located on Route 67, between Walloomsac, New York, and the Vermont border; 2 miles from the Vermont border. From Albany, take Route 7 east to Route 22, then north to Route 77. For more information, write to: Bennington Battlefield State Historic Site, RD 2, Box 11W, Hoosick Falls, NY 12090.

ORISKANEY BATTLEFIELD

It is open mid-May to October, Wednesday–Saturday and Monday 9 A.M. to 5 P.M., Sunday 1 P.M. to 3 P.M. It is located on Route 69, 2 miles west of the village of Oriskaney. From Westmoreland (Exit 321) of the New York State Thruway, take Route 233 to Route 69. For more information, write to: Oriskaney Battlefield, State Historic Site, Route 69, Box 275, RD 1, Oriskaney, NY 13424.

FORT STANWIX

Open daily from 9 A.M. to 5 P.M. from April 1 to December 31 except Thanksgiving and Christmas. For more information, write to: Fort Stanwix National Monument, 122 East Park Street, Rome, NY 13440.

SARATOGA BATTLEFIELD

There is a visitor center. Park roads are open daily from early April to November 30. The park entrances are 30 miles north of Albany, New York, on U.S. 4 and N.Y. 32. For more information, write to: Superintendent, RD 2, Box 33, Stillwater, NY 12170. Phone: (518) 664-9821.

BRANDYWINE

The visitor center is open Tuesday to Saturday, 9 A.M. to 5 P.M., Sunday 12 noon to 5 P.M. It is located near Chadds Ford on U.S. 1 (Baltimore Turnpike). For more information, write to: Brandywine Battlefield State Park, P.O. Box 202, Chadds Ford, PA 19317. Phone: (215) 459-3342.

THE STONE CHEW HOUSE

For more information, write to: Germantown Historical Society, 6401 Germantown Avenue, Germantown, PA 19122. Phone: (215) 844-0514.

RED BANK BATTLEFIELD

It is located on Hessian Avenue, off New Jersey Route 295, reached from Exit 23 off Route 295 (New Jersey Turnpike).

MONMOUTH BATTLEFIELD

The Monmouth Battlefield is open daily from 8 A.M. to 4 P.M. It is located on 347 Freehold-Englishtown Road on New Jersey Route 33. Take Exit 123, Garden State Parkway, and go west on Route 133. For more information, write to: Monmouth Battlefield State Park, 347 Freehold-Englishtown Road, Freehold, NJ 07728-9998. Phone: (908) 462-9616.

STONY POINT BATTLEFIELD

Open late April to October 31, Wednesday to Sunday, 8:30 A.M. to 5 P.M. It is located off Route 9 at Stony Point, New York, about 12 miles below West Point. For more information, write to: Stony Point Battlefield, P.O. Box 182, Stony Point, NY 10980. Phone: (914) 786-2521.

MOORES CREEK BATTLEFIELD

Open daily except Christmas Day and New Year's Day from 8 A.M. to 5 P.M. It is located 20 miles northwest from Wilmington, North Carolina. From there take U.S. 421 to junction with N.C. 210. Go west for five miles to park. For more information, write to: Superintendent, P.O. Box 69, Currie, NC 28435.

FORT MOULTRIE

The fort is open daily 9 A.M. to 6 P.M. in summer and 9 A.M. to 5 P.M. in winter, except Christmas

Day. Sullivan Island is reached from Charleston by U.S. 17N (business) to Mt. Pleasant and then right on S.C. 703. For more information, write to: Superintendent, Drawer R, Sullivan Island, SC 29482.

KINGS MOUNTAIN MILITARY PARK

From Charlotte, North Carolina, by I-85; from Spartenburg, South Carolina, by I-85, and from York by S.C. Route 81. For more information, write to: Superintendent, P.O. Box 40, Kings Mountain, NC 28086.

COWPENS NATIONAL BATTLEFIELD

It is located 11 miles northwest from I-85 exit Gaffney, South Carolina, and 2 miles southeast of U.S. 221 and Chesnee, South Carolina. The park entrance is northwest of the intersection of S.C. 11 and 110. For more information, write to: Superintendent, Box 308, Chesnee, SC 29332.

GUILFORD COURTHOUSE BATTLEFIELD

It is open daily 8:30 A.M. to 5:00 P.M., except Christmas Day and New Year's Day. It is located 6 miles from downtown Greensboro, North Carolina, off U.S. 220 on New Garden Road. For more information, write to: Superintendent, P.O. Box 9806, Greensboro, NC 27429. Phone: (910) 288-1776.

NINETY SIX HISTORICAL SITE

It is open daily from 8 A.M. to 5 P.M. except Christmas Day and New Year's. It is located two miles south of the town of Ninety Six, on S.C. Route 248.

YORKTOWN

Location: From Williamsburg via Colonial Parkway. From Newport News and Norfolk, via Routes 64, 105, and 17. For more information, write to: Superintendent, Colonial Historical Park, Yorktown VA 23690.

CHAPTER THREE

FORT MEIGS

It is open daily from April to October and charges $2.00 for adults, $1.00 for children. Location: West River Road (S.R. 65) in Perrysburg, Wood County, Ohio. Take I-475 to first interchange, Exit 2 and turn north to S.R. 65. Perrysburg is just south of Toledo and near the Ohio Turnpike. For more information, write to: Fort Meigs State Memorial, P.O. Box 3, State Route 65, Perrysburg, OH 43552. Phone: (419) 874-4121.

PERRY'S VICTORY AND INTERNATIONAL PEACE MEMORIAL

It is located on South Bass Island on Lake Erie about three miles from the mainland. From April through November, automobile ferries operate from Catawaba (3 miles) and from Clinton Point (10 miles). There is also year-round air service from Port Clinton. The memorial is open daily from April to late October. Location: Port Clinton is northwest of Sandusky, Ohio, on Route 2. Catawaba is off Route 53 north of Port Clinton. For more information, write to: Superintendent, P.O. Box 549, Put-in-Bay, OH 43456.

SACKETS HARBOR BATTLEFIELD

It is open late May to mid-October, 10 A.M. to 5 P.M., Wednesday through Saturday. It is located on Route 62 from Exit 44 off I-81 north of Syracuse, New York.

FORT WASHINGTON PARK

The fort and visitor center are open daily except January 1 and December 25. For more information, write to: Superintendent, National Capital Parks-East, 1900 Anacostia Drive, SE, Washington, DC 20020.

FORT MCHENRY

It is open daily from 8 A.M. to 5 P.M. It is located on the waterfront in downtown Baltimore. For more information, write to: Superintendent, Fort

McHenry National Monument and Historic Shrine, Baltimore, MD 21230. Phone: (410) 962-4299.

BATTLE OF PLATTSBURG

It is located at 48 Court Street, Plattsburg, NY 12901.

CHALMETTE UNIT

It is located six miles east of New Orleans. For more information, call: (504) 589-4428.

CHAPTER FOUR

THE ALAMO

It is open daily from 9 A.M. to 5:30 P.M. Location: Downtown San Antonio, Texas. For more information, write to: Daughters of the Republic Museum, P.O. Box 2599, San Antonio, TX 78199. Phone: (210) 225-1391.

SAN JACINTO BATTLEFIELD

The park and museum are open daily except December 24 and 25. It is located 22 miles east of downtown Houston off Texas Highway 225 east and north on Highway 134 (Battleground Road). For more information, write to: San Jacinto Battleground State Historic Park, 3523 Battleground Road, La Porte, TX 77571. Phone: (713) 479-2431.

PALO ALTO NATIONAL BATTLEFIELD

It is located outside of Brownsville 1 mile north of the city limits at the junction of Highway F.M. 1847 (Paredes Line Road) and Highway F.M. 511.

RESACA DE LA PALMA

It is located .7 mile north of Brownsville city limits on Highway F.M. 1847.

CHAPTER 5

FORT SUMTER NATIONAL MONUMENT

The fort is open daily from 9 A.M. to 6 P.M. except Christmas. For more information, write to: Superintendent, Fort Sumter National Monument, 1214 Middle Street, Sullivan's Island, SC 29482. Phone: (803) 883-3123. Tour boat schedules may also be obtained from Fort Sumter Tours, Inc., P.O. Box 59, Charleston, SC 29402. Phone: (803) 722-1691.

MANASSAS (BULL RUN) NATIONAL BATTLEFIELD PARK

The visitor center is open daily from 8:30 A.M. to 6:00 P.M. in summer and to 5 P.M. in winter and contains a slide presentation explaining the battle as well as a museum. As two battles were fought on this site, First and Second Manassas (Bull Run), there is information available for self-guided tours of each. The tour of First Bull Run includes the Confederate artillery position overlooking Matthew Hill and the Confederate line where General Jackson earned his famous nickname, "Stonewall." For more information, write to: Superintendent, Manassas National Battlefield Park, 12521 Lee Highway, Manassas, VA 22110. Phone: (703) 754-1861.

WILSON CREEK BATTLEFIELD

Wilson's Creek National Battlefield is off U.S. 60, about 3 miles east of Republic, Missouri. The visitor center of this 1,750-acre park is open daily from 8 A.M. to 7 P.M. except Christmas and New Year's Day and has films and maps to explain the battle, a museum, and informative material for self-guided tours. For more information, write to: Superintendent, Wilson's Creek National Battlefield, Box 75, Republic, MO 65738. Phone: (417) 732-2662.

FORT DONELSON NATIONAL BATTLEFIELD

Fort Donelson National Battlefield is about 1 mile east of Dover, Tennessee, on U.S. Route 79 and about 28 miles west of Clarksville. The visitor center is open daily from 8 A.M. to 4:30 P.M. except Thanksgiving Day, Christmas, and New Year's Day. The center includes a museum, a slide presentation, and articles tracing the fort's history. For more information, write to: Superintendent, Fort Donelson, P.O. Box 434, Dover TN 37058. Phone: (615) 232-5706.

PEA RIDGE NATIONAL MILITARY PARK

Pea Ridge National Military Park is 10 miles northeast of Roger, Arkansas, on State Route 71 and about 31 miles northeast of Fayetteville, Arkansas, on U.S. 62. The visitor center for this 4,300-acre park is open daily from 8 A.M. to 5 P.M. except Christmas and New Year's Day and includes a slide presentation of the battle and a museum with arms and photographs. The self-guided tour covers General Curtis's Headquarters, reconstructed Elkhorn Tavern, Union and Confederate artillery positions, along with other points of interest. For more information, write to: Superintendent, Pea Ridge National Military Park, Pea Ridge, AR 72751. Phone: (501) 451-8122.

GLORIETA PASS BATTLEFIELD

Glorieta Pass Battlefield is on U.S. Route 85 near Glorieta, New Mexico, 18 miles east of Santa Fe. The battlefield of Glorieta Pass, New Mexico, includes Pigeon's Ranch and Johnsons' Ranch and is a unit of Pecos National Historical Park, with headquarters at Pecos, New Mexico, about 25 miles east of Santa Fe on I-25. In early 1994, the battle sites were not fully developed but, even so, a visit to the area is worthwhile. To plan a visit, it is suggested to first contact the Pecos Park folk. For more information, write to: Superintendent, Pecos National Historical Park, P.O. Drawer 418, Pecos NM 87552. Phone: (505) 757-6414.

SHILOH NATIONAL MILITARY PARK

Shiloh National Military Park is off State Route 22, at Shiloh, Tennessee, about 25 miles northeast of Corinth, Mississippi, and around 110 miles east of Tennessee. The visitor center of this 3,800-acre park is open daily from 8 A.M. to 6 P.M., except Christmas Day. There is a 35-minute-long film and maps at the center that explain the battle along with material for self-guided tours, that include landmarks such as the Hornet's Nest, Peach Orchard, and Bloody Pond. For more information, write to: Superintendent, Shiloh National Military Park, Shiloh, TN 38376. Phone: (901) 689-5275.

FORT PULASKI NATIONAL MONUMENT

Fort Pulaski National Monument is on Cockspur Island, connected by a causeway to the mainland and about 15 miles east of Savannah, Georgia, via U.S. 80. The fort is open daily except Christmas Day from 8:30 A.M. to 5:30 P.M., with extended hours during the summer months. The visitor center contains a museum with exhibits and artifacts tracing the history of the fort. Arrangements can be made at the center for guided and self-guided tours of the fort. There is much to see at the old fort, such as sections of the brick wall damaged by Union shells, the Confederate defense system, the moat, prison, and room where Olmstead surrendered. For more information, write to: Superintendent, Fort Pulaski National Monument, P.O. Box 30757, Savannah, GA 31410-0757. Phone: (912) 786-5787.

McDOWELL BATTLEFIELD

It is located on U.S. Route 250. To arrange a visit or obtain information, write to: Lee Jackson Foundation, P.O. Box 8121, Charlottesville, VA 22906.

PORT REPUBLIC

Port Republic Battlefield is on U.S. Route 340 near Port Republic, Virginia. To visit, or for information, contact: Association for the Preservation of Civil War Sites, P.O. Box 1862, Fredericksburg, VA 22402.

MALVERN HILL BATTLEFIELD

The visitor center, located at 3215 East Broad Street in Richmond, is open daily except Thanksgiving and Christmas Day from 9 A.M. to 5 P.M. The center includes a museum and provides information for up to a 100-mile self-guided auto tour of all the park's battle and historic sites. The center also has a schedule of living history programs that take place there or on the battle sites. For more information, write to: Superintendent, Richmond National Battlefield Park, 3215 East Broad Street, Richmond, VA 23223. Phone: (804) 225-1981.

MANASSAS (BULL RUN)
NATIONAL BATTLEFIELD PARK

The over 3,000-acre Manassas (Bull Run) National Battlefield Park is near Manassas, Virginia, 26 miles southeast of Washington, D.C., at the intersection of I-66 and State Route 234. The visitor's center at the park entrance has a slide presentation of the battle and a museum with photos and artifacts to further explain what took place. As two battles were fought on this site—First Bull Run and Second Bull Run—there are separate self-guided tours for each. For more information, write to: Superintendent, Manassas National Battlefield Park, P.O. Box 1830, Manassas, VA 22110. Phone: (703) 454-1867.

HARPERS FERRY
NATIONAL HISTORICAL PARK

Harpers Ferry National Historical Park is on U.S. 340 at Harpers Ferry, West Virginia, and about 20 miles east of Frederick, Maryland, about 50 miles northwest of Washington, D.C., on U.S. 270. The visitors center is open daily from 8 A.M. to 5 P.M. except Christmas Day and New Year's Day. There is a film on the history of the town and material for self-guided tours. Much of the activity of the Civil War took place in the Maryland Heights area, also with stops on the self-guided tour. For more information, write to: Superintendent, Harpers Ferry National Historical

Park, Harpers Ferry, WV 25425. Phone: (304) 535-6371.

ANTIETAM NATIONAL BATTLEFIELD

Antietam National Battlefield and Cemetery is north and east of Sharpsburg, Maryland, along State 34 and 65, both of which intersect with U.S. 40, 40A, and I-70. The visitors center is north of Sharpsburg on State 65 and is open daily from 8 A.M. to 5 P.M., except Christmas Day and New Year's Day. There is a museum at the center with audiovisual exhibits explaining the battle and notices of special events. The numbered stops for self-guided tours are arranged in the sequence of the battle and include, among others, the re-built Dunker Church, North and East Wood, the Cornfield, Sunken Road (Bloody Lane), and Stone Bridge (Burnside Bridge). For more information, write to: Superintendent, Antietam National Battlefield, P.O. Box 158, Sharpsburg, MD 21783. Phone: (301) 432-5142.

THE CORINTH BATTLEFIELD

The Corinth Battlefield is in Corinth, Mississippi, on U.S. Route 45 and 72, about 8 miles south of the Tennessee border and about 80 miles from Memphis on State Route 78. The Battlefield contains monuments. Nearby is a National Cemetery with the graves of 7,000 Union soldiers and 3,996 "unknown" who died in the fighting in the general vicinity. The northeast Mississippi Museum in Corinth contains artifacts, maps, and photographs relating to the Civil War as well as maps for self-guided tours. The museum is open daily from 2 P.M. to 5 P.M. For more information, phone: (601) 286-6403.

PERRYVILLE BATTLEFIELD

Perryville Battlefield is at Perryville, Kentucky, near the intersection of U.S. Routes 68 and 150, 35 miles southeast of Lexington and 10 miles west of Danville. The 100-acre battlefield park appears much the same as when the battle took place. The battlefield museum, which includes a diorama of the battle is open daily from 9 A.M. to 5 P.M., April through October and at other times by previously made appointments. For more information, phone: (606) 332-8631.

FREDERICKSBURG BATTLEFIELD

The visitor center for the Fredericksburg Battlefield is at the foot of Marye's Heights on U.S. 1 (business). It can also be reached by the Orange Turnpike off I-95. The center, open daily except Christmas Day and New Year's Day from 9 A.M. to 5 P.M., has a museum and information for a self-guided tour that includes such sites as Sunken Road, Pontoon Bridge, and National Cemetery at Marye's Heights. For more information, write to: Superintendent, Fredericksburg and Spotsylvania National Military Park, 120 Chatham Lane, Fredericksburg, VA 22405. Phone: (703) 786-2880.

STONES RIVER NATIONAL BATTLEFIELD

Stones River National Battlefield is in the corner of Murfreesboro, Tennessee, 27 miles southeast of Nashville at Exit 78 off State Route 24. The visitors center, near the Old Nashville Highway, is open daily from 8 A.M. to 5 P.M. There is a museum and a film, as well as recorded guides for self-guided tours. Park officials suggest you allow at least two hours for a tour. For more information, write to: Superintendent, 3501 Old Nashville Highway, Murfreesboro, TN 37129. Phone: (615) 893-3501.

CHANCELLORSVILLE BATTLEFIELD

The visitors center at Chancellorsville is on State Route 3, about 9 miles west of I-95, and is open daily from 8 A.M. to 5 P.M. except Christmas Day and New Year's Day and provides detailed information for a self-guided tour. Salem Church and Zoan Church are between Fredericksburg and Chancellorsville on State Route 3. Stonewall Jackson's shrine at Guinea Station on Virginia 607 and 606 off I-95 includes the simple dwelling where Jackson died. For more information, write to: Superintendent, Fredericksburg and Spotsylvania National Military Park, 120 Chatham Lane, Fredericksburg, VA 22405. Phone: (703) 786-2880.

GETTYSBURG NATIONAL MILITARY PARK

Gettysburg National Military Park, containing almost 3,800 acres, is on U.S. Route 15, about 37 miles southwest of Harrisburg, Pennsylvania. The visitors center is open daily except Thanksgiving, Christmas, and New Year's Day from 8 A.M. to 5 P.M. and in summer until 6 P.M. The center contains an electric map explaining the battle and also has a museum. The center also provides information needed to make a self-guided tour of the battlefield by auto or on foot. Arrangements can also be made in advance for guided tours. Many believe the best way to explore much of the battlefield is on foot just as Meade's and Lee's men did. Some of the major points of interest are the National Cemetery, the Cyclorama Center, which contains a 356-foot-long painting of Pickett's Charge, McPherson Ridge, Little Round Top, Devil's Den, Wheatfield, Peach Orchard, Cemetery Ridge, and High Water Mark. Just east of the park is East Cavalry Battlefield Site. The main battlefield contains numerous monuments, statues, markers, and many cannon. For more information, write to: Superintendent, Gettysburg National Military Park, Gettysburg, PA 17325. Phone: (717) 334-1124.

The Battlefield at Brandy Station is about 8 miles northeast of Culpeper, Virginia, at Brandy Station on U.S. 29 and 15. The site is privately owned and there are historical markers on Fleetwood Hill, where much of the fighting took place.

CHAMPION HILL BATTLEFIELD

For a leaflet containing a map and information about the battle, write to the Jackson Civil War Roundtable at 806 North State Street, Jackson, MS 39201. Leaflets containing a map and information about the battle are available at the Vicksburg National Military Park for 50 cents.

VICKSBURG NATIONAL MILITARY PARK

Vicksburg National Military Park is located in the northeastern portion of Vicksburg, Mississippi. The park entrance and visitor center are on Clay Street (U.S. 80) and 1 mile off I-20. The center and USS *Cario* Museum are open daily except Christmas from 8 A.M. to 5 P.M. The museum, built around the remains of USS *Cario*, a Federal ironclad gunboat blown up by Confederate forces on the nearby Yazoo River, contains many artifacts and information regarding Civil War naval matters. The visitor center has an audiovisual explaining the siege and supplies data for self-guided tours that cover sixteen battlefield sites. For more information, write to: Superintendent, Vicksburg National Military Park, 3201 Clay Street, Vicksburg, MS 39180. Phone: (601) 636-0583.

PORT HUDSON
STATE COMMEMORATIVE AREA

Port Hudson State Commemorative Area is on U.S. Route 61, about 15 miles north of Baton Rouge, Louisiana. The visitor center and 40-foot-high observation tower are open daily except Thanksgiving, Christmas, and New Year's Day from 9 A.M. to 5 P.M. An interpretive program at the center describes the siege, and the museum contains many artifacts. The earthworks that dot the battlefield are good examples of this type of Civil War defense. For more information, write to: Port Hudson State Commemorative Area, 756 West Plains Port Hudson Road, Zachary, LA 70791. Phone: (504) 654-3775.

CHICKAMAUGA NATIONAL BATTLEFIELD

It is south of Chattanooga near Interstate 75. Park entrance is off U.S. Route 27 south of Georgia Route 2. There is a visitor center with a slide presentation and picnic tables near Bloody Pond. For more information, write to: Superintendent, Chickamauga and Chattanooga National Military Park, P.O. Box 2128, Fort Oglethorpe, GA 30742. Phone: (706) 866-2512.

CHATTANOOGA BATTLEFIELD

There is a visitor enter at Chattanooga at the intersection of I 59 and 79. For more information, write to: Superintendent, Chickamauga and Chattanooga National Military Park, P.O. Box 2128, Fort Oglethorpe, GA 30742. Phone: (706) 866-2512.

THE WILDERNESS BATTLEFIELD

The visitor center for the Wilderness Battlefield is at the Chancellorsville Battlefield, on State Route 3, about 9 miles west of I-95. The center is open daily from 8 A.M. to 5 P.M. except Christmas and New Year's Day and provides detailed information for self-guided tours of all four battlefields. The Wilderness Battlefield has an Exhibit Shelter on the Orange Turnpike showing how the battle was fought. Points of interest on the battlefield include the remains of the Wilderness Tavern, Widow Trapp Farm where Lee tried to lead an attack, and the Lacy House, which was Grant and Meade's headquarters. For more information, write to: Superintendent, Fredericksburg and Spotsylvania National Military Park, 120 Chatham Lane, Fredericksburg, VA 22405. Phone: (703) 786-2880.

THE SPOTSYLVANIA COURT HOUSE
BATTLEFIELD

The visitor center for the Spotsylvania Court House Battlefield is at the Chancellorsville Battlefield, on State Route 3, about 9 miles west of I-95. This center is open daily from 8 A.M. to 5 P.M. except Christmas and New Year's Day and provides detailed information for self-guided tours. There is an exhibit shelter on Brock Road within the Spotsylvania Court House Battlefield with displays explaining how the battle was fought. Points of interest on the battlefield site of Laurel Hill Engagement, Bloody Angle, and Lee's final line. There is a Confederate cemetery outside the battlefield just to the north of the village of Spotsylvania Court House. For more information, write to: Superintendent,

Fredericksburg and Spotsylvania National Military Park, 120 Chatham Lane, Fredericksburg, VA 22405. Phone: (703) 786-2280.

NEW MARKET BATTLEFIELD PARK

New Market Battlefield Park, administered by the Virginia Military Institute, is located off Exit 264 on I-81 which intersects with I-66 from Washington, D.C., and I-64 from Richmond. Within the 260-acre park is the Hall of Honor in memory of the cadets that took part in the battle. Inside the hall is an excellent war museum, a diorama of the battle, artifacts, and a film covering the Civil War in Virginia. The museum is open daily except Christmas from 9A.M. to 5P.M. For more information, write to: New Market Battlefield, P.O. Box 1864, New Market, VA 22844. Phone: (703) 740-3101.

COLD HARBOR BATTLEFIELD

The visitor center on Richmond's Broad Street, off I-95, is open daily except Thanksgiving and Christmas Day from 9 A.M. to 5 P.M. and contains a museum and information for self-guided tours. There is an Exhibit Center at Cold Harbor that explains how the battle was fought and the remains of Lee's earthworks are considered by many as outstanding. The Garthright House that served as a Union field hospital is only an exterior exhibit as the interior is not open to the public. For more information, write to: Superintendent, Richmond National Battlefield Park, 3215 East Broad Street, Richmond, VA 23223. Phone: (804) 226-1981. The North Anna Battlefield is on U.S. Route near Doswell, Virginia, and 15 miles north of Richmond on I-95. The battlefield is privately owned.

BRICE'S CROSS ROADS NATIONAL BATTLEFIELD

Brice's Cross Roads National Battlefield is 6 miles east of Baldwyn, Mississippi, on State Route 370 and 17 miles north of Tupelo, Mississippi, on U.S.

45. The site consists of only a few acres but much of the scene of the battle can be seen. There are no facilities or park personnel at the site but the staff at the visitor center at Tupelo National Battlefield Site will answer questions regarding Brice's Cross Roads. The Tupelo visitor center is within the city limits of Tupelo on State Route 6 about 1 mile west of the intersection with U.S. 45, also 1.2 miles east of the Natchez Trace Parkway. For more information, write to: Superintendent, Tupelo National Battlefield Site, R.R. 1, NT-143, Tupelo, MS 38801. Phone: (601) 680-4000.

KENNESAW MOUNTAIN NATIONAL BATTLEFIELD PARK

Kennesaw Mountain National Battlefield Park is located 3 miles north of Marietta, Georgia, and reached from U.S. 41 and I75. The visitor center and park are open daily from 8 A.M. to 5 P.M. except Christmas and New Year's Day. The center contains exhibits, an audio-visual presentation of the battle, and in summer, living-history programs. The self-guided auto tour includes Kennesaw Mountain where there is an observation platform, Pigeon Hill, Cheatham Hill, and Kolb's Farm. Distances from the center for walking tours are 2 miles, 5 miles, 10 miles, and 16 miles and can involve walking over difficult terrain. For more information, write to: Superintendent, Kennesaw Mountain National Battlefield Park, 920 Kennesaw Mountain Drive, Kennesaw, GA 30144. Phone: (404) 417-4686.

TUPELO NATIONAL BATTLEFIELD

Tupelo National Battlefield is within the city limits of Tupelo, Mississippi, on State Route 6 about 1 mile west of its intersection with U.S. 45. It is 1.2 miles east of the Natchez Trace Parkway. The battlefield is located near the site where the Confederate line was formed to attack the Union position. Park personnel at the visitor center can provide information and answer questions about the battle as well as that at Brice's Cross Roads. Both battlefields are administered by the National Park Service. For more information, write to: Superintendent, R.R. 1, Tupelo, MS 38801.

PETERSBURG NATIONAL BATTLEFIELD

The Petersburg National Battlefield visitor center is on State Route 36, about 2 miles east of I-95, and 25 miles south of Richmond on that Interstate. The battlefield is open from 8 A.M. until dark daily except Christmas and New Year's Day. The center has a film presentation that describes the siege and also furnishes information for two self-guided tours of the battlefield. Battlefield contains sixteen interesting sites that include the Crater, Fort Fisher, the largest earthen fortification of the battle, and Battery 8, captured by Union black soldiers. For more information, write to: Superintendent, P.O. Box 549, Petersburg, VA 23804. Phone: (804) 265-8244.

MONOCACY NATIONAL BATTLEFIELD

Monocacy National Battlefield is about 3 miles south of Frederick, Maryland, on I-270 or State 355, .1 mile after crossing the Monocacy River. The visitor center is open from 8:30 A.M. to 4:30 P.M. Wednesday through Sunday except Thanksgiving, Christmas, and New Year's Day. The center has an electric map program explaining the battle. For more information, write to: Monocacy National Battlefield, 4801 Urbana Road, Frederick, MD 21701. Phone: (301) 662-3514.

FORT MORGAN

Fort Morgan is 21 miles west of Gulf Shore at the western end of State Route 180 that connects via State Route 59 to I-10 from Mobile.

Fort Gaines is on nearby Dauphin Island and can be reached by ferry from Fort Morgan or by car from Mobile. It is open on the same schedule as Fort Morgan. Both forts are administered by the Alabama Historical Commission. The fort,

built in 1818, is open daily from 8 A.M. to 5 P.M. (to 6 P.M. in summer) except Thanksgiving, Christmas, and New Year's Day. The fort's museum contains many artifacts relating to its history. For more information, write to: Fort Morgan, 51 Highway 180 West, Gulf Shore, AL 36542. Phone: (205) 540-7125.

FORT FISHER

Fort Fisher State Historic Site is on the east side of the Cape Fear River, about 15 miles south of Wilmington, North Carolina, and 6 miles east of Southport via U.S. 421. The visitor center is open April 1 through October, Monday through Saturday from 9 A.M. to 5 P.M. and on Sunday from 1 P.M. to 5 P.M. From November 1 to March 31 it is open Tuesday through Saturday from 10 A.M. to 4 P.M. and closed Christmas and New Year's Day. The museum at the center has an audio visual program covering the fort's history as well as artifacts. Fort Fisher was the largest Confederate earthwork fort and about 10 percent of it remains. The sand of the other 90 percent of the original fort has been reclaimed by the Atlantic Ocean. For more information, write to Fort Fisher Historic Site, P.O. Box 169, Kure Beach, N.C. 28449. Phone: (910) 459-5538.

SAYLER'S CREEK

Sayler's Creek Battlefield State Park is 9 miles southeast of Farmville on U.S. 360 and State Route 617 and 59 miles west of Petersburg near U.S. 460. The 217-acre battlefield is open daily from dawn to dusk. There are descriptive markers along the roads that explain many aspects of the battle for those making a self-guided tour by car or on foot. For more information, phone: (804) 392-3435.

APPOMATTOX COURTHOUSE NATIONAL HISTORICAL PARK

The park is open daily from 8 A.M. to 5 P.M. except Thanksgiving, Christmas, New Year's Day, Washington's Birthday, Veterans Day, and Martin Luther King, Jr.'s birthday. The visitor center is at the old country courthouse at Appomattox and has a museum and slide presentation. The McLean House, the site of the surrender of General Lee to General Grant, is a reconstruction of the original. For more information, write to: Superintendent, Appomattox Courthouse Historical Park, P.O. Box 218, Appomattox, VA 24552. Phone: (804) 352-8782.

CHAPTER SIX

BATTLEFIELD OF FALLEN TIMBERS

It is open at no charge throughout the year from 8 A.M. to dark. Location: Exit first interchange on U.S. 24 southwest from I-475 and turn south about 1 mile to Fallen Timbers Memorial, located southwest of Maumee, Lucas County, Ohio, near Maumee River. For more information, write to: Toledo Metro Parks, 5100 West Central Avenue, Toledo, OH 43615. Phone: (614) 466-1500 or toll free 1-800-BUCKEYE.

TIPPECANOE BATTLEFIELD
STATE MEMORIAL

It is open from 10 A.M. to 5 P.M. daily from March through November, and from 10 A.M. to 4 P.M. December through February, except for Thanksgiving, Christmas, and New Year's Day. The memorial is 7 miles north of Lafayette, Indiana, just off the State Road 43 Prophet's Rock Road exit off I-65. For more information, write to: Tippecanoe County Historical Association, 909 South Street, Lafayette, IN 47901. Phone: (317) 742-8411.

HORSHOE BEND MILITARY PARK

There is a visitor center with exhibits and slide presentations providing information on the battle as well as the Creek Wars, Creek culture, and frontier life. There is a 2.8-mile nature trail through the battle site. It is open daily from 9 A.M. to 5 P.M. It is located on Alabama 49, 12 miles north of Dadeville and 18 miles northeast of Alexander City, which is around 70 miles southeast of Birmingham, Alabama. For more information, phone: Park Superintendent (205) 234-7111.

WASHITA BATTLEFIELD

The battlefield is open all year. It is located about .25 mile northwest of Cheyenne, Oklahoma, on U.S. Route 283. For more information, write to: Oklahoma Historical Society, Wiley Post Building, Oklahoma City, OK 73125. Phone: (405) 521-2491.

LITTLE BIGHORN BATTLEFIELD

It is located on the Crow Indian Reservation in southeastern Montana. The nearest cities are Billings, Montana, 65 miles northwest, and Sheridan, Wyoming, 70 miles south. For more information, write to: Superintendent, P.O. Box 39, Crow Agency, MT 59022.

BIG HOLE NATIONAL BATTLEFIELD

The battlefield is located 10 miles west of Wisdom on Montana 43. From Butte, Montana, take I-15 southwest to Divide, then Montana 43 to Wisdom. Coming from the west, Montana 43 intersects with U.S. 95 at state line between Salmon, Idaho, and Hamilton, Montana. For more information, write to: Superintendent, P.O. Box 237, Wisdom, MT 59761.

THE WOUNDED KNEE NATIONAL HISTORIC LANDMARK

There is a visitor center on the Reservation that can direct you to the Massacre Site. The Reservation is only a few miles from Pine Ridge on S.D. 87 and reached from Rapid City heading southeast on S.D. 40. Headquarters of Pine Ridge Reservation is just a short distance from Pine Ridge on S.D. 87. Pine Ridge is on S.D. 87 southeast of Rapid City. For more information, write to: Wounded Knee National Historic Landmark, Wounded Knee, SD 57794. Phone: (605) 867-5325.

CHAPTER 7

THE USS *Arizona* MEMORIAL

The visitor center is open daily from 7:30 A.M. to 5 P.M. The center and memorial are closed Thanksgiving, Christmas, and New Year's Day. For more information, write to: Superintendent, USS *Arizona* Memorial, 1 Arizona Memorial Place, Honolulu, HI 96818-3145. Phone: (808) 422-0561 or (808) 422-2771.

APPENDIX II

ARMED FORCES: ELEMENTS

Armies: The largest operational unit consisting of two or more corps and usually commanded by full general, lieutenant general, or major general. In the Civil War, Union armies might contain over one hundred thousand men. Confederate armies were generally considerably smaller. In the Revolutionary War, Washington's army often had less than ten thousand men.

Battalion: Five hundred men from two or more companies commanded by a lieutenant colonel. Battalion were common in the Revolution but not in the Civil War.

Brigade: Two thousand men from two or more regiments and commanded by a brigadier general.

Company: Formed from a number of platoons to give strength of one hundred men. Commanded by a captain.

Corps: Two or more divisions commanded by a major general in the Union army; often a lieutenant general in the Confederate army. Corps strength was around ten thousand. In the Confederate army, the corps as well as divisions and brigades were often named after their commander but in the Union army they were designated by numerals.

Detachment: A relatively small body of soldiers, usually commanded by an officer, sent on a specific assignment.

Division: The smallest unit capable of independent operation; included infantry and/or cavalry supported by artillery, engineers, and medical. Commanded by a major general; divisional strength in the Civil War was usually between six and nine thousand men. In the Revolution it was often as few as one or two thousand.

Platoon: About forty soldiers commanded by a lieutenant.

Regiment: Composed of a number of companies to give it a strength of around one thousand. Commanded by a lieutenant colonel or full colonel.

Squad: Generally less than ten soldiers; commanded by a sergeant.

Appendix III

Fortifications

Abatis: A barricade made by placing felled trees lengthwise, one over the other, with sharpened ends of branches facing outward toward the advancing enemy.

Approach Trenches: Often zigzag and dug at right angle to defenses to allow soldiers and guns to move from one parallel trench to one dug closer to the enemy fortifications.

Banquette: A raised step inside a parapet or trench for soldiers to stand on to fire on enemy.

Barbette: Earth or wood platform for fort's cannon.

Bastion: V-shaped projection of fort to allow enfilading fire—crossfire—on enemy.

Berm: Narrow space between ditch or moat around fort.

Breastworks: Protective barrier or wall made of whatever is available—earth, stone, fence rails, bales of hay, etc.

Causeway: Elevated roadway over fort's ditch or moat.

Chevaux-de-frise: Framework of heavy timber, often topped with pointed iron pikes, set at an angle to impede advancing attacking infantry, or sunk under water to prevent passage of enemy ships.

Citadel: A strong small fort built inside a larger fortification.

Counterscraps: Slope of ditch or moat surrounding a fort.

Covered Walkway: Roof over walkway connecting fort to its outer defenses.

Earthworks: Temporary fortifications made of earth, sand, or gravel.

Embrasure: Openings in fort outer wall to allow for placement of cannon.

Fascine: Long cylindrical bundles of brushwood, corn or sugar cane stalks, etc., bound together to fill trenches so attacking force can cross over them.

Gabion: Wicker basket or similar container, filled with earth, sand, stone, etc. to form a breastwork for infantry or protect artillery.

Loopholes: Small holes or slots in a defensive wall for musket and rifle fire.

Magazine: Storage room in fort for powder, ball, and arms.

Mine: An explosive charge placed under fortifications to blow an opening for attacking force to enter.

Palisade (also Stockade): Defensive wall made of logs, pointed at top with ends sunk into soil.

Parapet: Earth or stone walls of a fort.

Parallels: Trenches dug parallel to defensive wall. In the course of a siege, parallels connected by approach trenches are dug ever closer to the fortifications so cannon can be brought in close range.

Ramparts: Mass of stone or earth to elevate defenders.

Redoubt: A completely enclosed small, independent, and temporary earthwork.

Redan: V-shaped earthwork to protect artillery.

Revetment: Barrier against explosion or facing of masonry on fort's walls.

Salient: Portion of fortification pointing out toward enemy.

Sally Port: Main opening in fort so soldier and supplies can enter.

Stockade: See Palisade.

Works: Any kind of fortification. General Grant to the commander of Fort Donelson: "I propose to move immediately upon your works."

GENERAL GLOSSARY

Key to specific wars
FI: French and Indian Wars
AR: American Revolutionary War
1812: War of 1812
MW: War with Mexico
CW: Civil War
IW: Indian Wars

Artillery: Cannon mounted on carriage. Also referred to as gun.

Bateau (FI, AR): Flat-bottom boat about thirty-feet long and three-feet wide, propelled by oars, pole, or sail. Used to transport men and supplies on inland waters.

Battery: Unit of artillery, comparable to infantry company. Also one or more pieces of artillery in firing position.

Bomb or Bombshell: Hollow cannonball filled with gunpowder and ignited by a fuse.

Break Contact: To move away from enemy for tactical reasons.

Breech-loading: Any firearm loaded from the breech rather than from the muzzle.

Brevet: Honorary rank awarded for gallant action in battle. Did not include increase in authority or pay.

Broadside: Simultaneous firing of all cannon or guns from one side of a warship.

Broadsword (FI, AR): Heavy double-edged pointed sword.

"Brown Bess" (FI, AR): Common name for standard infantry musket introduced to British Army during reign of Queen Anne (1702–1714). Origin of nickname was from the early models which had barrels as well as stocks stained brown.

Buffalo Soldiers (IW): Nickname of black troops in West after Civil War.

Caliber: Power of any firearm based on the diameter of bore rather than weight of projectile.

Canister: Cannon shell filled with small iron pellets which act like buckshot when fired on advancing infantry or cavalry.

Carbine: A short-barreled musket or rifle, primarily carried by cavalrymen and dragoons.

Carronade (1812): Powerful but short-range ship's cannon best suited for close-in fighting.

Casualties: Number of men killed, wounded, missing, or taken prisoner in a battle.

Cavalry: Horse-mounted soldiers, often called troopers.

Colt Revolver (MW, CW, IW): Introduced during the War with Mexico, Samuel Colt's .44 caliber revolver was standard pistol in Civil War, although the Confederate forces continued to use the earlier heavy "Navy Colt."

Columbiad (CW): Heavy smooth-bore cannon used primarily for coastal defenses. Range in caliber eight, ten, and fifteen inches. It could fire a shell up to three hundred and twenty pounds.

Column: Formation of soldiers marching in long, narrow column. The order "By columns of fours" means ranks of four soldiers marching or riding abreast to form a narrow, long column. A column can also refer to a force of considerable strength.

Confederate Battleflag (CW): Distinctive red flag with blue bars, introduced shortly after First Bull Run as the Confederate national flag. It so closely resembled the Stars and Stripes that it caused some confusion among Confederate forces.

Congreve Rocket (1812): British rocket suitable for land or ship.

Contraband: Goods or property seized by a belligerent.

Countermarch: To reverse direction or march, returning to or near original position.

Cutlass: Short, single-edged sword, often with curved blade, carried by sailors.

Demonstration: To make a show of force without actually attacking. A feint.

Deploy: Position troops or artillery for battle.

Dragoon: Horse-mounted soldiers who often fought on foot but rode to battle site. Similar to cavalry.

Double-shotted (1812): Loading a ship's muzzle-loading gun with two cannonballs to increase its firepower.

Effective Range: Maximum distance a projectile can strike and still damage the target.

Enfilade, Enfiladed: Firing from side in order to sweep across the length of the enemy's position or his advancing columns.

Engaged (Effectives): Number of troops actually fighting in a battle as opposed to the total number available.

Envelopment: Attack on enemy flank to roll it sideways. In a double envelopment, both right and left flanks are attacked simultaneously.

Fieldpiece: A field gun. Any light piece of artillery that accompanies troops in the field.

Flank: End position of troops in a line of battle on each side of a marching column.

Flank Companies: Usually elite troops charged with protecting the flanks.

Flying Batteries (MW): Horse-drawn artillery mounted on carriages with large wheels so can be moved rapidly into firing position.

Forage: Food, especially for horses and mules.

Forced March: Marching with speed over a considerable distance.

Forlone Hope (AR): Body of soldiers sent on a dangerous and sometimes suicidal mission.

Fusilier (AR): British light infantry regiments so named because when formed in seventeenth century they were armed with a short musket called a fusil.

Garrison: A place where soldiers live, usually fortified.

Gatling Gun (CW, IW): An early crank-operated machine gun.

Grape or Canister: Similar to canister except pellets are smaller and more numerous as in a shotgun shell.

Grasshopper (AR): British light fieldpiece mounted on legs instead of wheels and when fired jumped about like a grasshopper.

Grenadiers (FI, AR): British and German mercenary elite troops. Regiments originally formed of tallest and strongest men to throw early-type hand grenade. Readily identified by their tall, brimless, miter-shaped hats.

Gun: A cannon. Artillery.

Henry Repeating Rifle (CW): First repeating rifle adopted by Union army and holding fifteen .44 caliber cartridges.

Hessians (AR): Mercenaries from German Duchy of Hesse employed by the British to fight in the American Revolution. The name soon applied to all British German mercenaries regardless of what part of Germany they came from.

Hotchkiss Cannon (IW): A light mountain fieldpiece.

Howitzer: Artillery piece with a relatively short barrel that could be elevated to fire shells at high angle to hit troops behind defenses.

Ironclad (CW): A wood vessel covered with protective armor of iron plates.

Jägers (AR): German for "huntsmen." German mercenary elite light infantry.

Lancers (MW): Cavalry or dragoons with arms that included a lance. A long spear with pointed metal head.

Legion (AR, IW): Force organized for a specific purpose and often consisting of infantry, cavalry, and artillery.

Light Infantry: Usually elite troops and not encumbered by all the equipment carried by the average soldier.

Linstock: Instrument to hold slow-burning match to ignite powder in a muzzle-loading cannon.

Lobsterbacks/Redcoats (AR): American Patriot's name for British soldiers in their scarlet jackets.

Long Gun (1812): Ship cannon with greater range than carronade.

Loyalist/Tory (AR): Americans who supported British in the Revolutionary War.

Minié Ball/Bullet (CW): Lead rifle bullet with hollow base that increased accuracy, range, and power.

Minutemen (AR): American patriots who in early days of war were prepared to come to fight British troops at "a minute's notice."

Mortar: Very short-barreled, large-bore cannon intended to destroy fortified positions.

Musket: Usually refers to smooth-bore, muzzle-loading shoulder gun.

Muzzle Loading: Any hand weapon or cannon loaded from front opening rather than from breech at other end.

Napoleon (CW): A bronze muzzle-loading fieldpiece used by both Union and Confederate forces.

Parole: Oath given by captured men to gain release on promise never to again fight against the captors.

Parrott Gun (CW): Union rifled canon with great range.

Partisans (AR, CW): Any irregular force; guerrillas.

Patriots/Rebels (AR): Americans who fought against the British in the Revolutionary War.

Pickets: Small body of troops in advance of main force to feel out enemy strength and warn of its presence.

Point-blank Range: Weapon so close to target that when fired is virtually unable to miss.

Poundage: Rating of gun by weight of ball it fires rather than caliber or diameter of its bore.

Provincials (FI, AR): American colonial troops serving under British.

Quarters: Place where soldiers live. Also term of surrender, "to ask for quarters."

"Quasi War": Undeclared naval war between the United States and France, 1798–1800.

Rank and File: Ordinary soldiers.

Reconnaissance in Force: Any operation, often by cavalry, seeking information on enemy and sometimes testing his strength.

Refuse a Flank: To reposition a flank so it cannot be turned by enemy.

Regulars: Officers and soldiers serving long-term enlistments in national army as opposed to short-term state militia and volunteers.

Resaca (MW): Dry channel of stream of river.

Rifle: Shoulder firearm with rifled bore as opposed to one with a smooth bore.

Rifled: Hand weapon or artillery with lands and grooves formed inside barrel to cause bullet or shell to rotate with increasing range and accuracy.

Saber: Heavy one-edged sword, often with curved blade, carried primarily by cavalry.

Salient: Body of men extending forward of main force.

Screen: Usually cavalry sent to keep enemy scouts from getting close enough to main force to learn its strength and position.

Sharps Breech-loading Rifle (CW): First truly successful shoulder weapon of this kind. So accurate it coined the term "Sharpshooter."

Small Arms: Weapons such as rifles, pistols, and swords carried by individuals as opposed to artillery.

Smooth-bore: Any firearm with a smooth rather than a rifled bore.

Spontoon (FI): Short spear carried by junior officers.

Spiking a Gun: Driving a metal spike through the touch hole of a cannon so the powder charge cannot be ignited.

Strategy and Tactics: Strategy is the overall planning of a large-scale military operation. Example: Union strategy included gaining control of the Mississippi River. Tactics is securing the strategic objective by the deployment of troops in the field. Example: Unable to take Vicksburg from the front, Grant circled around the city and took it from the rear, thereby gaining Union control of the Mississippi River.

"Swamp Angel" (CW): Heavy Parrott gun positioned in swamp seven thousand yards from its target of Charleston, South Carolina.

Swivel Gun (AR): Light fieldpiece on a swivel so it had a wide horizontal range.

Tactics: See Strategy and Tactics.

Torpedo (CW): A metal container with an explosive charge set in water to explode when struck by ship. Similar to modern naval mine.

Tory: See Loyalist/Tory.

Train: To aim a weapon; usually applies to artillery.

Trajectory: A projectile's path through air.

Troops/Troopers: Body of soldiers. "Troopers" usually refers to cavalrymen.

Unlimber: Disconnect an artillery piece from the horse or mule-drawn limber in preparation for going into action.

Van: The advance guard of a force on the march.

Volley: Soldiers or artillery firing in unison, generally on command.

Works: Fortifications.

BIBLIOGRAPHY AND SUGGESTED READING

(*Note*: Unless otherwise noted, listed publications are generally available at large public libraries and local public libraries in those states with an interlibrary loan system.)

GENERAL—ALL WARS

Black Americans in Defense of Our Nation. Blacks' role from 1770 Boston Massacre to Vietnam. Copyright 1990. U.S. Department of Defense. Government Printing Office, Washington, D.C.

Commager, Henry S., and Allan Nevins *The Heritage of America.* Firsthand narratives through World War II. Copyright 1939. Little, Brown and Company, Boston.

Goetzmann, William H., and Glyndwr Williams. *The Atlas of North American Explorations from Norse Voyages to the Race to the Pole.* Numerous maps in color include all major explorations of territory to become the United States. Copyright 1992. Prentice Hall, New York.

Langer, William L. *An Encyclopedia of World History.* Includes dates and brief description of major events in American history from Colonial times to 1952. Copyright 1952. Haughton Mifflin Company, Boston.

Lechie, Robert. *The Wars of America.* In 1,081 pages describes all wars from Colonial times to Vietnam. Contains a few black-and-white maps. Copyright 1981. Harper and Row, New York.

Lorant, Stefan. *The Presidency—A Pictorial History of Presidential Elections.* Text and illustrations cover major political events from Washington to Truman. Copyright 1952. The Macmillan Company, New York.

Manucy, Albert. *Artillery Through the Ages—A Short Illustrated History of Cannon, Emphasizing Types Used in America.* Reprinted 1985. National Park Service, Washington, D.C.

Matloff, Maurice, General Editor. *American Military History, Army Historical Series.* Authoritative work covers all nation's wars to Vietnam. First published 1969, partially revised 1973. Office of Chief of Military History, United States Army, Government Printing Office, Washington, D.C.

Natkiel, Richard. *Atlas of American History.* Two-color maps, illustrations, and brief text describe all American wars from Colonial times to invasion of Panama. Copyright 1986. First published by Brompton Books Corporation, Greenwich, Connecticut. Later edition by Dorset Press, a division of Marlboro Books, by arrangement with Brompton.

Roberts, Richard. *Encyclopedia of Historic Forts—The Military, Pioneer and Trading Posts of the United States.* Illustrated. Copyright 1988. The Macmillan Company, New York.

Williams, Harry T. *The History of American Wars from 1745 to 1918.* A Pulitzer Prize–winning author packs a large amount of facts into 415 pages. Copyright 1981. Alfred A. Knopf, New York.

FRENCH AND INDIAN WARS— COLONIAL WARS

Chidsey, Donald Barr. *The French and Indian War.* From Fort Necessity to fall of French Canada. Illustrated. Copyright 1969. Crown, New York.

Hamilton, Edward P. *The French and Indian Wars.* Covers all wars in the long conflict. Copyright 1963. Doubleday and Company, Garden City, New York.

Leach, Robert. *Flintlock and Tomahawk.* King Philip's 1675–76 war with the New England Confederation. Copyright 1958. The Macmillan Company, New York.

Peckman, Howard H. *The Colonial Wars—1689–1792.* Includes data on forts, arms, etc., as well as description of action. Copyright 1964. University of Chicago Press, Chicago.

AMERICAN REVOLUTION

Alden, John R. *The History of the American Revolution.* Copyright 1976. Alfred A. Knopf, New York.

Boatner, Mark M. *Encyclopedia of the American Revolution.* Covers leaders, battles, and includes maps. Copyright 1966. David McKay Company, New York.

Carrington, Henry B. *Battles of the American Revolution—1775–1781.* Numerous maps and charts. Copyright 1877. Promontory Press, New York.

Casey, William J. *Where & How the War Was Fought— An Armchair Tour of the American Revolution.* Covers existing battle sites along with other points of interest. Some maps. Copyright 1976. William Morrow, New York.

Early American Wars and Military Institutions. West Point, Military Series, Thomas E. Griess, Series Editor, Department of History, United States Military Academy, West Point. Illustrated and with many maps. Includes Revolution, War of 1812, Mexican War, and development of U.S. Army. Copyright 1986. Avery Publishing Group, Wayne, New Jersey.

Fleming, Thomas J. *Cowpen—Downright Fighting.* Illustrated description of battle. National Park Handbook 135, 1988. National Park Service, Washington, D.C.

Huddelson, F. J. *Gentleman Johnny Burgoyne—Misadventures of an English General in the Revolution.* Enjoyable reading. Illustrated. Copyright 1927. The Bobbs-Merrill Company, Indianapolis.

Middlekrauff, Robert. *The Glorious Cause—American Revolution 1763–1789.* Includes causes of war and how fought. Copyright 1982. Oxford University Press, New York.

Stemper, Sol. *The Bicentennial Guide to the American Revolution.* In three volumes. *The War in the North, The Middle Colonies,* and *The War in the South.* Includes interesting sites on way to battlegrounds. Copyright 1974. Saturday Review Press/E. P. Dutton, New York.

Ward, Christopher. *The War of the Revolution,* edited by John Richard Alden. This two-volume work is one of the best on the subject. Includes maps. Copyright 1952. The Macmillan Company, New York.

THE WAR OF 1812

Beirne, Francis F. *The War of 1812*. Includes land and sea battles. Eleven maps. Copyright 1949. E. P. Dutton, New York.

Caffrey, Kate. *Twilight's Last Gleaming—Britain vs. America 1812–1815*. Copyright 1977. Stein and Day, Briarcliff Manor, New York.

Coles, Harry L. *War of 1812*. History of American Civilization. Daniel Boorstin, editor. Copyright 1965. University of Chicago Press, Chicago.

MEXICAN WAR, 1846–1848

Eisenhower, John D. *So Far From God—The United States War With Mexico 1846–1848*. Copyright 1989. Random House, New York.

Reeder, Russel Porter ("Colonel Red Reeder"). *The Story of the Mexican War*. With maps and illustrated chapter heads. Copyright 1967. Meredith Press, New York.

Singletary, Otis A. *The Mexican War*. History of American Civilization. David Boorstin, editor. Several illustrations and maps. Copyright 1960. University of Chicago Press, Chicago.

Smith, Justin H. *The War with Mexico*. Two volumes. Copyright 1963. Peter Smith, Glouster, Massachusetts.

CIVIL WAR

American Civil War, The. West Point Military History Series, Department of History, United States Military Academy, West Point, New York. Thomas E. Griess, Series Editor. With illustrations. Accompaning separate Campaign Atlas available.

Copyright 1987. Avery Publishing Group, Wayne, New Jersey.

Anderson, Bern. *By Sea and River: The Naval History of the Civil War*. Copyright 1962. Alfred A. Knopf, New York.

Bearss, Edwin C. *Hardluck Ironclad*. Fate of USS *Cario*. Copyright 1966. Louisiana State University Press, Baton Rouge.

Bell, Irving W. *The Life of Billy Yank. The Life of Jonny Reb*. Copyright 1971. Louisiana State University Press, Baton Rouge.

Boatner, Mark M. *The Civil War Dictionary*. Covers people and events from A.A.G. to Samuel Zulick. Maps and diagrams. Copyright 1959. David McKay Company, New York.

Catton, Bruce. Three-volume The Centennial History of the Civil War:—*The Coming Fury, The Terrible Swift Sword, Never Call Retreat*. Copyright 1961, 1963, and 1965. Also author of *A Stillness at Appomattox*, Copyright 1953; *This Hallowed Ground*, Copyright 1956; and *Mr. Lincoln's Army*, Copyright 1956. All published by Doubleday and Company, New York.

Civil War Battlefield Guide, The. Edited by Frances H. Kennedy. Maps and text written by a number of authorities describe over 50 battles. Copyright 1990. The Conservation Fund, Arlington, Virginia.

Civil War Maps. An Annotated List of Maps and Atlases in the Library of Congress. Second edition compiled by Richard W. Stephenson, Geography and Map Division. Copyright 1989. Library of Congress, Washington, D.C.

Fellman, Michael. *The Inside War—Guerrilla Conflict in Missouri During the American Civil War*. Copyright 1989. Oxford University Press, New York.

Freeman, Douglas S. *Lee's Lieutenants.* Three-volume description of war in East and major commanders. Copyright 1948. Charles Scribner's Sons, New York.

Foote, Shelby. Three-volume *The Civil War: A Narrative. Fort Sumter to Perryville, Fredericksburg to Meridan,* and *Red River to Appomattox.* Copyright 1963. Random House, New York.

Grant, Ulysses S. *Personal Memoirs of U. S. Grant.* A two-volume classic that Grant finished as he was dying of cancer. Copyright 1885. Charles L. Webster and Company, New York.

Hicks, Roger W., and Frances E. Schultz. *Battlefields Of The Civil War.* Guide to major battlefields with maps, illustrations, and much factual information. Copyright 1989. Salem House Publishers, Boston.

Lawliss, Chuck. *The Civil War Sourcebook—A Traveler's Guide.* Illustrations, area maps, and details including points of interest at battlefields. Copyright 1991. Harmony Books/Crown, New York.

Macdonald, John. *Great Battles of the Civil War.* Maps, illustrations, and text on major battles. Copyright 1988. Collier Books/Macmillan, New York.

McPherson, John M. *Battle Cry of Freedom—The Civil War Era.* A fine one-volume account of this huge conflict. Copyright 1988. Oxford University Press, New York.

Mary Chesnut's Civil War. Her famous diary describing the war as viewed from the South. Edited by C. Vann Woodword. Copyright 1983. Yale University Press, New Haven.

Miers, Earl S. *The Web of Victory—Grant at Vicksburg.* Copyright 1955. Louisiana State University Press, Baton Rouge.

Novick, Sheldon, H. *Honorable Justice—The Life of Oliver Wendell Holmes.* Copyright 1989. Little, Brown and Company, Boston.

Pullen, John J. *The Twentieth Maine.* The volunteer regiment commanded by Colonel Joshua Chamberlain that held Little Round Top at Gettysburg. Copyright 1955. Lippincott, Philadelphia.

Roberson, James, Jr. *Civil War Sites In Virginia—A Tour Guide.* Copyright 1982. University Press of Virginia, Charlottesville.

Sifakis, Stewart. *Who Was Who in the Civil War.* By alphabetical order list names, brief biographical sketch, sometimes accompanied by a portrait of all important Union and Confederate commanders along with some others such as Lincoln, Jefferson Davis, and John Brown. Copyright 1988. Facts On File, New York.

INDIAN WARS

Axelrod, Alan. *Chronicle Of The Indian Wars—From Colonial Times to Wounded Knee.* Numerous illustrations and several maps. Copyright 1993. Prentice Hall, New York.

Stewart, Edgar L. *Custer's Luck.* Includes conflict with Plains Tribes and Custer's career covering battle at Washita and Little Bighorn. Copyright 1955. University of Oklahoma Press, Norman.

Utley, Robert M. *Custer Battlefield—History and Guide to the Battle of the Little Bighorn.* National Park Service Handbook #132.

    With Wilcomb Washburn. *The American Heritage History of The Indian Wars.* Extensively illustrated. Copyright 1977. American Heritage Publishing Company, New York.

Waldman, Carl. Maps and illustrations by Moly Braun. *Atlas of the North American Indian.* From prehistory to 1986 and includes all wars. Copyright 1985. Facts On File, New York.

Other Sources

Additional data describing sites and action was obtained from National Park Service "National Register of Historic Places Inventory—Nomination Form." Forms include information on *Fort Ticonderoga/Mount Independence, Princeton Battlefield, Oriskany Battlefield, Monmouth Battlefield, Brandywine Battlefield Park, Camden Battlefield, Alamo Plaza Historic District, Resaca de la Palma Battlefield, Port Hudson Battlefield, Tippecanoe Battlefield State Memorial, Battle of Fallen Timbers, Washita Battlefield,* and *Wounded Knee National Historic Landmark.*

INDEX

BOLDFACE PAGES LOCATE MAPS; *ITALICIZED* PAGES LOCATE PHOTOGRAPHS.